Cruising Guide to Germany and Denmark

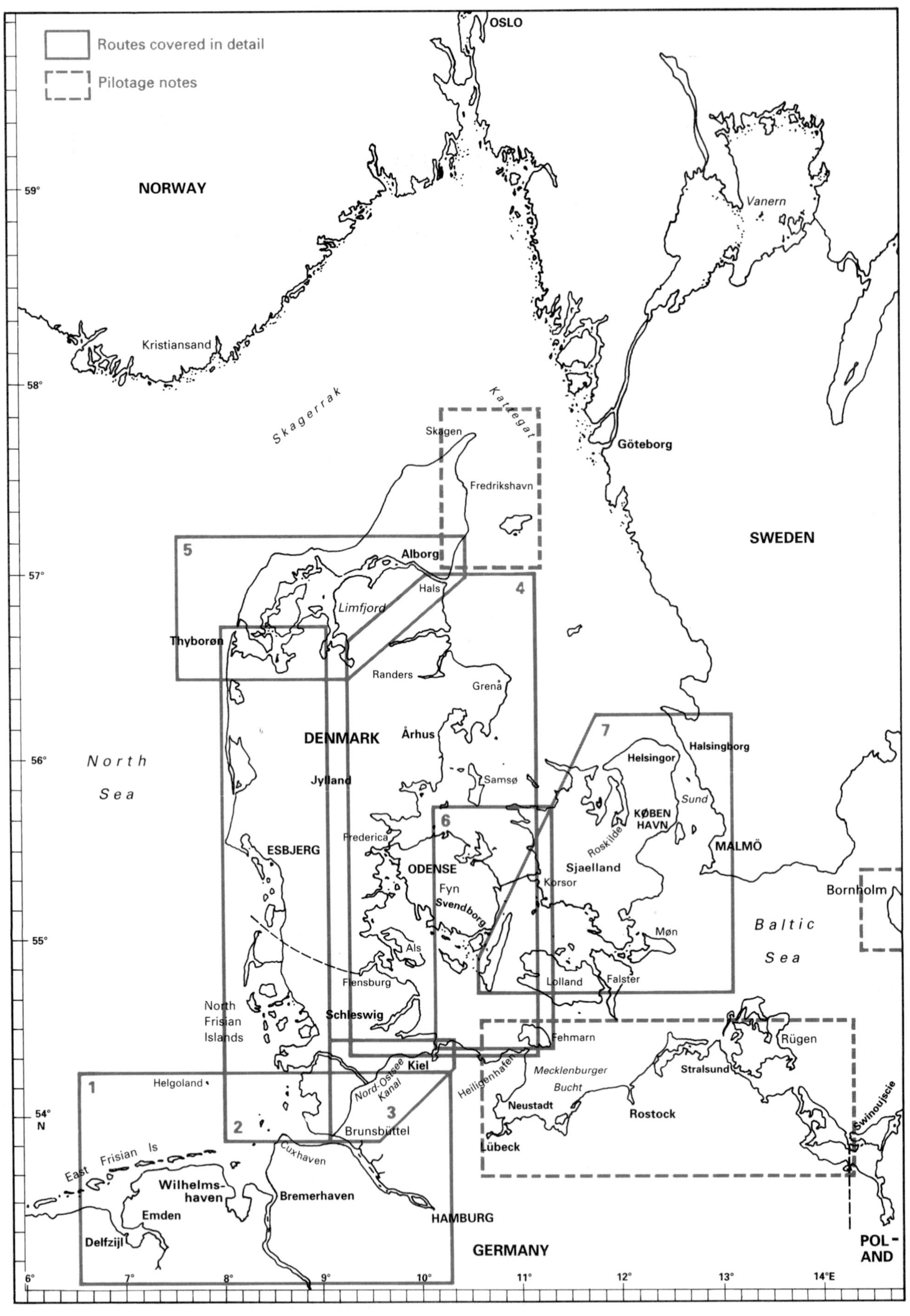
Routes covered in detail
Pilotage notes
OSLO
NORWAY
Vanern
Kristiansand
Skagerrak
Kattegat
Skagen
Göteborg
Fredrikshavn
SWEDEN
5
Alborg
Hals
4
Limfjord
Thyborøn
Randers
Grenå
7
DENMARK
Århus
Halsingborg
Helsingor
North
Sea
Jylland
Samsø
Sund
6
KØBEN HAVN
Roskilde
Frederica
MALMÖ
ESBJERG
ODENSE
Sjaelland
Korsor
Fyn
Bornholm
Svendborg
Baltic
Sea
Møn
Als
Flensburg
Lolland
Falster
North Frisian Islands
Schleswig
Fehmarn
Rügen
Kiel
Mecklenburger Bucht
Heiligenhafen
Stralsund
1
Helgoland
Nord-Ostsee Kanal
3
Neustadt
Rostock
Swinoujscie
2
Brunsbüttel
Lübeck
East Frisian Is
Cuxhaven
Wilhelmshaven
Bremerhaven
Emden
HAMBURG
Delfzijl
GERMANY
POL-AND
59°
58°
57°
56°
55°
54° N
6°
7°
8°
9°
10°
11°
12°
13°
14°E

Cruising Guide to Germany and Denmark

Passages, harbours and pilotage in the German Bight and the southwest Baltic

---

BRIAN NAVIN

Imray Laurie Norie & Wilson Ltd
St Ives Cambridgeshire England

Published by
Imray, Laurie, Norie & Wilson Ltd
Wych House, St Ives, Huntingdon
Cambridgeshire PE17 4BT, England
☎ (01480) 462114 *Fax* (01480) 496109
1994

British Library Cataloguing in Publication Data.
A catalogue record for this book is available from the British Library.

ISBN 0 85288 191 6

This work has been corrected to November 1994.

CORRECTIONAL SUPPLEMENTS

Imray pilot books are amended at intervals by the issue of correctional supplements. Supplements, if available, are supplied free of charge with the books when they are purchased. Further supplements are available from the publishers. The following should be quoted:

1. Name of book
2. Date of edition (above)
3. Date of last supplement (if applicable)
4. Name and address to which supplement should be sent on a stamped addressed A4 envelope

CAUTION

Every effort has been made to ensure the accuracy of this book. It contains selected information, and thus is not definitive and does not include all known information on the subject in hand; this is particularly relevant to the plans, which should not be used for navigation. The author and publishers believe that it is a useful aid to prudent navigation, but the safety of a vessel depends ultimately on the judgement of the navigator, who should assess all information, published or unpublished, available to him.

PLANS

The plans in this guide are not to be used for navigation. They are designed to support the text and should at all times be used with navigational charts.

Printed in Great Britain by
The Bath Press, Avon

Contents

PREFACE AND ACKNOWLEDGEMENTS, vi

INTRODUCTION
Other Imray pilot books, 1
Scope of this book, 1
Central European Time, 1
Telephoning, 1
Currency and coinage, 1
Tourist information addresses, 1
Chart agents and bookshops, 2
Charts, 2
Books, 3
Customs formalities and other regulations, 3
Lands of the sea raiders, 4
Symbols and definitions, 6

PART I. THE NORTH SEA COASTS

1. **The German Bight**
   Pilotage overview
   Area covered, 7
   Tidal heights and ranges, 7
   Tidal streams and currents, 7
   Weather, wind, fog and ice, 13
   Major lights, 14
   Marine and Aero RDF beacons, 14
   Decca coverage, 14
   Coast radio stations, weather forecasts, Navtex, 14
   Lifeboat stations, 14
   Charted nature reserves, 15
   Offshore approaches to the German Bight coasts, 15
   Approaches East Frisian islands, 15
   Borkum and the Ems estuary approaches, 16
   Approaches Jade and Weser entrances, 17
   Approaches Elbe entrance, 17
   Approaches North Frisian islands, 18
   Approaches Jutland west coast, 18
2. **The German Frisian coast and the Elbe**
   Route 1. Emden to Hamburg via the watt channels, Wilhelmshaven, Bremerhaven and Helgoland, 19
3. **The Schleswig-Holstein and Jutland west coasts**
   Route 2. Cuxhaven to Thyborøn via the North Frisian islands, 47
4. **The Nord-Ostsee-Kanal and the Eider river**
   Route 3. North Sea to Kiel via the Nord-Ostsee-Kanal or via the Eider river and the Nord-Ostsee-Kanal, 59
   3A Brunsbüttel to Kiel via Nord-Ostsee-Kanal, 62
   3B Eidersperrwerk to Kiel via Eider river and Nord-Ostsee-Kanal, 67

PART II. THE BALTIC COASTS

5. **Southwest Baltic**
   Pilotage overview
   Area covered, 73
   Anchoring and mooring in nontidal waters, 73
   Currents and water levels, 75
   Weather, wind, fog and ice, 77
   Water and air temperatures in the sailing season, 77
   Lights and buoys, 78
   Fishing stakes and buoys, 78
   Marine and Aero RDF beacons, 78
   Decca coverage, 79
   Coast radio stations, weather forecasts, Navtex, 79
   Lifeboat stations, 80
6. **The Jutland east coast and the Lille Bælt**
   Route 4. Kiel to the Limfjord entrance via the Lille Bælt, 81
7. **The Limfjord**
   Route 5. A cruise round the Limfjord, 117
8. **South Fyn and the Store Bælt**
   Route 6. Kiel to Odense via South Fyn and the Store Bælt, 131
9. **South Sjælland and the Sound**
   Route 7. Kiel to Roskilde via Smålands Farvandet and the Sound, 149
10. **The German Baltic coast and Bornholm**
    Passage notes
    The German coast from Kieler Bucht to the Polish border, 177
    Bornholm and Christiansø islands, 186

APPENDIX
I. Charts: British Admiralty, German, NV *Sportschiffahrtskarten*, Danish, 189
II. Water levels in the southwest Baltic harbours, routes 4, 5, 6 and 7, 199
III. Telephone numbers of harbours, 201
IV. Bibliography, 203
V. Glossary, 204

INDEX, 205

Preface

Denmark and neighbouring Germany provide one of Europe's most fascinating cruising coastlines. To a first-time visitor there is a bewildering variety of yacht harbours and anchorages. This book concentrates on the information the yacht skipper needs most – navigation and pilotage – rather than on the best restaurants, bars and nightlife, which any good tourist guide will tell you about. However, some brief words are given, wherever it seems appropriate, about any major local features or scenery of interest to the tourist.

To simplify the picture in a region of scattered islands and deeply indented coastlines, the passage and harbour information is given in sequence along each of the seven routes chosen. As a result a few harbours, particularly in Denmark, have been excluded, but the vast majority are covered.

This book together with my previous two books should enable the English, Danish or German yachtsman to navigate to most harbours between the English and Swedish coasts.

ACKNOWLEDGEMENTS

Piloting a 10m boat across the busy North Sea and into hundreds of harbours along a labyrinthine coastline is a team task and definitely not one for the single-hander. I would like to express my gratitude above all to my wife, Barbara, who accompanied me to the top of every creek and harbour, kept an immaculate ship, helped to lay up each winter and shared in driving 1,000 miles across Europe on several occasions. I would also like to thank the other people who have crewed for me, shared the driving and helped to lay up: son Robert, daughter Sarah, Alex Blatchford, Ron and Jan Woolhead, Peter Giles, Arthur Somers, Mike and Beatrice Last and David Fowler.

This type of guide book is made possible by the wealth of information available from the UK, German and Danish hydrographic offices and their staffs of many years past, to whom I would also offer my deepest thanks.

Many thanks, once again, are due to the editorial and design team at Imray, Laurie, Norie and Wilson for their exceptionally high professional standards, particularly in the layout, chartwork and illustration of this complicated book.

Brian Navin
Southminster, Essex
1994

INTRODUCTION

OTHER IMRAY PILOT BOOKS

There are two other pilot guides in this series by the same author:

North Sea Passage Pilot
Harbours and pilotage on the East Coast of England, France, Belgium & the Netherlands.

Cruising Guide to the Netherlands

For the Baltic in general, see
The Baltic Sea RCC Pilotage Foundation. Compiled by Barry Sheffield. Edited by Oz Robinson.

SCOPE OF THIS BOOK

This guide covers the North Sea and Baltic coasts of Germany and Denmark as well as the Kiel canal (Nord-Ostsee-Kanal) and Eider river system connecting the two areas, and includes a brief diversion across to the Swedish side of the Sound.

Part I is a guide to the North Sea coasts and Nord-Ostsee-Kanal/Eider river, and Part II to the Baltic coasts. Each part commences with a pilotage overview, followed by chapters covering a range of cruising routes – three in Part I and four in Part II. Chapter 10 contains notes on pilotage for the Baltic coast of Germany and the isolated Danish island of Bornholm (not covered in the seven route plans).

CENTRAL EUROPEAN TIME

Northern Germany and Denmark are on Central European Time, which is one hour ahead of UT (i.e. add one hour to UT to obtain CET, in other words it is the same as British Summer Time). As in the UK, there is also a summer-time period, usually from the end of March to the end of September, when an hour is added to CET, i.e. add two hours to UT or one hour to BST to obtain local summer time. Remember that the times of the tides in the Admiralty *Tide Tables* for the four standard ports on the North Sea (Helgoland, Wilhelmshaven, Cuxhaven and Esbjerg) are in CET throughout, i.e. time zone −0100 is prominently stated at the top of the appropriate tidal pages. Therefore, if you are sailing in the region during these six 'summer' months and you have changed your watch to local summer time, which I would strongly advise you to do, you must always add one hour to the Admiralty's tidal times in order to obtain the local times of HW and LW.

TELEPHONING

From the UK the international and country code is (00 49) for Germany. As in the UK, there are also local area codes, each beginning with 0, when dialling within Germany. These precede the local number if you are dialling from outside the local area. For example, (040) 38 99 28 is a number in Hamburg dialled from outside Hamburg. Dialled from the UK this number would be (00 49) 40 38 99 28; dialled within Hamburg it would simply be 38 99 28. German telephone numbers in this book are preceded by the 0 and the local area code, all in brackets. The telephone code to the UK from Germany is (00 44), which replaces the 0 preceding the UK area code.

In Denmark there are no area telephone codes. Dialling from abroad to Denmark requires the international code and the country code plus the Danish number. For example, from the UK the Danish number 52 41 00 76 is obtained by dialling (00 45) 52 41 00 76. In Denmark it is simply necessary to dial the number. The telephone code to the UK from Denmark is (00 44), which replaces the 0 preceding the UK area code.

CURRENCY AND COINAGE

Germany The Deutschmark (DM) is divided into 100 pfennigs. Coins are of 1, 2, 5, 10 and 50 pfennigs, and 1, 2 and 5 DM. Banknotes are of 5, 10, 20, 50, 100, 500 and 1000 DM.

Denmark The Danish krone (Dkr) is divided into 100 øre. Coins are of 5, 10, 25 and 50 øre, and 1, 2, 5 and 10 Dkr. Banknotes are of 5, 10, 20, 50, 100, 500 and 1000 Dkr.

TOURIST INFORMATION ADDRESSES

Denmark

In the UK the most useful address is:

Danish Tourist Board, 55 Sloane Street, London SW1X 9SY. ☎ (0891) 600109 (automatic information service), (0171) 259 5958/5959.

In Denmark their address is:

Danish Tourist Board, Bernstorfgade 1, DK-1577 København V. ☎ 33 11 14 15/33 11 13 25

The British Embassy in København is:

British Embassy, Kastelvej 36–40, DK-2100 København Ø. ☎ 01 26 46 00.

The Danish national yachting authority is:

Dansk Sejlunion, Idraettens Hus, Brøndby Stadion 20, DK-2600 Glostrup. ☎ 02 45 55.

In the larger towns and resorts of Denmark there are branch offices of the Danish Tourist Board. These can be contacted by post, addressing the letter simply to Turistbureauet, followed by the name of the town.

A useful Danish telephone number for Baltic weather information (in English) is:

Danish Weather Service ☎ 97 10 17 95.

Germany

In the UK the most useful address is:

German National Tourist Office, 65 Curzon Street, London W1Y 7PE. ☎ (0891) 600100 (automatic information service), *Fax* (0171) 495 6129.

The most useful yachting associations in northern Germany are:

Deutscher Segler-Verband, Grundgenstrasse 18, D-22309 Hamburg. ☎ (040) 632 0090.

Deutscher Motoryacht Verband, same address as above, ☎ (040) 630 8011.

British Kiel Yacht Club, BFPO 108. ☎ (0431) 398833.

A useful address for weather information is the Hamburg sea-weather bureau:

Deutscher Wetterdienst Seewetteramt, Bernhard-Nocht Strasse 76, D-20359 Hamburg. ☎ (040) 31900.

CHART AGENTS AND BOOKSHOPS

British Admiralty charts and other publications referred to in this guide may be ordered from Imray Laurie Norie & Wilson Ltd, Wych House, The Broadway, St Ives, Huntingdon PE17 4BT, England. ☎ (01480) 462114 *Fax* (01480) 496109.

The most useful addresses for obtaining charts and other nautical publications in this area are:

Datema Gmbh, Am Seedeich 39, D-27572 Bremerhaven. ☎ (0471) 79 98 15.

Seekarte (Kapt A Dammeyer), Korffsdeich 3, D-28217 Bremen. ☎ (0421) 39 50 51 *Fax* (0421) 39 62 23 5.

Rauschenplat bookshop, Deichstrasse 21, D-27472 Cuxhaven. ☎ (04721) 3 71 37.

Neubauer bookshop, Schillerstrasse, D-27472 Cuxhaven. ☎ (04721) 3 88.

Bade & Hornig GmbH, Herrengraben 31, D-20459 Hamburg. ☎ (040) 37 48 110 *Fax* (040) 36 64 00.

Eckhardt & Messtorff GmbH, Röedingsmarkt 16, D-20459 Hamburg. ☎ (040) 37 48 42 22 *Fax* (040) 37 30 28.

[1]**Nautischer Dienst (Kapt Stegmann & Co),** Maklerstr 8, D-24159 Kiel. ☎ (0431) 33 17 72.

Iver Weilbach & Co A/S, Tolbodgade 35, København ☎ 33 13 59 27 *Fax* 33 93 59 27.

1. Herr Stegmann, who runs this operation, has a chart shop close by the locks at the Holtenau entrance to the Nord-Ostsee-Kanal, well placed for collecting charts en route either for the Baltic or for western European waters.

CHARTS

The area is very well covered by the national surveying authorities and by yachting publishers. Both the official hydrographic and the small-craft yachting charts are available. The official sea charts, of course, vary in size, while the small-craft charts are available in convenient chart-table sizes, usually *circa* 59 x 42 cm, and in series packs. Appendix I shows the coverage of the main chart series available. Four of the main chart sources are detailed below.

British Admiralty charts are most useful in the German Bight, but their coverage of the Frisian islands is limited. The Admiralty *Tidal Stream Atlas (NP 253) North Sea Eastern Part*, with 13 hourly tidal plans based on Dover, is useful for tidal planning in the German Bight and as a quick chart-table reference for the turn of tide in the Jade/Weser and Elbe entrances.

German Seekarten und Sportbootkarten The German official sea charts or the pleasure-craft charts (the latter available in series packs) are essential for the German North Sea harbours and river entrances. These charts are well provided with harbour insets, while the yachting sets include additional notes on weather, lights etc.

Danish official sea charts and søsportkorten The latter are pleasure-craft charts, sold in two series, which are somewhat small in scale. Based on the official sea charts, they often need to be read with a magnifying glass. The Danish hydrographic charts are excellent.

NV Sportschiffahrtskarten This group of four series packs of small-craft charts (plus some one-offs such as the Nord-Ostsee-Kanal, the Schlei, and a *Lotsenkarte*/pilot chart with winds and currents) is published by Nautische Veröffentlichung and covers the Danish/German Baltic. The charts are standard chart-table size and include harbour insets and sea-current charts.

The small-craft charts are cheaper than the official versions, often cover wider areas and are yet cheaper when bought in series packs. At the time of writing, for example, it was possible to cover the whole of the SW Baltic comprehensively at 50 to 60 per cent of the price of the equivalent official charts by using the NV *Sportschiffahrtskarten* sets or a combination of these and Danish small-craft charts. Individual copies of the latter were available at 60 per cent of the price of the official Danish charts.

Frequent corrections are available for the official charts in this list, although of course these can also be used for the yachting charts, providing you are well briefed on the comparative coverage of the official chart series. British yachtsmen should note carefully that Admiralty *Notices to Mariners, Weekly Editions* include corrections for Denmark and the Baltic, but that the Admiralty's quarterly *Small Craft Editions* do not cover these areas.

A reasonable selection of charts to cover the whole area would be: Admiralty approach charts for the German Bight; German hydrographic *Sportschiffahrtskarten* sets for the Frisian coast, Weser, Elbe, Nord-Ostsee-Kanal and the Eider; Danish hydrographic charts for the Danish North Sea coast and the Limfjord; and NV *Sportschiffahrtskarten* sets for the whole of the SW Baltic, supplemented by the occasional more detailed Danish chart for a shallow-water area.

BOOKS

A tidal almanac is essential for the German Bight and its coastal area. Admiralty *Tide Tables, Volume 1 (NP201)* is adequate for the whole area, with its four standard ports – Helgoland, Wilhelmshaven, Cuxhaven and Esbjerg – and their secondary ports, covering most of the main harbours in the area. Tidal-current information (tidal diamonds) is included in all the North Sea charts recommended above.

The Admiralty lists are also useful: *List of Lights and Fog Signals, Vols B (Southern and Eastern Sides of the North Sea NP75)* and *C (Baltic Sea NP76); and List of Radio Signals, Volume 1, Part 1 Coast Radio Stations (NP281(1)) and Volume 3 Radio Weather Services (NP283)*. Do not forget to buy the printed correction supplements which go with all of these books. Both series are also frequently amended in the weekly Admiralty *Notices to Mariners*.

The Admiralty's two volumes of sailing directions are well worth using: *North Sea (East) Pilot (NP55)* and *Baltic Pilot Volume 1 (NP18)*. Again you need to buy the supplements, which are somewhat infrequent, leaving the books a little out of date. Allowing for possible corrections of detail, however, the broad picture of weather, currents and pilotage directions coupled with the fact that they are in English makes them most useful.

Finally, there are many yachting pilot books on the area, but the most useful and up to date are in German or Danish (apart from the one you are now reading!), so you will need to do some homework and take dictionaries. It is possible to cover only a small selection here – there are many others.

Nordseeküste, in two volumes, by Jan Werner (German Bight from Den Helder to Esbjerg), and two books of aerial photographs and pilotage notes: *Deutsche Nordseeküste* and *Deutsche Ostseeküste* (both DK Edition Maritim), by Nils Bahnsen and Jürgen Chr. Schaper. All three books published by Delius Klasing Verlag.

Der Grosser NV Hafenlotse, an essential adjunct, is a series of four pilot books coinciding with the four areas covered by the NV *Sportschiffahrtskarten* packs and published by the same company. A similar four-book series, *Der NV Landgangslotse,* deals with the tourist aspects of each area.

A single Danish book provides succinct and easily translatable reference material (particularly on yachting facilities and harbour plans) for all of the Danish harbours and in summary form for some German and Swedish Baltic harbours – *Komma's Havnelods,* published by Komma & Clausen. This is also available in German as *Hafenführer Dänemark,* published by DK Edition Maritim.

There are at least two books on anchorages in Denmark: *Ankerplätze in Dänemark* by Jan Werner, published by DK Edition Maritim, and *Ankern in Dänemark* by Gerti and Hans Claussen, published by Die Barque GmbH.

CUSTOMS FORMALITIES AND OTHER REGULATIONS

Both countries

From 1 January 1993, if you live in the EU you are allowed to move your tax-paid pleasure craft between EU countries without restriction, although it is probably wise to carry proof of tax-paid status by obtaining the EU Single Administrative Document from your local customs and excise authority.

Another easing of the regulations from January 1993 concerns dutiable goods. Yachts which arrive in an EU country from another EU country (or, in Denmark, from another Scandinavian country or Greenland) carrying dutiable goods under the permitted limit no longer need to report to customs. It must be stressed, though, that if you are at all worried about the customs status of any goods you have aboard you should report to the nearest customs office on arrival.

Foreign vessels must be registered (British yachts by one of the two official methods). Crew must have valid passports. There are no restrictions on crew changes.

It is always advisable when under sail and engine to display the motoring cone as per the International Collision Rules. In Germany they are particularly keen on this.

Germany only

Helmsman's certificates are required for German nationals, so it is wise for British yachtsmen to carry an RYA Helmsman's (Overseas) Certificate or another appropriate RYA qualification and a VHF Certificate of Competence. Children under 15 are not allowed to steer a vessel under way in German waters.

As in the Netherlands, in Germany yachts must carry aboard copies not only of the International Regulations for Preventing Collisions at Sea but also of the local German Collision Regulations and the Rules for the Nord-Ostsee-Kanal, even if the skipper is unable to read German.

Denmark only

Persons who have been outside Europe, the USA or Canada in the fourteen days before their arrival must have an International Smallpox Vaccination Certificate.

Lands of the sea raiders

Denmark – Europe's most stable democratic kingdom

'From the wrath of the Northmen, O Lord, deliver us.' Nothing could be further from the character of the modern Danes and north Germans than what is implied by this 10th-century prayer of north European churchmen. The origin of the Vikings is shrouded in mystery. In the ninth and tenth centuries they hit northwestern (and eastern) Europe like a bolt from the blue, extending their depredations well beyond those of their predecessors and contemporaries, the Angles, Saxons, Jutes and Frisians. They left their mark throughout the Mediterranean, western Russia, Turkey and Greenland, and as far afield as North America, long before Columbus.

The Vikings' relatives who stayed at home in Denmark established a nation which, after struggling with a long series of regal despots, is now one of Europe's most stable welfare states and constitutional monarchies. Nevertheless, the 19th and 20th-century history of Denmark's southern frontier and of the north German plain has been a bloody one.

The mysterious origin of the sea invaders

Until the end of the 8th century the history of Scandinavia and northern Germany is dim. The German Bight, Jutland and the SW Baltic coastal areas were ruled by warring petty kings and chieftains. Jutes, Angles (named after Angeln in southern Jutland and now in Germany – see Route 4), Saxons from Holstein, and islanders from the Frisian North Sea coasts were the earlier invaders of England, the low countries and France. In the 5th century a petty king of Jutland sent his generals Hengist and Horsa to conquer Thanet, Kent and the Isle of Wight with an army of Danes, Angles, Saxons, Jutes and Franks. England is named after the Angles who later overran most of East Anglia, the Midlands and Northumbria, while the Saxons left their mark on Sussex, Essex and Middlesex. In around 780 the first Viking raid on England is reputed to have occurred, and in 1014 the Danish Canute became King of England and later of Denmark, although the English-Danish constitutional connection died with him in 1035.

812 AD is the first proven date in Danish history, when King Gottfried and Emperor Charlemagne fixed the frontier of what was to become the kingdom of Denmark at the Eider river. Gottfried may later have constructed the famous Danevirke defensive wall across the Jutland peninsula, although Denmark's first official king, Gorm the Old, who ruled from around 900 to 940, is claimed by some to have this honour. Norse – the language north of the Eider river – had emerged many hundred of years earlier, but by around 1000 Danish, Norwegian and Swedish began to emerge as separate sister languages.

Roskilde's Viking-ship museum (Route 6), on Sjælland island, is organised around five Viking ships, found in 1962 in a narrow part of the fjord where their 11th-century owners sank them and covered them with stones to block the passage of Norwegian invaders. The ships are a deep-sea trader, a Baltic merchant ship, a warship, a longship and a ferry/fishing boat.

The Danevirke

Constructed in the 9th century, this earthwork is now entirely within the boundary of modern Germany. Its object was to defend the narrowest neck of the Jutland peninsula (no, not the route of the modern Nord-Ostsee-Kanal!), between Hedeby (Haitabu; see Route 4), the dark-ages seaport at the head of the Schlei river, and Holingsted, on the Trene river, which joins the Eider river running into the North Sea.

Queen of all Scandinavia

Under the Valdemar kings in the 12th, 13th and 14th centuries Denmark expanded by conquest into northern Germany and along the southern Baltic coasts and then lost these areas. A resurgence of Danish power occurred in 1387 due to the Kalmar Union with Norway under Queen Margarethe; this lasted for more than 400 years. In 1397 Sweden joined the Union ruled by the 'Queen of all Scandinavia', which at the end of the century also included Finland, Iceland and Greenland. The break-up of the Union began when Sweden left, soon after the 'Stockholm Bloodbath' perpetrated by Christian II in 1520.

Drove roads and *kroer*

The development of cattle droving on a large scale began just after the Union was formed. With it came the drove roads, which were highly important routes until the railway era. There were three major drove roads down the Jutland peninsula; although these have mostly disappeared under the modern roads, there are some remaining protected stretches. Along these roads developed the *kroer* (jugs) or inns for the drovers, and again some of the originals remain, although a wide variety of more recent *kroer* are equally tempting to the modern traveller.

København

København (Route 6) or 'Købmanns Havn' (merchants' port) developed from the 11th century onwards, becoming the main city of the Kalmar Union in 1397. A fortified stronghold, it was destroyed twice by fire in the 18th century and later came under Nelson's bombardment. A few fortifications such as the Kastellet remain, together with some 17th and 18th and a wealth of 19th-century buildings.

Kronborg castle

Kronborg castle (Route 6), in Helsingør (the Elsinore of Shakespeare's *Hamlet*), looks over the narrowest part of the Sound towards Sweden. Originally built in 1420, it was rebuilt around Shakespeare's time, burnt down and rebuilt in the 17th century, using tolls levied on passing shipping, and renovated in 1924.

Kronborg castle.

Monarchies and wars

The 16th and 17th centuries were marked by wars in the Baltic, in which Denmark was occasionally allied with but more often fought against Sweden. 1660, when Denmark changed from an electoral kingdom into a hereditary monarchy, marked the beginning of a gradual improvement in the country's fortunes, including some naval success in the 1700–1720 war with Sweden. Many relics of the 17th and 18th-century Swedish wars are to be found in the castles, palaces, churches and town museums of the Store Bælt and the Sound (Routes 6 and 7).

Forced to become part of the Continental Blockade in the Napoleonic wars, Denmark joined battle with Great Britain; in 1807 København withstood Nelson's bombardment, but at the Treaty of Kiel in 1814 the country lost Norway to Sweden and Helgoland to Great Britain.

H.C. – Denmark's most famous literary son

Denmark, with 5 million people, is a small country, so it is not surprising that it took until the 19th century to produce a world-renowned writer. Not until the late 20th century did Danny Kaye's Hollywood film put Hans Christian Andersen's name, as well as that of 'wonderful Copenhagen', onto the lips of the world. A cobbler's son born in Odense, capital of Fyn, H.C. Andersen lived from 1805 to 1875, and was contemporaneous with Dickens, whom he knew and visited. He moved early to København, remained unmarried and travelled for most of his life throughout Europe, writing novels and fairy tales. Although he neglected Odense (Route 5), his birthplace is his most lavish memorial (as Stratford is Shakespeare's), preserving an extensive museum of mementoes, his parents' house and a waterfront park.

Battle of the Dybbøl

In 1849 Denmark became a parliamentary democracy, and the second half of the 19th century was marked by the wars for Schleswig-Holstein, in the neck of the Jutland peninsula. Denmark occupied Schleswig in 1850. In 1864 it was defeated by Prussia and Austria and forced to cede the duchies of Schleswig, Holstein and Lauenburg. During this war the famous Dybbøl hill battle was fought, enabling the Prussians to invade the island of Als. Two museums and various monuments (Route 4) commemorate the battle.

The 20th century

Arguably one of the more rational and certainly one of the luckier countries of Europe, Denmark remained neutral in the First World War, during which the country adopted a more democratic constitution. In the early 1920s it began electing social democratic governments. Iceland became an independent kingdom during the First World War, becoming a republic in the Second World War. In 1920, as a result of the First World War, the Danish-speaking northern part of Schleswig voted by plebiscite to rejoin Denmark, so once more Dybbøl hill could fly the Dannebrog. The Danes claim that this is one of the world's first national flags, and legend has it that it was handed down from heaven. When you are cruising in Denmark, the flag is prominent everywhere, on shops, houses, factories and public buildings. I have even seen rowing boats flying enormous versions of it, and most yachts have oversized fishtail Dannebrog ensigns.

In the Second World War, Denmark, after signing a nonaggression pact with Germany, was occupied. A resistance movement developed and helped Denmark's Jewish population to escape, mainly to Sweden via Sjælland's most northerly fishing port, Gilleleje (Route 7).

In 1973, Denmark became one of the more controversial members of the EU.

North Germany's turbulent naval and military history

The strategic location of Germany's northern plain, together with its short Frisian North Sea coastline, separated from the German Baltic coast by the Jutland peninsula, is the root cause of the region's turbulent military and naval history in the 19th and 20th centuries. In the late 19th century control of Schleswig-Holstein (see above), at the neck of the Jutland peninsula, was wrested from Denmark by its considerably larger southern neighbours.

The Nord-Ostsee-Kanal

The Nord-Ostsee-Kanal (Route 3) was opened by the Kaiser in 1895, at the height of the European nations' competition for naval supremacy, and this established the Kieler Förde's strategic importance as a naval base; prior to this, Wilhelmshaven (Route 1), on the Jade, had been Germany's major naval port. The canal, almost as a postscript to the military objective, has developed into one of the world's busiest shipping routes. Over long stretches it is now edged with mature woodland, with picturesque sidewaters like a Danish fjord's, and it is difficult to see it as an entirely man-made waterway.

The Second World War had a devastating impact on the southern part of this region and the cities of Wilhelmshaven, Kiel and Hamburg have since been completely rebuilt. However, many of the smaller towns and villages on the Frisian coast and islands came through unscathed, retaining many of their old buildings. This is even more the case further north, where historic towns such as Rendsburg, Friedrichstadt (both on Route 3), Schleswig, Kappeln and Flensburg (all on Route 4) are architectural delights. The Hanseatic cities of Lübeck, Wismar, Rostock and Stralsund, on Germany's Baltic coast (see Chapter 10 for notes on the Hanseatic League), also have a wealth of medieval buildings.

Bridging the Store Bælt and the Sound

At the time of writing this book, the Jutland peninsula and Fyn were joined by a fixed railway bridge (33m clearance) and a road bridge (44m clearance) across the narrow part of the Lille Bælt (see Route 4). However, Fyn was still not connected to Sjælland across the Store Bælt, the main communication here still being the car/train ferry with the trains shunted on and off at each landing place (there is an interesting museum on the history of this ferry service at Korsør, see Route 6). However, Denmark's major project of the 20th century, the Store Bælt bridging and tunnelling project, was well under way and due to be completed by 1996. The bridge clearance at the western end of this project is 18m and at the eastern end will be 65m so if you are cruising in the area make sure you have up-to-date charts and keep a listening watch on VHF Ch 16, and if necessary contact the bridge on its working and information Ch 11, when you approach.

There is no doubt that Europe's biggest infrastrucure project of the 21st century will be the Dkr20 billion ($3 billion at 1990 prices) Øresund bridge and tunnel, to be built from København to Malmø in Sweden, which was originally agreed between the two governments in 1991. Like the British with the Channel Tunnel, the Swedes have been reluctant to give the final go ahead and there has been strong environmental opposition on the grounds that the bridge will impede saltwater flows into the already polluted Baltic – although, surprisingly to the layman, the bridge is not across the narrowest part of the Sound but is in an island-scattered area. However, the Swedish government was reported to have given the green light in June 1994, a decision warmly welcomed by Denmark, and tenders were to be collected. The completion of the project will almost certainly be after the year 2000, but surveying and construction will be a long, drawn out event, so once again, therefore, whenever you are cruising in this area make sure you have up-to-date charts and listen in on VHF Ch 16 or to whatever working channel is finally allocated when the time comes.

SYMBOLS AND DEFINITIONS

General

km kilometre(s)
kn knot(s)
M nautical mile(s)
m metre(s)

Used in route descriptions

Distances

In addition to an overall distance quoted at the beginning of each route plan, the plans also quote the approximate shortest safe distances between the main destinations, and this mileage is quoted immediately before each major destination.

Lit The expression 'lit' is used of some buoys, harbour entrances and bridge opening spans. It means that buoys have navigational lights and that a harbour entrance or bridge opening has one or more lights on one or both sides of the navigable passage.

Anchorage

Tidal streams, currents and water levels (in Baltic)

Fixed bridge

Lock or lock complex

Opening bridge

Difficult local weather and wind conditions

Walk-aboard moorings for yachts (could be a commercial harbour, a fishing harbour or a landing stage, rather than a yacht harbour). A major problem, particularly in many tiny (often 100m-long) harbours, is to find boxes, i.e. pairs of posts, which are wide enough to take 3–4m-beam yachts.

Yacht havens with more than about 100 moorings usually, though not always, have showers, toilets, water and electricity, and those with 200 or more virtually always have these facilities.

Yacht havens which, in the estimation of the author at time of writing, have at least 200 yacht spaces are indicated by a *. The author tries to estimate more accurately the numbers of moorings for yacht havens with 400 or more. These are the places where repair facilities are likely to be extensive.

PD Where petrol and diesel fuel are available at or close to the harbour at the time of research into this book, this is denoted in brackets as P and/or D. The minimum depth or range of depths in the harbour – below chart datum in the North Sea or mean sea level (MSL) in the Baltic – is also given.

→ Notes covering the passage route to next harbour.

Used on plans

Bn Beacon
Hbr Harbour
Lt Light (i.e. on a buoy or beacon/tower)
Lts in Line Lights in line
Tr Tower

PART I
THE NORTH SEA COASTS
1. The German Bight

Pilotage overview

AREA COVERED

Chapter 1 of this book covers that area of the North Sea eastwards and southwards of a line from the northern end of the Jutland peninsula to the Ems estuary.

It examines in detail three cruising routes for yachts in the area: along the southern and eastern coasts and across the southern end of the peninsula to Kiel.

TIDAL HEIGHTS AND RANGES

See also Chapters 2, 3, 4

Tide tables

Admiralty *Tide Tables, Vol 1. European Waters (NP192)*

The German Bight is subject to that familiar north European phenomenon – semidiurnal tides. However, they tend to be less fierce than in the southern North Sea: tidal ranges in the open sea are smaller than in the Dover Strait and Thames estuary areas, and in the rivers Ems, Jade, Weser and Elbe ranges are less than those in the Westerschelde and the London river.

The tidal range increases eastwards along the north German coast and in the rivers, and decreases northwards along the Jutland coast to a negligible level at the Skagerrak. Similarly, differences between the springs and neaps ranges vary in the same directions. At Borkum the springs range is 2·7m and the neaps range 2m, a difference of 0·7m; at Cuxhaven in the Elbe entrance the figures are 3·4m and 2·5m, a difference of 0·9m, and at Hanstholm in north Jutland both ranges are a tiny 0·3m.

Times of HW are progressively later along the German coast eastwards and continuing northwards to north Jutland. In the rivers, the HW time is later the further upstream one goes. In the table below, HW Borkum is at about the same time as HW Dover.

TIDAL STREAMS AND CURRENTS

Tidal atlas

Admiralty *Tidal Stream Atlas. North Sea – Eastern Part (NP253)*

In the German Bight, since the predominant winds are from the two westerly quadrants, an underlying ¼kn current sets in an anticlockwise direction round the bay – i.e. in a north to northeasterly direction off the north German coast and in a northerly direction off the Jutland peninsula. This current is overborne by the semidiurnal tidal currents: in the Admiralty *Tidal Stream Atlas* the current is incorporated as a retardation or acceleration of the tidal streams in the hourly tidal plans.

Because of the limited tidal ranges, tidal currents in the open-sea parts of the German Bight tend to be slower than those in the southern North Sea. The tidal currents in the former area's constricted rivers are, however, as fast as those in the latter area's rivers. Off the N German coast N of Norderney the average maximum hourly streams at neaps and springs on both flood and ebb are around 0·7/1·4kn. Off the Jutland coast close N of Horns Rev the streams are weaker at 0·3/0·6kn. In the central German Bight the maxima are 0·4/0·7kn. By contrast, the river streams range from average maxima of 2·5/3kn in the Randzelgat entrance to the Ems through 2·5/3·75kn in the Aussenjade and Weser channels to 3·5/4·25kn in the Elbe off Cuxhaven. Timing arrival at these entrances so as to have a favourable tide is therefore critical – any yachtsman who has spent hours pushing a foul tide into the entrance of the Westerschelde or the Thames after an exhausting overnight passage will know what I mean.

HW Dover coincides with HW Borkum. Streams out of the Elbe, off Cuxhaven, start at HW Dover +1·5hrs. They start an hour earlier (HW Dover +0·5) off Borkum to the W and in the southern German Bight generally. Ingoing streams start 6.25 hours later, at HW −4·5 in the Elbe and at HW −5·5 near Borkum. Off this north German coast there are periods of slack water starting from around an hour and a half before these turns of tide.

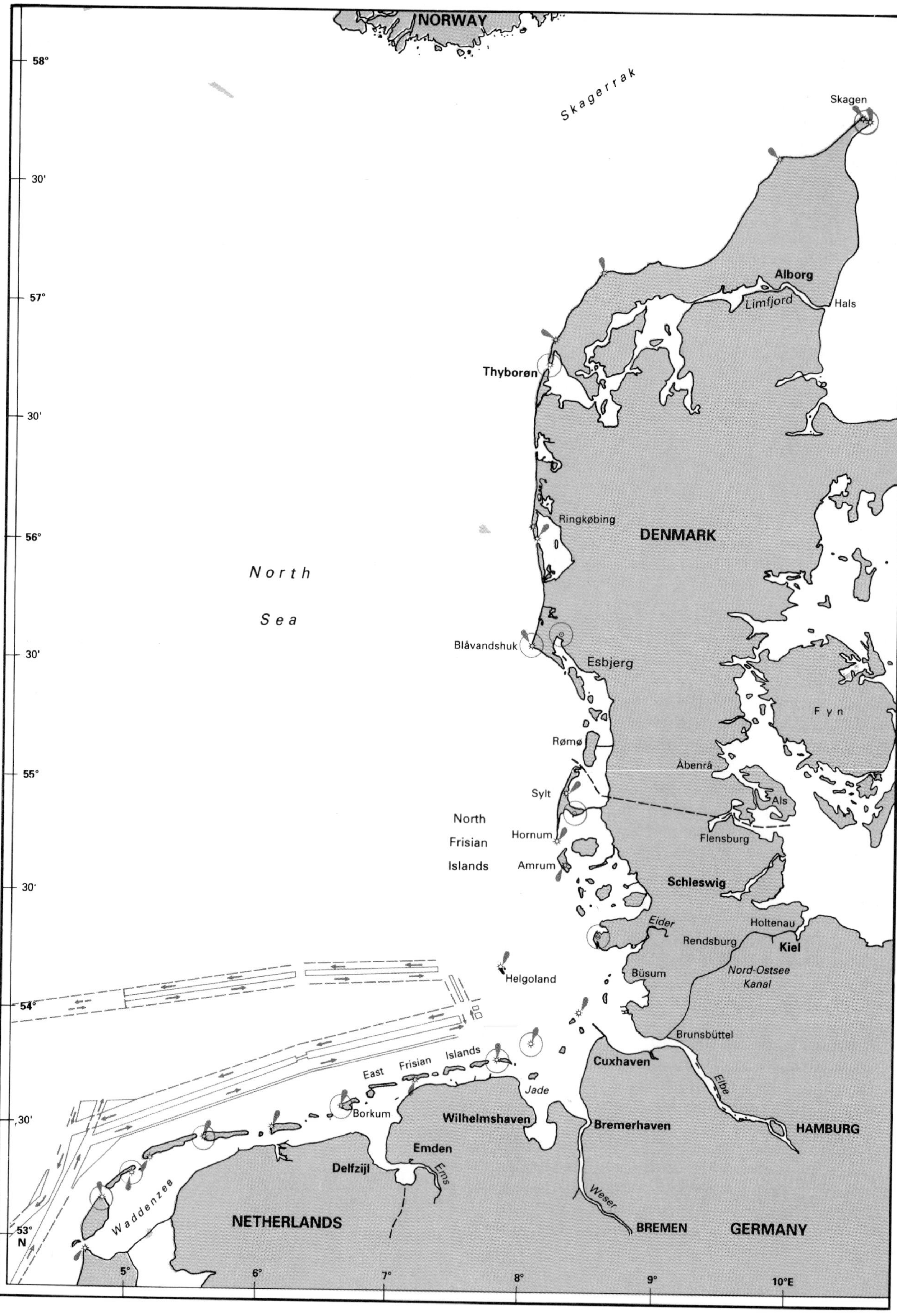
NORWAY
58°
Skagerrak
Skagen
30'
57°
Alborg
Limfjord
Hals
Thyborøn
30'
Ringkøbing
DENMARK
56°
North
Sea
Blåvandshuk
Esbjerg
30'
Fyn
Rømø
55°
Åbenrå
Sylt
Als
North
Frisian
Islands
Hornum
Flensburg
Amrum
30'
Schleswig
Eider
Holtenau
Rendsburg
Kiel
Helgoland
Büsum
Nord-Ostsee
Kanal
54°
Brunsbüttel
East
Frisian
Islands
Cuxhaven
Jade
Elbe
30'
Borkum
Wilhelmshaven
Bremerhaven
HAMBURG
Emden
Delfzijl
Ems
Waddenzee
Weser
NETHERLANDS
BREMEN
GERMANY
53°
N
5°
6°
7°
8°
9°
10°E

Approximate times and ranges of tides in the German Bight

	HW	*Springs (metres)*			*Neaps (metres)*		
	(time)[1]	*MHW*	*MLW*	*Range*	*MHW*	*MLW*	*Range*
North German coast eastwards							
Emden (Ems)	+0033	3·5	0·0	3·5	3·1	0·4	2·7
Borkum (Fischerbalje)	−0047	2·7	0·0	2·7	2·3	0·4	1·9
Norderney (Riffgat)	−0027	2·7	0·0	2·7	2·4	0·4	2·0
Helgoland	**0000**	**2·7**	**0·0**	**2·7**	**2·3**	**0·4**	**1·9**
Langeoog Ostmole	+0002	3·0	0·0	3·0	2·6	0·4	2·2
Spiekeroog Reede	+0003	3·1	0·0	3·1	2·7	0·5	2·2
Wangerooge West	+0007	3·2	0·0	3·3	2·6	0·5	2·1
Neuharlingersiel	+0016	3·2	0·0	3·2	2·8	0·4	2·4
Alte Weser Lt (Weser)	+0023	3·2	0·0	3·2	2·8	0·4	2·4
Hooksiel (Jade)	+0052	3·8	0·0	3·8	3·3	0·5	2·8
Wilhelmshaven (Jade)	+0110	4·2	0·0	4·2	3·7	0·6	3·1
Cuxhaven (Elbe entrance)	+0115	3·4	0·0	3·4	2·9	0·4	2·5
Bremerhaven (Weser)	+0143	4·0	0·0	4·0	3·6	0·4	3·2
Brünsbuttel (Elbe)	+0212	3·1	0·0	3·1	2·7	0·2	2·5
Glückstadt (Elbe)	+0317	3·1	0·0	3·1	2·7	0·2	2·5
Stadersand (Elbe)	+0353	3·2	0·0	3·2	2·9	0·2	2·7
Schulau (Elbe)	+0419	3·3	0·0	3·3	3·0	0·2	2·8
Seemannshöft (Elbe)	+0443	3·5	0·0	3·5	3·2	0·1	3·1
Hamburg (Elbe)	+0452	3·6	0·0	3·6	3·2	0·1	3·1
Northwards from the Elbe to Jutland							
Büsum	+0052	3·7	0·0	3·7	3·2	0·5	2·7
Eidersperrwerk	+0115	3·6	0·0	3·6	3·1	0·4	2·7
Tönning (Eider)	+0243	3·5	0·0	3·5	3·0	0·4	2·6
Friedrichstadt (Eider)	+0336	n/a	n/a	n/a	n/a	n/a	n/a
Nordfeld (Eider)	+0343	n/a	n/a	n/a	n/a	n/a	n/a
Husum	+0206	3·8	0·0	3·8	3·4	0·5	2·9
Amrum-Hafen	+0142	2·9	0·0	2·9	2·6	0·3	2·3
Hörnum	+0223	2·2	0·0	2·2	2·0	0·2	1·8
List	+0251	1·9	0·0	1·9	1·7	0·2	1·5
Rømø Havn	+0232	1·9	0·0	1·9	1·6	0·3	1·3
Grådyb Bar	+0133	1·5	0·0	1·5	1·2	0·3	0·9
Blåvandshuk	+0140	1·8	0·0	1·8	1·4	0·3	1·1
Esbjerg	+0255	1·6	−0·1	1·7	1·4	0·2	1·2
Torsminde	+0335	0·9	0·0	0·9	0·7	0·1	0·6
Thyborøn	+0450	0·4	0·0	0·4	0·3	0·1	0·2
Hanstholm	+0515	0·3	0·0	0·3	0·3	0·0	0·3

Note Data are approximate and should not be used to estimate actual times and heights, which should be obtained from tide tables.

1. Time is in hours/minutes relative to HW Helgoland

Off the north Jutland coast and in the north German Bight the stream, albeit a weaker one, turns in a clockwise direction from S-going at HW Dover −2·5, through SW and W to NW-going at Dover +6, and round through N, NE, E and SE back to S-going. There are approximately two hours of slack water during the turn from S through to W-going (HW Dover +1 to +3), and at the change from NE through to SE-going (HW Dover −5 to −3).

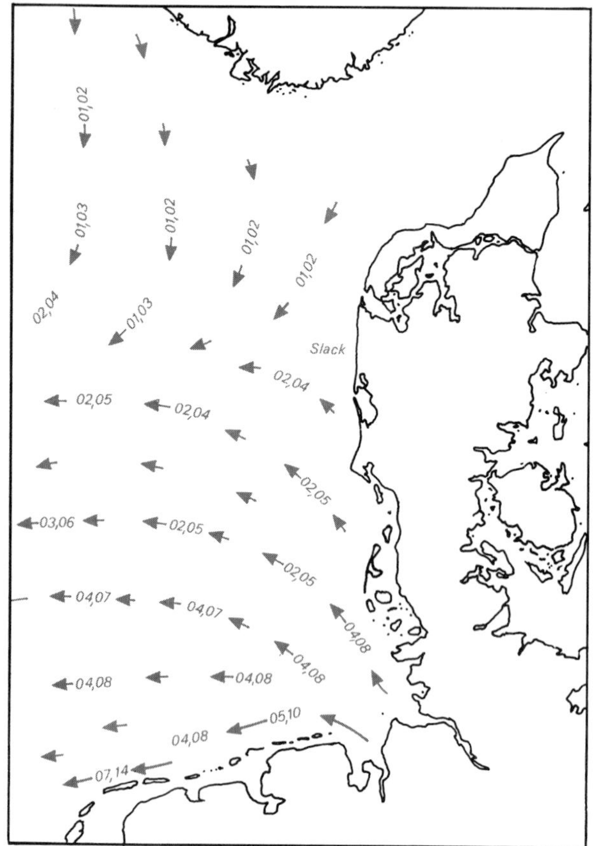

2hrs after HW Dover

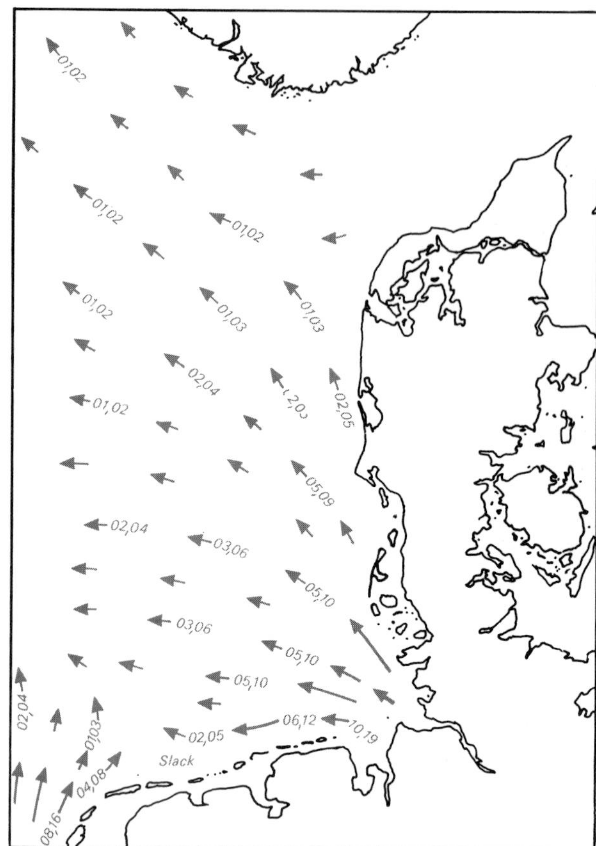

5hrs after HW Dover

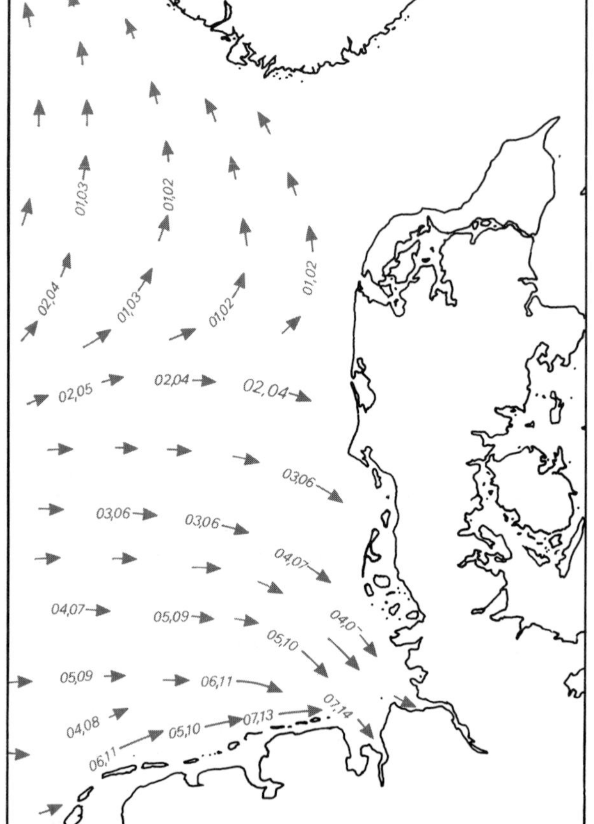

4hrs before HW Dover

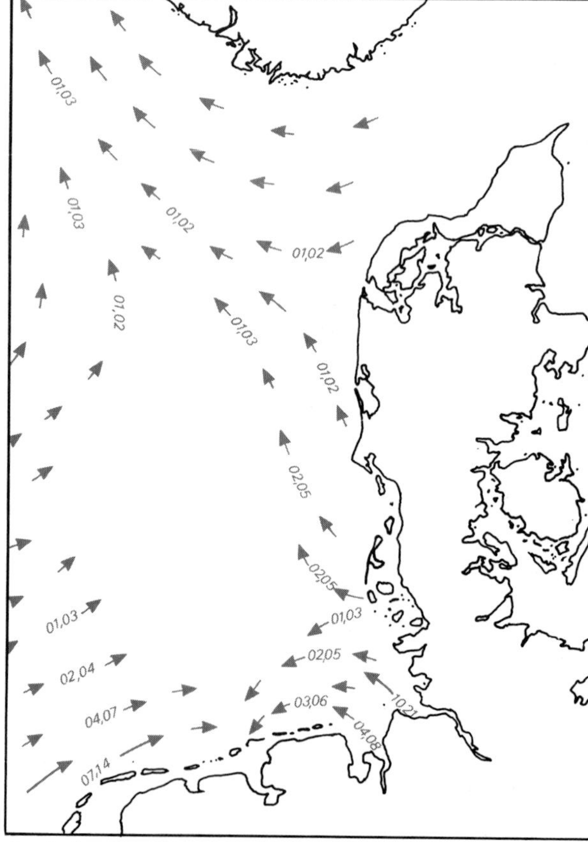

6hrs before HW Dover

Tidal streams in the German Bight. Arrows show rate in knots at neaps and springs e.g 01,02 0.1 knot at neaps 0.2 knots at springs

Tidal streams[1]

Position	*Start times (direction)*	
Based on HW Helgoland:		
Ems Outer Grounds	−0600 (E)	+0020 (W)
Randzelgat (W of Borkum)	−0600 (Flood)	−0015 (Ebb)
Osterems entrance	+0555 (Flood)	−0030 (Ebb)
2·5M N of Juist water tower	−0545 (S then E)	−0005 (ENE then W)
Juister Wattfahrwasser (1M SW E end of Juist)	−0540 (NE)	+0020 (SW)
Channel directly W of Norderney	+0550 (Flood)	−0010 (Ebb)
1·5M N of centre Norderney	−0525 (WSW then E)	+0035 (NW then W)
Accumer Ee (2·5M N of Langeoog church)	−0510 (E)	+0020 (NW then W)
Otzumer Balje (4M NW of Spiekeroog church)	−0520 (E)	+0055 (W)
Harle (4M NW of Wangerooge Westturm)	−0535 (E)	+0040 (Ebb)
Helgoland (1·5M SW of Lt)	−0515 (SE/Flood)	+0045 (NW/Ebb)
Based on HW Wilhelmshaven		
Aussenjade (NE of Wangerooge)	−0650 (Flood)	−0050 (Ebb)
Innenjade (near Hooksiel)	−0610 (Flood)	HW (Ebb)
Alte Weser Lt tower	−0610 (Flood)	HW (Ebb)
Bremerhaven (Nordschleuse)	−0450 (Flood)	+0120 (Ebb, variable)
Bremen(Industriehaven)	−0240 (Flood)	+0220 (Ebb, variable)
Based on HW Cuxhaven		
Elbe 1 LtV[2]	−0620 (Flood)	−0030 (Ebb)
Cuxhaven fairway	−0410 (Flood)	+0130 (Ebb)
Brunsbüttel	−0330 (Flood)	+0220 (Ebb)
Seemannshöft (approach to Hamburg)	−0100 (Flood)	+0410 (Ebb)
Based on HW Helgoland		
W coast of Schleswig-Holstein, 8°W and seawards	+0530 (S/Flood)	−0030 (N/Ebb)
Norderpiep (8°37'E)	−0535 (E/Flood)	+0110 (W/Ebb)
Süderpiep (8°32'E)	−0430 (E/Flood)	+0120 (W/Ebb)
Eider entrance approach (8°27'E)	−0430 (S−E/Flood)	+0125 (NE−W/Ebb)
Mittelhever (8°25'E)	−0440 (E/Flood)	+0115 (W/Ebb)
Rütergat (8°23'E)	−0430 (NE/Flood) (approx)	+0115 (SW/Ebb) (approx)
Vortrapptief (channel between Sylt and Amrum)	−0350 (ESE/Flood)	+0110 (WNW/Ebb)
Rømø Havn entrance	−0215 (NNE/Flood)	+0345 (SSW/Ebb)
Esbjerg Roads(off Færgehavn, also approx same Grådyb Bar)	−0305 (ESE/Flood)	+0315 (WSW/Ebb)
Hvide Sande (2M off)[3]	−0455 (S/Flood)	+0120 (N/Ebb)
Thyborøn Kanal (off entrance)[4]	+0100 (N/Flood)	−0400 (S/Ebb)

1. Note that data are approximate; actual times, directions and rates of stream should be obtained from tidal diamonds on charts.
2. Strong winds influence the duration, direction and rate of streams. Flood/ebb duration can be reduced by as much as 2 hours (E winds on flood), or increased by up to 2¼ hours (NE winds on ebb). Flood/ebb direction can be deflected by from 15 degrees anticlockwise (NE winds on ebb) to 35 degrees clockwise (N/NE winds on flood, S winds on ebb) depending on wind direction. Rates are increased or decreased by up to ½kn when the wind is with or against the stream, respectively. Off Nordergründe, 3M S of Elbe 1 LtF, strong winds can produce even greater changes than these.
3. Weak streams much affected by wind.
4. S to W winds increase rate and duration of N-going stream and reduce S-going flow; if long duration then N-going flow may continue several days. N to E winds have contrary effect.

Finally, no description of the area's tides is complete without a warning about the occasional exceptional tides. Persistent NW and northerly winds of storm force can drive water into the North Sea, creating a storm surge which is particularly severe if it coincides with HW and spring tides. Water levels can be increased by 3m or more above the normal tidal predictions. Winds from other directions and, more importantly, high atmospheric pressure can cause negative surges, which can reduce water levels by 2m or more. Again these effects tend to be greater nearer to the Elbe entrance, with its funnelling effect, and the highest recorded tides in some German ports have ranged from 3·6 to 4 m above MHW, and the lowest from 2 to 2·3m below MLWS. Navigational warnings of these hazards can be obtained from the area's radio services and of course from Navtex.

Winds and barometric pressure in the German Bight.

Helgoland from the south – offlying Hengst rock at west end, wind generator at east end on Vorhafen wall.

WEATHER, WIND, FOG AND ICE

Weather and wind conditions are extremely variable and seldom remain the same for more than a few hours on any passage. Across the seasons pressure averages 1012/1015 millibars, but with the passage of depressions and intervening high-pressure ridges through or to the N or S of the region it can fluctuate hourly. It can fall as low as 950 millibars in a deep depression, bringing a series of rapid changes in wind strength and direction.

While the depression systems generally move eastwards or northeastwards towards the Skagerrak, the occasional depression runs southeastwards straight into the Bight. In winter the depressions tend to cross the region more directly than in summer, when they cross to the N of the region. Spring (March to May) and autumn (September to November), when the depression tracks are moving northwards or southwards, are the most variable weather periods.

Less frequently, more stable conditions may last for up to a week or more, due to the spreading of high-pressure air, usually from the Azores region of the Atlantic in summer (June to August) and from Siberia in winter (December to February). Pressure can then occasionally reach 1050 millibars, with light, more variable conditions prevailing except on the edge of the system, where the isobars may be compressed by adjacent depressions, creating strong persistent winds.

October to March is the period with most gales and May to July the period with the least, while the frequency of gales is higher to the N of the region near the Skagerrak. In the sailing season, the strongest winds tend to occur in late summer and autumn.

The predominant winds are from the two westerly quadrants and tend to be more southwesterly in winter and northwesterly in summer, so that summer gales tend to be onshore on both north German and Jutland coasts. Early in the sailing season (March to May) there is most chance of getting winds from the NE quadrant, but this is more so in the southern corner of the bay than off northern Jutland. Throughout the sailing season there are relatively few winds from the SE quadrant.

Locally, winds tend to be deflected along the coasts, and in periods of warm summer weather onshore sea breezes develop near midday. However, most winds are onshore. Heavy cross seas occur when SW gales veer W or NW and when wind is against the ebb tide in the outer parts of the Elbe, Weser and Jade estuaries.

The channels behind the Frisian islands which edge the Bight from Horns Rev near Esbjerg round to the Ems estuary (and continue westwards in the Netherlands) are extremely well protected in any weather, but the outer shoals of these islands facing seawards are treacherous in most onshore weather above Beaufort force 4, as also are the big estuaries, particularly during the ebb. North of Horns Rev the Danish coast has few harbours of refuge, and the 20-metre contour, though steeply shelving, is generally a good 5 to 10 miles offshore, so it pays to keep well offshore, navigating carefully in order to avoid a lee shore situation developing in the persistent onshore wind conditions.

Fog in the region occurs mainly in late autumn, winter and early spring (October to March) and much more rarely in late spring, summer and early autumn (April to September). The most frequent fog is in the inner corner of the German Bight around the North Frisian islands, and in the Elbe, Jade and Weser estuaries, with the influence of the nearby land. In the December to March period, according to the Admiralty *Pilot*, it here averages between 8 and 18 per cent, although again in the May to September period it varies from only 1 to 3 per cent.

Ice is limited to the estuaries of the region, and particularly the Jade and the Elbe, during December, January and February, but varies considerably from year to year; there has been less in recent years.

In sum, therefore, it is much easier during the sailing season to sail from W to E in the region, but long passages risk strong onshore winds on arrival on either the Danish or the German coast. Early in the season there could be 'windows' in the weather when sailing westwards is easier, as well as lighter weather for sailing in general. However, in the very early season, particularly in the islands and estuaries of the inner bight, there is a risk of fog.

MAJOR LIGHTS

A 250M arc of 47 lights with 15M range or more surrounds the German Bight (including three pairs of leading lights and three light floats/vessels with 17m range: TW/Ems, Deutsche Bucht and Elbe). Although they stretch from Germany's Borkum island in the SW to Hanstholm on Jutland's northern coast, there are only seven lights on Denmark's 200M stretch of coast, the remaining 40 being on Germany's 130M of coast and islands.

Twenty of the lights are of 15–19M range (two of these in Denmark), 27 are of 20M or more range (five in Denmark).

Eighteen of the lights, all in Germany, are coloured, sector lights for approach warning of danger zones, while several of the longer-distance ones have additional directional flashing lights or are one of a pair of leading lights. The seven longest-distance lights are (see Admiralty *List of Lights* for characteristics) Borkum Kleiner (Dir30M) and Campen (Dir30M) on the Ems estuary, Helgoland (28M), Voslapp Rear (27M) on the Jade estuary, Tegeler Plate (27M) on the Weser estuary, Grosser Vogelsand (29M) on the Elbe estuary and Hanstholm (26M) on the northern Danish coast. Between the last two there is a large gap, although there is a 23M-range light on Blåvandshuk, at the root of the dangerous Horns Rev. There are several major lights on the Frisian islands in the 20–25M-range category.

MARINE AND AERO RDF BEACONS

Marine radiobeacons in the area transmit under the system established on 1 April 1992: the RDF set's beat-frequency oscillator (BFO) must always be used, and each station broadcasts individually and continuously (not as a member of a group), giving the identification signal at least twice for approximately 13 seconds followed by a long dash for approximately 47 seconds. Problems can be encountered from interference overlap between neighbouring (and sometimes distant) beacons on frequencies which are close together.

Name	*Freq. (kHz)*	*Ident.*	*Range (miles)*	*Position*
Borkum Kleiner Lt	302	BE	20	53°34'·8N 6°40'·1E
Deutsche Bucht LtF	312	DB	20	54°10'·7N 7°26'·1E
Wangerooge Lt	309·5	WE	20	53°47'·5N 7°51'·5E
Helgoland Lt	312·5	DHE	70	54°11'·0N 7°53'·0E
Elbe LtF RC	298	EL	20	54°00'·0N 8°06'·6E
Alte Weser Lt RC	309	AR	20	53°51'·9N 8°07'·7E
Nordholz(Aero)	372	NDO	30	53°47'·2N 8°48'·5E
Westerland/Sylt (Aero)	286	SLT	25	54°51'·4N 8°24'·7E
Donna, Dan Oilfield (Aero)	355	DON	75	55°28'·2N 5°08'·1E
Blåvandshuk Lt RC	296	BH	50	55°33'·5N 8°05'·1E
Thyborøn Lt	306	TN	100	56°42'·5N 8°13'·0E
Skagen W Lt RC	298·5	SW	50	57°45'·0N 10°35'·8E

DECCA COVERAGE

There is excellent Decca coverage of this area for coasting vessels from the Frisian Island Decca Chain (9B):

Station	*Place*
Master	Finsterwolde (53°12'N 7°06'E in the Netherlands' Groningen province)
Red slave	Høyer (55°01'N 8°42'E on Danish mainland E of Sylt)
Green slave	Heiloo (52°36'N 4°44'E in the Netherlands' North Holland province)
Purple slave	Zeven (53°17'N 9°16'E on German mainland NE of Bremen)

COAST RADIO STATIONS, WEATHER FORECASTS, NAVTEX

Following is a list of the area's VHF coast radio stations. If marked with a star they are also MF radio stations. For further information (frequencies, traffic lists etc.) see Admiralty *List of Radio Signals.*

Station	*VHF channels*	*Position*
Norddeich*	16, 86, 28, 61	53°38'N 7°12'E
Bremen	25, 28	53°05'N 8°48'E
Helgoland	3, 27, 88	54°11'N 7°53'E
Elbe-Weser	1, 23, 24, 26, 28, 62	53°50'N 8°39'E
Hamburg	25, 27, 82, 83	53°33'N 9°58'E
Eiderstadt	25, 64	54°20'N 8°47'E
Nordfriesland	5, 26	54°55'N 8°19'E
Blåvand*	2, 16, 23, 25	55°33'N 8°07'E
Skagen*	16, 1, 2, 3, 4, 64, 83, 19	57°44'N 10°34'E

BBC shipping forecasts are given on Radio 4 at 0033, 0555, 1355 and 1750 (UT). Netherlands coastguard transmits near-gale warnings only (not forecasts) in English on Navtex (station P). Norddeich Radio broadcasts strong-breeze warnings for the German Bight in English on MF at 0133, 0533, 0900, 0933, 1300, 1333, 1733, 2100, 2133. The best source of local weather forecast information is the yacht clubs throughout the region.

LIFEBOAT STATIONS

There are thirty lifeboats based in this area, i.e. an average of one per 12 miles of coastline. Seven of these are beach-type lifeboats based in the Frisian islands, and the rest are fixed-engined and cruising-type lifeboats, of which 11 are based in Germany and 12 on the inhospitable Danish coast. In the following list, places whose names are in bold have motor or cruising lifeboats and the rest have beach lifeboats.

Lauwersoog (Netherlands)
Oosterburen (Schiermonnikoog, Netherlands)
Borkum
Norderney
Baltrum
Langeoog
Neuharlingersiel
Helgoland
Wangerooge
Horumersiel
Wilhelmshaven

Fedderwardersiel
Bremerhaven
Cuxhaven
Büsum
Nordstrand, Strucklahnungshörn
Amrum Haven
Hafen von List
Rømø Havn
Sønderho
Esbjerg
Hvide Sande
Torsminde
Thyborøn
Vorupør
Hanstholm
Torup Strand
Slette Strand
Løstup
Hirtshals Havn

CHARTED NATURE RESERVES

In the *wattenmeer* (drying mudflats) of the East and North Frisian islands certain areas are designated by the German authorities as Zone 1 nature reserves. These are marked by green pecked lines on the German charts. These zones are closed to navigation from three hours after to three hours before HW, i.e. during the main drying period, and anchoring, drying out and landing in the areas is not permitted at any time. However, there is one critical navigational concession – the marked channels through Zone 1 areas are excepted from the above rules, so it is permissible to anchor on the edges of and navigate in these channels at all times.

Offshore approaches to the German Bight coasts

The closing approach to most of these coasts should be made in settled or moderate weather, since in most cases wind direction creates a lee shore or at best a wind parallel to the coast on both S and E coasts of the Bight. In the Elbe approaches in the corner of the Bight winds from the NW quadrant against an ebb tide are particularly uncomfortable.

The only safe deep-water harbour approach channels are to the Ems, the Elbe and the Esbjerg. All of the other *seegats* are shallow, making pilotage difficult. They should only be approached in moderate weather towards the top of a rising tide when their offing buoys have been found. Most of the Danish Jutland harbours also have narrow, shallow and difficult entrances.

Two approximately parallel TSSs (Traffic Separation Schemes) off the east Frisian coast, together with a third linked TSS connecting the two near the Deutsche Bucht LtF, dictate the long-distance approach of yachts to harbours in this area. The two main schemes are marked by lit lateral buoys, with the flood direction eastwards.

Yachts approaching the German East Frisian islands from the N or heading northwards from the islands must cross these schemes at a right-angled heading to the traffic. Alternatively, they can navigate along the Inshore Traffic Zone directly N of the islands, entering or leaving its eastern end near Wangerooge.

Helgoland is an ideal deep-water harbour of refuge in the corner of the Bight, with no traffic restrictions, which can be approached from several directions to obtain a lee. Here yachts can wait for a window in the weather in which to approach any of the East or North Frisian islands or enter the Elbe.

Approaches East Frisian islands

See also Chapter 2, Route 1

This 60M stretch of coast is fringed by a line of sandbanks and sandy, partially wooded islands some two to five miles off the mainland, to which they are connected by tidal sandflats crossed by winding channels. Gently shelving offshore banks N of the islands assist a seawards approach by depth sounding, but prevalent onshore winds often mean heavy seas.

There are some navigable, well buoyed and lit *seegats* between the islands through which to run for shelter, with harbours of refuge behind the western end of each island, but curtaining banks across many of the entrances make this an extremely dangerous coast in even moderate onshore winds. The low, flat islands and dunes make visual identification from seawards difficult unless conspicuous charted objects (mainly light towers and beacons with varying topmarks, all marked on the charts) are carefully sought out. The E-going flood tide near the island coasts tends to set towards the land, and when the tide turns it does so in an anticlockwise direction.

The *seegats* range from pointing N at the eastern end of the chain to pointing W at the western end. Strong winds from these directions against the ebb kick up steep seas in the channels and breaking seas on their fringing banks. The banks tend to shelve offshore, so depth sounding is a useful aid. It is essential to find the offing buoy for the beacons before entering the channel. It may have been moved from its charted position when you arrive, so beware, even if you think you have an up-to-date chart, and seek out the buoy and its subsequent channel-marking buoys.

There are eight major *seegats*, of which the Westerems is by far the safest and least restricted, with two deep-water channels. Two *seegats* are unmarked (or poorly marked) and shallow, and should not be navigated except by locals: the Osterems, E of Borkum, and the Wichter Ee, between Norderney and Baltrum. The remaining five (including the Blaue Balje, at the E end of Wangerooge), though marked, are curtained to the north by shoals inside the 5-metre contour which in places dry out. Going out along the buoyed channels across these shoals at low water in order to catch the flood eastwards is therefore dangerous, and even in light weather conditions it is advisable

Starboard withies at Eidersperrwerk. The German *watt* channels are well maintained.

not to cross before half-tide rising. Finding the entrances from offshore is also difficult, as their offing buoys are frequently moved. Wangerooge is a particular problem; although superficially it looks a good launching pad for crossing the outer Jade/Weser estuary to catch the flood into the Elbe, the *seegats* at each end have soundings of 1m and less in their outer grounds.

All the *seegats*, without exception, are dangerous in winds of over force 4 and from virtually the whole 180 degrees of the two northern quadrants. In sum, if you are familiar with the difficult English east and south coasts, these *seegats* are much, much more difficult than the Chichester, Deben or Ore bars. The descriptions of the seaward approaches below exclude the many charted topmarked beacons on the islands.

Borkum and the Ems estuary approaches

The Dutch/German border begins in the Westerems W of Borkum and follows the river to the Dollart. W of Borkum the approach is via either the Westerems channel or the more southerly Hubertgat. Both have large offing buoys and well buoyed channels, and both enter the Randzelgat W of Borkum and are convenient for the Fischebalje approach channel to Borkum and its yacht harbour. Of the two offshore channels, only the well lit Westerems is recommended for a night approach. There is also a buoyed (unlit) *seegat* providing a very tricky approach to the Oosterems N of Borkum across the Juister Riff.

Approaching from the north from seawards, Borkum island has two areas with high dunes, making it look like two islands from this angle. Several landmarks cluster at the W end of the island, including the Grosser lighthouse, Grosser beacon, an old lighthouse and a water tower.

Three major lights assist in seawards approaches W of Borkum: Borkum Kleiner light (30M range), Borkum Grosser light (24M range) and Campen (30M-range directional light), on the mainland, which gives the approach along the Randzelgat and inner Westerems channels.

Juist is a low-lying strip of dunes rising to 20m at the W end. A hotel and a water tower are roughly in the centre of the island. It is not recommended that strangers navigate round either end of the island from seawards, since the approach channels are unmarked. The best approach to the drying harbour halfway along the southern side of the island is on a rising ride from Norderney along the Busetief and the Juister Wattfahrwasser.

Norderney has a line of 20m dunes along most of its N coast, with the highest, Weisse Düne (white in appearance), near the centre. The town at the W end has conspicuous buildings, a church and a water tower nearby; in good visibility the 133m-high radio towers on the mainland NE of Norddeich can be seen behind. Norderney lighthouse (23M range), a tall octagonal brick tower, is near the island's centre.

The Norderneyer Seegat, leading to the harbour, is itself 5–15m deep, but is approached from offshore via two much shallower buoyed (unlit) channels across the outer grounds, the northwesterly-trending Schluchter and the northeasterly Dove Tief, both with lit offing buoys placed outside the 10m contour. Depths vary and are often less than 2m; sometimes the channels silt up completely and the buoys are withdrawn. Schluchter is better protected from NE winds. In strong onshore winds entry or exit is not advised.

Baltrum has dunes (only up to 15m high) at its W end and two nonprominent landmarks: Neue Kirche, near the dunes and on some bearings obscured by them, and Ost beacon, at the E end with a diamond topmark. The Wichter Ee *seegat*, between Norderney and Baltrum, is not recommended for navigation, since it is unmarked and the outer grounds dry in places.

Langeoog has 15–20m dunes on its N coast and a church and a water tower at its W end. In clear weather Esens church spire on the mainland behind can be seen.

The Accumer Ee *seegat*, between Baltrum and Langeoog and leading to the yacht harbour, has a lit offing buoy. Depths in the main channel are good, but to reach it requires following a shallow, mainly unlit buoyed northerly-trending channel crossing the outer grounds, with depths below 2m and again sometimes silting up. In strong onshore winds entry or exit is again not advised.

Spiekeroog has dunes up to 20m in height at its W end, where the village is situated, and is low-lying in the E.

The *seegat* here is very similar indeed to that at Norderney, with a deep-water channel off the W end of the island and two shallow buoyed (sparsely lit) approach channels across the outer grounds, each with offing buoys (one lit). These are the Westerbalje and the N-trending Otzumer Balje, both of which have depths below 2m and occasionally silt up. In strong onshore winds entry or exit is again not advised.

Wangerooge, with dunes rising to only 15m, has a conspicuous 64m-high light (23M range) and a Gothic-looking 52m-high west tower, both at its W end. There is also a disused lighthouse in the centre of the island.

The Harle channel is located almost centrally between the ends of Spiekeroog and Wangerooge islands, with shoal depths on each side but depths of over 17m in the main channel. An unlit buoyed channel leads across the outer grounds to a lit offing buoy, with varying depths, often of less than 2m. In strong onshore winds entry or exit is again not advised.

Vintage German centre-plater, tailored for the *watt* channels.

The Blaue Balje, between Wangerooge and the small island of Minsener Oog at the Jade entrance, is a deep (up to 21m) channel off the end of Wangerooge, with an unlit buoyed channel across the shallow outer grounds to its lit offing buoy. Depths here are again constantly changing, with some under 2m. In strong onshore winds entry or exit is again not advised.

Helgoland approaches

See Chapter 2, Route 1

Approaches Jade and Weser entrances

The outer entrance of the Jade and Weser estuaries is marked by a number of offshore light towers which are good visual as well as night marks. These include the Mellumplate (24M range), in the Jade entrance, and three in the Weser entrance: Alte Weser (22M), Tegeler-Plate (21M) and Hohe Weg (19M).

The main (buoyed and lit) dredged ship channel into the Jade estuary, the Wangerooger Fahrwasser, leads from the southern end of the Jade approaches TSS N of Wangerooge around Minsener Oog and into the entrance. There is also a buoyed but unlit deep channel, Mittelrinne, useful for pleasure craft coming from the Weser or Elbe and running into the main channel from the N between Strandplate and Mittelplate shoals.

The Weser estuary has a much more complex scattering of shoals than the Jade, with two major entrance channels, the Tegeler Rinne to the N and the safer and better marked big-ship channel, the Hohewegrinne, to the S. The latter starts about 5M N of the eastern end of Wangerooge and runs between the Mellum Plate and Tegeler Plate shoals. The Tegeler Rinne is marked; it is used mostly by fishing vessels or yachts crossing the Nordergrunde to and from the Elbe.

At LW in northerly winds many shoals in the estuaries, particularly the Tegeler Plate, can build up heavy breaking seas.

Approaches Elbe entrance

See Chapter 2, Route 1

There is a wide area of drying shoals and dead-end channels between the Weser and Elbe entrances. Crossing this often lee shoal via its tortuous *watt* channels is only for those with local knowledge. The main shipping channel into the estuary starts at the Elbe LtFl (17M range). Chapter 2, Route 1 details the main marks seen on the approach to Cuxhaven.

The prevailing winds being from the westerly quadrants, approach is often in lee conditions. The tidal streams are strong and can be deflected by strong winds (see tidal streams table above). The worst conditions in the estuary are in NW gales against the ebb, while on the flood strong N to NW winds can set a vessel southwards onto the Nordergrunde during approach.

Approaches North Frisian islands

This 90M stretch of coast from the Elbe estuary to Blåvandshuk and its offlying Horns Rev has similarities with the East Frisian islands in the inhospitality of its approach and pilotage. In some ways it is worse: not only are the North Frisians low-lying, with dunes rising to 30m at most, but they have a more complex network of islands and sandflats, and the 10m contour, with the exception of the area in front of Sylt, is 5 to 10M offshore of the outer islands, compared with only 3 to 5M in the East Frisians. In a few respects it is better: the channel-marking buoys extend further offshore and the offing buoys are also further offshore, but this is often little consolation for a long bumpy trek over 3–5m shallows, along channels which can funnel force 3–5 winds to much higher strengths.

The area, again, is frequently a lee shore, with seas breaking on the outer grounds, particularly near low water in rough weather. Tidal range is relatively small, though larger in the S nearer to the Elbe estuary, and it always pays to use the tidal streams. The neaps/springs ranges at Esbjerg, for example, are a mere 1·2/1·7m, and those at Büsum 2·7/3·7m (see list above).

For a night approach the main channels are marked by lit buoys, and there is a series of lights on the offshore sides of the islands varying from 11 to 23M in range, so that on clear nights passage from Helgoland at the southern end of the islands is rarely out of sight of lights.

See Chapter 3 for description of the main seamarks and coastal landscape on Route 2.

Blåvandshuk, 23M range, guardian of Denmark's Horns Rev.

Approaches Jutland west coast

The 170M of coast from Blåvandshuk to the Skagerrak contrasts with the Frisian coast. Although it too is low-lying sand and dunes, offshore beyond these are narrow lines of shallow sand ridges, parallel to the coast and extending up to about half a mile offshore, where they steeply shelve into the sea.

Although the tidal range is small and the currents are relatively weak, winds are again often acutely or directly onshore, and closing the coast in strong onshore winds is not advised. After persistent strong winds, wind-driven currents along the shore often overbear the tidal currents for several days, more frequently in a northerly direction.

A series of charted, topmarked beacons and occasional light towers and churches are the main landmarks. *See Chapter 3 for description of the main seamarks on Route 2.*

2. The German Frisian coast and the Elbe

Route 1
Emden to Hamburg via the *watt* channels, Wilhelmshaven, Bremerhaven and Helgoland

Commentary

See also Chapter 1, Approaches – Westerems to the Jade. Approaches – Jade and Weser entrances. Approaches – Elbe entrance

Although draught is no problem in the major rivers – the Ems, Jade, Weser and Elbe – a few shallow areas in the German *watt* channels determine the maximum draught with which it is feasible to cruise the full length of this route. It is normally about 1·4m – possibly as much as 1·5m in appropriate tidal and weather conditions.

There are, to echo Erskine Childers' *The Riddle of the Sands*, seven *wattfahrwassern* from Borkum to the Jade, one behind each of the seven islands. Of these, the two shortest (but also the shallowest) are behind Borkum and Baltrum. Each is about four miles long; according to the German charts, each gives about 1·5/1·6m of water at MHWS and 1·2/1·3m at MLWN, and dries well above chart datum at LW. There is another, deeper channel further S at Borkum, used in the route below, which is a safe detour for vessels of up to about 2m draught and also useful at neaps, but there is no alternative at Baltrum. Nor is it possible to bypass Baltrum by going out to sea via its western *seegat*, since the Wichter Ee is unmarked, treacherous and only for people with local knowledge (*see also Chapter 1, Approaches – East Frisian islands*).

Theoretically, the main *watt* channels behind the five remaining main islands give at least 1·8m of water at MHWS (over 2m behind Norderney and Langeoog). There is a final additional channel in the route below – into the Jade behind Minsener Oog (yes, Childers was wrong, this double island is to be added to his seven) – and this also gives over 2m at MHWS.

But all this is academic: the sands are constantly moving and the charts are only rough indicators. You must follow the withies and buoys religiously on a rising tide and never be surprised to find you are 'nudging' the ground. It is also worth visiting the clubs to quiz the yachtsmen who have arrived from the opposite direction on their experiences of the next *watt* channel.

Withies with branching heads or besoms and red fluorescent tapes are the northern-channel markers (port when entering harbours). Two withies close together mark the junction of two channels. Withies with bound-down heads and green fluorescent tapes, of which there are few, are southern-side markers (starboard when entering harbours). The deepest part of the *watt* channel is not close to but usually around 50m or so away from the withies. You should always be aware of the soundings and do an occasional cross-channel test run. Red and green lateral buoys (mainly spars) replace the withies in the deeper approach channels to the *wattfahrwassern*, and at the eastern end of the *wattfahrwassern* care must be taken to examine the German charts for the large arrows which indicate the direction of the buoyage, which is not always with the direction of the flood.

The simple tactic for cruising eastwards or westwards is to leave a harbour at the earliest practicable time on the flood (depending on distance) in order to arrive at the next destination on a rising tide or somewhere approaching the top of the tide and follow the withies and buoys as you find them on the chart (they may have been moved, so your Decca positions will only be approximate guides). The distances between harbours are often well within a rising-tide period. As it is better to travel at springs, which gives 1 to 2 feet more water, than at neaps, these short trips are usually towards the middle of the day.

One further point: behind the longer islands the shallowest part of the *watt* channel tends to be about two-thirds of the island's length along, nearer the eastern end, so timing is a little more tricky when travelling westwards (the route below is eastwards). If you take the ground by accident (or by design) you will almost certainly be fairly close to the withied channels, so you have no need to worry about Zone 1 nature reserve restrictions (see Chapter 1).

The Zone 1 nature reserve areas tend to be S of and at the eastern end of each island, and also on the landward side of the mudflats S of each *seegat*.

There are five major cities on this route. Hamburg dominates all, with its nightlife and every possible amenity, but its yachting facilities are limited, although you can pick a marina further down the Elbe and travel in by public transport or taxi. Cuxhaven has the best yachting facilities along the coast and is architecturally a pleasant town. Bremer-

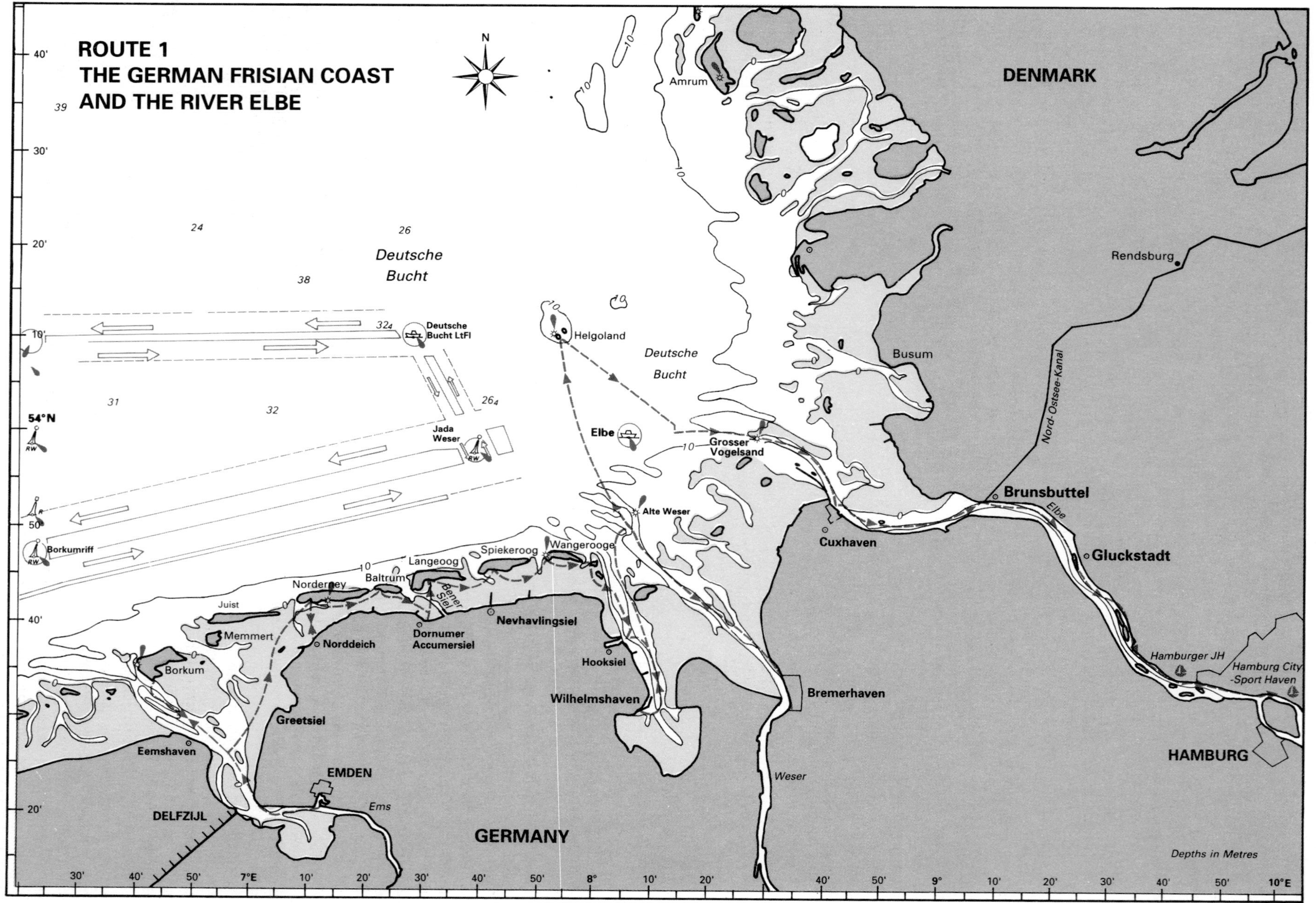
ROUTE 1
THE GERMAN FRISIAN COAST
AND THE RIVER ELBE
N
DENMARK
GERMANY
HAMBURG
Hamburg City
-Sport Haven
Hamburger JH
Gluckstadt
Brunsbuttel
Elbe
Nord-Ostsee-Kanal
Rendsburg
Busum
Cuxhaven
Bremerhaven
Weser
Amrum
Deutsche Bucht
Helgoland
Elbe
Alte Weser
Grosser Vogelsand
Deutsche Bucht LtFl
Jada Weser
Borkumriff
Wangerooge
Spiekeroog
Langeoog
Baltrum
Norderney
Juist
Memmert
Borkum
Bener Siel
Nevhavlingsiel
Hooksiel
Wilhelmshaven
Dornumer Accumersiel
Norddeich
Greetsiel
EMDEN
Ems
Eemshaven
DELFZIJL
54°N
7°E
8°
9°
10°E
Depths in Metres

haven's Columbus centre, with its nearby floating ship collection, is well worth visiting. Wilhelmshaven is a somewhat austere city, but has a very wide range of amenities. Emden has very limited facilities for pleasure craft and only a few attractions for visitors, including museums and some historic ruins.

The towns and villages on the N German coast tend to be rather bare and austere, and are often dominated by high sea walls. The islands are more picturesque; although they are crowded seaside resorts, this means that they have many attractions and restaurants. The islands, despite the crowds, manage to retain a somewhat time-warped 19th-century character, with classical seafront buildings, ferry harbours, dazzling white sandy beaches, green woodlands, grasslands with ponies and cattle, and – dream of the greens – restrictions and even some bans on cars in favour of horse transport, bicycles with trailers and the odd municipal electric vehicle.

Along the Elbe, there are some interesting old towns and villages in the side waters, particularly if you are prepared to do some mud-hopping on the return trip from Hamburg.

Apart from the main-line connections at Emden and Hamburg, at each end of this route, if you wish to meet crew the best places are Norderney and Norddeich (there is a main-line railway connection as well as a ferry between the two), Wilhelmshaven, Bremerhaven and Cuxhaven. The *siel* towns are connected by bus services, and there are ferries from the mainland to each main island harbour.

Distances

325M overall. 285M to Brunsbüttel only. 169M to Brunsbüttel if visits to Leybucht, the Jade, the Weser and Helgoland are excluded.

Tides, depths and currents

See Chapter 1 for tidal times and ranges by harbours

Times of HW are progressively later along the German coast eastwards, and upstream along each of the four rivers Ems, Jade, Weser, and Elbe. HW Borkum (which approximates to HW Dover) is about two hours earlier than HW Cuxhaven, and HW Hamburg is about three and a half hours later still. HWs at Emden, Wilhelmshaven and Bremerhaven are from one to one and a half hours after HW at their river entrances (see Chapter 1 for more precise data).

Similarly, the tidal range increases eastwards along the coast and along the rivers. At Borkum the spring range is 2·7m, at Cuxhaven 3·4m and at Hamburg 3·6m; at Emden, Wilhelmshaven and Bremerhaven the figures are 3·5m, 4·2m and 4·0m respectively. The neaps range along the coast tends to be progressively larger in the same direction, being smaller than the springs range by 0·8m at Borkum and by 1·1m at Wangerooge west. Along the rivers the differences change very little (0·8m at Emden, 1·1m at Wilhelmshaven, 0·9m at Bremerhaven and Cuxhaven, and there is actually a reduction to 0·5m at Hamburg).

The flood tide runs into the *seegats* and spreads eastwards and westwards round the back of each island. The ebb runs out in the opposite direction.

Persistent strong winds can affect the sea level: northwesterlies have been known to increase the water level by an extreme of 3–3·5m above MHW, and southeasterlies reduce it by 2m above MHW.

There is a multitude of drying harbours along this route, all the way to the outskirts of Hamburg, in many of which you will sink into soft mud. However, the distances between the deeper-water harbours are in all case moderate, so you will have no problem if you do not wish to take the ground.

Weather

With the exceptions of the short *seegat* crossings, the approaches to Helgoland and the outer grounds of the Jade/Weser and Elbe estuaries, most of this route is well protected from winds from most directions. In these exposed areas, winds from the NW quadrant in particular are to be avoided.

Charts

Note Chart datum and chart soundings are based on mean low water springs (MLWS) on all charts except the Dutch chart, which is based on mean lowest low water springs (MLLWS). Heights are based on mean sea level (MSL) except on British Admiralty charts, where mean high water springs (MHWS) is the base.

British Admiralty (note that there is no chart to cover most of the *watt* channels of the East Frisian islands) *126, 1507, 1875, 3261, 3262, 3266, 3268, 3368, 3369, 3405, 3406, 3407, 3509, 3510, 3761.*

German hydrographic *2, 3, 4, 5, 6, 7, 44, 46, 47, 48, 81, 87, 88, 89, 90, 91.*

German hydrographic *Sportbootkarten* *3010, 3014, 3015.*

Dutch small-craft chart *1812.*

A multitude of drying harbours – Spiekeroog at low water.

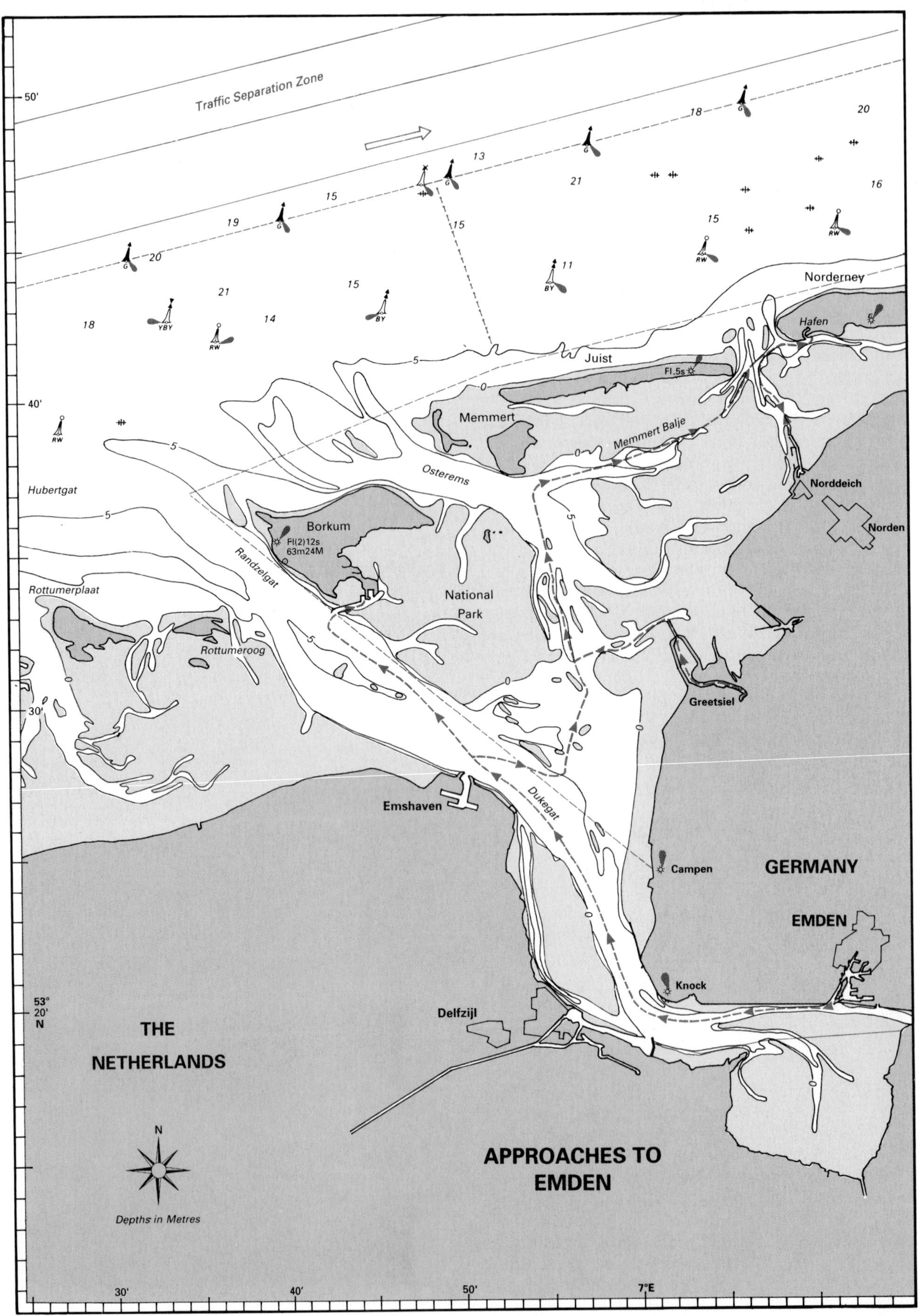

Traffic Separation Zone
Norderney
Hafen
Juist
Fl.5s
Memmert
Memmert Balje
Osterems
Norddeich
Norden
Hubertgat
Borkum
Fl(2)12s
63m24M
Randzelgat
National
Park
Rottumerplaat
Rottumeroog
Greetsiel
Emshaven
Dukegat
Campen
GERMANY
EMDEN
Knock
Delfzijl
THE
NETHERLANDS
APPROACHES TO
EMDEN
Depths in Metres

Route description

EMDEN

This highly commercial port has limited attractions for pleasure craft, and Delfzijl's yacht haven, in the Netherlands on the opposite bank of the Ems, is arguably, a more comfortable starting point for the trip to Borkum. In Emden, the easiest moorings to pick up are at the pontoons of **Emder Segel-Vereins** (3m depth) on the E side of the Aussenhafen just before the lock, but these suffer from swell from passing vessels (and in SW winds). Alternatively, pass through Nesserland lock (VHF Ch 13; in summer open 0600–2200, but Sundays and holidays 0800–1200) and then through an opening railway bridge; there are moorings either in the old **Ratsdelft** basin (3m), in front of the Rathaus, or through another opening bridge in the Falderndelft basin (4·6m). Both moorings are very convenient for the town but have few amenities. The yacht moorings in **Jarssumerhafen**, in the SE corner of the port complex, are in an extremely unprepossessing industrial dock basin a considerable distance from the town.

The town's tourist attractions are a ruined medieval church, a waterside Renaissance gate, a museum of modern art, and one of Europe's largest collections of armour at the Ostfriesisches Landesmuseum.

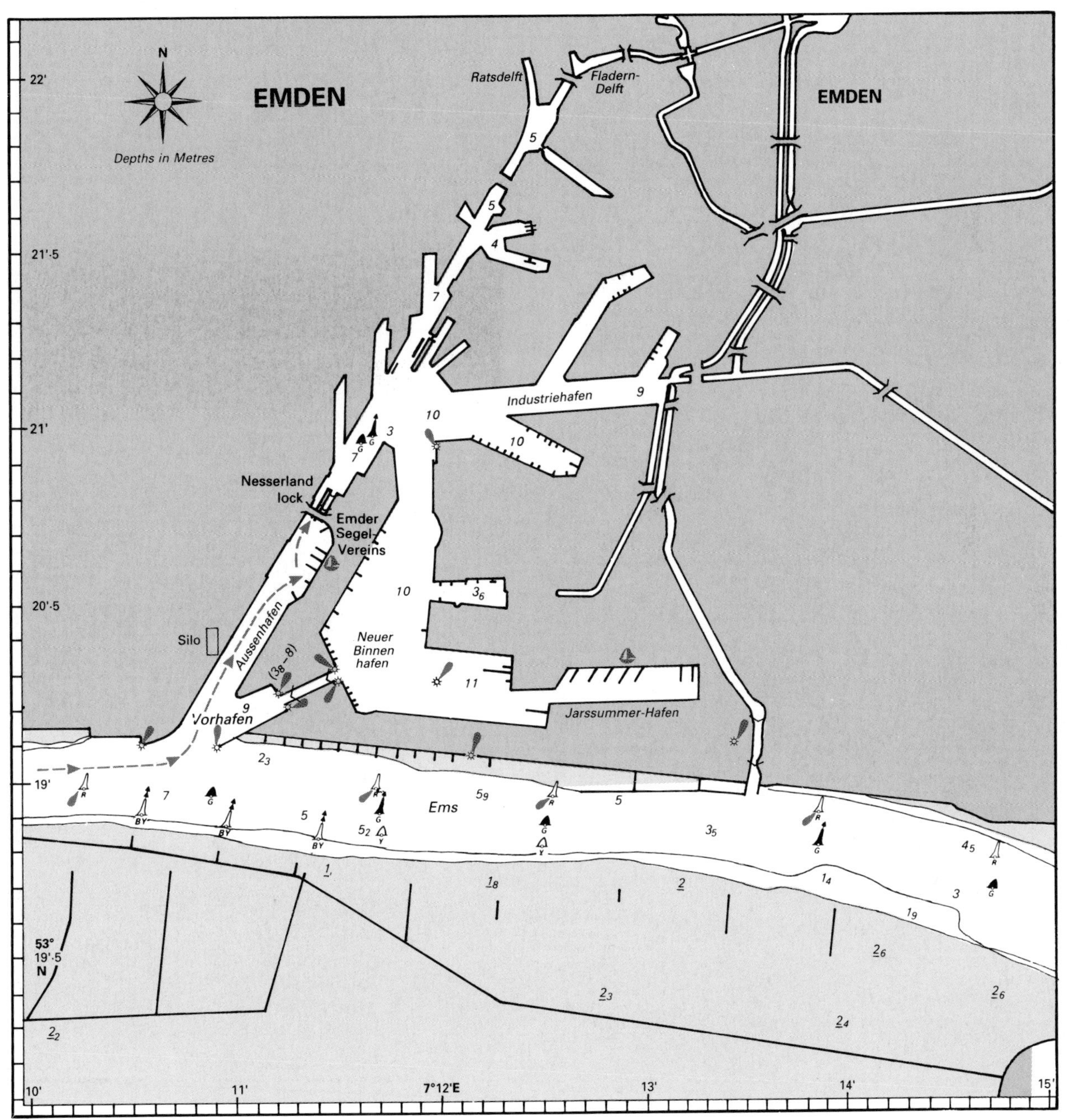

Obsolete Deutsche Bucht LtV in the Ratsdelft, Emden.

→ This is an extremely easy passage. After the narrow Emden Fahrwasser, it keeps in 5–10m water outside the starboard edge of the generously buoyed (mainly lit) main shipping channel. At night there are two sets of lights in line near Emden, a sector light on the Knock bend, Campen's directional light along the Randzelgat and a sector light at the entrance to Borkum's Fischerbalje approach channel. This channel is buoyed (some lit, 4–6m depth). Borkum yacht haven is immediately to port, before the commercial harbour.

26M
BORKUM

The yacht haven (1·8–2·5m, PD*) has most facilities, but is in an isolated spot some 5km away from the busy seaside resort clustered along the shore to the NW. The town has all the usual attractions, and can be reached either by the harbour-town train or on bicycles hired from the harbourmaster.

THE EMS

This distance requires starting at HW Emden at latest to obtain the benefit of a full ebb, since HW averages 1 hour 20 minutes later than at Borkum, so that there are only about 5 hours of ebb downstream. Off Emden's entrance the ebb can reach a maximum of about 2·2kn at +0330hrs HW Borkum; off the bend at Knock it can reach 2·8kn at +0300hrs HW Borkum, and off Borkum 2·8kn at about +0200hrs HW Borkum.

The most difficult weather on this passage is a northwesterly against the ebb from the Knock bend onwards.

Crossing the Ranzelgat approaching Borkum.

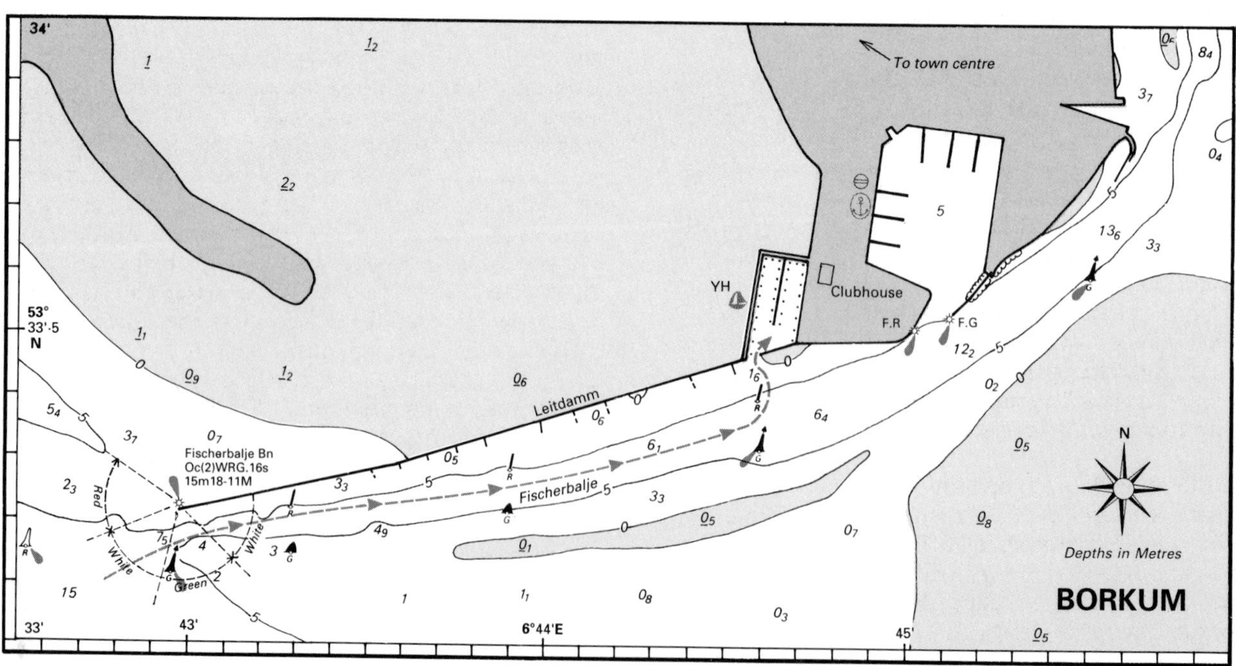

Borkum's new yacht harbour.

Leybucht and Greetsiel. Lower Saxony's plan for the area.

DIVERSION TO GREETSIEL (LEYBUCHT)

(18M return to main route above – not included in total mileage)

→ Halfway between Nos O32 and O30 (Osterems) red buoys head northeastwards past a W cardinal buoy joining the Ley channel (L-series buoys) at a T-junction. Follow these buoys carefully northeastwards (red to port, they are spindly and about half a mile apart and visibility needs to be reasonable) along the zig-zagging channel towards the yellow lit beacon and green buoy off the end of Leysiel entrance channel. Round the green buoy (keep it to starboard) and head southwards between the breakwaters, marked by posts, into the outer lock basin. Opening is usually prompt, but use VHF Ch 17 and tie up to a post, if necessary.

« The lock and opening bridge at Sperrwerk Leysiel are serviced on request between 4 hours before and 3 hours after HW Norderney; in season 24 hours daily except on Fridays after 2200, Saturdays (service 0500–2200), Sundays and holidays (service from 0500 onwards).

→ The Leybucht project is due for completion in 1995, but the dam and lock are now fully operational and water levels in Speicherbechen lake and the channel to **Greetsiel** are maintained at MHW. The 4M-long buoyed (unlit) and withied channel is 3m deep if you keep to the centre. Dredging has left the fishing harbour 4·5m deep (there are sometimes spaces along the wall); the new yacht harbour to port just before the fishing harbour has 1·5–2m of water and a clubhouse barge (showers, bar etc.). This busy German tourist village, is reminiscent of Dutch canal villages, with its leafy square, pavement cafés, two windmills, and a large crab-fishing fleet with huge booms and nets lining the harbour's edge.

→ After returning to the Leysiel lock channel entrance, there are two possible departure routes: either, retrace the Ley channel and continue to its junction with the Memmert Balje to join the route to Norderney above; or, follow the partly buoyed but mainly withied Nordeicher Wattfahrwasser, a somewhat shallow *watt* channel only to be taken on the second half of a rising tide, northwards to Norddeich entrance.

RANDZELGAT, OSTEREMS, MEMMERT WATTFAHRWASSER, BUSETIEF

This distance requires a departure on the early flood so that the shallowest part of the Memmert Wattfahrwasser is crossed towards the end of the flood.

→ If your vessel is shoal draught and can take the ground you might risk taking the short route via the Borkumer Wattfahrwasser close to the island (not included in route below), but this is so shallow that you need to leave near the top of the tide, which means you could find yourself negotiating the Memmert Wattfahrwasser on a falling tide.

As often in cruising, the longer route is safer. This involves retracking southeastwards along the N side of the Randzelgat, past the Emshörn light beacon and Emshörn Z1A platform, to the first of the Osterems (O) series of unlit spar buoys leading northwards (do not cut the corner; keep green buoys to port, red to starboard). You will thus be sure of at least 2m of water in the shallow southern end of the channel at this time of tide. At the extreme N end of the buoyed channel, make sure you clear the Kopersand spit to the E before following the Memmert Balje/Wattfahrwasser (M series of mostly red spar buoys). The spars are followed by withies (keep them to port) across the Memmert *watt*, then more red spar buoys (still keep to port), to the point where they enter the Busetief channel. At this point a group of buoys to the W of the course marks the start of the Juister Wattfahrwasser. Continue heading northeastwards, noting that the buoyage direction now reverses (green to port, red to starboard). Follow the Busetief (unlit buoys, 2–4m) into the Riffgat (some lit buoys, 10m-plus depths) off Norderney Hafen, then go hard to port

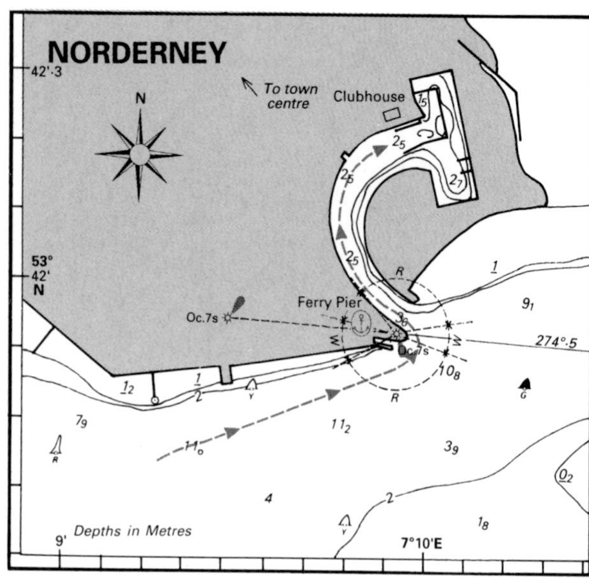

(with care) round the sector light and along a 2·5–3·6m-deep channel to the yacht haven at the NE end.

Greetsiel's crab-fishing fleet.

Departure along Norddeich's entrance channel. No we weren't preparing to cycle over the *watts*!

Norderney yacht harbour looking from the west.

31M
NORDERNEY

⛵ ⚓ The yacht haven (1·5–2·7m, PD*) has all facilities but is nearly 2km from town, so bicycles need to be hired. There is a possible anchorage E of the harbour entrance over sand on the N side of the channel.

The main features of Germany's oldest spa and 19th-century royal holiday centre are its elegant sea-facing facades and its central parklike square, where you can sit at an outdoor café and listen to a German band. The restaurants are many and varied and the nearby beaches inviting. In one side street a pyramid of 61 stones, each from a different German state, commemorates Kaiser Wilhelm's unification of Germany.

It is an easy trip to Juist from here; although its harbour dries out, if you do not want to take the ground it is possible to visit for an hour or two towards the top of the tide and then return to Norderney.

Norderney SC on the west side of the yacht harbour.

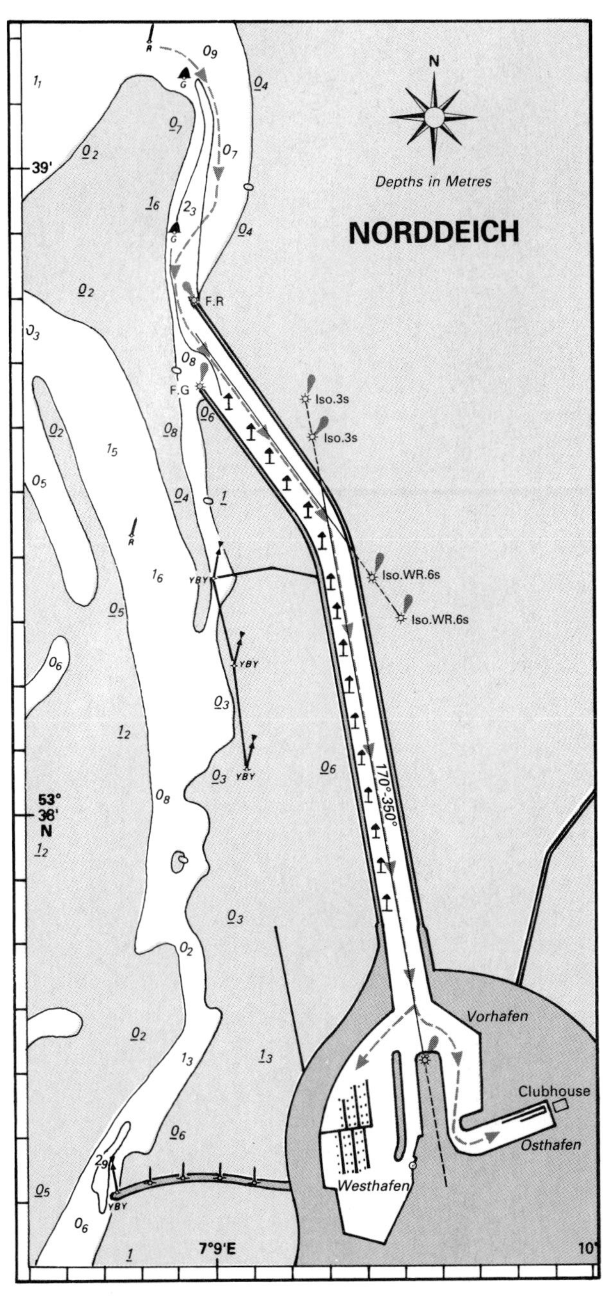

BUSETIEF

A passage on the second half of the flood is recommended to newcomers so that the trickier latter part of the route can be negotiated nearer to HW.

→ Follow the Busetief (buoyed, some lit) SW and southwards, keeping out of the way of the ferry of course, to the lit W-facing entrance piers and the 1M-long approach channel to Norddeich, marked by starboard-hand withies on the W side.

6·5M

NORDDEICH

Visitors should moor in the Westhafen yacht haven, although occasionally there is space on the pontoons of the local yacht club in the Osthafen (2·5m, PD★). The yachting facilities are equal to those at Norderney, but the town has limited attractions compared with Norden, a larger and architecturally interesting historic town some 4km inland.

BUSETIEF, RIFFGAT, NORDERNEYER WATTFAHRWASSER, BALTRUMER BALJE

A passage on the second half of the flood is recommended, piloting the Norderneyer Wattfahrwasser nearer to HW.

→ Return along the Busetief and follow the Riffgat and Norderneyer Wattfahrwasser. Both of the latter channels are marked by unlit, mainly red spar buoys, with a short stretch of port-hand withies across the *watt*. From the green light buoy at the end of this channel, at the eastern end of Norderney, a direct course is taken to round the sector light at the end of Baltrum's northern mole (S cardinal beacon to starboard when entering). The course then leads along the S side of this mole through the entrance and hard to starboard to the yacht pontoons at the NE corner.

14M

BALTRUM

A small harbour without fuel and with limited facilities; it is best to enter at half-tide and above. The yacht haven dries out at its inner edges, but there is water at the outer pontoons. The holiday resort is about 1km away. The island has no cars at all, only horses and bicycles, and the town/village is small – which some may find a relaxing change from the previous stop.

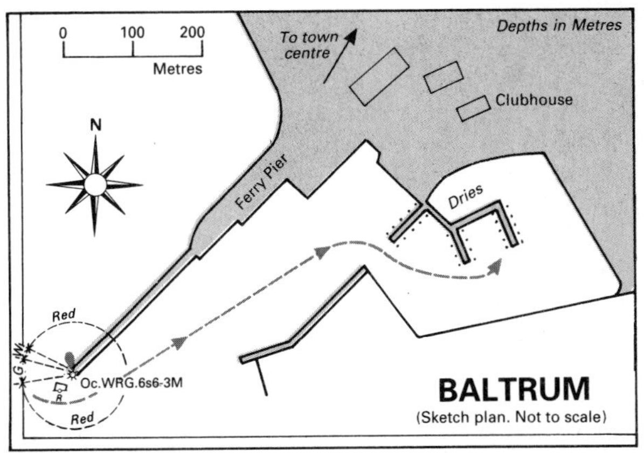

Baltrum. Approach from west.

Baltrum. Rounding entrance wall with its offlying buoy.

Baltrum ferry pier. These Frisian ferries often have only 1·2m draught!

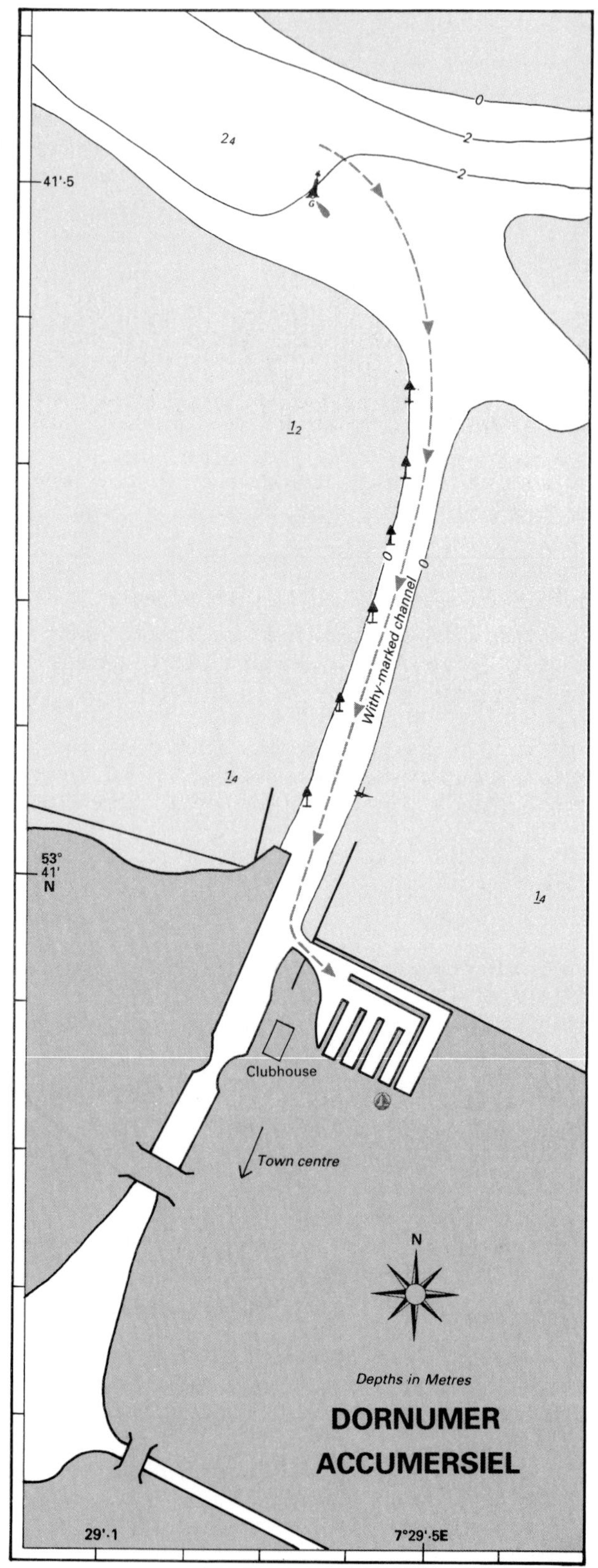

BALTRUMER BALJE, BALTRUMER WATTFAHRWASSER, ACCUMERSIELER BALJE

Again a passage on the second half of the flood is recommended, crossing the very shallow Baltrumer Wattfahrwasser on a rising tide before HW.

→ Follow the red unlit spar buoys of the Baltrumer Balje southwards, then follow the port-hand withies of the Baltrumer Wattfahrwasser in a wide loop eastwards and northwards to where more red spars (still keep to port) lead to a green light buoy at the entrance to the Accumersieler Balje. Follow the buoyed channel southeastwards, then head from the green light buoy southwards along the shallow (1m at LW) approach channel (starboard-hand bound-down withies) into the harbour, and turn hard to port just inside the entrance (unlit) into the yacht haven.

7·5M

DORNUMER ACCUMERSIEL

The harbour (D, and P nearby but not in yacht haven) has limited space and is shallow and almost drying; if you do get a place you will probably touch and sink into the mud at the pontoons, unless you are very shallow draught. A short midday visit is probably the best. Dornumersiel is a rather suburban village about 10 minutes' walk away.

Dornumer Accumersiel. Looking back along the approach channel. Yacht harbour entrance is hidden beyond the building to the right.

ACCUMERSIELER BALJE, DOLLART

For this very short distance the last two hours of flood are as good as any, to give plenty of water in the Accumersieler Balje.

→ Return to the Accumersieler Balje entrance and turn eastwards, carefully rounding the Neiderplate spit. Follow the Dollart buoyed (unlit) channel and go hard to port round the harbour's sector light on the W mole; follow the starboard-hand withies towards the pontoons at the NW end. Dredging and harbour extension had been under way when we made our visit, and a floating baffle protecting the SE side of the harbour had to be rounded carefully to reach the pontoons.

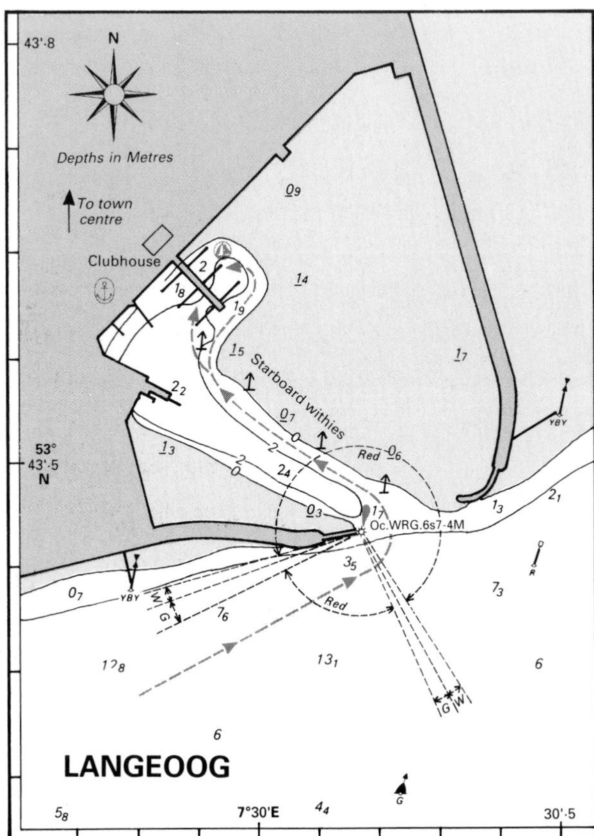

4M
LANGEOOG

The yacht haven (1·8–2·2m, PD nearby, not in yacht haven*) is about 2·5km from the village, which can been reached by rail or bicycle – or dare I suggest walking!

Langeoog entrance. Approaching from south.

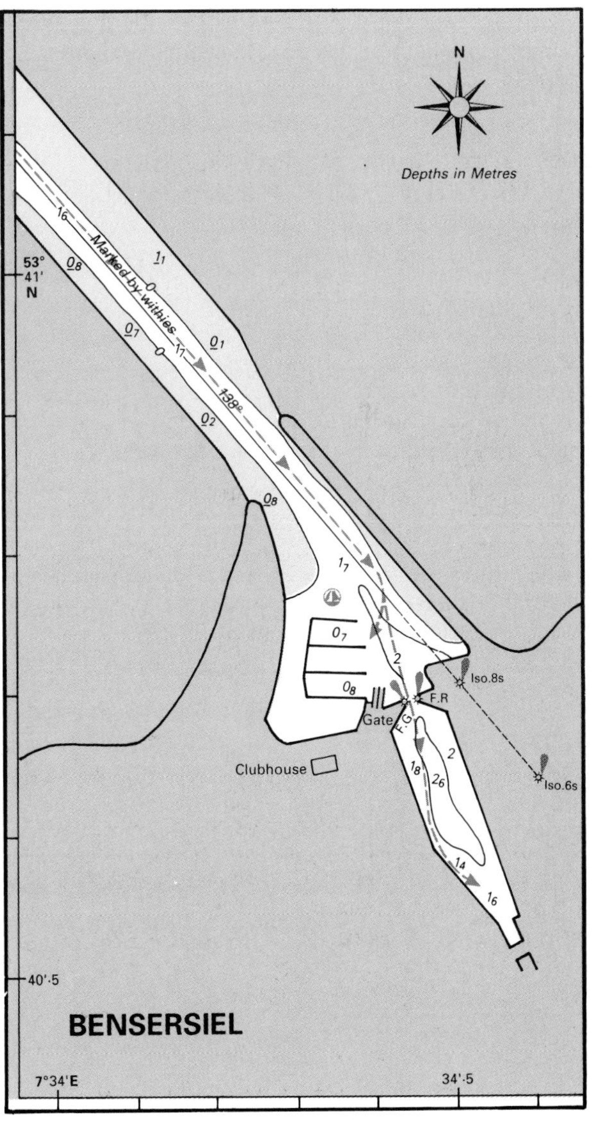

Langeoog yacht harbour.

↳ Another easy one-hour passage, probably best made by newcomers on the last two hours of flood.

→ The route lies southeastwards along a buoyed (some lit, mainly 5m-plus) channel, with two directional sector lights to help at night, on the ends of Langeoog's western and Bensersiel's eastern outer breakwaters. Follow the 1·5M-long Bensersiel approach channel (1·6m, lights in line), with withies on each side and E cardinal beacons, and pass into the outer yacht haven, turning to starboard for the pontoons.

4M
BENSERSIEL

⛵ At some states of tide you may possibly touch on some of the pontoons in the outer yacht haven (0·8m and 0·7m, PD*). It is sometimes possible to lie in the deeper (1·8m-plus) inner commercial/fishing harbour alongside the wall or another vessel. There are shopping facilities in the village, which is behind and dominated by its high sea wall.

STÜVERSLEGDE, NEUHARLINGERSIELER WATTFAHRWASSER, SCHILBALJE

↳ Although there is the shallow Nieuharlingersieler Wattfahrwasser to cross towards the end and you will be pushing some flood in the Schilbalje, this is an easy short route, to be taken on the second half of the flood.

→ The route returns along the approach channel, then turns eastwards along the red buoys of the Stüverslegde. From the point where a double withy marks the junction of two *watt* channels, follow the port-hand withies of the 4M-long Neuharlingersieler Wattfahrwasser over the drying *watt*, then pass Neuharlingersiel entrance and continue northwards along the buoyed (some lit; the buoyage now changes to red to starboard and green to port) Schilbalje channel to Spiekeroog's entrance light. Finally, follow the 1M-long entrance channel (withies on each side) to the yacht haven pontoons (to starboard), or raft along the quayside (to port).

En route, it is easy to call in for lunch at **Neuharlingersiel** (D, 1·5m), a small and delightful historic fishing harbour where part of the *Riddle of the Sands* film was shot. The 1M entrance channel is marked by withies (starboard hand) on the W side, with a light at the northern end, and has 0·7m charted depths. There is little room for visitors, and you may have to lie alongside a fishing vessel in the inner harbour if there is no room at the outer-harbour pontoons.

There are two other routes from the W across the *watts* to Spiekeroog. The first (7·5M long) starts by heading from Langeoog along the short Langeooger Wattfahrwasser (buoys and withies) into the Hulbalje (buoyed, direction remains red to port), at the eastern end of the island. Enter the Schilbalje (buoyed, direction remains red to port since you are now sailing with the flood tide) with a favourable tide to reach Spiekeroog entrance. The second route is along the Stüverslegde, as in the route from Bensersiel (above). At the double withy at the end of the buoyed channel, however (see Bensersiel route), take the port-hand channel (withies May to mid-September) which leads across the Stüverslegde drying *watt* into the Hulbalje (buoyed, direction still red to port), and then continue along the Schilbalje channel with the tide (buoyed, red to port) to Spiekeroog.

Fishing vessel in the German *wattfahrwassern*.

10M
SPIEKEROOG

⛵ The yacht-haven pontoons dried out to soft mud on our visit. (PD is nearby, but not in yacht haven). The island is worth a cycle tour; it is partly wooded and has a 17th-century church displaying some of the remains of a Spanish Armada wreck.

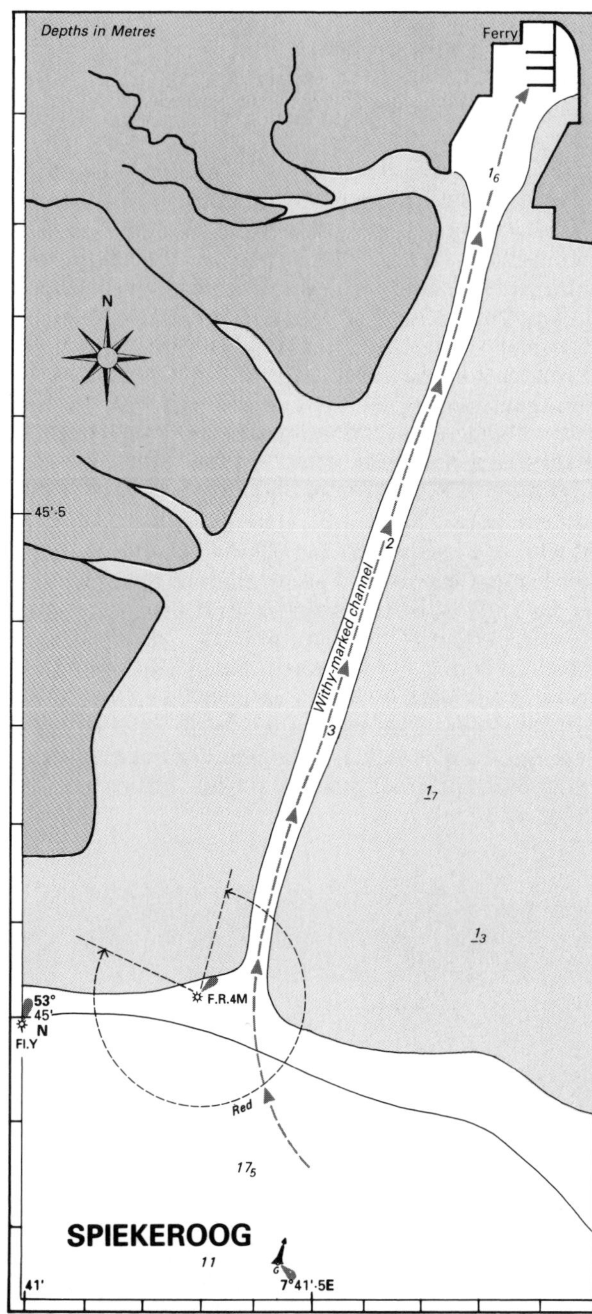

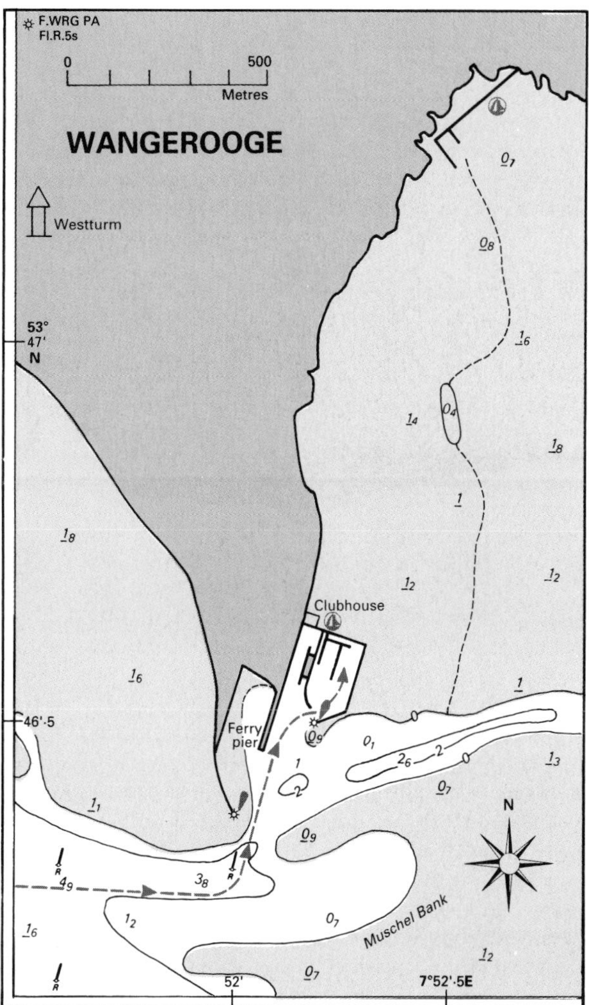

SCHILBALJE, LANDBALJE, HARLESIELER WATTFAHRWASSER, DOVE HARLE

↳ As with the previous passage, the second half of the flood is the best time, in order to cross the Harlesieler Wattfahrwasser on the rise.

→ The route follows the buoyed (some lit) Schilbalje and Landbalje channels and then continues along the port-hand withies of the Harlesieler Wattfahrwasser, into the Dove Harle (buoyed in direction of SE-going, incoming tide), and to the RGR middle-ground buoy (there are a red light and a green buoy some 0·2–0·3M to the W of this). From this buoy the route leads directly to the F.R light on Wangerooge's western mole, then heads N into the harbour. Wangerooge's Gothic Westturm spire and the nearby pillar of its high light are unmistakable on approach.

Neuharlingersiel. Picturesque fishing harbour used in the film *Riddle of the Sands*.

10M

WANGEROOGE-WESTANLEGER

The ferry pier is to port, and to starboard is the entrance (green light to starboard) to the yacht haven (0·6m, so you may touch on some pontoons at some states of the tide). The facilities are limited. Transport to the town, which is 5km away in the centre of the island, is by train. The walks along the sea wall and dunes are worthwhile. The Westturm is now a youth hostel; there is a small museum in the old lighthouse in the town.

Wangerooge Westanleger. Keep withies to starboard and enter yacht harbour between the yellow and green beacons.

Another visit (not included in the mileage below – it is 5M from Wangerooge) worth making in the last two hours of the flood is to **Harlesiel**. The route returns to the RGR middle-ground buoy and follows the green buoys of the Carolinensieler Balje to Harlesiel light beacon (6M range). Keeping the beacon to starboard, proceed along Aussentief von Harlesiel (following the E side of the breakwater, which is submerged near the top of the tide and is marked by starboard-hand withies), first southwestwards for 0·8M and then S by westwards to the entrance (red light). There is a short training wall, again submerged at HW, on the E side of the final entrance approach. Vessels wait at the quayside on the W side of the outer harbour for the lock, which opens when the outer water level is equal to the inner. The inner harbour is 0·5M long to the bridge at Carolinensiel, and there are a few yacht moorings on each side of the channel beyond the lock (PD). The somewhat suburban village is another 1–2km along the Harle creek.

WANGEROOGE WATTFAHRWASSER, BLAUE BALJE, MINSENER BALJE, MINSENER OOG WATTFAHRWASSER, DIE JADE

Again the second half of the flood is best, negotiating both *wattfahrwassern* well before HW with the last of the flood in the Jade. If you wish to make the complete passage to Wilhelmshaven, missing out Hooksiel, an earlier start (at about one hour after LW at Wangerooge) is recommended, although this will almost certainly mean 'nudging' the ground on the early part of the route. Off Schillighörn in the Jade the flood can reach up to 2·4kn at −0430hrs HW Wilhelmshaven.

→ There are two routes from Wangerooge entrance. The first leads directly eastwards for 1M, following the port-hand withies over the drying *watt* and joining the deeper Wangerooger Wattfahrwasser (alternative name: Telegraphenbalje) at a double withy. The second, if you wish to start as early as possible on the tide, leads southwards and westwards (sounding round the Muschelbank and the red spar buoy at its SW corner) and then directly into Wangerooger Wattfahrwasser, following the withies into the Blaue Balje (red spar buoys to port). It continues round the N side of the GRG middle-ground buoy and southeastwards into the winding Minsener Balje, which initially follows the S side of the Hauptdamm (marked by cardinal danger buoys at the ends of its breakwaters) and then becomes a buoyed channel (green unlit buoys to starboard). This leads to the Minsener Oog Wattfahrwasser, where port-hand withies lead over the *watt* directly into the Jade. The route then leads in deep water (around 10m) outside the main channel navigation buoys, heading southwards to the offing buoy at Hooksiel.

Hooksiel entrance and lock from the green offing buoy.

The Jade, Weser, Elbe and Eider estuaries (Brunsbüttel to Helgoland)

This route passes the entrance to the starboard-hand withy-marked winding Wanger Aussentief channel (about 0·5m at LW) to **Wangersiel/ Horumersiel** (PD nearby but not in yacht haven), where you can lie at the pontoons, if you can find a place, but where some of the moorings round the sides dry.

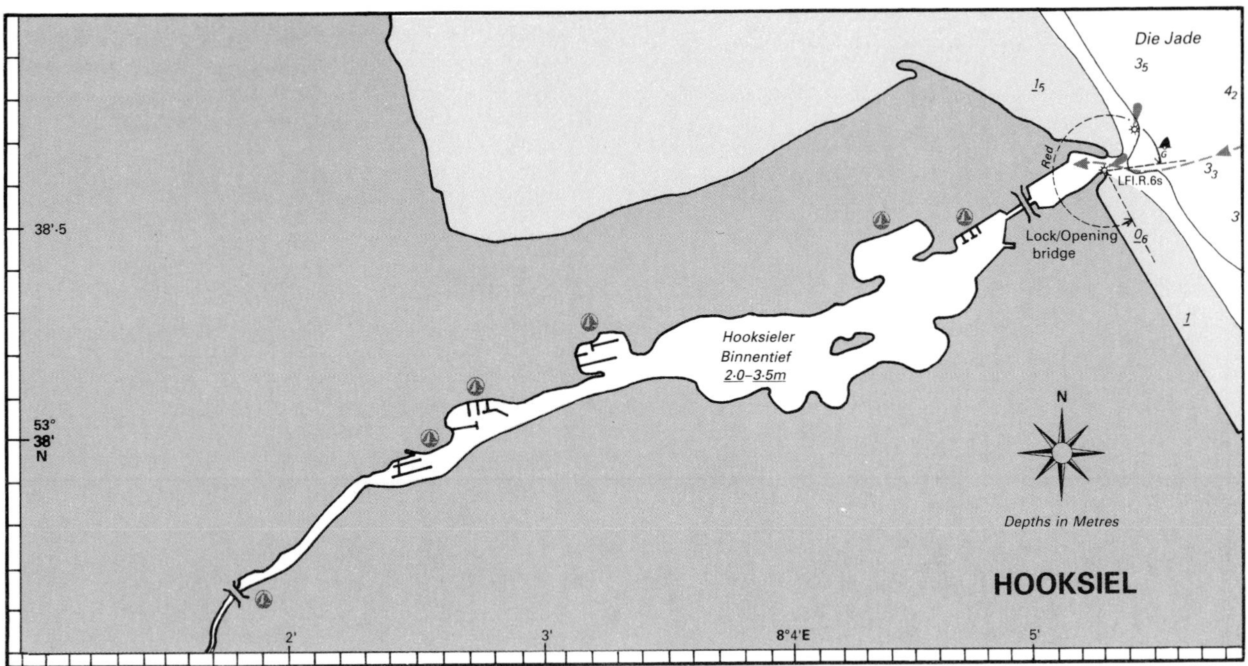

15M

HOOKSIEL AND HOOK MEER

The entrance (sector light) is approached directly from the N side of the green offing buoy, and is available at all states of tide (2·5m). Vessels wait for the lock and opening bridge at the northern quayside in the outer harbour. There is a frequent lock-opening schedule (☎ (04425) 285/687/430); you will need to fly the N flag. This is the largest yachting complex on the North Sea coast of Germany, with all facilities and at least four sets of mooring pontoons, in the small bays on the N side of the Hook Meer (2–3·5m, PD*) and at its head near its small holiday village.

THE JADE

Jade Rivier radio on VHF Ch 20, 23, 16 has information broadcasts in German on Ch 20 at 10 minutes past the hour.

Yet another easy (2-hour) passage, which can be taken any time on the flood.

→ The route leads outside the W edge of the deep-water channel (buoys, many lit) in 5–10m. Take care to give good clearance to the tanker-mooring piers, which extend up to 700m out towards the fairway. There are several sector lights on each shore, and along the main channel there are three sets of lights in line, plus the directional sector light, Arngast (16–21M range, red round tower, white band, 2 galleries), on the final main reach past the Neuer Vorhafen. There is considerable naval and commercial traffic in this river.

Rüstersiel is a small yacht haven (2m, PD nearby but not in yacht haven). Enter just before the tanker piers through a (drying) outer harbour and sluice gate (open two hours before to two hours after HW) and then proceed 0·7M along the Maade on the N side. If you wish to continue the remaining 0·7M to lie at the yard by the N quayside of this suburb, then you must pass through an opening bridge (manned 0700–1700 on weekdays). This area of mixed fields and industrial sites is about 5km from the centre of Wilhelmshaven.

→ The entrance (lit) to the **Fluthaven** is to starboard some 0·7M after passing the entrance (lit) to the Neuer Vorhafen. Follow the wall (the end of the Leitdam on the opposite side of the fairway is marked by an unlit N cardinal buoy) past a sector light and turn hard to starboard round the second sector light into Nassau Hafen.

10M

WILHELMSHAVEN

Wilhelmshaven, Germany's main naval port on the North Sea, founded in 1856, has been rebuilt after heavy wartime bombing. It is a lively city, with spacious docks, parks, a few remaining old buildings, and many cultural centres, including a theatre and museum. **Nassau Hafen** (1·7–2·7m, PD), in the tidal Fluthafen, has a single 100m-long floating pontoon (so you can forget your warps, even though there is a 3·7–4·2m tidal range), to which boats are rafted; there is a clubhouse nearby. If you have the time, there are far more moorings along the S side of the **Grosser Hafen** (*). This is entered by passing through the lock (VHF Ch 16, 13, or harbourmaster VHF Ch 16, 11) in the Alter Hafen, S of the entrance to the Fluthafen, and then continuing westwards through the opening Kaiser Wilhelm Brücke (9m clearance closed). It is worth walking along the Südstrand seafront, with its nearby aquarium.

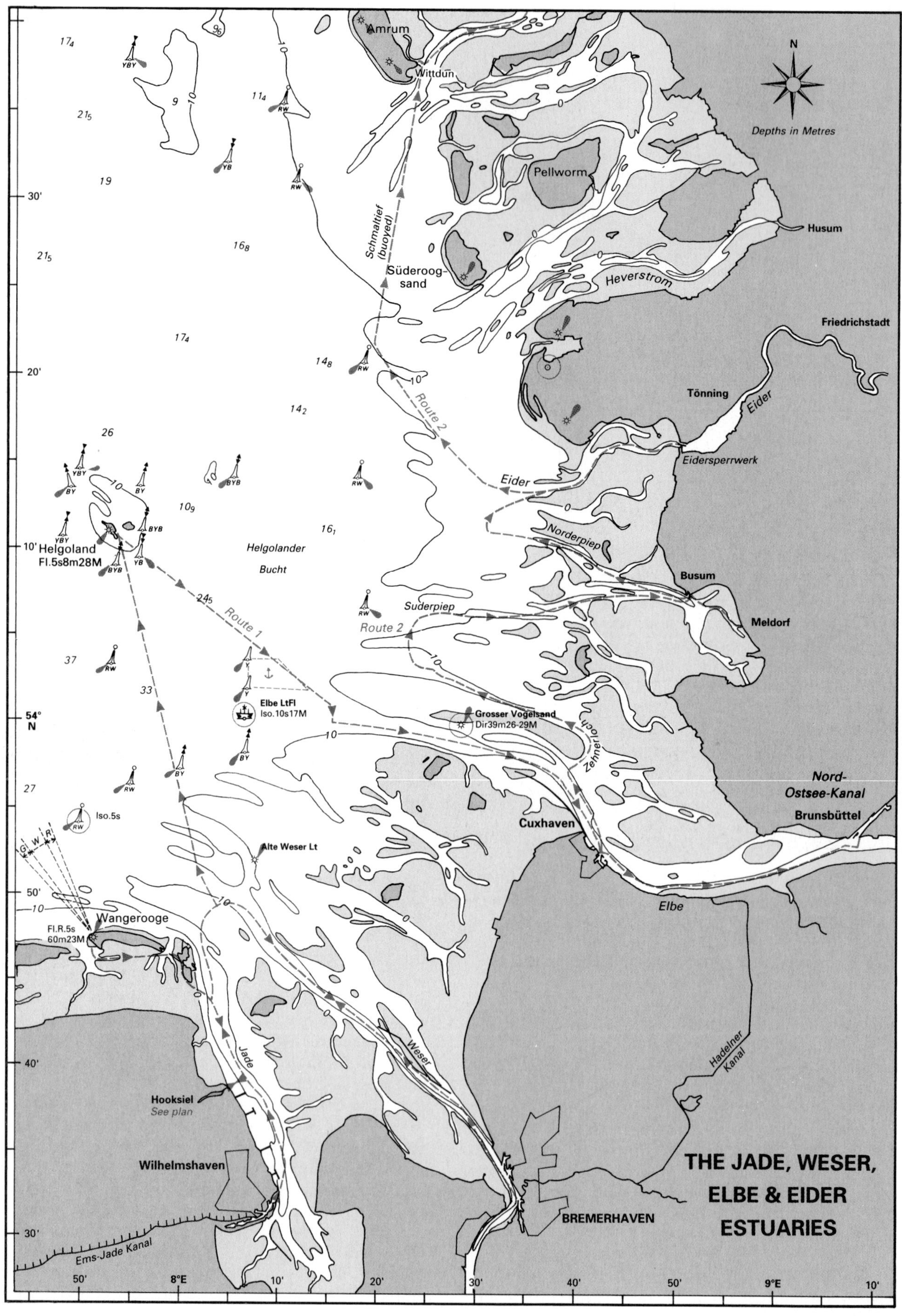
THE JADE, WESER, ELBE & EIDER ESTUARIES
Depths in Metres
N
Amrum
Wittdün
Pellworm
Husum
Schmaltief (buoyed)
Süderoog-sand
Heverstrom
Friedrichstadt
Tönning
Eider
Route 2
Eidersperrwerk
Norderpiep
Busum
Meldorf
Suderpiep
Helgoland Fl.5s8m28M
Helgolander Bucht
Route 1
Elbe LtFl Iso.10s17M
Grosser Vogelsand Dir39m26-29M
Zehnerloch
Nord-Ostsee-Kanal
Brunsbüttel
Cuxhaven
Elbe
Iso.5s
Alte Weser Lt
Wangerooge
Fl.R.5s 60m23M
Jade
Weser
Hadelner Kanal
Hooksiel
See plan
Wilhelmshaven
BREMERHAVEN
Ems-Jade Kanal
54° N
8°E
9°E

THE JADE, MITTELRINNE, THE WESER (HOHEWEGRINNE, FEDDERWARDER FAHRWASSER)

Bremerhaven Weser Rivier is the station controlling merchant shipping, on a series of VHF reporting channels, along the various reaches of the river Weser. It sends out information broadcasts in German at 20 minutes past the hour on VHF Chs 2, 4, 5, 7, 21, 22, 82, and at 30 minutes past the hour on Chs 19, 78, 81. Communication with *Pilots* is on VHF Chs 6 and 16.

U-boat in Bremerhaven's historic ships collection.

Wilhelmshaven.

Bremerhaven.

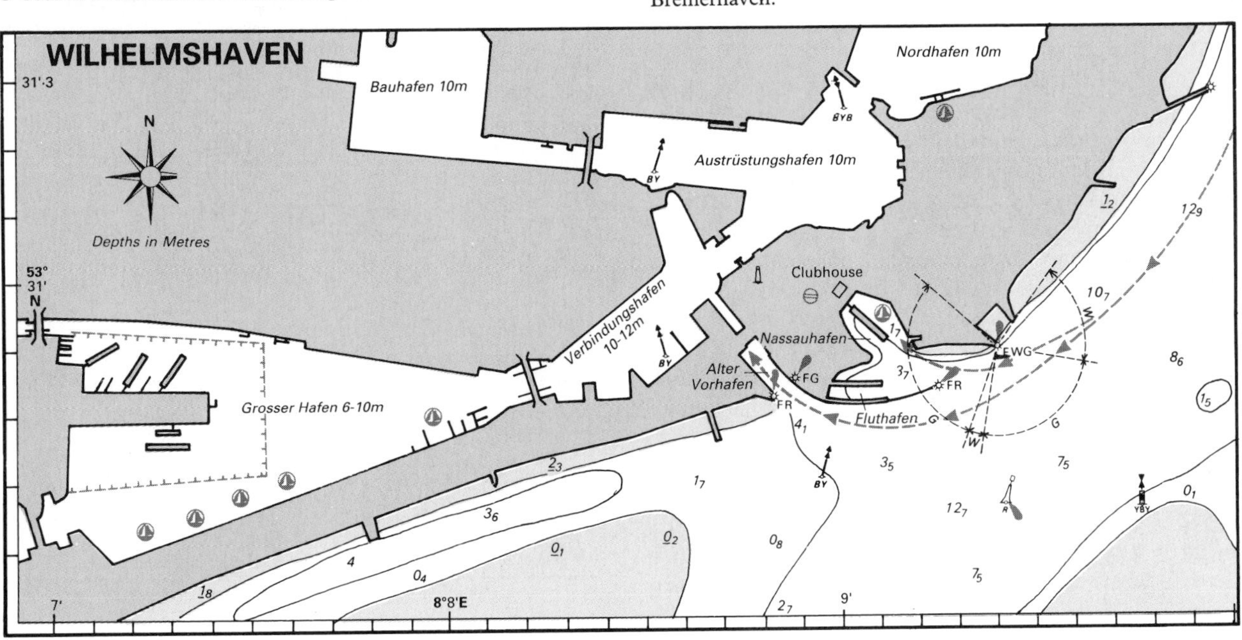

If you wish to sail directly to Helgoland and miss out Bremerhaven, then timing and currents are virtually the same as for Bremerhaven (below), starting at HW Wilhelmshaven. For the passage from estuary to estuary described below, it is necessary to leave Wilhelmshaven with a full ebb, go down to the entrance and take the flood up the Weser.

Crossing the outer shoals can be very uncomfortable in northerly winds, which can build up heavy breaking seas on the ebb.

→ The main route follows the extreme eastern edge of the Jade channel (buoyed, mainly lit, deep water, 10m plus) northwards to the buoyed (unlit spars) Mittelrinne channel. Cross (or round by sounding, depending on weather) the Jadeplate/Mittelplate sandbank (falling tide nearing LW, so take care) into the Weser, then head southeastwards along the outside of the western outer edge of the buoyed (mainly lit, over 10m-deep water) Hohewegrinne and Fedderwarder Fahrwasser to Bremerhaven.

A night passage should only be attempted in good weather, due to the problem of rounding the Mittelplate spit into the Weser. The unlit buoys of the Mittelrinne channel are a problem here, and a sharp lookout, together with use of the sectors of the Mellumplate light (23–24M range, red square tower with white band) to the S, bearings on the Weser fairway lit buoys to the N, and frequent sounding, is needed to back up your Decca/GPS positions.

Directional sector lights, Tegeler Plate (16–21M range, red pillar with projecting gallery and white lantern on top) and Hohe Weg (15–19M range, red 8-sided tower), lead down the initial reaches of the main channel. Another sector light at Robbennordsteert and several sets of lights in line complete the main channel route to Bremerhaven. Just over 1M southwards, past the second of the two entrances to the commercial Überseehafen, the entrance (lit) into Bremerhaven's Vorhafen is hard to port in deep water (6m plus), and here there can be a cross-tidal stream of up to 1·5kn on entry or departure.

→ There is a possible short cut for intrepid mudscrapers which reduces the distance between the two major ports by about 25M, but local knowledge is advisable. It follows the Kaiserbalje, a drying *watt* channel which can be crossed towards the top of a rising tide. This channel is entered to starboard about 6M N of Wilhelmshaven, and crosses a Zone 1 nature reserve. It is marked by withies from May to mid-September, and leads directly across the southern end of the Hohe Weg bank into the Fedderwarder Priel (unlit buoys, over 5m deep). This is followed northwards to join the Fedderwarder Fahrwasser, and the route then continues as above. Southwards (in the opposite direction to the route) along Fedderwarder Priel at **Fedderwardersiel** there is a fishing harbour and also a yacht haven, both of which dry out. The problem with this route is that after crossing the Kaiserbalje there is very

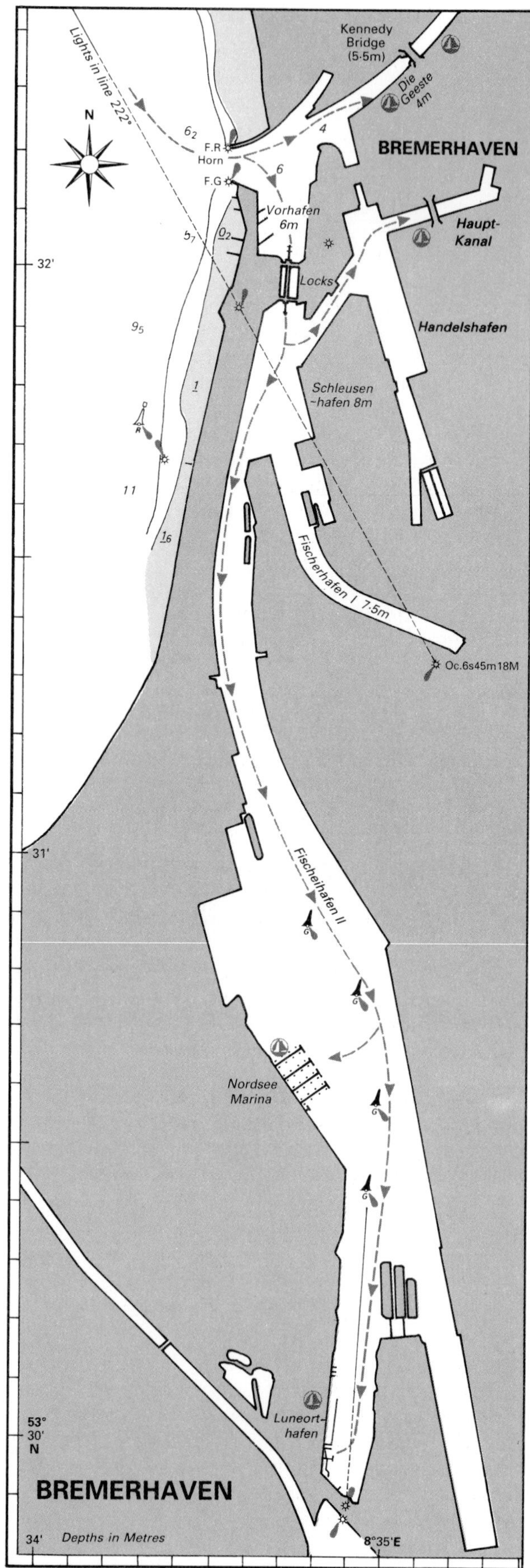

little flood stream left for the remaining 10M to Bremerhaven, and pushing a strong ebb up the Weser is a problem.

47M
BREMERHAVEN

Wasser und Schiffahrtsamt, Bremerhaven (the Weser navigation office), can be reached on ☎ (0471) 4 83 50. There are four possible mooring places. The moorings in **Die Geest** (4m) are alongside the SE quay, on either side of the flood barrage (closed when the water level is 1m or more above MHW) with its Kennedy bridge (bascule, 5·5m clearance closed). These are tidal, so you need to tend warps (3·6–4m tidal range), and they are not peaceful, although convenient for the city centre.

To reach the three nontidal moorings it is necessary to pass through the Fishereihafenschleuse, the lock into the southern fishing harbour complex. Entry (day and night) is requested by the sound signal 'Q' (two long, one short, one long blast), and departure by 'N' (one long, one short blast). The **Haupt-Kanal** (4m) is E of the southern exit from the lock along the Hafenkanal and across the Handelshafen. There are head and stern moorings along each side and a manned swing bridge about halfway along the basin; it is very convenient for the city centre. **Nordsee-Marina** (*) and **Luneort-hafen** (*) pontoon moorings are on the W side of **Fishereihafen II** some 2–3M S of the lock, and are extremely remote from the city.

Although uninteresting architecturally, for the seafarer Bremerhaven is fascinating, since it is Germany's biggest fishing port and the home of the German Museum of Navigation, with its 14th-century Hanseatic cog, dredged up in the river near Bremen. It also has, next to the large Columbus shopping centre, a huge array of floating historic vessels, including a U-boat, one of Germany's last wooden sailing ships, an Arctic exploration vessel and various fishing vessels and warships.

THE WESER (FEDDERWARDER FAHRWASSER, HOHEWEGRINNE, ALTE WESER) AND ELBE NORTH SEA APPROACHES

Departure from Bremerhaven at the top of the tide gives roughly five hours, i.e. half of the passage, down-tide and the other half cross-tide, initially with a W by N-going ebb abaft the beam, but reversing on the approach to Helgoland to an E by S-going flood on the bow. If anything, therefore, an early start, say an hour before HW Bremerhaven, will probably maximise the more favourable ebb. In the Fedderwarder Fahrwasser near Robbenplate the Weser's outgoing stream can reach up to 3·8kn at +0300hrs HW Bremerhaven, while off the Alte Weser light at the entrance the figure is 2·4kn at +0210hrs HW Bremerhaven.

In southwesterlies this can be a fast passage, if somewhat choppy in the crossing to Helgoland with wind against tide.

→ The route retraces the passage down the Weser close to the E side and outside the main shipping channel (mainly in 10m and over). It continues past the Alte Weser sector light (17–22M range, red pillar with wide top platform and lantern, 2 white bands, black base, floodlit) and along the Alte Weser channel out to A1 and A2 lit red and green buoys at the extreme outer entrance. The route then heads directly for Helgoland Oost light buoy (E cardinal), during which passage both the Alte Weser light and the Helgoland light (the latter 28M range, brown square brick tower, white balcony) can be seen in normal visibility at night. This part of the route crosses the main shipping route from the Elbe across to the TSS N of the Frisian islands, so an extra careful lookout should be kept for crossing ships.

APPROACHES TO HELGOLAND

Approach to the harbour on the SE end of Helgoland is via the two leading lights on Düne and a lit buoyed channel in 7–11m depths, turning to port through the W-facing entrance (lit) into the Vorhafen.

Helgoland, lying some 23M N of Wangerooge, is a conspicuous red sandstone rock, 55m high, with a conspicuous lighthouse in the centre, a 99m radio mast to its NW and a prominent isolated rock (Hengst) off the NW end of the island. The island shelves gently at the SE end near the harbour. Düne is a low sandy island 0·5M E of the main island, with prominent leading lights (rear a tower and front a framework). Rocky shoals from 5m to drying trail in a northwesterly to southeasterly direction around and from each end of the two islands, almost joining up in the Wal shoals, between the islands. Here depths in the main channel, over a stony bottom, are around 5–6·4m; the deeper Nordreede and Südereede channels lead to it.

Shelter between the islands is limited, and in rough weather, particularly from NW or SE, steep seas can build up in the central channels. Even in the inner Südhaven, where yachts lie, there can be a pronounced scend, and it is very uncomfortable indeed in westerly storms.

48M
HELGOLAND
Helgoland and approaches

VHF Ch16, 67, *Helgoland Port*. Definitely a short-stay harbour of refuge. Visitors raft to pontoons (5m plus, restaurant and showers nearby) in the N of the **Südhafen**, the unlit entrance of which is at the N side of the Vorhafen. In summer there are huge rafts of yachts. A red light at the entrance signal station indicates that it is full, and you must then anchor on the W side of the **Vorhafen** (contact the harbourmaster by VHF to pay your dues) –

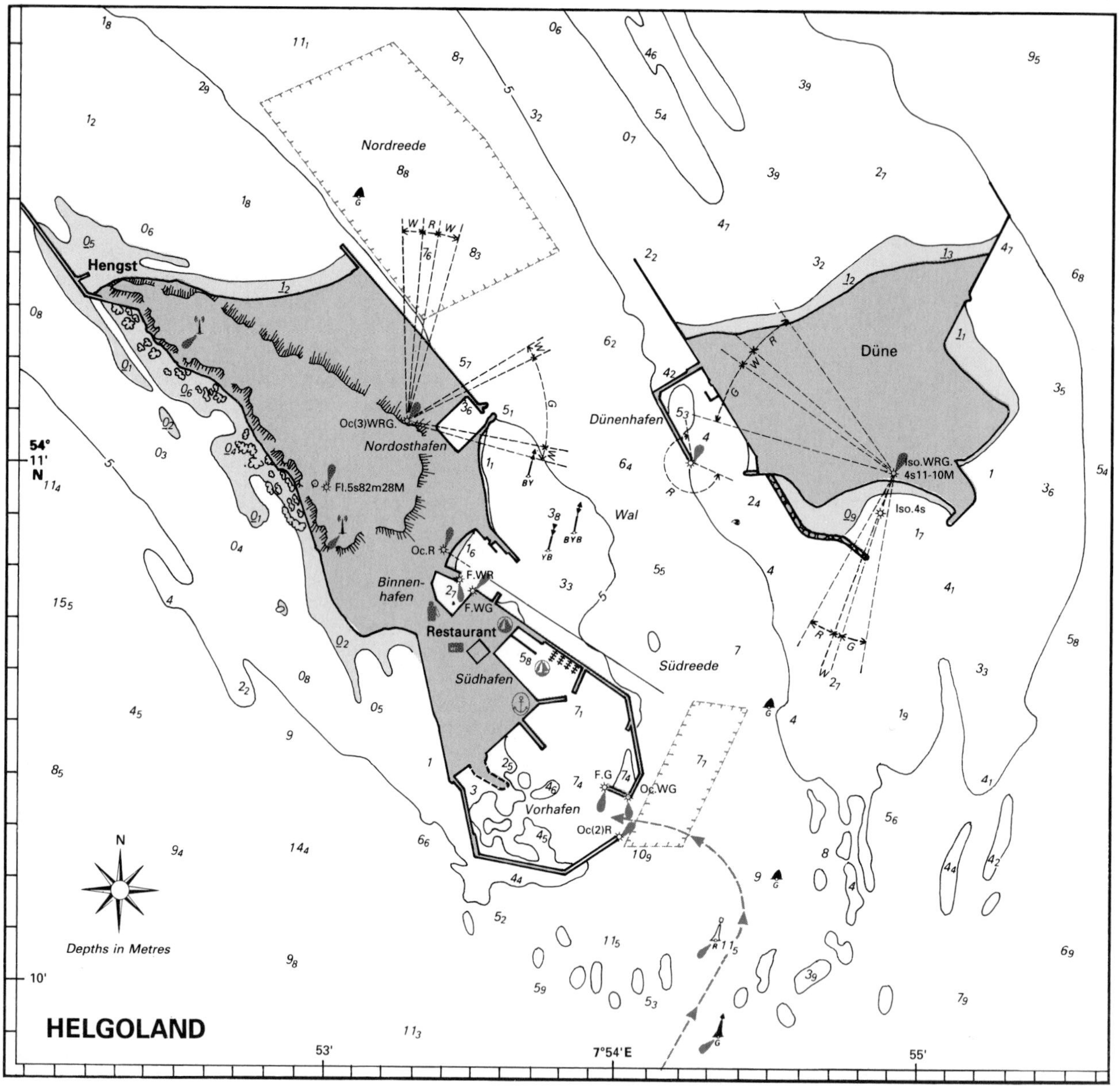

uncomfortable in SE to E winds – or you can trek round to, and raft up on the quays of the southern section of the **Binnenhafen** (PD), the next basin to the N (also uncomfortable in easterlies), but keep clear of the refuelling pontoon (southern corner) and the northern section of the basin which is reserved for liberty boats of trippers from the many ferries which anchor in the Südreede. **Nordosthafen** is for local vessels and **Dünenhafen** is banned to pleasure craft. The town, an easy walk (bicycles banned), is crammed with duty-free shops.

Previously occupied by the British, Helgoland was exchanged for Zanzibar and became German in 1890. When it was bombed in the Second World War the islanders were evacuated, and the island served as a bombing target for the RAF until its return to Germany in 1952; it is now a highly popular duty-free resort.

Helgoland. Vorhafen and Südhafen from the hill above.

THE ELBE ENTRANCE

Rivierzentrale Cuxhaven has information broadcasts for the E part of the German Bight in English and German on VHF Chs 19, 18, 5, 21, 3, at 5 minutes to the hour.

To maximise the Elbe entrance flood inwards for this distance a start at −0600hrs HW Helgoland is required.

The worst conditions in the estuary are in NW gales against the ebb, while on the flood strong N to NW winds can set a vessel southwards onto the Nordergrunde during approach (*see also Chapter 1, Approaches: Elbe entrance*).

The course initially leads southeastwards to the outer Elbe buoys on the northern side of the channel close W of Grosser Vogelsand shoal. The shipping channel is crossed at right angles to its S side and followed eastwards outside the buoys along its outer edge, mainly in over 10m. The wide, deep, well lit, buoyed and beaconed shipping channel into the estuary starts at the Elbe LtFl (17M range) to the W of this point. This is followed in succession by the Grosser Vogelsand light (26M, helicopter platform and wide gallery on red pillar with white bands), a radar hut on Scharhörn, Neuwerk light (16M range, square brick tower with small cupola on top) and nearby beacon and radar tower, and the Kugel beacon (triangular framework) on the coast N of Cuxhaven, while the buildings of Cuxhaven usually appear after Neuwerk has been sighted.

Cuxhaven yacht haven is the second entrance (lit) to starboard, NW of the short round radar tower with a platform on top. There can be a crosscurrent of up to 3·6kn on the flood and 4·2kn on the ebb across this entrance, so watch out!

Cuxhaven's modern yacht harbour.

35M

CUXHAVEN

Cuxhaven port radio communicates on VHF Chs 12, 14, 16 at all hours. **Cuxhaven** yacht haven (2·5–3m, PD nearby but not in the yacht haven*) is a spacious marina with a luxurious yacht club. It is a short walk over the sea wall into the backstreets of the old town, while beyond is a more modern shopping centre. The city has all amenities.

Another yacht haven (**Marina Cuxhaven**) was in course of construction at time of writing. This is SW of the opening bridge and lock at the end of the Alter Hafen, and could be complete by the time you are using this book. The Alte Hafen is entered from the Vorhafen, the next entrance (lit) along the waterfront after the main yacht haven.

THE ELBE

Rivierzentrale Brunsbüttel has information broadcasts in English and German on VHF Chs 4, 67, 18, 22, 5, 21, 3 at 5 minutes past the hour.

Strategy for travelling upstream or downstream on the Elbe

The full 57M trip upriver from Cuxhaven to Hamburg's City-Sport Hafen is possible on a single flood tide, since there is an average of just over nine hours' rise from LW at Cuxhaven to HW at Hamburg. You will need to average just over 6kn with the tide, or about 4–5kn boat speed.

In the opposite direction, downriver, of course, there is a problem, since there is only a 3 to 4-hour fall of tide if you start at HW Hamburg. If you have a powerful engine you could try starting at LW Hamburg, pushing the weaker tide in the upper reaches and taking the faster ebb later in the lower reaches, but the most comfortable way is to break the return passage into two halves (say at Glückstadt), starting at about 1 hour before local HW in each case. Alternatively, the downstream direction is by far the better in which to visit a few selected drying and half-tidal harbours along the river.

Very careful planning indeed is needed if you wish to visit some of the many drying harbours and half-tidal creeks along the Elbe. Although this book covers most of them in consecutive order moving upstream, this is the more difficult direction in which to visit them. It is only possible to leave such harbours relatively close to HW, which leaves very little flood tide for the ensuing trip upstream, so the distance to the next drying harbour must be short if you wish to enter on the same tide near HW. The situation to avoid is one in which you motor out into the river near HW and continue upstream for an hour to find that you are pushing a strong adverse current and that there are no adequately deep harbours of refuge within reach. It is always preferable to use only the deeper harbours going upstream and to visit your selected harbours on the return passage downstream.

As a backup to your planning, there are several places behind the various longitudinal islands and

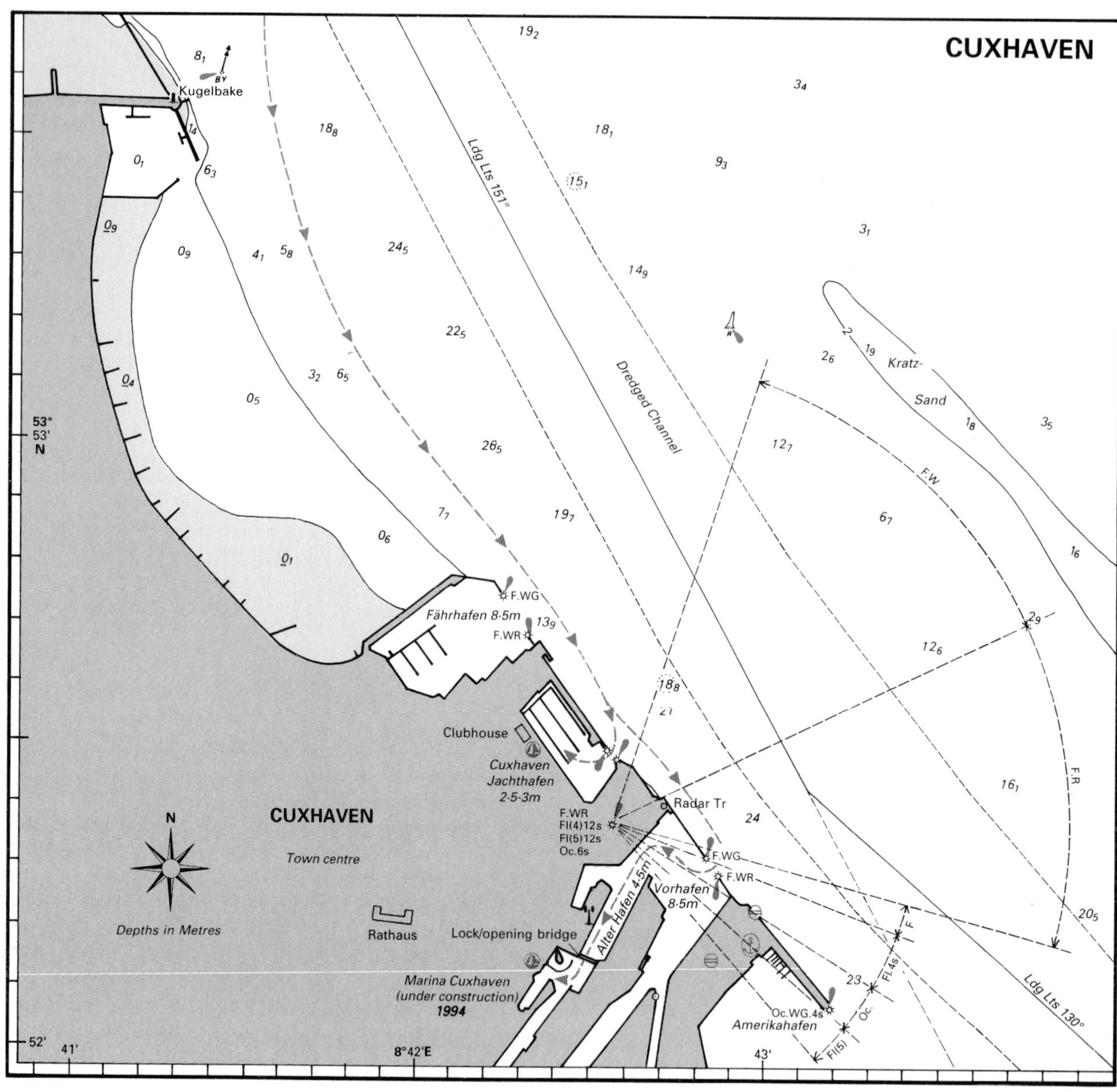

banks along the river where you can anchor in complete protection, well away from the main fairway and the swell from its many commercial vessels.

In most of the small harbours along the Elbe space is limited, so you may have problems finding a box, but offsetting this, visiting yachts are often relatively few. You may certainly find it difficult to find a box wide enough to take your boat if it is a beamy one. Many of the harbours have clubhouses or restaurants nearby, but in most, particularly on weekdays, you will have to take your chances on being able to get a shower at the club or a guesthouse.

A final warning: in the side channels which lead to many of these harbours it is advisable to keep down your speed to 4·5kn (8kmph) maximum, and in many of the more important ones this is the legal limit.

Passage, for this first 3–4 hour trip, should be timed to coincide with the flood, which can reach up to 3·6kn off Cuxhaven entrance at −0230hrs HW Cuxhaven and 2·6kn off the Nord-Ostsee-Kanal entrance at −0140hrs HW Cuxhaven. HW Brunsbüttel averages +0102hrs HW Cuxhaven.

→ The route continues along the outer starboard edge of the main channel (mostly light buoys and light towers, with two major sets of lights in line at Altenbruch and Brunsbüttel). There is a wide steep-sided shoal shelf to beware of on the S side of the river in this stretch. There is busy shipping traffic on the whole of this route to Hamburg, so care should be taken to keep out of the fairway as much as possible.

There are four possible mooring places (see below) on this section of the passage (excluding Neufeld, along a drying creek on the N bank, which is too difficult for a visitor, and excluding the deep-water yacht haven inside the Brunsbüttel entrance to the Nord-Ostsee-Kanal). Three of these are half-tide-plus approaches, so 1–2 hours before HW is the best time for entry. The fourth (River Oste) is best approached 1–2 hours after LW. It is possible to lie afloat in two of the harbours.

S bank **Altenbruch**, SE of Cuxhaven, dries to hard sand, so it must be entered near HW and is only for boats which can dry out upright.

S bank Leading southwards from the E side of the Medem light beacon (B triangle on B column) is a little more than half-tidal (0·8m sounding) unlit withied channel, the river Medem. On the W side of the river beyond the junction with the Hadelner Kanal, some 0·5m S of the entrance, is **Otterndorf**. At the pontoons on the W side here vessels with a draught of 1·5m (possibly a little more) can stay afloat. There is a pleasant riverside restaurant nearby. At the pontoons on the E side of the head of this basin you will lie in soft mud. There are also floating moorings in the **Hadelner canal**, beyond and S of the lock. HW Otterndorf averages about 20 minutes after HW Cuxhaven.

S bank The river Oste is buoyed (unlit) and navigable for 80km as far as Bremervörde (upper reaches beyond the scope of this book). The depth in the entrance channel is around 1·5m, possibly a little more, so a prudent approach should be made, at the earliest, 1 hour after LW. HW at the entrance averages about 40 minutes after HW Cuxhaven. There is a flood barrage with a lifting bridge (clearance 5·75m closed) 2·5M from the entrance, manned from 0500 to 2200 daily and opened on two long blasts on the whistle or on using VHF Ch 69. The first floating moorings are at **Neuhaus**, 3·5M SE of the Oste sector light beacon (black tower, red band and red lantern) at the entrance. HW Neuhaus averages about 1 hour after HW Cuxhaven.

N bank **Brunsbüttel Alter Hafen**, close W of the locks on the N bank, is half-tidal (0·5m bar). It is entered along a drying withied (mainly port-hand) channel W of a small sector light on its eastern mole. Visiting vessels will usually have to sit in the mud at the guest pontoons at the northern end.

17M

BRUNSBÜTTEL

See Chapter 4

THE ELBE: BRUNSBÜTTEL TO GLÜCKSTADT

↳ Another 2–3 hour flood-tide passage, with a stream which can reach up to 2·6kn off Brokdorf at −0120hrs HW Cuxhaven. HW Glückstadt averages +0207hrs HW Cuxhaven (i.e. +0105 HW Brunsbüttel).

➜ The route continues along the outer starboard edge of the main channel (mostly lit buoys, lights in line and sector lights). This starboard-hand bank has wide difficult shoals, so you should keep close to the channel buoys. The river is crossed at right angles before passing the Rhinplatte N sector light (red pedestal on dolphin, keep it to starboard) and continuing along the buoyed (unlit) Glückstadter Nebenelbe (3–6m), turning hard to port through the entrance (lit) of Glückstadt Aussenhafen.

⚓ There are five mooring possibilities (see below) en route to Glückstadt, all of which dry out to varying degrees. Three of these are half-tide-plus approaches; the remaining two, in the river Stör, can be entered at all states of tide.

N bank **St Margarethen** dries; its creek can only be entered near HW and is only for boats which can dry out upright.

S bank **Freiburg**'s difficult approach is from No. 65 green buoy southeastwards behind the drying Freiburg Reede, keeping 250m offshore in 2–4m, then hard to starboard round the green entrance beacon at the end of the breakwater (Freiburg Radar tower is a prominent landmark at the root of this breakwater). Freiburg Hafenpriel is only navigable near HW. The moorings, many of which dry out, are in a western side-creek, or on the NW bank and at the quay at the head. There is a flood barrage en route which is only closed if the water level exceeds 0·8m above MHW. HW Freiburg averages approximately 1 hour 45 minutes after HW Cuxhaven.

E bank The river Stör has lights in line at the entrance and a closely buoyed (unlit) channel to the flood barrage. The entrance bar has about 2·5m, so it is available at all states of tide, depending, of course, on the moorings you will be using. HW at the entrance averages about 2 hours after HW Cuxhaven. The barrage is only closed if the water level rises more than 1m above HW; a sound signal of two long blasts or a call on VHF Ch 9 obtains access through its lifting bascule bridge (clearance 7m closed). There are drying moorings at **Störloch**, in soft mud in the small harbour behind the E wall (0·6m in the entrance and 0·9m on the northern pontoons), extending NE from the flood barrage, and also alongside at the pontoon (1·2m, so you will probably touch at LW) at the picturesque village of **Wewelsfleth**, 1M further along on the N bank. There are other moorings (beyond the scope of this book) along the Stör.

W bank **Wischhafen** is approached either along the 2·5M-long buoyed (unlit) Wischhafener Fahrwasser or directly from the east along the short 2–3m fairway (buoyed and lit) through the Brammer-bank. Both channels enter the Wischhafener Süderelbe, which has an 0·9m bar at the entrance, so is half-tidal. This is followed by a flood barrage with an opening bridge (clearance 6·3m closed), both of which are normally open (if closed, two long blasts is the request signal for the bridge to open); 1·4M from the entrance on the N bank there are drying moorings at Wischhafen. Anchoring is permitted at the northern end of the Wischhafener Fahrwasser outside the fairway, but you will be about 400m offshore without landing possibilities.

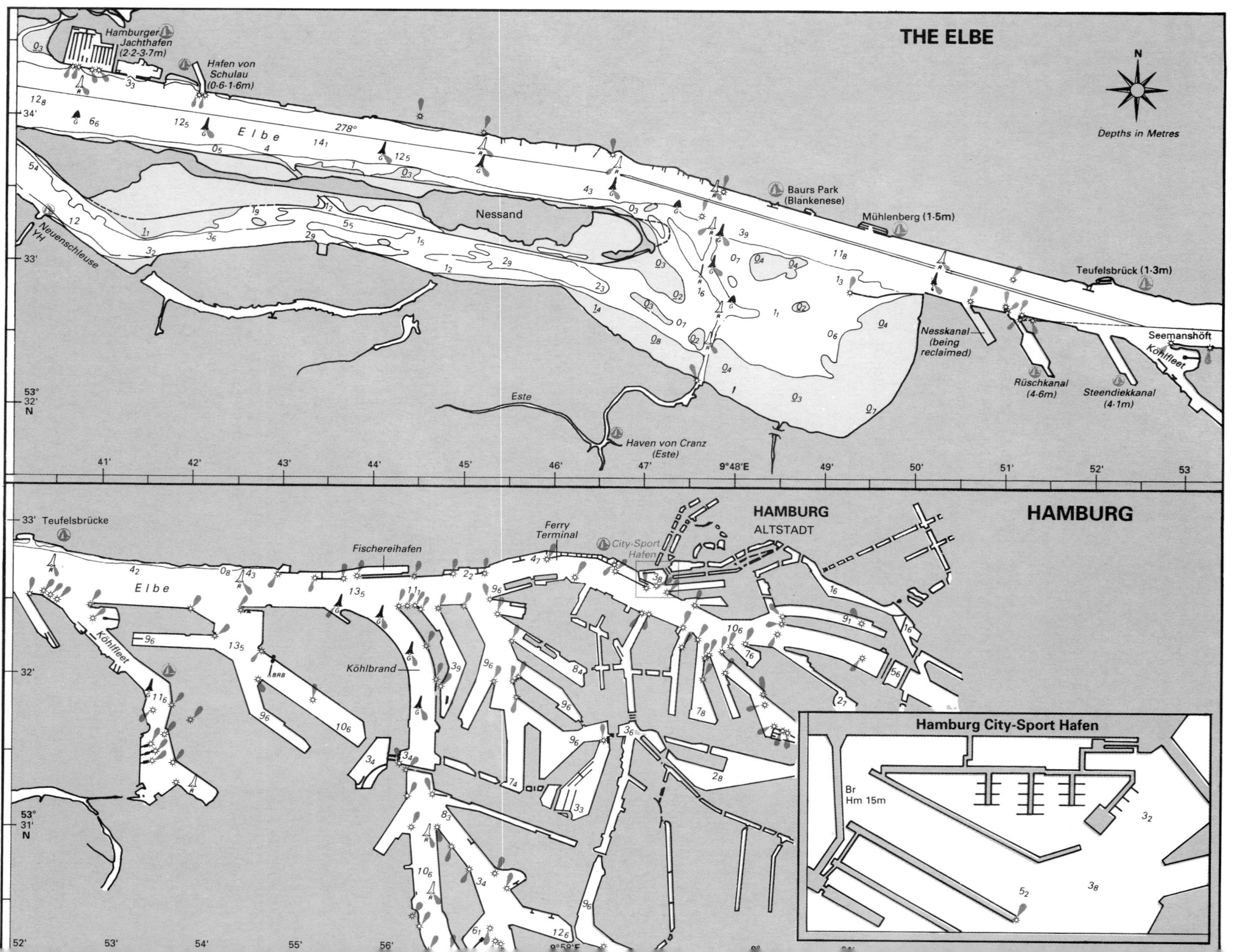

THE ELBE
N
Depths in Metres
Hamburger Jachthafen (2·2-3·7m)
Hafen von Schulau (0·6-1·6m)
Elbe
278°
Nessand
Neuenschleuse YH
Baurs Park (Blankenese)
Mühlenberg (1·5m)
Teufelsbrück (1·3m)
Seemanshöft
Köhlfleet
Nesskanal (being reclaimed)
Rüschkanal (4·6m)
Steendiekkanal (4·1m)
Este
Haven von Cranz (Este)
53° 32' N
9°48'E
HAMBURG
HAMBURG ALTSTADT
Teufelsbrücke
Fischereihafen
Ferry Terminal
City-Sport Hafen
Elbe
Köhlfleet
Köhlbrand
53° 31' N
Hamburg City-Sport Hafen
Br Hm 15m

12M

GLÜCKSTADT

There is plenty of water at the moorings at the SE corner of the **Aussenhafen** (D), and if these are crowded at weekends the S quay can be used – the N quay is for commercial traffic. For a long stay, there are moorings on the N side of the **Binnenhafen** (the showers and WCs are located here), after passing through the basin entrance, which opens from two hours before to half an hour after HW. This historic town, once part of Denmark, was developed by immigrants, particularly from the Netherlands, and has many interesting old buildings.

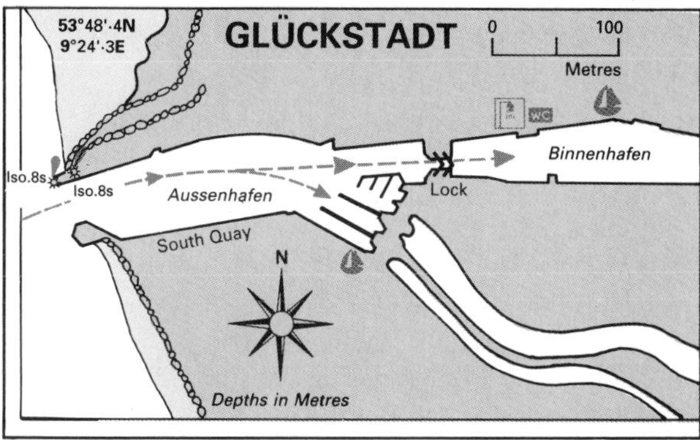

⚓ There is a reasonable daytime anchorage outside the harbour behind the Rhinplatte, at the southern end outside the fairway.

THE ELBE: GLÜCKSTADT TO HAMBURG

This 28M passage requires a good part of a full flood, with the strength of the stream progressively weakening from a maximum of 2·4kn at −0430hrs HW Hamburg, near Pagensand, to 2·0kn at −0400 hrs HW Hamburg at Seemannshöft, and 1·8kn at −0420hrs HW Hamburg at St Pauli pier, Hamburg. At St Pauli pier, which is just below City-Sport yacht haven, the tide begins ebbing at +0020hrs Hamburg. HW Hamburg averages +0337hrs HW Cuxhaven (i.e. +0135hrs HW Glückstadt).

→ The route follows the Glückstadter Nebenelbe fairway (buoyed, unlit, 3–9m) southwards to the final green buoy, crosses the Elbe fairway at right angles and continues along the outer starboard edge of the main channel (mostly lit buoys, lights in line and sector lights). For the next 17M to Hamburger yacht haven there are wide shoals on each side of the river, with a series of sandbar islands. The main fairway, however, is well buoyed.

From the Hamburger yacht haven eastwards, the N bank has wooded hills and country houses as Hamburg's Altona suburbs are approached, while a complex dock area covers the whole of the S bank. The buoyage continues until just before Nesskanal on the S bank; it is best to keep just outside the green buoys, which are close to the 5m contour. From Nesskanal, simply keep to the steep-to starboard side, but watch out for exiting traffic when crossing each dock entrance.

There are about a dozen possible mooring places along this stretch to Hamburger yacht haven (see below), at least eight of which dry out; most of these, having half-tidal approaches, must be entered 1 hour or at most 2 hours before local HW. In three, possibly four, you can stay afloat, but two of these (on the Krückau and Pinnau rivers) have sills, so again you are limited by time. Another (Brunshausen) has a deep-water approach, but the moorings must be entered 2 hours after LW. The last (Neuenschleuse) is a riverfront yacht haven with no problems.

E bank **Bielenburg** dries, suffers from swell and is too small to consider entering.

W bank **Ruthenstrom** has an 0·4m bar at its entrance and shallow/almost drying moorings over 1M down near the lock.

E bank **Kollmar**, in the approaches to the channel behind Pagensand, is a small, directly entered, but drying harbour.

W bank **Barnkruger Loch** is a tiny drying harbour on the W bank with an extremely difficult approach along the unbuoyed channel inside the Schwartztonnen-sand and 0·5M along a drying creek to the drying moorings by the bridge. Not recommended to the newcomer.

E bank **Krückaumündung** is one of the better moorings in this stretch, with 1–3m water (deepest at the northern end) at the pontoons. The approach is along the Pagensander Nebenelbe channel (2·5–6m approaching), at the N end of the Pagensand; the Krückau channel entrance is to port (sector light on black dolphin on starboard side of entrance). The harbour is 0·7M along the channel, which shoals to 1·1m after passing through a (usually open) flood barrier/swing bridge (two long blasts if closed, when clearance is 7m). The approach then leads hard to starboard through a very narrow entrance, with a sill which has 2·3m at HW and gates which are open from 2 hours before HW to HW. 200m E of these entrance gates there is a waiting pontoon which dries over mud. To avoid sitting here, entry at about 1 hour before HW is best. HW Kruckaumündung averages approximately 2 hours 30 minutes after HW Cuxhaven.

E bank **Pinnaumündung**, with 2·5–3m of water, is the second reasonable mooring inside the yacht haven. Continuing along towards the southern end of the Pagensander Nebenelbe (buoyed, unlit, minimum depth 2·6m), the Pinnau channel entrance is to port (keep close to sector light on red dolphin on port side of entrance, withied channel, minimum 1·5m depth). The harbour is 1M along the channel, through a (usually open) flood barrier/swing bridge (two long blasts if closed, when clearance is 7m), then hard to port through a very narrow entrance, with gates which are open from 1 hour before to half an hour after HW. There are other moorings along the Pinnau which are outside

The yacht pontoon at Pinnaumündung.

Hamburger Jachthafen at Wedel.

the scope of this book. HW Piennaumündung averages approximately 2 hours 40 minutes after HW Cuxhaven.

W bank **Abbenfleth**, on the Bützflether Süderelbe creek, has a drying bar and channel; the stem and stern moorings 0·4M from the bar on the W bank dry to soft mud. The creek entrance has two triangular leading marks on the S side. These are not reliable deep-water marks, and entry near HW is best. The flood barrage and bridge en route are normally left open.

W bank **Brunshausen** (Stadersand, Port Radio: VHF Ch 11, 12, 16) pontoons (Segler-Verein Stade) are 0·7M down the river Schwinge on the N bank. The river-entrance (front light of lights in line, white tower with red band is on S side) depth is 3m, and as you may just touch at LW on the pontoons, it is better to enter at around 4 hours before HW. There is an open flood barrage with an opening bridge (6·3m clearance closed, two long blasts to request opening) just before the moorings. There are moorings further along the Schwinge, but they are outside the scope of this book. HW Stadersand averages +0238hrs HW Cuxhaven (i.e. +0036hrs HW Glückstadt).

E bank **Haseldorf** is a drying harbour 1M along the withy-marked Dwarsloch, on the southern side at the head of the channel. The village with its castle is 2km away. The S side of the Dwarsloch entrance is marked by Juelssand sector light (white tower near house with B roof).

N bank **Hetlinger Schanze** is a tiny yacht haven entered directly from the river; you will touch at the pontoons (0·5m). There is little space.

S bank The winding **Lühe** creek has 3·8m in the entrance at HW – i.e. hardly any at all at LW – and several pontoons about 0·5M along the creek also dry. On the downstream side of the entrance there is a front light of lights in line (white tower with red band). Just inside the entrance is a flood barrage with a lifting bridge (6·2m clearance closed), which operates during most daylight hours Mondays to Thursdays and offers a more restricted service on Fridays, weekends and holidays (☎ 041 42 25 35).

S bank (Hahnöfer Nebenelbe): Just above the Lühe entrance the wide buoyed (unlit) Hahnöfer Nebenelbe (2–4m) heads off the main river behind Hankskalbsand. **Neuenschleuse** is a small yacht haven entered directly on the S side of this channel, with 1·5m at the visitors' pontoon, on the W side of the harbour.

28M (to Hamburg City-Sport Hafen)
HAMBURG
Port radio VHF Ch 14, 13, 6, 73

⛵ From Hamburger yacht haven to the City-Sport Hafen there are some six yacht havens on the N bank, and around five on the S bank. Four of the latter are in leafy but somewhat remote oases in the unprepossessing S bank dock complex W of the junction with the Süderelbe.

N bank With nearly 2000 boxes, **Hamburger Jachthafen** (2·2–3·7m deep, PD*), at Wedel, is the largest and best equipped yacht haven on the Elbe. It is entered directly from the river through either of two lit entrances, both angled slightly upstream. It is here that you should get your mast lowered if you wish to go upriver beyond Hamburg to the canal to Lübeck and the Baltic. There are nearby rail and road connections to central Hamburg.

N bank **Hafen von Schulau** (lit entrance, 0·6–1·6m) is a small commercial and pleasure-craft harbour which seems to have silted up a little in recent years, so entry at LW is best avoided. HW Schulau averages +0304hrs HW Cuxhaven (i.e. +0102hrs HW Glückstadt).

S bank **Este** river is entered from a buoyed (some lit) channel with a minimum of about 1·3m, and 1m at Buxtehude, 7M away. There are two flood barrages with opening bridges (6·7m and 4·7m clearance closed) within about three quarters of a mile of each other, manned during daylight hours and contacted on VHF Ch 10 or requested to open with the usual two long blasts on the foghorn (☎ 040 7 45 91 62 – both are controlled from the same office). There is a small shallow yacht haven on the E side just after the second barrage.

N bank **Baurs Park (Blankenese)** is a tiny harbour for small boats (unlit entrance), opening directly onto the river.

N bank **Mühlenberg** (1·5m, unlit entrance) is a small yacht haven entered directly from the river. It is below a pleasant wooded park.

S bank **Nesskanal**, **Rüschkanal** and **Steendiekkanal** (*) are large former commercial docks, all with lit entrances, converted either entirely or in part into yacht havens with stem and stern moorings.

S bank **Köhlfleet** is a large commercial dock with a few yacht moorings on the E side about 0·8M from the entrance (lit).

N bank **Teufelsbrücke** (1·3m, unlit) has a direct entrance and a similar wooded aspect to Mühlenberg, but is smaller; you may touch at LW.

N bank **City-Sport Hafen** is a relatively new yacht haven for short-stay visitors to central Hamburg. After passing St Pauli pier, with its large ferry ships, and the entrance to the Niederhaven, the entrance to the yacht haven is to port, passing across the entrances to Brandenburger Hafen to port and Sandtorhafen to starboard. The pontoons, with facilities, are close inshore.

There are plenty of restaurants, night life and tourist attractions in **central Hamburg** within easy reach of City-Sport Hafen. You can take a Hafenrundfahrt on one of the nearby ferry boats. You can walk north and eastwards to the main shopping area and the beautiful Binnenalster and Aussenalster lakes beyond, and visit the imposing 19-century Rathaus, five churches, the Kunsthalle and several other museums, and the daring expressionist architecture of the Chilehaus. Alternatively, you can take a slightly longer walk or bus-ride westwards to Altona which used to be a city of its own in the past. Here you can visit the weekly Fischmarkt held on the waterfront, visit its Rathaus and museum, take a stroll along the Reeperbahn or eat in one of its Portuguese restaurants.

→ It is 40M from this point to Lauenburg, where the Elbe-Lübeck-Kanal (35M long) enters the river and vessels need to lower their masts: the maximum height of vessel is 4·2m and the maximum draught 2m. Vessels wishing to lower their masts are advised to do so at the Hamburger yacht haven at Wedel, 11M below City-Sport Hafen, where there are extensive facilities. At the other end of the Lübeck-Kanal, just beyond Lübeck, masts can be raised again at the boatyards on the W side of Teerhof Island and at Schlutup on the Untertrave.

Hamburg City-Sport Hafen.

3. The Schleswig-Holstein and Jutland west coasts

Route 2
Cuxhaven to Thyborøn via the North Frisian islands

Commentary

See also Chapter 1, Approaches – The North Frisian islands. Approaches – Jutland west coast.

The route below is selected for descriptive convenience, placing two disparate coastal areas under a single chapter heading. It is not recommended as one for a small yacht to attempt in a single continuous cruise, but parts of it could be incorporated into other cruises. For example, after a North Sea crossing to Esbjerg or Helgoland, en route to the Baltic, different sections of the route could be used to reach the Limfjord, the Eider river or the Nord-Ostsee-Kanal.

During the prevailing westerlies, the outer coastline of the peninsula is a lee shore. The coastline N of Horns Rev is smooth and barren, with a few difficult harbours of refuge; the southern part has extensive, intricate, shifting shoals to negotiate, with westward-facing (i.e. usually windward-facing) river entrances in between, before its harbours are reached. You will need up-to-date, detailed charts (the German and Danish hydrographic series are recommended). As the islands and coastline are low-lying, you must navigate carefully by the light towers, church towers and beacon markers throughout the area, and in the southern channels by the buoys and withies, if possible on a rising tide on a first visit. In these channels, where the shoals are constantly changing, you must navigate by the actual buoys and withies as they appear en route, since they are liable sometimes to be moved from their charted positions.

Since the prevailing weather is onshore, it is important to choose moderate conditions when following the northern coastline or crossing the outer shoals between the buoyed channels in the S. The route described below is the simplest and safest, but not the shortest, since it assumes that the visiting vessel is not shoal draught. The southern area has a complicated labyrinth of channels and gutways, more even than the Thames estuary, and there are many shoal-draught, rising-tide routes available other than those dealt with here, where local knowledge helps.

The route below, for example, bypasses the possible diversion to Husum along the Heverstrom, which requires accurate timing and pilotage. Similarly, the part of the route from Wyk southwards round Amrum to Hörnum on Sylt is much longer than the HW short cut across the drying bank between the two islands.

With the exception of the major ferry port of Esbjerg, most of the towns are primarily fishing harbours and seaside holiday centres, of varying but usually limited architectural and historical interest. The countryside is generally low-lying and much more sparsely wooded than the east coast of the Jutland peninsula, with some spectacular sand-dune country in places such as Sylt and along the north Jutland coast.

There is only one significant, purpose-built yacht harbour, at Meldorf near Büsum. All the rest on this coast are relatively small and usually part of commercial or fishing harbours.

Finally, it must be stressed that the route is selective; there are many other harbours on the islands and mainland in Schleswig-Holstein which could have been visited.

Distance

337M including visit to Tönning, overlapping with Chapter 4 (Eider river and Nord-Ostsee-Kanal route across the peninsula). The distance is the same if the passage route starts at Helgoland instead of Cuxhaven.

Tides, currents, depths and weather

See also Chapter 1 for tidal details by harbour.

The tidal range, the differences between springs and neaps, and the stream rates are all at their greatest in the Elbe estuary. They decrease northwards to minimal levels near Thyborøn and the Skagerrak, so tidal timing is far more critical on the first half of this route, between Cuxhaven and Esbjerg, which is also the area with shifting banks and shoal-water pilotage.

Persistent winds from about force 5 upwards in the German Bight affect the sea level: easterlies reduce the water level and winds from the two western quadrants increase it. Some channels have 1m or less of water at MLWS, and in these it can be seen just how tricky pilotage in the area can be. Wind direction can also affect the duration and the rate of the tidal streams in the area.

The route below gives a wide berth to the outer banks in order to remain in at least 5m where possible, particularly when doubling round from one channel into the next. In settled weather it is possible to reduce the distance by cutting across the outer ends of the banks in lesser depths. It is wise to avoid the outer banks in any onshore winds from force 5 upwards and certainly to keep in depths of 10m or more in these uncomfortable conditions.

Charts

Note Chart datum and chart soundings are based on mean low water springs on all charts except on Danish charts *93/93S, 99* and *108/108S*, where they are based on mean sea level. All heights are based on mean sea level.

German hydrographic *44, 81, 82, 83, 103, 104, 105, 106, 107, 108, 109.*
German hydrographic ***Sportbootkarten*** *3013, 3014* (part).
Danish hydrographic *93, 94, 99, 108.*
Danish *Søportskort Serie 2* *93S, 94S, 108S.*

Route description

OPTIONAL APPROACH FROM HELGOLAND

An optional approach to the route below is in deep water directly from Helgoland to Büsum via the Süderpiep offing buoy and the Süderpiep channel, cutting out Cuxhaven and the tortuous passage round the Elbe sandbanks. This is a much simpler route; the distance to Büsum from Helgoland is 35M, exactly the same as the distance from Cuxhaven.

CUXHAVEN

See Chapter 1, Route 1 for harbour information.

ELBE, ZEHNERLOCH, NORDER ELBE, SÜDERPIEP

Given the length of this leg, it is best to take the last of the ebb out of the Elbe and the flood up the Süderpiep channel, taking advantage of the strong streams and arriving in the final approaches on a rising tide. This will mean rounding the outer banks at around LW, so they should be given a wide berth, depending on weather conditions. The spring ebb off Cuxhaven can reach as much as 4·2kn at around +0450hrs HW Cuxhaven, and that in the Zehnerloch 3·3kn at +0420hrs. In the Süderpiep, the mid-flood reaches about 2·3kn maximum at springs. HW Büsum averages −0023hrs HW Cuxhaven.

Even in moderate winds from the NW and SW quadrants there can be considerable seas over the outer banks and in the outer channels of the Elbe entrance, particularly with cross-tidal streams, and in strong winds from these directions passage should not be attempted.

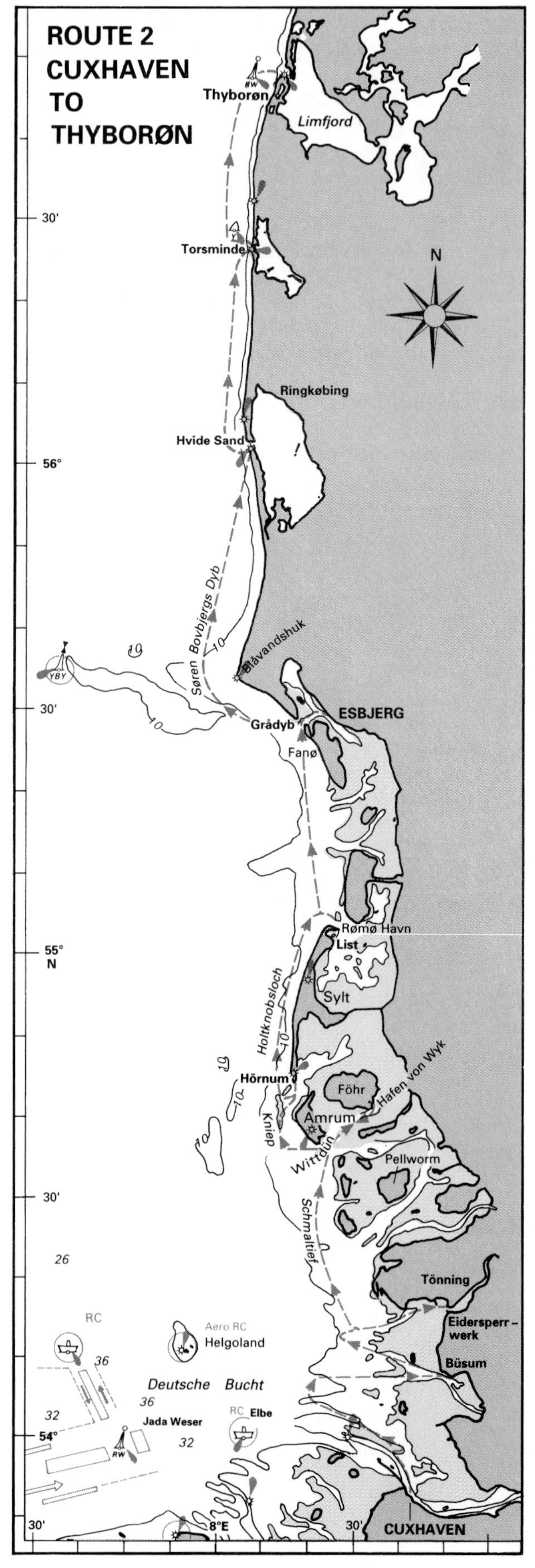

→ From Cuxhaven, the starboard edge of the Elbe deep-water channel outside the buoys (all lit) should be followed north-northwestwards in 6–7m. 0·5M N of RWR light beacon 'W', turn northeastwards along the Zehnerloch channel (over 6m deep, buoyed, one lit at the northern end). Then turn northwards and westwards, rounding into the Norderelbe buoyed (some lit) channel. Turn northwards near the end of the buoyed channel, keeping outside the 5m contour and clear of the ends of the two tongues of sand on either side of the Falsches Tief, then turn eastwards along the Süderpiep buoyed (some lit – mainly red buoys on N side of the channel) channel. Follow the buoys carefully to remain in the channel along the N side of the 5M-long middle-ground sand bar (just dries in places) approaching Büsum. This will ensure depths of over 5m, and in many places over 10m and up to 20m. There is a sector light at the root of Büsum's W mole, with a white sector directed along this northern channel and red and green sectors to N and S of the white light. Büsum is not visible from seawards, and the Tertius (rectangular topmark) and Blauortsand (framework) beacons on the shoals to the N of this approach are the first landmarks.

35M

BÜSUM

« The lit harbour entrance is approached along lights in line and then through a flood barrage gate. This is closed when the water level exceeds 0·4m above MHW, when vessels must lock through (VHF Ch 11, 16). There can be very strong cross-tidal streams in the entrance at half-tide, and on the flood there is an anticlockwise rotation. The yacht haven (PD) is in basin IV, immediately to starboard after the main entrance. Keep clear of the narrow drying patches on each side of the basin's entrance, remaining in 2·5m depth, and stay at the SW end, as the NE end of the basin dries. An alternative to the yacht harbour is to lie alongside a fishing vessel in Basin II, but if you are directly against the wall here don't forget to tend your warps for the large tidal range.

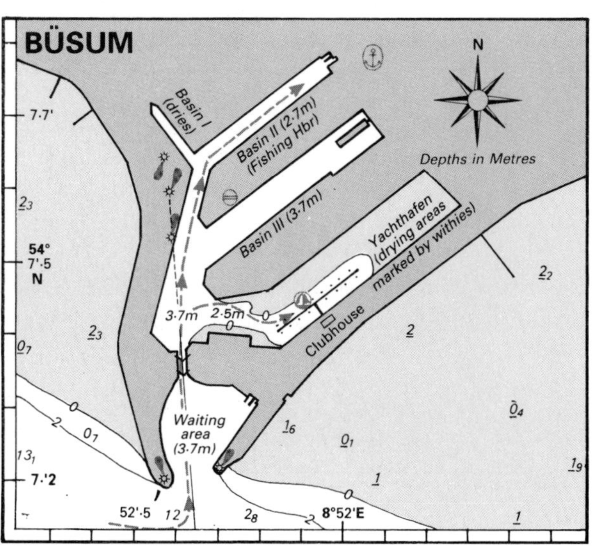

Inner side of Büsum lock from Basin III.

The town is a holiday resort and fishing port, similar in many ways to Norderney.

MELDORFER BUCHT

→ « Büsum should be left about 2 hours before HW with the flood; there willl then be plenty of water along the Kronenloch (range of tide is 3·8m at springs and 2·8m at neaps, and the times at Meldorf are only a minute or so later than at Büsum). The route follows a channel (unlit) marked with lateral spar buoys and withies, and near the lock with cardinal beacons on the S side, where the water is deeper. The lock (unlit at time of writing) is not on VHF, but it is wise to contact the lock-keeper by telephone in advance (☎ 048 32 71 81), as the lock is closed above certain water levels.

4M

SPORTHAFEN MELDORF

The harbour (PD*, 2–6m on the pontoons, shallow around the sides of the basin) has full facilities, including a shop, but the surrounding area is somewhat bleak; bicycles are a useful asset.

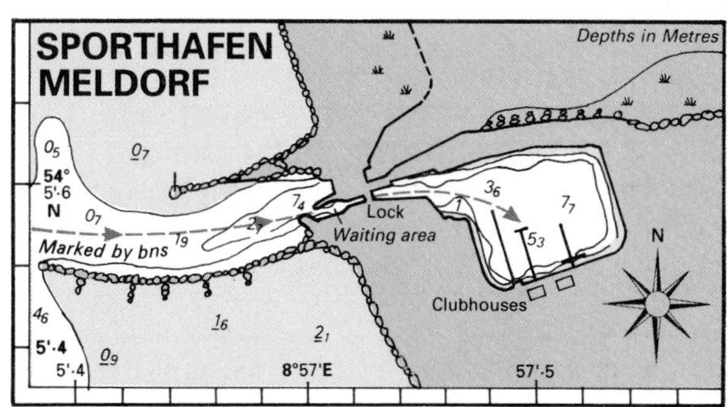

MELDORFER BUCHT, NORDERPIEP, EIDER ENTRANCE CHANNEL

A similar distance to the first leg of the passage route, so again a departure along Kronen Loch and the Norderpiep on the ebb and an arrival at the Eidersperrwerk on the flood are necessary, since the Eider approach channel is shallow and should be navigated on a rising tide. In the Norderpiep at the outer end of the channel the ebb reaches about 2·3kn maximum at springs; at the outer end of the Eider channel the ingoing flood reaches only 1·2kn maximum at springs. HW Eidersperrwerk averages +0023hrs HW Büsum, and HW Tönning is +0150hrs HW Büsum, so there is plenty of time to use the tide in this direction – the reverse is true when returning in the opposite direction.

→ Return past the entrance of Büsum and turn northwestwards out of the main channel just S of the Blauortsand beacon, following the buoyed Norderpiep channel (over 6m, spars, all unlit). This maintains depths of at least 6m until the 3–4m bar at the end of the channel is reached. Turn northwards near the Norderpiep buoy at the end of the buoyed channel, keeping outside the 5m contour and clear of the sand spits to the E, and pick up the outer buoys of the Eider channel (buoyed, a few lit), then carefully follow this eastwards to the Eidersperrwerk. There is a 3–4m bar at the outer end of the Eider channel; this is followed by a 6m-deep (plus) section. There is then a very tricky northern loop across two 1·5–3m patches where the depths just outside the marked channel are 1m and less. Finally, the approach to the dam crosses 2–3m patches. A rising-tide approach, to add at least 1m (and up to 3·5m) to these charted depths, is definitely called for.

St Peter sector light (red tower with B lantern, 11–15M range) and the prominent buildings of St Peter-Ording to its N are on the mainland, due N of the deep outer section of the entrance channel.

34M
EIDERSPERRWERK
See Chapter 4

EIDER RIVER
See Chapter 4

5M
TÖNNING
See Chapter 4

EIDER RIVER, EIDER ENTRANCE CHANNEL, MITTELHEVER, SCHMALTIEF

This is a long leg which could take nine hours or more, but well over half of it is along the Eider river and channel and across the Mittelhever approaches, so it is advisable to use the benefit of a complete ebb tide by either starting at the Eidersperrwerk or leaving Tönning an hour before local HW. This gives plenty of water along the tricky Eider channel and also ensures arrival at around half-tide rising, with time to seek out a berth in the shallow approach channel or the harbour of Amrum. The ebb in the outer Eider channel has a maximum rate of 1·2kn; in the Schmaltief and Norderaue channels the flood can reach up to 2·5kn. HW Amrum averages +0027hrs HW Eiderssperrwerk.

→ Return to the Eider offing buoy (RW, lit) at the end of the Eider channel and head north-northwestwards to the Mittelhever offing buoy (RW, lit), keeping in 8–12m throughout. Take a northerly course to the Schmaltief buoy (unlit), then follow the buoyed (unlit) Altes Schmaltief and Schmaltief channels (ST series of spar buoys). There are bars at the southern (3–4m) and northern (2–3m) ends of these channels and a deep section (7m plus) in the middle, so this is a route for fine weather.

In rough conditions it is advisable to sail offshore, taking the deeper, buoyed (some lit) Rütergat channel, further N, which approaches Amrum in a northeasterly direction. There are northern (1–4m) and southern (3–4m) shoals (buoyed) to be avoided at the outer end of this channel.

From the last of the Schmaltief buoys, the route lies northeastwards along the buoyed (some lit) deep-water channel (10–20m and over) to the Amrum-Hafen offing buoy (lit). Taking care to keep N of the southern spit after rounding the lit buoy to its N, follow the channel westwards close past the ferry harbour (look out!) to Wittdün harbour, keeping N of the port-hand withies (upward branches) on its southern side and sounding to keep in the channel in 2m minimum depth. Amrum-Hafen lights in line are of use for finding the offing buoy but not for following the channel.

There are low light-coloured sand dunes, a major light, Amrum (red tower, white bands, 23M range), and a minor sector light, Wriakhörn (framework tower, 7–9M range), at the S end of the island.

47M
AMRUM

⚓ This is a tiny harbour, so do not be surprised if you have to anchor. The yacht moorings are on the two southern pontoons, to stern-posts (1m soundings, so you will probably ground; Yachtclub Amrum has showers and WCs). A good anchorage in 3–4m over sand is in the channel N of the harbour, landing by dinghy at the harbour. The ferry/holiday resort town, with shops and restaurants, is about 1km SE of the yacht haven.

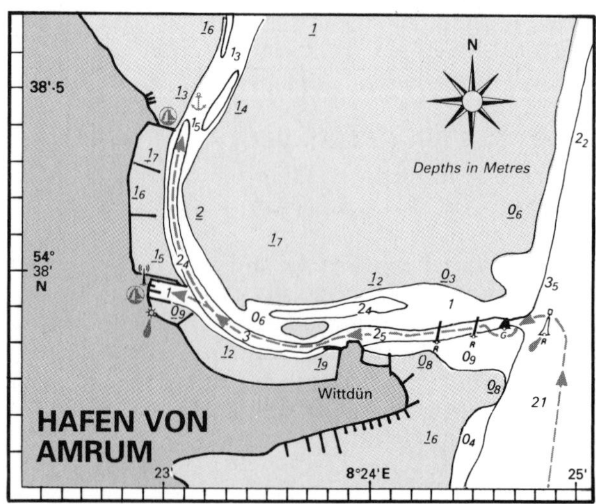

NORDERAUE, FÖHRER LEY

A short run to be taken on the flood. At mid-tide the current can average up to 2·5kn in the Norderaue.

→ Follow the buoyed (some lit) Norderaue channel (10–20m plus deep), turning northwards just before the Föhrer Ley lit buoy and proceeding along the channel of this name (buoyed, unlit, 6m plus). Wyk island is low-lying, and the church at Nieblum and the church and clocktower/spire at Wyk are helpful marks. Hafen von Wyk entrance is approached from southeastwards, keeping inside the charted white sector of the sector light on its S mole. Cross N of and give a wide berth to the ferry-harbour entrance, then turn W and northwards to dogleg round the northern mole (in 1·5–2·5m depth) into the yacht haven. The fishing harbour and Alter Hafen are to the S of the yacht haven.

8M

FÖHR/HAFEN VON WYK

This is one of the largest yacht havens in this area, although it probably has fewer than 200 berths. It has crane and yard facilities (D), and 1–1·7m charted depths, so you should be able to lie afloat. Harbour office of the commercial harbour: VHF Ch 11 and 16. The holiday resort 1km or more away has a 13th-century church.

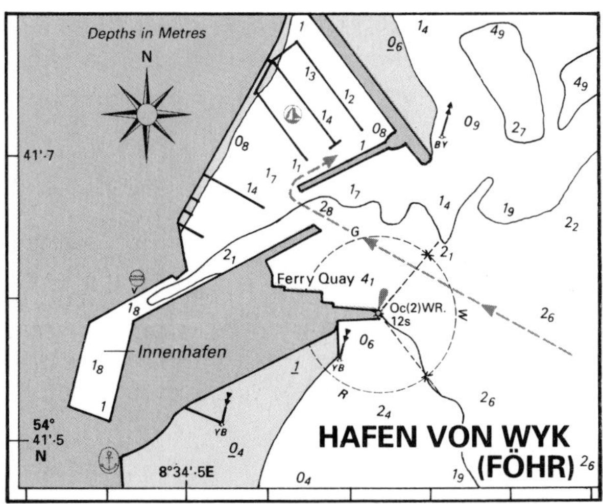

NORDERAUE, KNIEP, VORTRAPPTIEF

The critical depths on this route are in the Kniep channel W of Amrum, where a rising tide helps. Either start at low water and make a hard push to Amrum, or better still take the last of the ebb to Amrum and anchor until say two hours after LW before taking the rising tide N to Hörnum, where HW averages some 41 minutes after HW at Amrum. At the northern end of the Vortrapptief channel just off Hörnum-Odde the spring mid-flood averages up to 3·6kn and at neaps 2kn; it is only fractionally less on mid-ebb.

→ Return past Amrum's approach channel, then follow the buoyed (KN series, unlit, red to starboard, and most of the buoys are red) Kniep channel W and northwestwards round Amrum. Charted soundings can be little as 2·6m here, so again in winds from the SW quadrant it can be uncomfortable. Looking eastwards, Amrum island has dunes rising to 30m in the centre and N, while Nebel church and two windmills are near the middle of the island. Next follow the Vortrapptief deep-water channel (buoyed, some lit, lights in line, mainly 10–20m depths) northwards into Hörnum Reede to Hörnum entrance (lit).

Sylt island's southern peninsula, Hörnum, consists of 15–30m dunes, with the conspicuous Hörnum light (red tower, white band, 20M range) at the S end, and a 193m radio mast 3M N of this.

23M

SYLT/HÖRNUM

The entrance route is a dogleg round first the E (Schutzmole) then the N mole (a long blast on the whistle is the regulation at this point) to the pontoons/posts (2·1–3·1m depth) at the N end of the harbour. Anchoring and fishing are forbidden S of the harbour entrance, but there are anchoring possibilities to the N. This is primarily a busy small commercial harbour and tourist centre. The yacht haven has limited facilities. The built-up area is a short walk away.

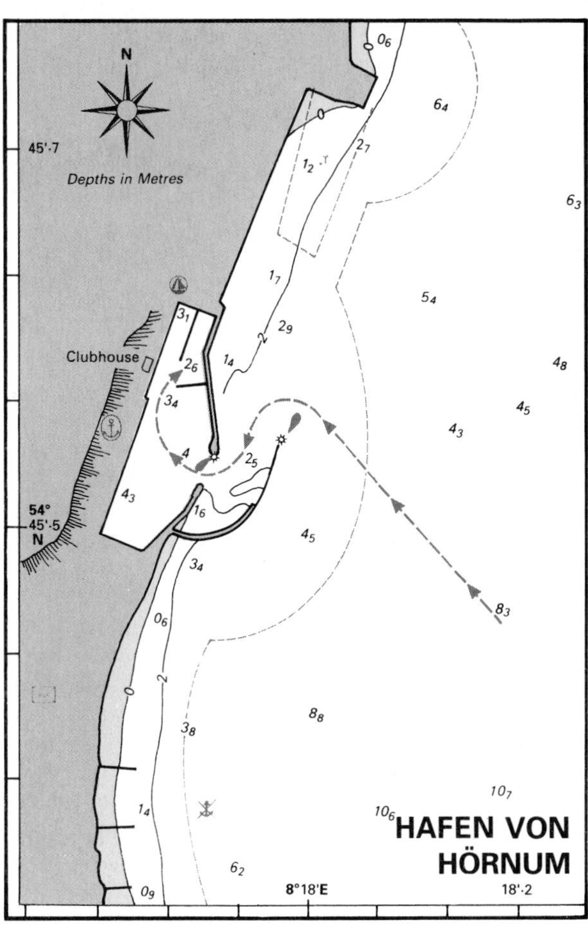

Hörnum, Sylt, 20M range, red tower with white band.

Hörnum. A tiny harbour, looking northeast towards the yacht pontoons.

VORTRAPPTIEF, HOLKNOBSLOCH, SYLT OFFSHORE, LISTER LANDTIEF, LISTER LEY

This passage distance again calls for a departure at about half-ebb and arrival on the flood, crossing the shallow Lister Landtief on a rising tide. This means that much of the run along the W coast of Sylt is cross-tide, with the current setting westwards, but it then moves anticlockwise, backing southwards then eastwards and sweeping into the Lister Tief just after local LW. In the inner Lister Tief the spring flood averages a maximum of 2·6kn, but it is only 1·6kn in the S-trending Lister Ley. HW List averages 28 minutes later than HW Amrum.

→ Return along Vortrapptief, turning southwestwards along Holknobsloch channel (buoyed unlit, HK series), and cross the outer bar (3–4m) to the offing buoy. Then head northwards, keeping 2–3M offshore in around 10m, shoaling to around 6m approaching the Lister Landtief.

The centre of Sylt, Westerland, is heathland, with a water tower and a church tower nearby. Further N is the conspicuous 51m Rote Kliff, with Kampen light tower (16–20M range, white tower, B band) nearby and a disused light tower yet further N. The N part of Sylt, List Land, has dunes rising to 30m and two light towers on its extreme northern end: List West (10–14M range, white tower, red lantern) and List Ost (10–14M range, white tower, red band and red lantern).

The Lister Landtief channel is marked (two unlit red buoys, 2–4m depth) and leads into Lister Tief, where the steep-shelving S shore can be followed relatively close to in over 10m. The lit green buoy marking the eastern spit is then rounded and the Lister Ley channel (buoyed, unlit, over 10m) followed to the harbour entrance.

33M
SYLT/LIST

The ferry (to Rømø) pier is S of the entrance, which is lit. The harbour is entered by heading N and then doglegging round the W mole to the yacht pontoons (1·1–2·6m), which are in the southern half of this tiny harbour with limited facilities. There are anchoring possibilities to the N of the entrance, but much more peaceful conditions will be found in 3m over sand on the W side of the Irrtief channel by continuing SW from the harbour.

The main villages/towns on Sylt (Westerland, Kampen, Wenningstedt and List) are all connected by bus. Westerland is the largest, with a casino,

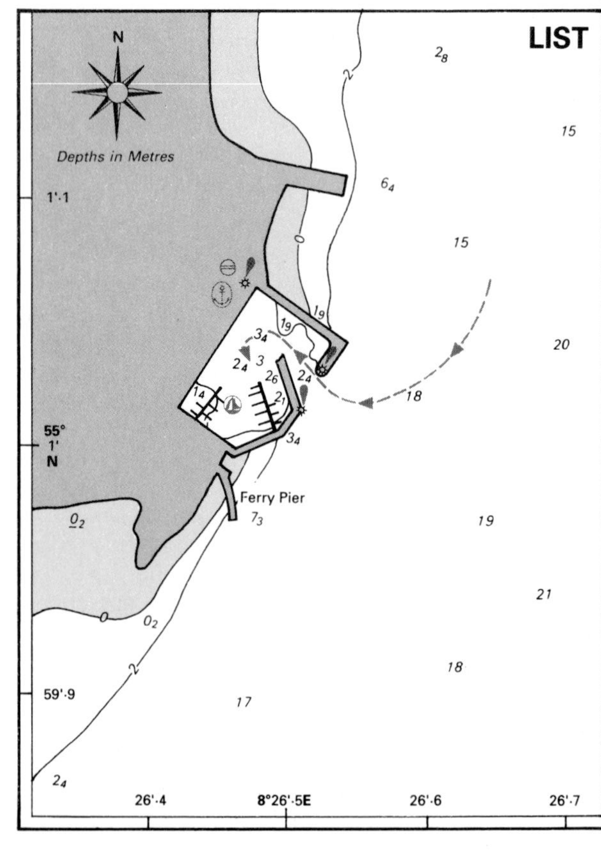

good restaurants and shops. It is within easy reach of the magnificent beaches along the W side of Sylt, and is connected to the mainland by train (even if you come by car you must load it onto the train, remaining in the car). List Land, at the N of the island, has strange, outer-space-like scenery, with contorted dunes covered in heather.

List. Entrance to another small harbour.

LISTER LEY, RØMØ DYB

↳ For this short passage taking the late flood to Rømø is probably best, making a short push out of List, following the Lister Ley, then continuing with the tide along Rømø Dyb marked channel (buoys and beacons, some lit) to the lit harbour entrance.

Rømø, the first of the Danish North Frisian islands, is low-lying, with dunes rising to 18m, a church tower some 3M from the S end, and a prominent hotel in the centre.

7M

RØMØ/RØMØ HAVN

⛵ Harbour office: VHF Ch 16, 10, 12, 13. This is a larger harbour than List, with an outer and an inner entrance (both lit), entered directly from the E. The ferry pier is S of the channel between the two entrances and the yacht pontoons are on the N side of the inner harbour (2m, D). It is possible to anchor further along the channel N of the harbour entrance in 3m. Shopping facilities close W of the harbour.

Rømø is connected by a road on a causeway to the Danish mainland. It has marshes, heathland and sandy beaches, as well as many old thatched farmhouses, including the Commander's House at Toftum, in which there is a museum.

LISTER TIEF, OFFSHORE OF FANØ, GRÅDYB

↳ This is another 6/7-hour leg, with a departure early on the ebb or even before HW recommended to maximise the amount of N-going tide offshore, although the streams are relatively weak. Arrival will be early on the flood: HW Esbjerg averages +0023 HW Rømø, but outside at the Grådyb Bar HW is well over an hour earlier, i.e. averaging −0101hrs HW Rømø. In any case, there is plenty of water in the Grådyb dredged channel, while the maximum spring rate in Esbjerg roads is 2kn and the tidal range at Esbjerg is only 1·2–1·7m.

Rømø. Entrance to the outer harbour.

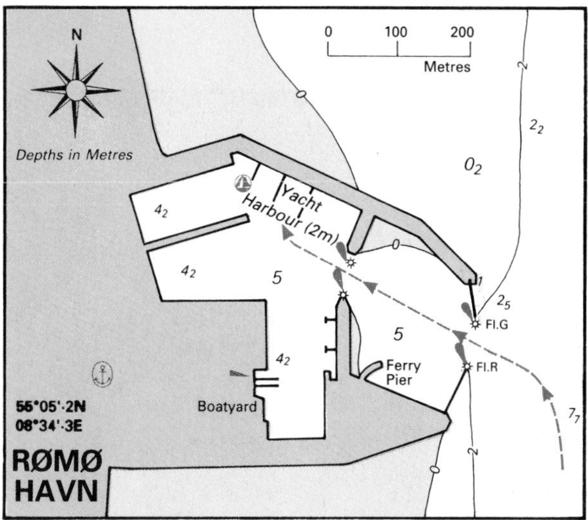

➞ Return to and along Lister Tief channel (buoyed, some lit) to Lister Tief offing buoy (lit, RW). Then head directly northwards for Grådyb's No. 1 outer channel buoy (lit, N cardinal). Follow the buoyed (lit) channel (also with several sets of lights in line) to the fishing-harbour entrance (lit, second entrance of Esbjerg complex).

On this route, much of which is 5M or more offshore, Fanø can be seen as a line of white dunes, with a church and windmill at Sønderho at the S end and beach hotels and a church at Nordby in the N. Approaching Esbjerg's Grådyb channel, a water tower and two church towers at Esbjerg and Jærne can be sighted.

⚓ If, en route, you have to run for shelter and anchor, the best place is in the Knude Dyb, behind the Keldsand; the entrance bar to this channel (buoyed, unlit, with mainly red buoys) has 2–4m. The Juvre Dyb, further S, leading to the backs of Rømø and Manø islands, has a much shallower, trickier bar, and although buoyed it is not recommended for visitors.

39M
ESBJERG

⚓ Harbour office: VHF Ch 16, 12, 13. The major commercial and ferry harbour complex of Esbjerg is not (at time of writing) geared up for visiting yachts, although plans are being made, so the best place to lie is in the **fishing basin** alongside one of the smaller vessels, by agreement. There are some pontoons for yachts and a small clubhouse at the shallow S corner of the next basin, **Trafikhavn**, but the approach is tricky and empty spaces are few.

Another option is to lie at **Nordby**, on Fanø island opposite. This is approached along Fanø Lo (marked, lit, lights in line, dredged to 2·7m); visitors can lie alongside the quay (Søndre Havnebro, 1·6–2·9m) or continue on to the small yacht haven (1·9m, unlit entrance, limited facilities) at the head of the channel.

Finally, there is a well protected anchorage in 2–3m (but remote from Esbjerg) in Ho Bugt, near the head of the buoyed (unlit) Hjerting Løb channel, which branches off N from the Grådyb before reaching Esbjerg.

Esbjerg was a tiny fishing village until the founding of the modern port in 1868. Its main architectural interest is therefore in its large Victorian buildings, particularly those in its pedestrian shopping street, Kongensgade. The water tower in the hillside park overlooking the harbour is near a museum of modern Danish art. There is a town

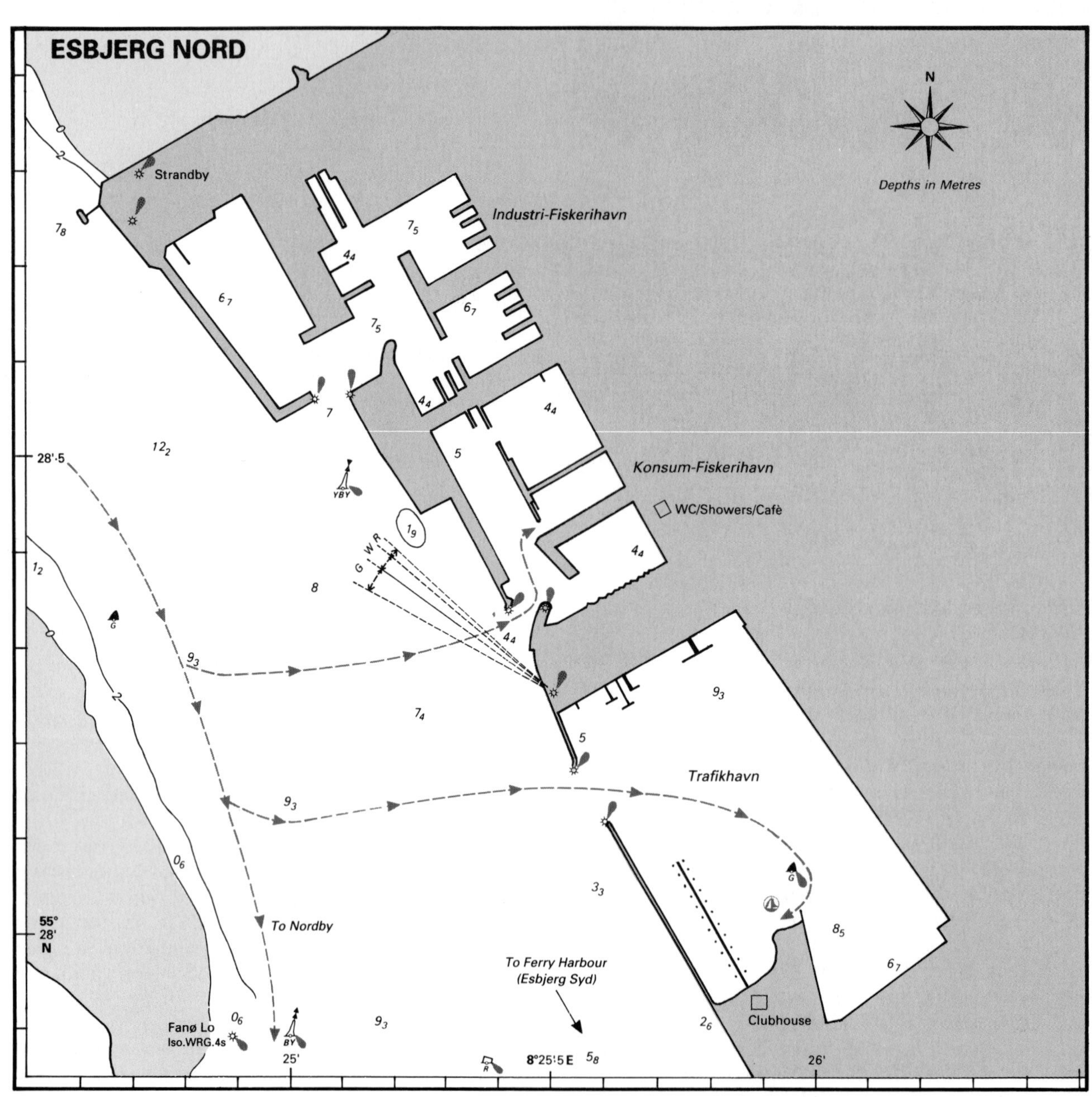

museum in Norregarde, and also a fisheries and maritime museum and an aquarium.

Esbjerg. Yacht pontoons in Trafikhavn.

Esbjerg. Fishing harbour from inside, looking towards the entrance.

SLUGEN, SØREN BOVBJERGS DYB, OFFSHORE

This is probably a 9-hour run, so a start at 2 hours before HW Esbjerg, pushing some tide along the Grådyb, obtains the full benefit of the N-going stream and only a hour or two of weak opposing current at the other end. HW Blåvandshuk averages −0115hrs earlier than HW Esbjerg, so the passage through Søren Bovbjergs Dyb is at about 2–3 hours after HW with a strong N-going stream (the flood southwards is not as strong). The streams along the coast further N all the way to Thyborøn are weak (spring rate around 0·75kn in either direction) and regular only in calm weather. There is an underlying persistent N-going current, the 'Stryget', which is normally weaker than the tidal stream, but can be strengthened by S–SW winds.

→ W Settled weather is essential for this tricky passage with no harbours of refuge, and the three harbours described below should never be approached in strong onshore winds. On the first part of the route, Skallingen is a low dune (up to 10m high) peninsula stretching northwestwards from the Grådyb channel to the prominent light tower at Blåvandshuk (white square tower, 23M range). The offlying Normands Dyb and Slugen channels are inside the notorious Horns Rev, which stretches over 20M out to sea to an offlying W cardinal buoy. The route takes the inshore channel. N of Blåvandshuk, a series of (charted) beacons and church towers provide the main landmarks among the dunes.

From Esbjerg, return to the Grådyb channel No. 1 buoy, then turn northwestwards to the first lit red buoy of Slugen channel (buoyage direction from here is red to port, green to starboard). Follow Søren Bovbjergs Dyb (buoyed, mainly green, one lit), and from the last buoy follow the coast northwards, keeping about 2 M off, to the harbour entrance. Hvide Sande light (14M range, 19m-high grey framework tower) is close S of the inner entrance to the harbour, and Lyngvig light tower (white round tower, 22M range) is 3M N of this.

All along this coast from Fanø island to about 10M N of Thyborøn anchoring, fishing and landing are forbidden within a band which extends approximately 1M offshore. This is marked on the chart.

48M
HVIDE SANDE

Harbour/lock office: VHF Ch 16, 12, 13. Visitors should contact the harbourmaster on VHF (a) to check the water levels over the bar and (b) to be allocated a berth. Approach directly from seawards when the visibility is adequate and the entrance is in sight. As well as the 14M-range light (see above), there is an entrance light on the end of the N outer mole, which extends beyond the entrance. There are pairs of entrance lights on the outer and inner entrances and three pairs of lights into the various basins. The entrance to the Østre (eastern) basin of the Sydhavn, which is also the approach to the Kammersluse, is to starboard past the entrance to the western basin of the Sydhavn. Visitors can

Hvide Sand from Nordhavn looking towards entrance.

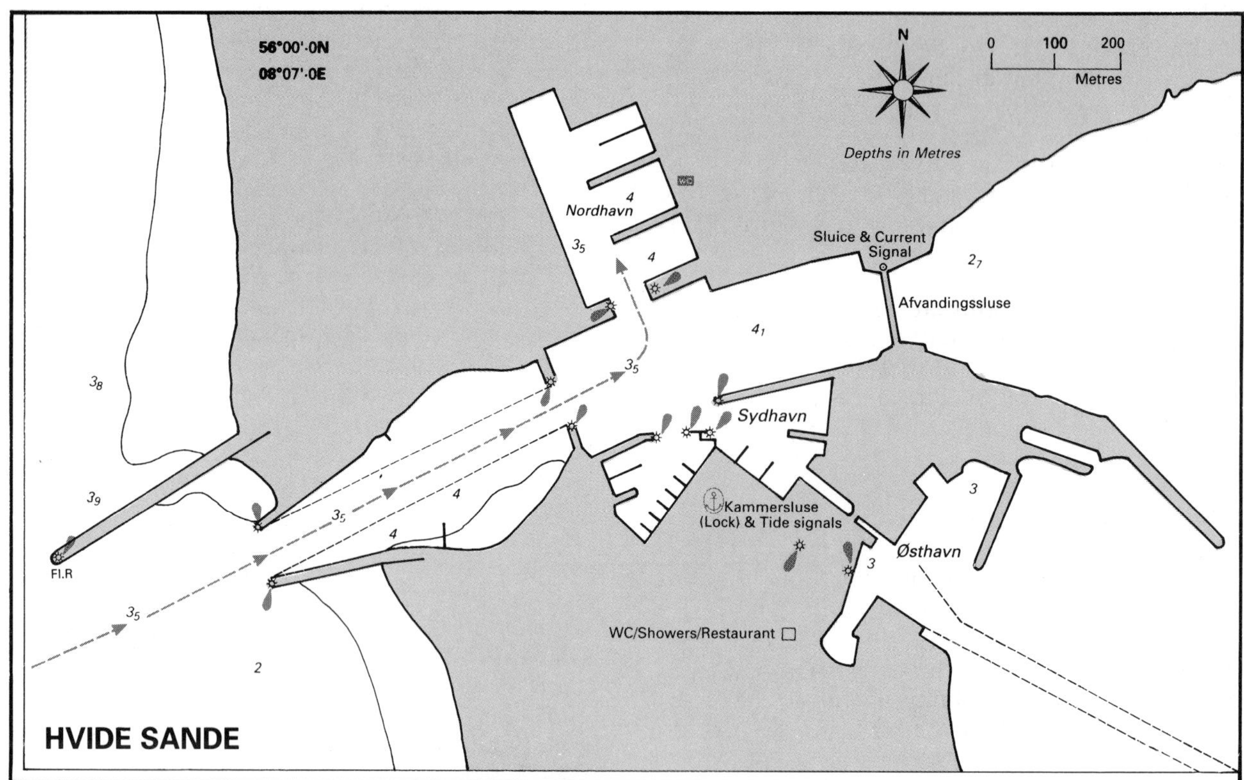

Beacons on the Jutland west coast near Hvide Sande.

usually stay in the Nordhafen (4m, PD, a long walk from the small, relatively modern town).

There is an extremely strong current out of the entrance when the drainage sluice at the E end of the harbour is open. On the northern side of this, a current signal mast shows black cone point up/green over white light – strong ingoing current; black cone point down/white over green light – strong outgoing current.

The tidal range in the harbour is 0·8m. Strong westerlies can raise sea level by up to 3·1m and easterlies lower it by 2m. Close N of the current signal mast (see above) is a water-level signal mast, on a 19m mound, which shows water-level signals relative to MSL. The night signal lights are: white/white(horizontal) zero or above MSL; Y −0·25m; Y/Y(vert) −0·5m; Y/Y/Y(vert) −0·75m; R −1·0m; red/white(vert) 1·25m; R/Y/Y(vert) −1·5m; R/Y/Y/Y(vert) −1·75m. The day signals are: 2 long cylinders side by side zero or above MSL; 1 cone −0·25m; 2 cones −0·5m; 3 cones −0·75m; 1 short cylinder −1·0m; 1 short cylinder with 1 cone −1·25m; 2 cones −1·5m; 3 cones −1·75m.

RINGKØBING AND RINGKØBING FJORD

(not included in total distance)

In the 17th century, Holmesland Klit, the sandbank protecting Ringkøbing Fjord from the North Sea, had a huge gap to the S of Hvide Sande. By 1915 this had closed, leaving only a tiny gap into the fjord at Nymindegab at the extreme southern end. By 1931 this gap had also been closed, and the lock and sluice at Hvide Sande were inaugurated.

The fjord can now be entered through the Kammersluse lock and opening bridge at certain levels of tide and then followed along a dredged (2·7m) channel. The fjord has depths of 2–4m. Ringkøbing Havn (2–3m, single light at entrance) is 6M away at the NE corner of the fjord, and is approached along a dredged channel (2·8m) marked by spar buoys. Visitors should use the **Gamle Havn** (the old harbour, the NE one of the three basins), although the yacht haven to its S is also possible. The pretty, gabled town is close by. There are other pleasure-craft harbours further S along the fjord's E and S shores.

Ringkøbing is the market centre for a wide area, and was a seaport in the 13th century before Holmesland Klit isolated the fjord from the sea. Most of its buildings date from the 17th century; there is also an 18th-century church, an early 19th-century Rådhus (town hall) and a good museum.

OFFSHORE

This passage takes under 6 hours. The tidal streams are weak, but in calm weather when wind is of little relevance the passage can be done on a single N-going ebb (starts at +0120hrs after HW Helgoland). In persistent SW-quadrant winds the N-going flow can be strengthened and continue for days. Strong NE winds give the opposite S-going effect.

→ The route leads northwards about 2M offshore, passing a series of (charted) beacons and church towers. Torsminde light (14M range, 25m-high grey framework tower) is 100m N of the harbour entrance.

28M

TORSMINDE

Harbour/lock office: VHF Ch 16, 12, 13 (except between 1300–1400 and 0000–0300). As at Hvide Sande, visitors should always contact the harbour on VHF (a) to check the water levels over the bar and (b) to be allocated a berth. Approach directly from seawards when visibility is adequate and the entrance is in sight. Moorings are at the pontoons in the Vesthavn (3m, PD), which is entered hard to starboard between its entrance lights.

As at Hvide Sande, there is an extremely strong current out of the entrance when the drainage sluice at the E end of the harbour is open. On the southern side of the drainage sluice a current signal mast shows similar signals to that at Hvide Sande (see above).

The tidal range in the harbour is 0·5–0·6m and, again as at Hvide Sande, strong westerlies can raise sea level by up to 3·0m and easterlies lower it by up to 1·8m. On the northern side of the drainage sluice a water-level signal mast shows similar signals to that at Hvide Sande (see above). Only vessels with lowering masts can pass through the lock into Nissum Fjord, which is a bird sanctuary.

At Torsminde is a seamen's church (originally a lifeboat shed) commemorating the many lost at sea in this area, and further S is a memorial to the 1,400 British sailors drowned in 1811 in the wrecks of the RN ships *George* and *Defence*.

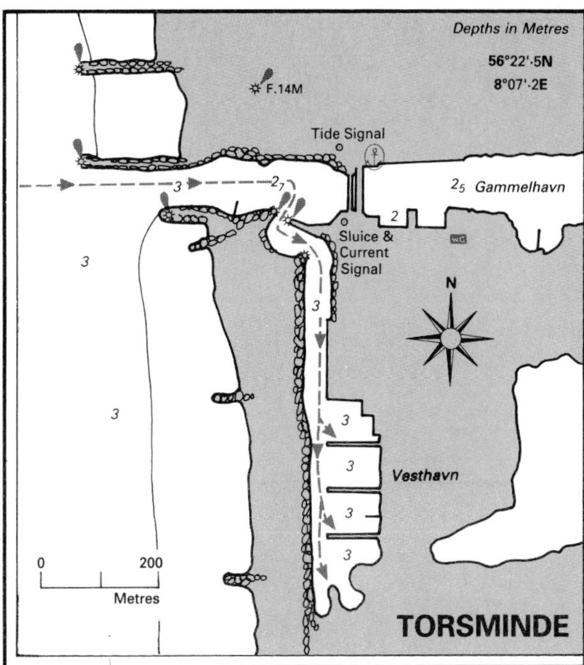

Torsminde outer entrance looking westwards.

OFFSHORE

A very similar leg to the previous one, with tidal currents usually of less importance than wind. In calm weather the start can be on the northerly stream, starting at 1 to 2 hours after HW Helgoland. In strong winds streams can be increased in rate and prolonged in duration (see previous leg).

→ Another passage northwards about 2m offshore, with beacons, a large number of church towers, Bovbjerg light (16M range, red round tower 26m high on a 38m dune) about halfway along the route and Thyborøn light (16M range, 17m-high framework tower) on the S side of the Thyborøn entrance.

N of Thyborøn entrance, Lodbjerg (23M range, 35m-high tower on 13m dune) and Hanstholm (26M range, 23m-high tower on a 42m chalk headland) are the major S approach lights to the Skagerrak, which is beyond the scope of this book.

In approaching Thyborøn from offshore after a North Sea crossing, the first landmarks raised are Vestervig and Gjettrup churches to the N of the harbour, and Nørre-Nissum and Tørring churches and the high ground N of Lemvig to the S of the harbour. A sector light combined with lights in line on Agger Tange, followed by a second set of lights in line, leads E and southeastwards into Thyborøn Kanal entrance, where the buoyed (some lit) channel leads southwards into the Søndre Dyb. The lit harbour entrance is hard to starboard about 1M S of the Kanal entrance.

26M

LIMFJORD ENTRANCE/THYBORØN KANAL

See Route 5, Chapter 7 for details of Thyborøn harbour complex.

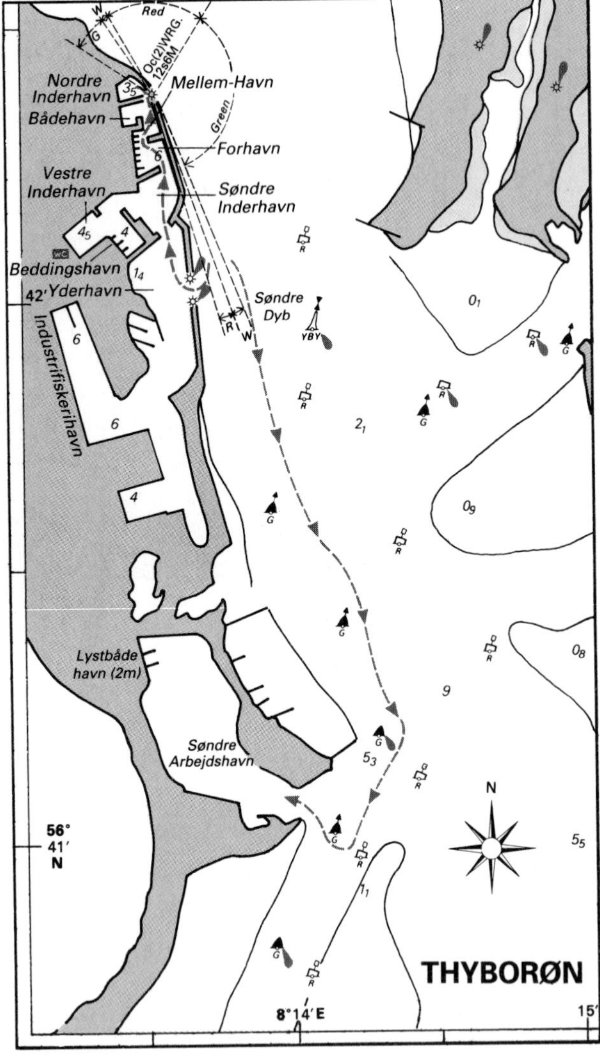

HARBOURS NORTH OF THYBORØN

The 110M of smooth inhospitable coastline between Thyborøn and Skagen is lined with dunes and has sand ridges a few cables offshore, so navigation needs to be in deep water (10–20m or more) with a very cautious eye on the weather. There are two large commercial/fishing/ferry harbours (their towns are small) which are good refuges for yachts: **Hantsholm** is 30M N of Thyborøn; **Hirtshals** is just over 50M beyond that and about 40M from Skagen harbour (see end of Chapter 6 – a wide detour is needed to round the end of Skagen point). Each harbour is tucked behind the eastern side of the western promontories of the two northernmost wide shallower (mainly 1·0–20m depths) bays: Jammer Bugt and Tannis Bugt. Each of these promontories has a major light (named after the harbours), with 26M and 25M ranges respectively and offshore buoys marking their short offshore spits. Each harbour has lit outer and inner entrances and is approached from approximately northwest to northeast in 7m of water with 4–7m depths in the basins. Permission to enter and directions for a berth must be obtained (VHF Ch 16) in advance from the harbourmasters.

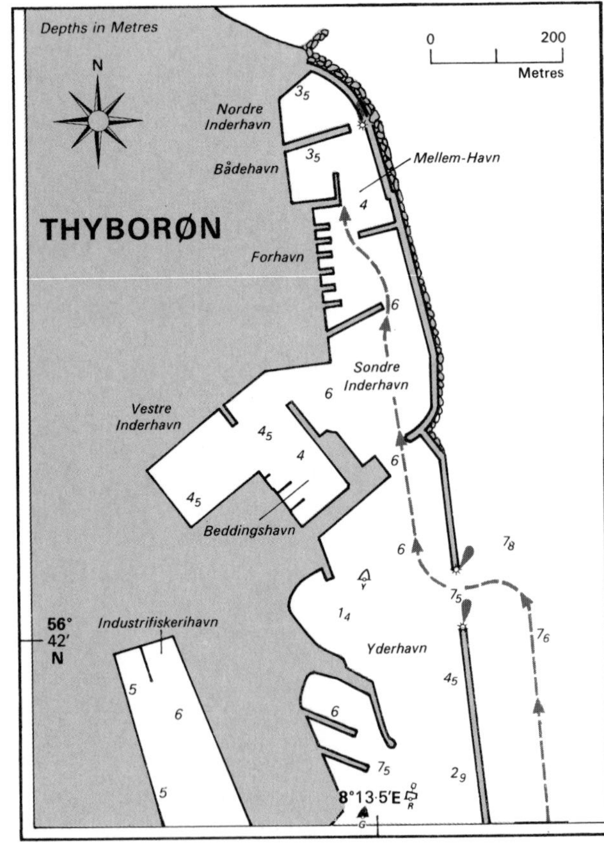

4. The Nord-Ostsee-Kanal and the Eider river

Route 3
North Sea to Kiel via the Nord-Ostsee-Kanal or via the Eider river and the Nord-Ostsee-Kanal

Commentary

A canal connecting the North Sea and the Baltic was first mooted in the 14th century, but did not materialise until 1784, when the 3·5m-deep Eiderkanal, connecting the Eider river at the Obereidersee with Holtenau, was opened, during the rule of the mentally retarded King Christian VII of Denmark.

In 1887, after Schleswig-Holstein had become part of the German empire, the Kaiser laid the foundation stone for a much shorter (100km, compared with 173km for the Eider system), wider and deeper canal directly across the peninsula from the Elbe to Kiel to satisfy increasing military demands. The Kaiser Wilhelm Kanal, as it was first called, remains an engineering masterpiece. It was opened in 1895 and had a simple double lock at each end, at Brunsbüttel and Holtenau (there are now two double locks at each end). A 1·5M stretch of shallow canal, with a lock and opening bridge at Gieselau, provided an alternative connection to the sea for shallower-draught vessels, via the western reaches of the river Eider.

The Kiel canal, or rather the Nord-Ostsee-Kanal, is wide, with plenty of passing space and high elegant bridges. After a hundred years of growth, its mature forested banks give it the appearance of a Danish fjord. There are three lakes in which to lie, surrounded by woods, in the northern half of the canal. The Obereidersee's (entrance Km 66 on the N bank) leafy yacht harbour is a short walk from the centre of the ancient town of Rendsburg; the Borgstedter See (Km 70 on the N bank) has a few floating moorings near the bridge, and the Flemhuder See (Km 85·5 on the S bank) is a delightful tree-surrounded anchorage. The Gieselau-Kanal, on the N bank (Km 40), is another quiet backwater in which to lie for a night. The yacht harbours at each end of the canal and a couple of other official mooring places near the banks are less comfortable stopovers, due to noise and swell from passing ships.

Rendsburg has a main-line railway station, if you wish to leave the boat for a few days and go sightseeing S to Hamburg or N to Schleswig and Jutland.

If you have time to spare and wish to visit the North Frisian islands, the Eider river and Gieselau-Kanal route winds tortuously through rolling woods and pastures with cattle and sheep. Tönning fishing harbour and the Dutch-style town of Friedrichstadt are at the seaward end, and there are many picturesque villages with stopping places in the quiet nontidal upper reaches.

Both routes are protected from weather and even in a westerly gale the Nord-Ostsee-Kanal is merely dappled with tiny white caps. However, in a head wind – i.e. usually when travelling W – the Nord-Ostsee-Kanal can be a hard push, demanding a good, reliable engine.

Except at Düsternbrook at the end, there are no large marinas on this route. Rendsburg is a modest size, probably having fewer than 200 berths.

Distances

Route A (Nord-Ostsee-Kanal only) 56·5M, of which Nord-Ostsee-Kanal only 54M.

Route B (Eider river and Nord-Ostsee-Kanal) 83·5M.

Depths, buoyage, bridges and locks

The Nord-Ostsee-Kanal is dredged to 11m depth (based on mean sea level for the Baltic and Elbe combined). It is somewhat less (7–10m) near the Alte schleusen (125m long) at each end of the canal, which are for smaller vessels and pleasure craft. The larger (310m long) Neue schleusen at each end are for large commercial vessels. The six bridges on the canal all give clearances of 40m.

The Binneneider (the Gieselau-Kanal and the Eider river to Nordfeld) has a minimum depth of 3m and is buoyed (unlit) on some of the difficult bends. It has three locks, at Gieselau, Lexfähre and Nordfeld (modest charges at each), and an opening bridge at Pahlen (not serviced on Sundays or public holidays).

The Eider river from Nordfeld to the sea is tidal (see below) and marked by withies and buoys (unlit to Tönning). Although a minimum of around 2m depth is charted as being available close to the buoys (depths on the German chart are to MLW from Nordfeld to Tönning and to MLWS from Tönning seawards), these soundings are unreliable. Given this situation it is advisable, as a visitor, to

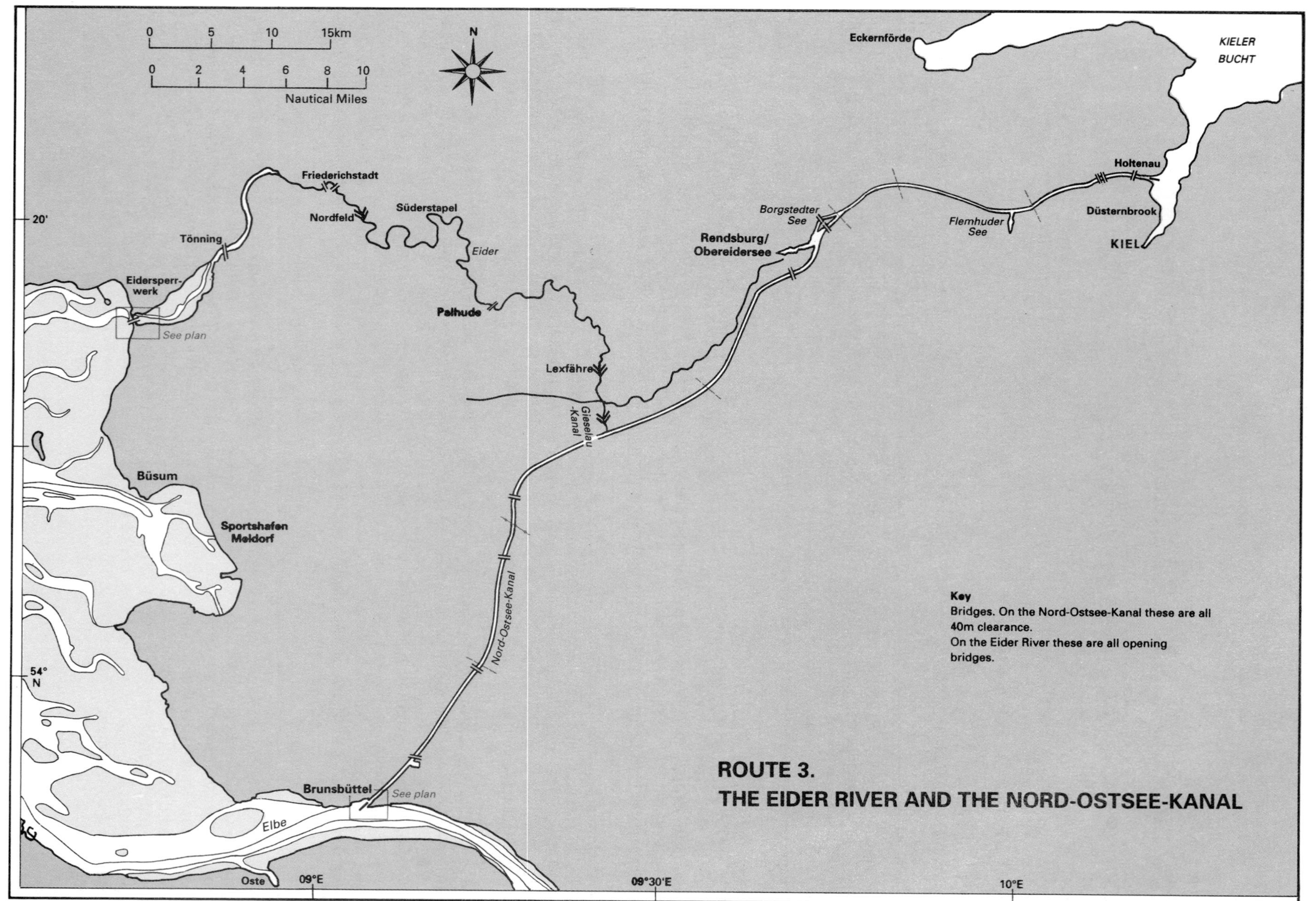
0 5 10 15km
0 2 4 6 8 10
Nautical Miles
N
Eckernförde
KIELER BUCHT
Holtenau
Düsternbrook
KIEL
Flemhuder See
Borgstedter See
Rendsburg/ Obereidersee
Friederichstadt
Nordfeld
Süderstapel
Eider
Tönning
Eidersperr-werk
See plan
Palhude
Lexfähre
Gieselau -Kanal
Büsum
Sportshafen Meldorf
Nord-Ostsee-Kanal
Key
Bridges. On the Nord-Ostsee-Kanal these are all 40m clearance.
On the Eider River these are all opening bridges.
ROUTE 3.
THE EIDER RIVER AND THE NORD-OSTSEE-KANAL
Brunsbüttel
See plan
Elbe
Oste
20'
54° N
09°E
09°30'E
10°E

navigate this 16M of river on the top half of the tide and preferably on a rising tide, even when going downriver. This, of course, helps to make the entry into Tönning (parts of which dry out) and Friedrichstadt (where there is a bar) close to HW. This timing is useful in getting to the Eidersperrwerk near to HW, ready for a prompt departure out to sea with the full ebb. At the Eidersperrwerk the neaps range is around 2·6m and springs range 3·5m, and similar assumptions can be used for the 16M tidal stretch above this to Nordfeld. There are three opening bridges (none of which are serviced on Sundays or public holidays) on these reaches: a road bascule bridge above Tönning, and a railway swing bridge below and a road bascule bridge above Friedrichstadt.

The Eider river from the Gieselau-Kanal junction eastwards to the railway embankment at Rendsburg (it is now cut off from the Obereidersee) has only 1·5m minimum depth and is impractical for boats with fixed masts to navigate, since it has three fixed bridges with clearances of only 4m.

Throughout the Eider river/canal system, with the exception of the Eidersperrwerk, the locks and bridges do not operate on VHF.

Tidal times and depths on the tidal reaches of the Eider

Times

Tidal differences (hours) based on HW and LW Büsum:

	HW	*LW*
Ausseneider	−0024	n/a
Süderhoft	+0009	+0044
Eidersperrwerk	+0025	+0126
Schülpersiel	+0200	n/a
Tönning	+0144	+0223
Friedrichstadt	+0241	+0339
Nordfeld	+0247	+0358

Tidal differences (hours/minutes) based on Helgoland:

	HW		*LW*	
Time (based on UT +1 hr)	0100 and 1300	0600 and 1800	0100 and 1300	0800 and 2000
Büsum	+0054	+0049	+0000	+0028

(Data above are from Admiralty *Tide Tables*)

Mean tidal depths (in metres based on MLWS) at the Eidersperrwerk:

(Hours)	*Springs*	*Neaps*
LW	**0·0**	**0·4**
−5	0·3	0·7
−4	1·0	1·2
−3	2·1	1·9
−2	2·9	2·5
−1	3·3	2·9
HW	**3·5**	**3·0**
+1	3·3	2·9
+2	2·8	2·5
+3	1·9	1·8
+4	1·0	1·0
+5	0·3	0·5
LW	**0·0**	**0·4**

Regulations relevant to pleasure craft

Maximum speed on the Nord-Ostsee-Kanal 15 kmph (8·1kn), on the Gieselau-Kanal 10kmph (5·4kn) and from Tönning to Friedrichstadt on the Eider river 15kmph (8·1kn).

On the Nord-Ostsee-Kanal the entrance locks are manned 24 hours a day. Pleasure craft may use the canal from sunrise to sunset; engines must be used, and sailing without an engine is banned, as are fishing, shooting and hunting.

The Eider river and canal system is so tortuous and narrow that you will almost certainly be forced to motor or sail under engine for considerable distances.

There are small dues payable at each of the three Binneneider locks, which are slightly higher for single boats locking through.

The Gieselau-Kanal is for use only in daylight. Use of the lock is forbidden when there is a red light on its signal mast.

Nord-Ostsee-Kanal dues, which were very reasonable at time of writing, are collected from pleasure craft at the Holtenau end. Skippers must obtain a ticket from the kiosk on the N side of the lock complex (which also sells charts, as does the Nautischer Dienst bookshop on the S side of the locks). The ticket is handed over for checking at the harbour office on the central island before locking through.

Pleasure craft should keep close (but not too close) to the starboard side of the canal, since passing ships can throw up a wash which sometimes grounds small vessels. Three vertical red lights at certain signal points on the Nord-Ostsee-Kanal mean that yachts should wait – usually to give way to particularly large vessels. As well as keeping out of the way of ships, yachts should watch out for and give way to the many ferries across the canal.

Charts

Note German chart *104* enables you to use Decca or GPS to find your position in the winding Eider river. On this chart, chart datum and soundings are based on mean low water springs below Tönning and on mean low water neaps from Tönning to Nordfeld; above Nordfeld the Eider has 'around 3m at normal water levels'. Heights on the tidal Eider are to mean sea level. Soundings and heights in the Nord-Ostsee-Kanal are to canal mean level.

German hydrographic *42 Nord-Ostsee-Kanal, 104 Eider river.*

German hydrographic *Sportbootkarten* *3009.*

NV Sportschiffahrtskarten *NOK Nord-Ostsee-Kanal.*

British Admiralty *2469 Nord-Ostsee-Kanal.*

Route description

3A BRUNSBÜTTEL TO KIEL VIA NORD-OSTSEE-KANAL

BRUNSBÜTTEL

« Outside Brünsbuttel locks entrance in the Elbe and close E of the very easternmost mole next to the Alte schleusen is a waiting area for pleasure craft, with two posts in deep water, from either of which it is possible to swing (uncomfortably). Vessels should fly Flag N at the crosstrees and contact the lock on VHF Ch 13 (Kiel Kanal I). A loudspeaker tells pleasure craft when they can enter. The signals on the locks relevant to yachts are: red light = entrance forbidden; white light over red light = prepare to enter; white light = yachts can enter. In the lock, pleasure craft moor to floating pontoons, upon which crew can stand.

Beyond the locks, the pleasure-craft moorings (stem and stern box moorings, PD nearby but not at the moorings) are on the northern side of the Binnenhafen, behind the end of the Neue schleusen. They are subject to considerable noise from ships locking through, towering over the moorings. There are showers and toilets, and the town shops are a short walk away, but unless you walk to a garage there is no fuel.

→ Continuing along the canal, there is a 40m bridge at Hochdonn (Km 19), as well as a ferry and an official waiting place (includes pleasure craft) with bulky dolphins at Weiche Dückerswisch (Km 21–22).

21M
GIESELAU-KANAL ENTRANCE

After passing under another 40m-clearance bridge at Grünental (Km 31), the Gieselau-Kanal enters on the N bank at Km 40·5. 1·5M along this sidewater are its lock and lifting bridge, with alongside moorings at pontoons on each bank before the lock.

→ There is another 40m-clearance railway bridge just before the bend at Rendsburg. This spectacular piece of engineering was built in the early years of the century; I recommend the view of the Obereidersee area from the train as it sweeps round the bend across the bridge. The deep Obereidersee entrance (W bank Km 66) is between a shoreside beacon (white light) and a red light buoy about 200m to the N.

15M (including 1.5 from lake entrance to the yacht haven)
RENDSBURG/OBEREIDERSEE

Vessels should keep to the centre of the narrow Obereiderenge channel before it widens out into the

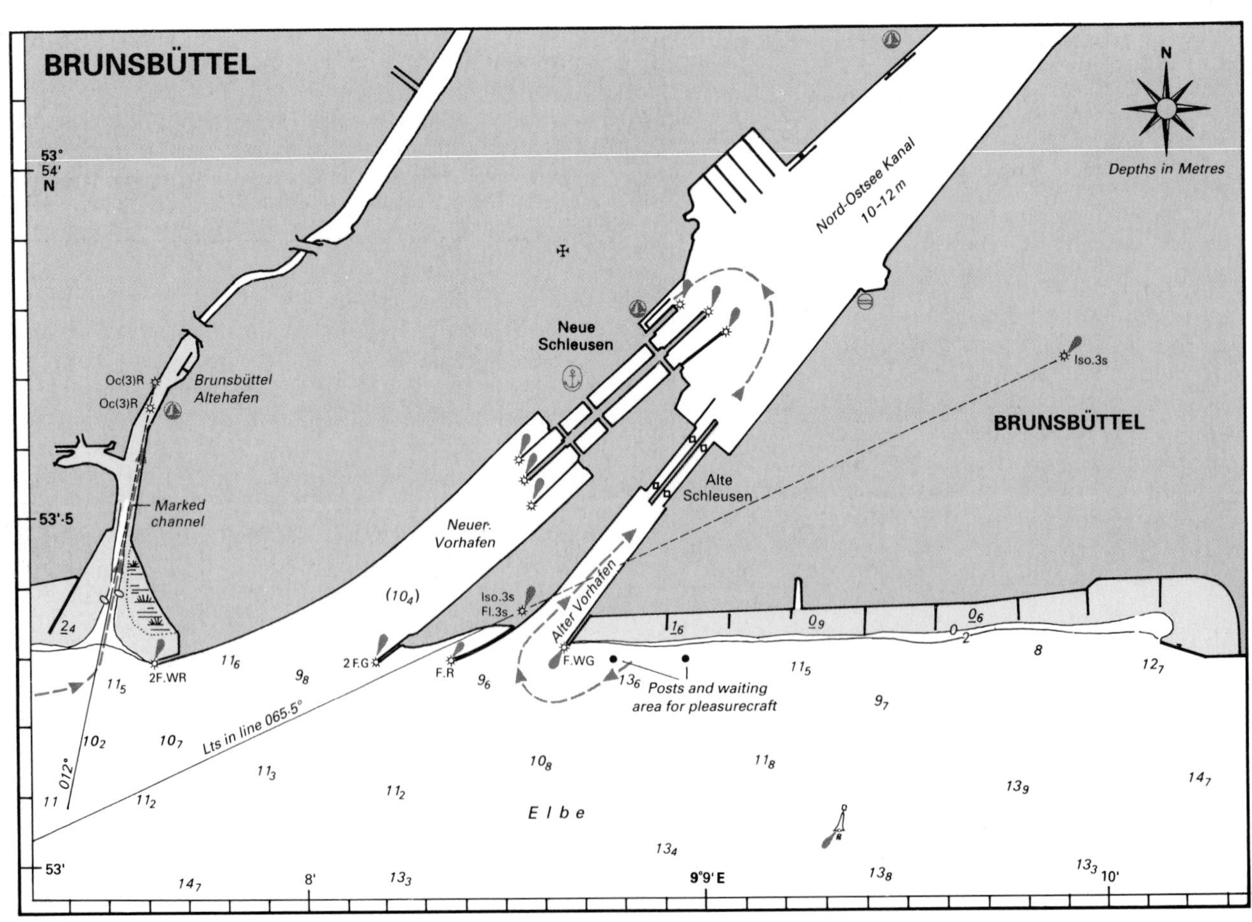

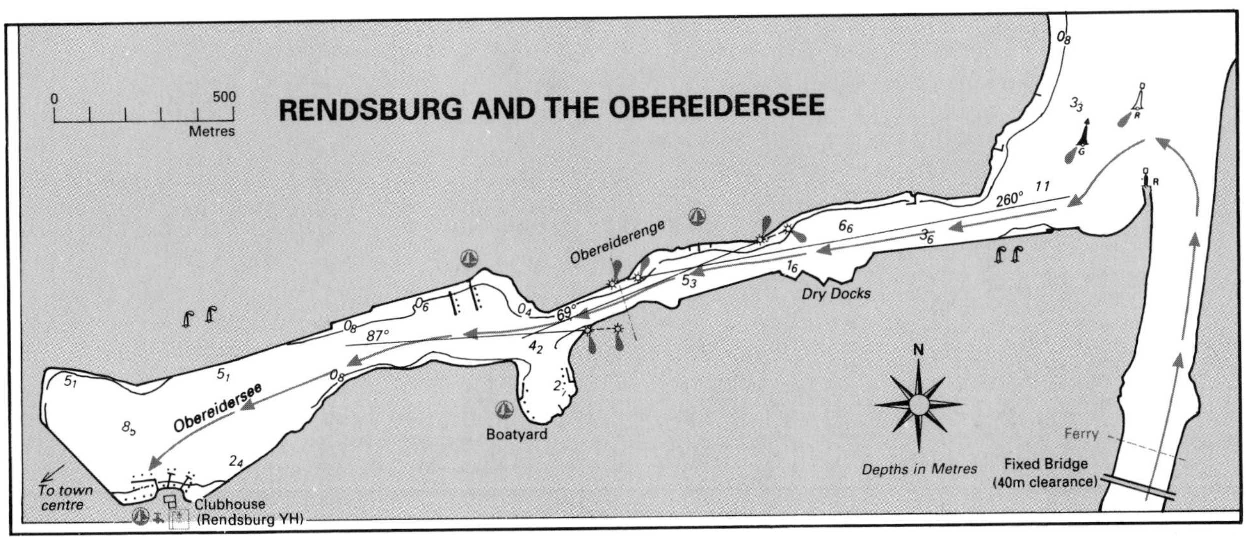

Rendsburg's tree-surrounded yacht harbour.

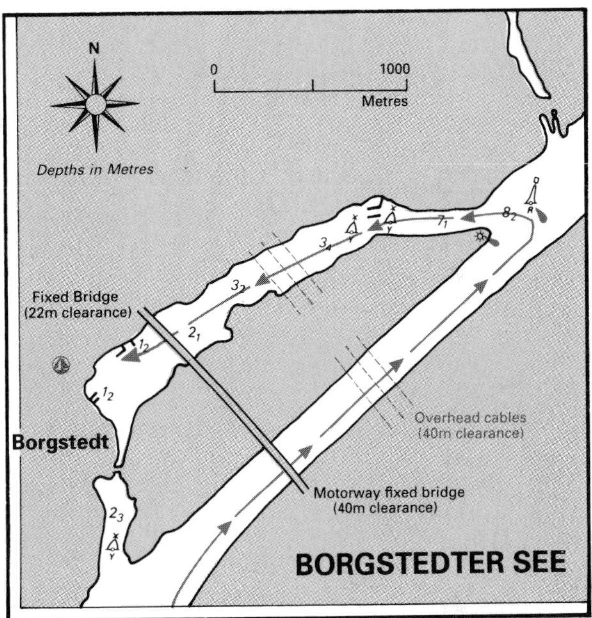

Obereidersee proper, keeping in about 5m. There are two mooring places on the N side of the latter channel and a boatyard in the small bay to the S. However, the best place for visitors is at Rendsburg yacht haven (PD), on the S side of the Obereidersee, taking up a berth on one of the outer pontoons and then seeing the harbourmaster. The yacht haven is only a short walk from the railway station and the medieval city with its Altstädter Markt, the 16th-century Rathaus with its museum, and many ancient buildings.

→ There is a 40m-clearance motorway bridge in the next short stretch, with red (to port) and green (to starboard) lit buoys on the approach. The entrance to the Borgstedter See is beyond on the N bank at Km 70.

3·5M (to entrance from Rendsburg yacht haven)

BORGSTEDTER SEE

A The Borgstedter See is entered close S of a red light buoy. Keep to midchannel, passing to the S of

Approaching Rendsburg. One of the Nord-Ostsee-Kanal's 40m bridges.

two yellow buoys (3–4m depth, but only 2m near the bridge), and anchor. The shoreside moorings beyond the 22m-clearance bridge are shallow.

→ A series of red lit buoys marks the northern bank on leaving; the next reaches are scenic and surrounded by woods. The entrance to Flemhuder See is at Km 85·5 at the end of a row of dolphin posts, just before the small lock entrance to the Achtenwehrer Schiffahrtskanal.

8M
FLEMHUDER SEE

A This beautiful lake is surrounded by wooded hills. There is a recommended anchorage for pleasure craft, marked by four yellow buoys, at its northern end in 2·2–5m of water, although further southwards there are other possibilities if you keep to the middle of the lake.

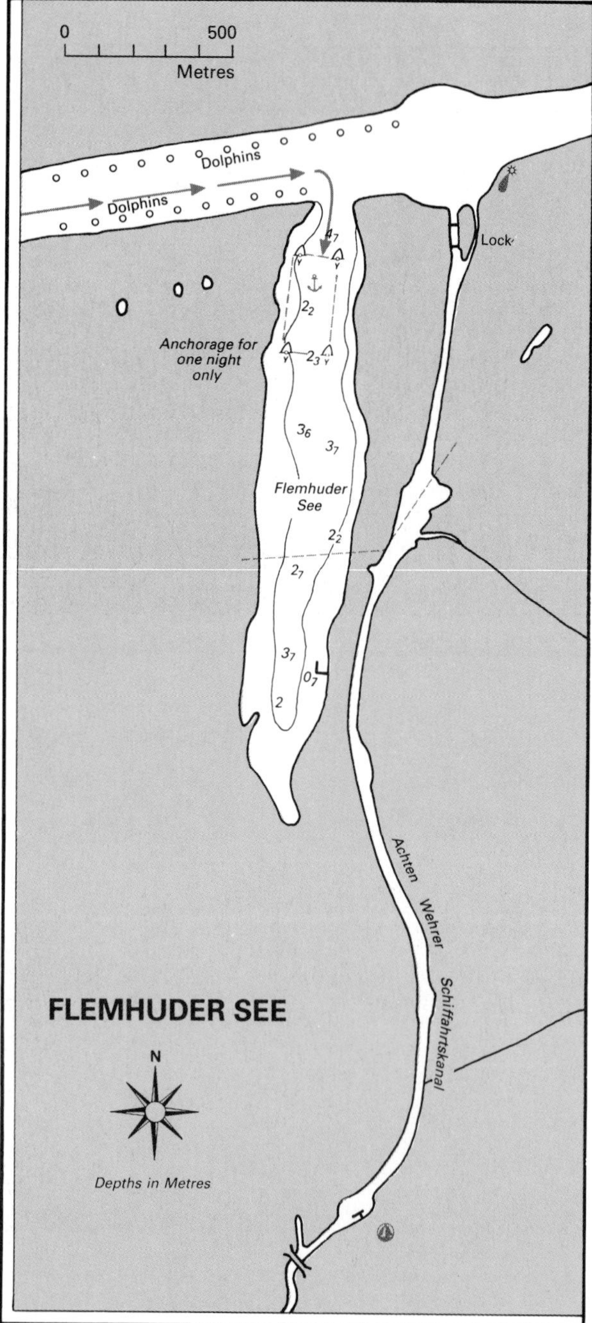

→ There is another 40m rail and motorway bridge at Suchsdorf (Km 93·5), and the 40m-clearance Holtenauer road bridge is at Km 96·5 just before the approach to the Holtenau locks.

7M
HOLTENAU

« Holtenau lock can be called on VHF Ch 12 (Kiel Kanal IV). Again there are loudspeakers, and light signals similar to Brünsbuttel's. It is possible to tie alongside on the N side of the lock complex just W of the Alte schleusen to wait for the lock to open. In the lock, as at Brünsbuttel, pleasure craft moor to floating pontoon; payment for passage (see above) is made at this point.

Moorings (D from a barge, P nearby but not at moorings) are head and stern to the long pontoons close N of the outlet from the Alte schleusen. There are shops a short walk away at Holtenau and a bus service to Kiel to the S.

→The route now leads southwards in deep water (10–14m), past the sector light on the Nordmole of the Scheerhafen S of the entrance and past the northern suburbs of Kiel, directly to the green light buoy off Düsternbrook yacht haven.

2M
KIEL (DÜSTERNBROOK) AND KIELER FÖRDER

See Chapter 6

Holtenau Alte Schleusen from a mooring on north side of the Binnenhafen.

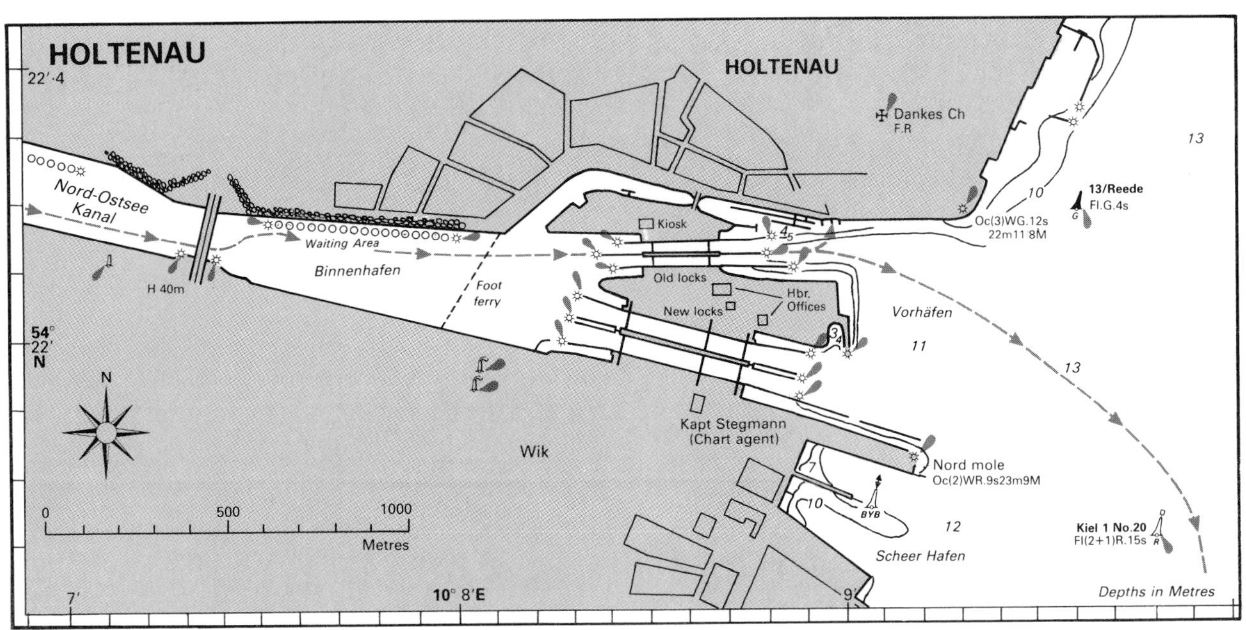

Holtenau. Yacht harbour alongside the lock exit channel.

Nord-Ostsee-Kanal railway bridge.

Holtenau. Inside the old lock. Harbour office to the right.

Nord-Ostsee-Kanal. Beauty and the beast: wooded banks and container shipping.

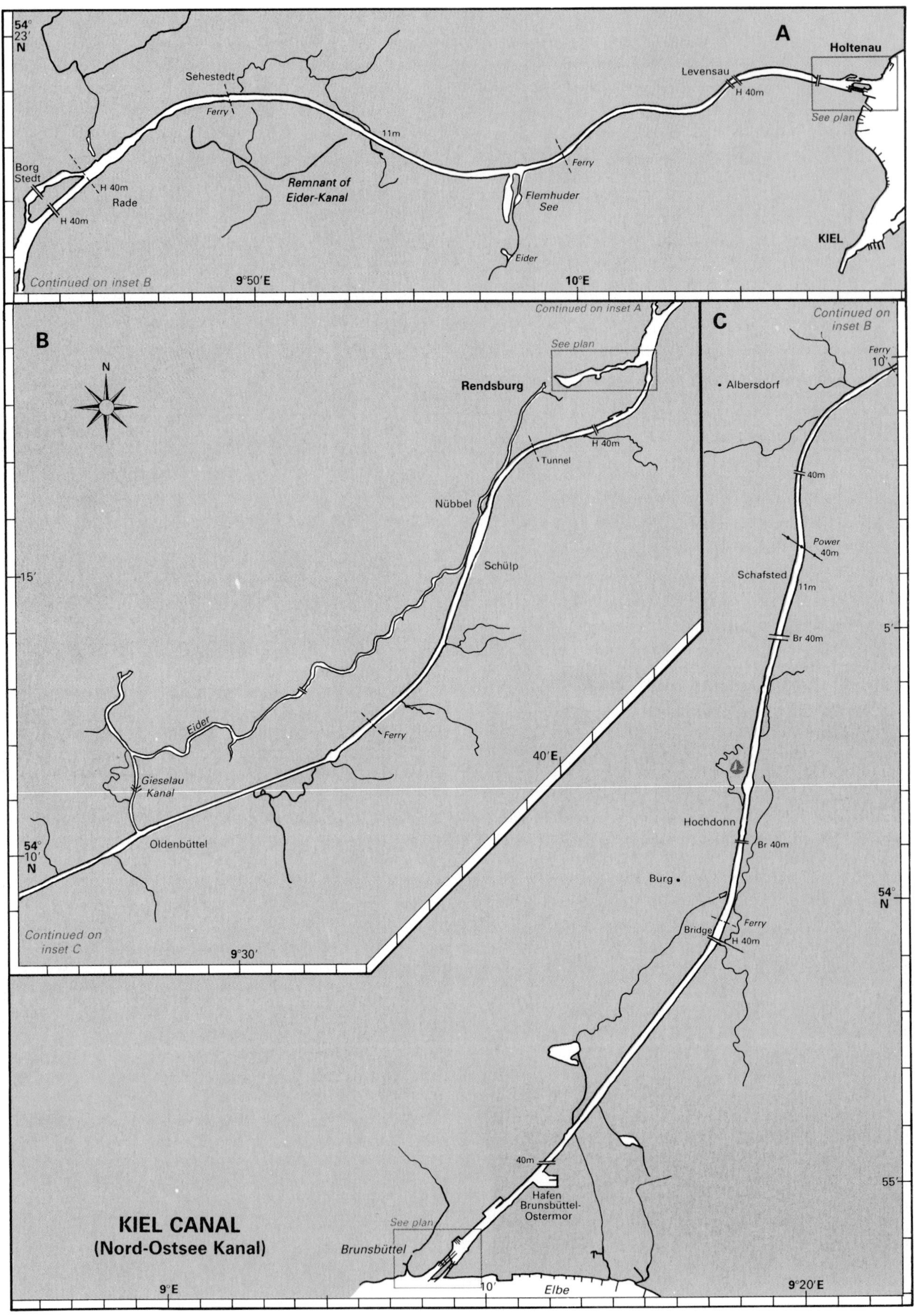
A
Holtenau
Levensau
H 40m
See plan
Sehestedt
Ferry
11m
Borg Stedt
H 40m
Rade
H 40m
Remnant of Eider-Kanal
Ferry
Flemhuder See
Eider
KIEL
Continued on inset B
9°50′E
10°E
54° 23′ N
B
Continued on inset A
See plan
Rendsburg
H 40m
Tunnel
Nübbel
Schülp
15′
Eider
Ferry
40′E
Gieselau Kanal
Oldenbüttel
54° 10′ N
Continued on inset C
9°30′
C
Continued on inset B
Ferry
10′
Albersdorf
40m
Power 40m
Schafsted
11m
5′
Br 40m
Hochdonn
Br 40m
Burg
54° N
Bridge
Ferry
H 40m
40m
Hafen Brunsbüttel-Ostermor
55′
KIEL CANAL
(Nord-Ostsee Kanal)
See plan
Brunsbüttel
9°E
10′
Elbe
9°20′E

Route description

3B EIDERSPERRWERK TO KIEL VIA EIDER RIVER AND NORD-OSTSEE-KANAL

EIDERSPERRWERK

The dam is a flood-control barrier (opened in 1975), operated occasionally, which leaves the river Eider tidal for the full 16M beyond to Nordfeld lock. To the N of the flood barrier are a lock and opening bridge through which vessels must pass. These, though operated on a 24-hour basis, are only effectively available on a rising tide up to HW and until at the latest 2·5 hours after HW, when sluice drainage often takes place (the sluicing gates having been closed from about half an hour after HW), causing a 2–5kn outgoing current. At half-tide there is also a strong cross-tide in the approaches to the outer basin, which is dredged to 2·2–2·5m. Vessels waiting for the lock can moor along the moles of the western outer basin or at the quays of the eastern inner basin. The lock-keepers are available on VHF Ch 14 or ☎ 048 33 22 11, and they will instruct you where to moor, depending on the shipping present.

→ ⚓ The river winds through wide drying flats to Tönning and has a minimum of about 2m depth (MLWS) in the closely buoyed (a few lit) channel. There is a good sheltered anchorage about 2·5M inland close N of red buoy No. 68 near the entrance to a creek crossing the Kattinger Watt. If you wish to time perfectly a full tidal run directly to Nordfeld without visiting Tönning or Friedrichstadt, this is a good place from which to start. 1M beyond this anchorage is the entrance to a drying creek; 0·5M along the E side of this lies **Schülpersiel** yacht haven, where most boxes dry out, but there is a little more water alongside the wall at the southeastern corner. The entrance to the creek is round three cardinal beacons (a N and 2 E), nudging along the creek on a rising tide.

Eidersperrwerk. Leaving the lock. The lowering dam sections are to the right.

5·5M

TÖNNING

Y Hafen von Tönning (PD) is a historic fishing and trading harbour dating from the 17th century. It has an easy deep-water (6m plus) approach, but the entrance (lit both sides) has a strong crosscurrent at half-tide. The harbour channel has at least 3m at MHW but its N and S quays mostly dry out to soft mud at LW, so you may gently lean – and you must tend your warps. The Eider drainage programme (notice outside harbourmaster's office, N quay) does cut out the occasional LW period, leaving you afloat. The Eiderkade, an alternative deep-water

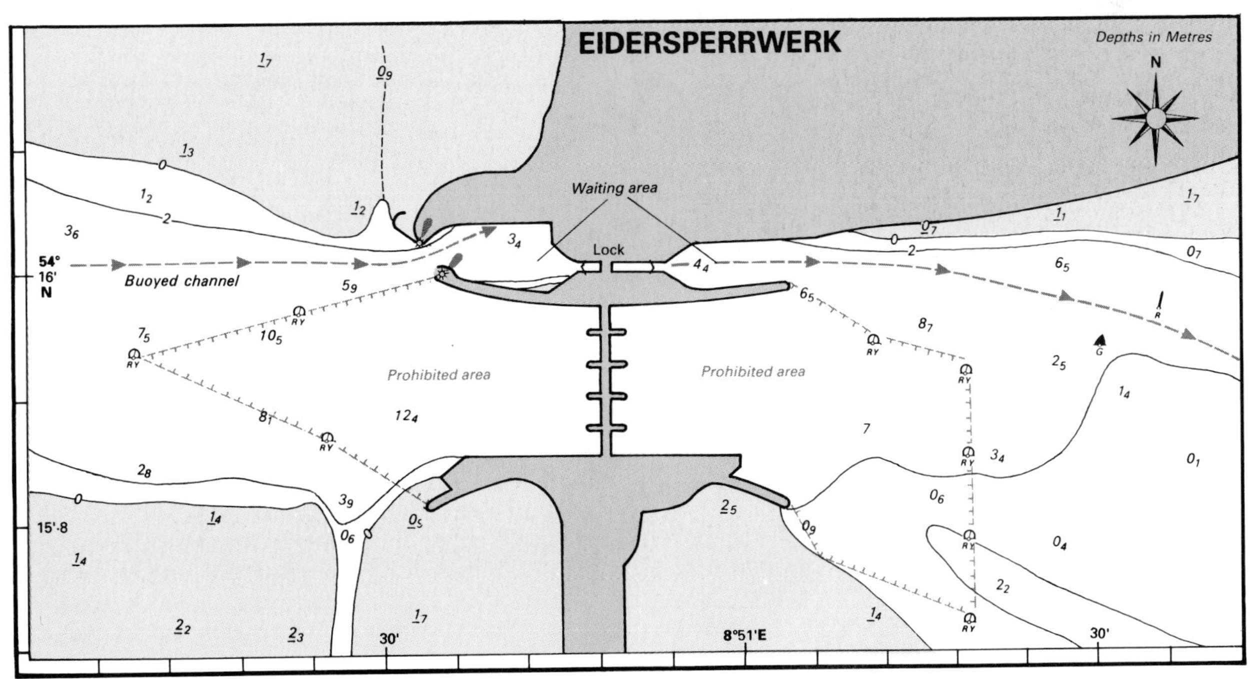

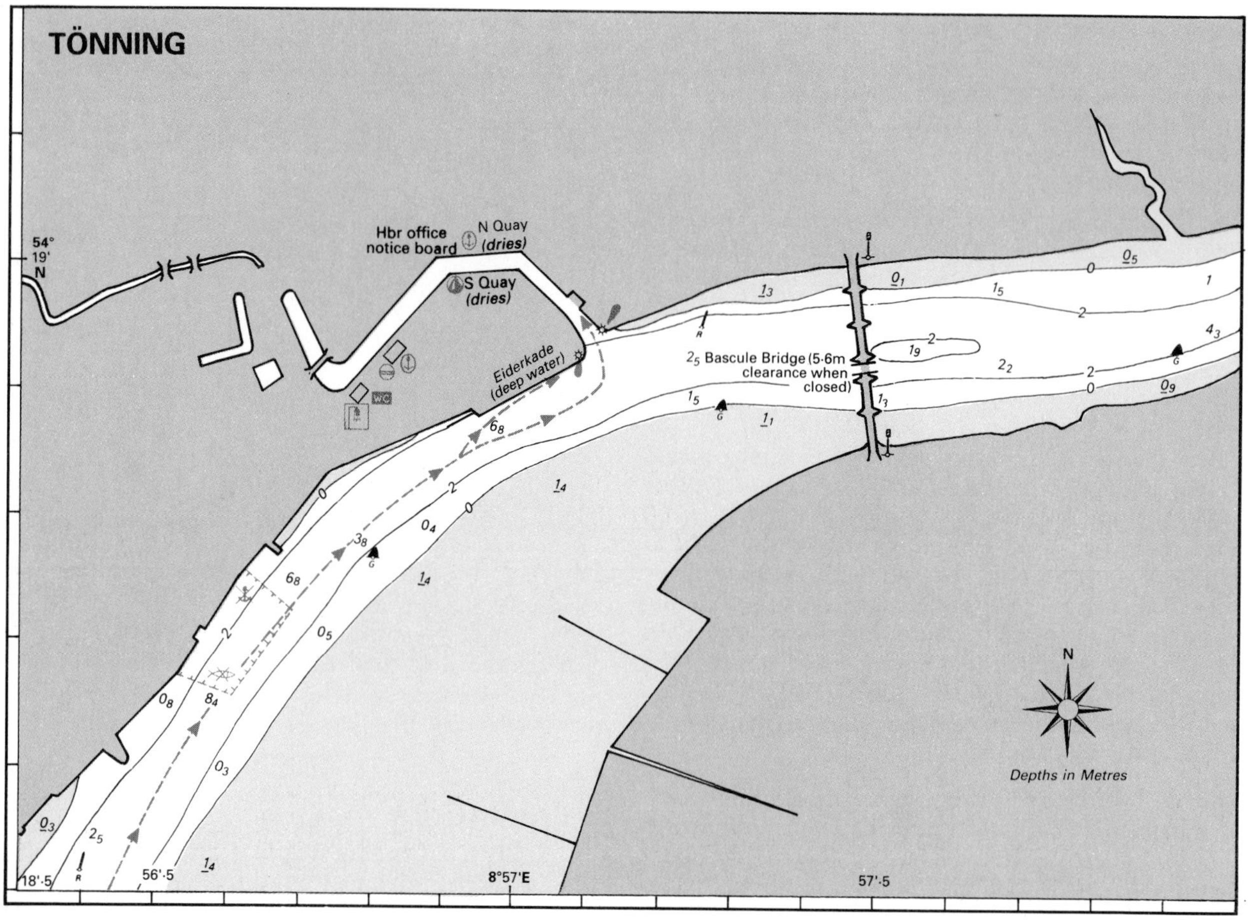

TÖNNING

Hbr office notice board
N Quay (dries)
S Quay (dries)
Eiderkade (deep water)
WC
2_5 Bascule Bridge (5·6m clearance when closed)
54° 19' N
18'·5
56'·5
8°57'E
57'·5
N
Depths in Metres

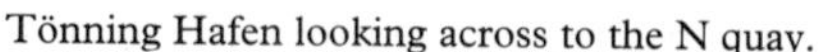

Tönning Hafen looking across to the N quay.

Tönning. Slipway at head of Torhafen.

mooring W of the harbour entrance, is aligned west-southwesterly on the open river and this, together with its posts, offers an uncomfortable mooring.

→ The river winds on, marked mainly by port (branching and with fluorescent red tapes) and starboard (downwards bound and with green tapes) withies, and a few unlit buoys. The river must be taken on a rising tide, as it is easy to stray out of the channel into less than 2m (MSL) soundings. The road bridge (bascule, 5·6m clearance above MSW when closed) E of Tönning and the railway bridge (swing, 3·9m clearance above MSL) W of Friedrichstadt are both manned in the season from 0700 to 1900 from Monday to Saturday, but not on Sundays or public holidays; a sound signal of two long blasts obtains service. The opening of the railway bridge depends, of course, on times of trains.

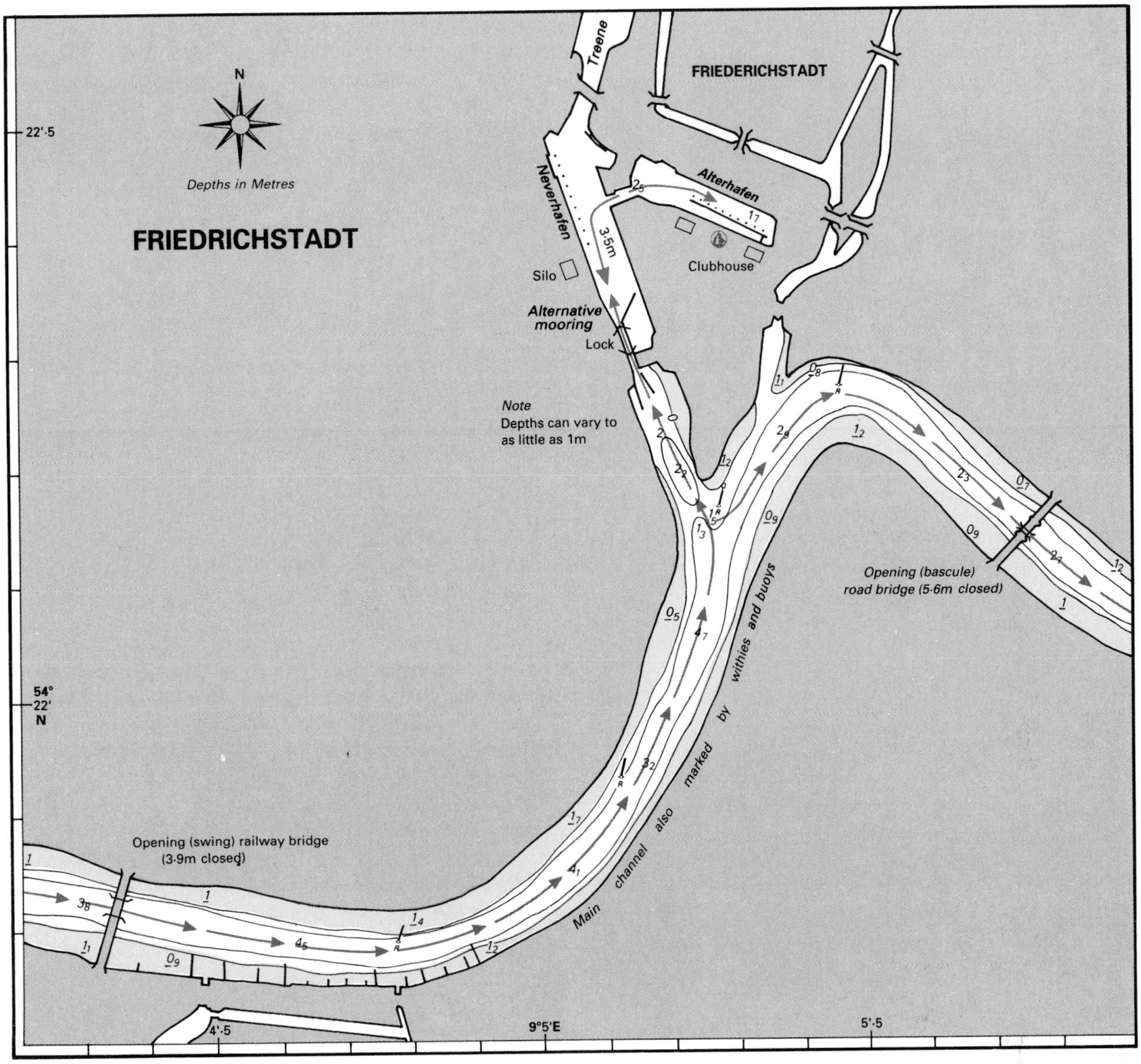

FRIEDRICHSTADT

Depths in Metres

FRIEDERICHSTADT

Treene

Neverhafen

Alterhafen

Clubhouse

Silo

Alternative mooring

Lock

Note
Depths can vary to as little as 1m

Opening (bascule) road bridge (5·6m closed)

Main channel also marked by withies and buoys

Opening (swing) railway bridge (3·9m closed)

22′·5

54° 22′ N

4′·5

9°5′E

5′·5

Double bascule road bridge. Gezeiteneider, east of Friederichstadt.

8·5M

FRIEDRICHSTADT

The unlit entrance is S of red buoy No. 112 on the W bank. There is a shallow bar (1·3–1·5m) across the entrance, emphasising the need for a rising-tide approach. The lock into the Neuer Hafen is 2·7m deep, but the approach channel can be as little as 1m, so it is doubly advisable to pick a rising tide. There are waiting posts to tie alongside in the approach channel. The lock is manned in the main season (May to August) from Monday to Saturday 0700–1900, Sundays and holidays 0900–1000 and 1700–1800, with slightly reduced service periods outside this season. The Neuer Hafen beyond is 3·5m deep with mooring possibilities along the W wall. A right-angled swing to starboard leads into the 1·7–2·5m-deep Alter Hafen, with stem and stern moorings. It is a very short walk to the old town and the shops to the N.

Friederichstadt's 'street' canals.

Friederichstadt town square. Imported Dutch seventeenth century architecture.

Nordfeld lock. Preparing to enter from the Binneneider.

This town is a jewel of early 16th-century Dutch architecture in a most unlikely area. It was founded by Dutch immigrants in 1619 under the patronage of Duke Friedrich III of Schleswig. With a tree-surrounded market place and canals with humpback bridges, it is a miniature Amsterdam, well worth a visit.

The route continues with the rising tide along the withy-marked channel with occasional unlit buoys on the bends. The bascule road bridge above Friedrichstadt, when closed, has 5·6m clearance above MSW, and is manned and signalled as described above for the two bridges below Friedrichstadt.

2·5M

NORDFELD LOCK

« This lock (Km 78) is manned from Monday to Saturday 0600–1900 and on Sundays and holidays 0600–1000 and 1600–1800. There are mooring posts in the approaches to the lock and on the inland side which lead to a red buoy (leave to port) SE of the lock.

→ « From now on the river is peaceful and flat with high dyked banks, often covered with trees. It has a minimum depth of 3m; the tricky bends are marked by numbered lateral buoys (unlit). The opening bridge at Pahlhude (Km 46) has 3·5m clearance closed and is manned from Monday to Saturday 0700–1900, but not on Sundays or public holidays. The opening bridge and lock at Lexfähre (Km 26) are manned from Monday to Saturday 0800–1900 and on Sundays and holidays 0800–1000 and 1600–1900.

Lexfähre lock.

Binneneider. The bend at Süderstapel.

Locking out at Gieselau to head for the Nord-Ostsee-Kanal.

Alte Eider pontoon moorings.

Alte Fährehaus inn, River Eider.

There are over a dozen charted places where boats can moor by the bank or at jetties. The three most significant ones, near small towns or villages for shopping, in succession moving upstream, are **Süderstapel** (Km 61, camping site N bank with stem and stern moorings and showers and toilets), **Pahlhude** (Km 46, stem and stern moorings), and **Lexfähre** (Km 26), where there are stem and stern moorings at the Alten Fährhaus (a restaurant, with showers and toilets nearby), 300m above the lock on the W bank, and similar moorings 150m NE of these at yacht club Eider on the E bank. Süderstapel has a thriving colony of storks near its church.

30M
GIESELAU-KANAL/LOCK

After the right-hand fork into the Gieselau-Kanal just over 1M below Lexfähre, this lock and opening bridge are at a quiet spot just under 1M down the canal. Service hours are from Monday to Saturday 0800–1300 and 1400–1800, and on Sundays and holidays 0800–1000 and 1600–1800. There are jetties on either side of the canal beyond the lock for tying alongside (see Route 3A above). Vessels are allowed to remain for one night only.

37M (to Düsternbrook)
GIESELAU LOCK TO KIEL (DÜSTERNBROOK)

See above Route 3A for description of rest of this route

PART II
THE BALTIC COASTS
5. Southwest Baltic

Pilotage overview

AREA COVERED

Part II of this book covers that area of the Baltic lying within the encircling Danish, German and Swedish coasts from Skagen southwards to Kiel, eastwards and northwards round Falster and Møn and along the Sound to its northern entrance. Chapter 10 contains some brief notes on the German coast E of Kieler Förde and on the outlying Danish island of Bornholm.

Four cruising routes for yachts in the area are examined in detail; three of these fan outwards from Kiel, going northwards, and one is a trip round the Limfjord.

ANCHORING AND MOORING IN NON-TIDAL WATERS

The reflex action for the North Sea yachtsman is to turn his boat's head into the tide before anchoring, picking up a mooring or coming alongside. This involves dowsing the mainsail and sometimes the jib as well and usually involves engine power to counteract the effect of the tide on the yacht's way. If anchoring, he will also have estimated how far the tide is likely to fall, in order to let out the correct length of chain or warp, and make sure he doesn't ground at LW. In North Sea waters, therefore, he must know the times, directions and rates of the tidal streams, and the tidal heights.

The Baltic yachtsman's reflex when mooring in his well sheltered waters is to turn the boat's head into the wind, since the effect of current is usually much weaker. He will be looking for a fixed minimum depth of water to cover most possible falls in water level – i.e. probably a sounding of around 2–4m, depending on his vessel's draught.

There are, of course, often situations in both the North Sea and the Baltic where wind and current are equally balanced or one is stronger than the other in the least expected direction. In this case the helmsman has to look at the lie of other boats on their moorings to gauge his approach, or take the way off his vessel in order to test out the direction of drift to obtain the best heading for anchoring. In the Baltic, the local current may not always be in the same direction as the local wind, due to the lie of the land and the weather over a wider area, so looking at moored vessels and drift testing are just as important as in the tidal North Sea. Again before mooring a considered estimate of likely current direction is essential, but there is no need for tide tables or atlas.

In harbours and marinas mooring is almost universally four-cornered, with two head ropes (short enough for you – and your wife – to climb easily ashore over the pulpit) to the pontoon cleats (or metal loops), and two stern warps bowline-looped to stern posts. Scandinavian boats have pulpit rails with a downwards U-bend in front of the forestay, which occasionally includes a small platform at the bottom to make it easier to climb aboard. Pontoons are mainly (not always) fixed rather than floating, and as there can be small changes in the water level it is not advisable to leave a boat with the warps sweated bar tight; some play should be allowed. Most Germans and Danes have a rubber snubber halfway along each head rope, which stops the straining and jerking of the foredeck cleats or samson post as well as giving a blissful night's sleep aboard. For boats of over 3m in beam it is sometimes difficult to find boxes with posts which are wide enough apart (although the posts are often usefully flexible!), particularly in the many smaller harbours, and it is often necessary to lie alongside walls or across boxes, or to anchor outside. In a few small harbours (for example, on the islands of Anholt and Ven) there are no stern posts, and yachts are expected to lie to a stern kedge anchor, which can create problems if ground tackle becomes entangled ('a guy on the island of ...... is making a fortune with snorkel and flippers', joked one yachtsman).

It is not advisable to anchor overnight in less than 3m of water; it is often preferable to stay in about 4m in the protected anchorages mentioned in the route plans in this book. Always hoist an anchor ball during the day and use an anchor light at night.

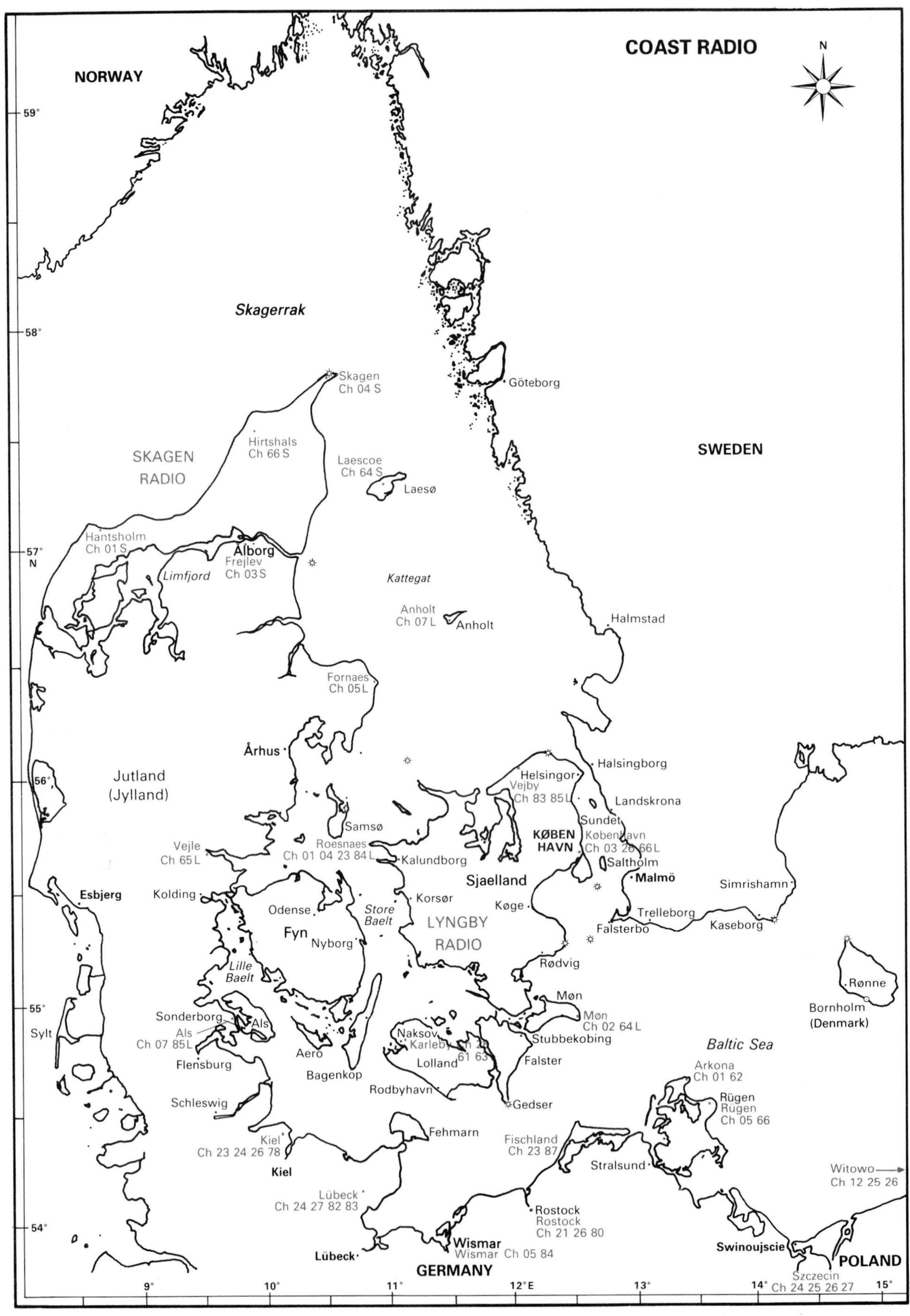
COAST RADIO
N
NORWAY
Skagerrak
SWEDEN
Skagen
Ch 04 S
Göteborg
Hirtshals
Ch 66 S
SKAGEN
RADIO
Laescoe
Ch 64 S
Laesø
Hantsholm
Ch 01 S
Ålborg
Frejlev
Ch 03 S
Limfjord
Kattegat
Anholt
Ch 07 L
Anholt
Halmstad
Fornaes
Ch 05L
Århus
Jutland
(Jylland)
Halsingborg
Helsingor
Vejby
Ch 83 85L
Landskrona
Samsø
Sundet
KØBEN
HAVN
København
Ch 03 26 66L
Saltholm
Malmö
Vejle
Ch 65L
Roesnaes
Ch 01 04 23 84L
Kalundborg
Sjaelland
Simrishamn
Esbjerg
Kolding
Korsør
Køge
Trelleborg
Odense
Store
Baelt
Falsterbo
Kaseborg
Fyn
Nyborg
LYNGBY
RADIO
Rødvig
Lille
Baelt
Rønne
Møn
Bornholm
(Denmark)
Sonderborg
Als
Als
Ch 07 85L
Møn
Ch 02 64 L
Sylt
Naksov
Karleby
Stubbekobing
Baltic Sea
Aero
Lolland
Falster
Flensburg
Bagenkop
Arkona
Ch 01 62
Rodbyhavn
Schleswig
Gedser
Rügen
Rügen
Ch 05 66
Fehmarn
Kiel
Ch 23 24 26 78
Fischland
Ch 23 87
Kiel
Stralsund
Witowo
Ch 12 25 26
Lübeck
Ch 24 27 82 83
Rostock
Rostock
Ch 21 26 80
Wismar
Wismar Ch 05 84
Swinoujscie
Lübeck
GERMANY
POLAND
Szczecin
Ch 24 25 26 27
59°
58°
57°
N
56°
55°
54°
9°
10°
11°
12°E
13°
14°
15°

Many of the anchorages described are over sand; others are over mud or clay. In the more sheltered coves there is often grassy weed. There are occasionally large stones scattered over the bottom, even in sheltered spots, and strong winds from certain directions can sometimes reduce the tidal levels, so in these conditions it is advisable to anchor in deeper water. Finding the right depth in sheltered anchorages is no problem, since the German and Danish fjords and bays are shallower than those of Scotland or Norway and their edges do not shelve as steeply. There are many anchorages available in around 4m of crystal-clear water, within a few hundred metres of a narrow, embracing beach or low sand cliff crowned by a hill or a wood which gives protection from the weather. The places to avoid anchoring at all costs are in narrow sounds where there are strong throughgoing currents.

If you read the lie of the land and the wind direction, choosing anchorages in this area is easy. In many of the anchorages described in this book there are one or two Danske Sejlunion mooring buoys (usually yellow, sometimes with 'DS' marking), which can be picked up for 24 hours maximum by vessels of up to about 15 tonnes' displacement, and are sometimes occupied by several boats (the first comer being the 'marshal').

For those who read some German there are at least two excellent pilot books on Danish anchorages (see Appendix VI), and even to non-German speakers these could be useful purely for their plans showing the locations of the anchorages.

CURRENTS AND WATER LEVELS

Current charts/water levels:

- The Danish pilot book *Komma's Havnelods* (a German translation, *Hafenführer Dänemark,* is published by DK Edition Maritim) gives charts of N-going and S-going wind currents in the main SW Baltic channels, and likely water-level changes in each harbour for different wind directions and for MHW.
- German NV *Sportschiffahrtskarten* packs include charts of N and S-going currents in some detail.

The Kattegat has a tidal range of 0·3m; the rest of the Baltic is effectively nontidal (though many of the harbours and constricted fjords have ranges of 0·1 to 1·0m – see Appendix IV). There are few significant tidal currents, so tidal times are usually irrelevant (and unavailable) to passage-making. The Baltic is like a huge freshwater river fed by its surrounding tributaries and water-saturated land, flowing outwards through the Kattegat and Skagerrak into the North Sea and sliding over the top of a deep ingoing subsurface saltwater current from the North Sea. The predominant current is westwards along the NE German coast/Fehmarn Bælt and northwards through the Lille Bælt, the Store Bælt and the Sound. This is modified locally by the actual lie of the coasts and islands, with races near headlands and in narrows, and eddies in bays.

However, the overall regional wind pattern, particularly at the 'mouth' of the river in the Skagerrak, can strengthen, weaken or even reverse the direction of the normal outgoing current. Persistent winds of force 3 or over from NE through E and S to SW tend to strengthen this outward current, which can reach over 2kn in the narrower channels. Persistent strong westerly winds in the Skagerrak can reverse the current to a southerly or ingoing direction throughout most of the area. Winds in the remaining NW–N sectors have little effect on the N-going current in the Kattegat, but S of this in the Belts and the Sound they can reverse the current to an ingoing one southwards or, in Fehmarn Bælt, eastwards, although they need to be over force 3 to do this; anything less simply weakens the N-going current.

In moderate winds in the Kattegat the average current speed is usually below 0·2kn, and only in the N near Skagen and Læso does it exceed 1 knot. In light winds the outgoing current of the Baltic is dominant. In strong winds the surface current can reach 1–2kn. In the SW Baltic proper amongst the islands the currents can be fast and the outgoing currents usually last longer. They can vary from less than 1 to over 2kn and are considerably modified by constricted straits, open bays etc. In moderate winds the average current is below 0·2kn.

The strongest streams are in the Snævringen (narrows) from Fredericia to Fanö between Jutland and Fyn, in the Fehmarn Bælt between Lolland and Germany, in the eastern channels of Smålands Farvandet between Sjælland and Falster/Mon (where they are also tidal in settled weather), and in the northern narrows of the Sound. During storms they can be up to 6kn in some of these places, and there is only one direction most pleasure craft can make in those conditions! There are also back-eddies of the current near the banks and at bends, while current changes can be accompanied by opposing currents in the same channel and even by a central stream with opposing currents on each side.

The above remarks apply to the open-water areas of the SW Baltic; the fjords in the mainland and in the islands are cul-de-sacs, and in most of these the current into or out of the fjord is directly wind-driven, the Kieler fjord being a good example. N of Fyn, however, there is an underlying six-hourly tidal flow in many of the fjords; this can be severely distorted by persistent and/or strong winds, which, depending on direction, extend or reduce and strengthen or weaken the ebb or flood stream.

Wind strength and direction, as well as affecting current, can raise or lower the overall water level by up to 0·9m in open waters, and by even more in constricted channels, harbours and anchorages, which can be critical for harbours with 2m or less of water. At the southern end of the Jutland coast, in Kolding's 3m-deep harbour at the top of the fjord, for example, a strong westerly can reduce the water level by up to 1·5m and an easterly increase it by the same amount. At Norsminde, a tiny 2·2m-deep harbour in the N of the area, a strong southerly can

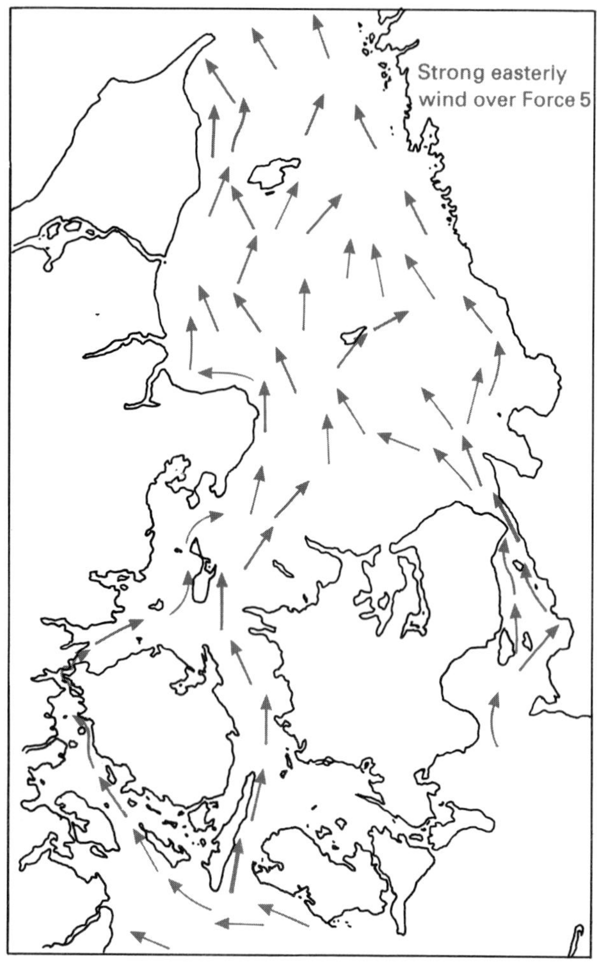

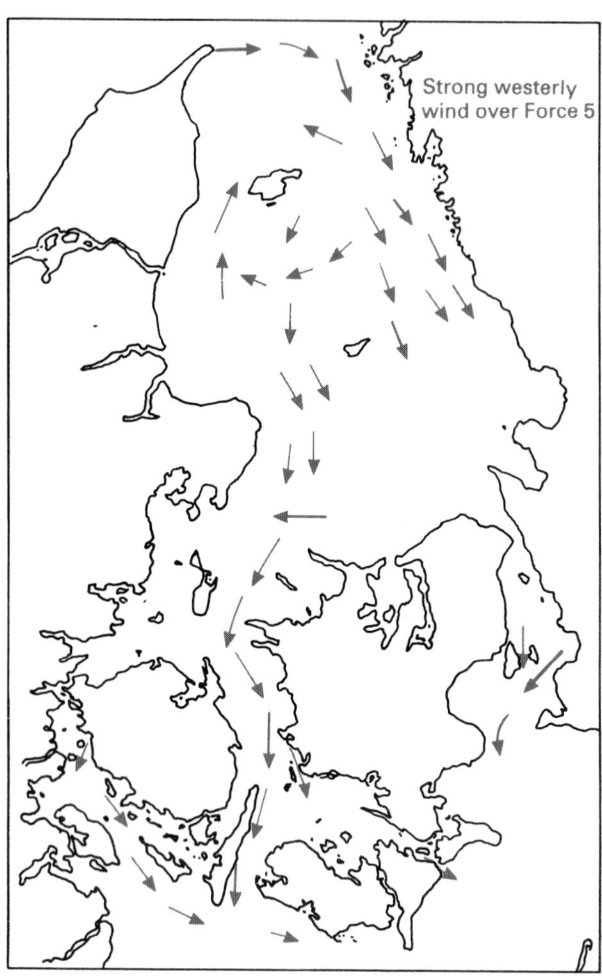

Surface currents in the Baltic Sea

Yacht harbour at head of Randers Fjord, March. A light coating of ice and no boats.

reduce the depths by 1m. Again this effect is most exaggerated in the Snævringen, where S to SW winds can lower sea level by up to 1·7m and N to NE winds raise it by up to 1·4m.

WEATHER, WIND, FOG AND ICE

Since the area is landlocked the weather is not as extreme as in the North Sea. Gales are infrequent and mainly confined to the September to April period, and, apart from in the northern Kattegat, the limited fetches tend to produce only moderate seas and swell. Most depressions tend to move N of the area in the sailing season and winds are highly variable in direction, with more chance of southerlies and easterlies than in the North Sea, particularly in the early part of the season. Because of this variability in wind direction it is doubly advisable to be constantly aware of the weather pattern in order to avoid wind shifts, which can set vessels onto a lee shore in these complex coastal waters, particularly early and late in the season.

WATER AND AIR TEMPERATURES IN THE SAILING SEASON

For those of us from the more temperate climes of Atlantic Europe a list of average monthly air and water temperatures is a useful cruise-planning tool. The season starts a little later and finishes a little earlier than on the English east coast, but always remember that the weather is highly variable. April is definitely chilly: Århus' mean air range for April is

Wind strength and direction
(per cent; average Beaufort strength in brackets)

	Kieler Bucht			Bornholm			Kattegat		
	Apr	*Jul*	*Oct*	*Apr*	*Jul*	*Oct*	*Apr*	*Jul*	*Oct*
N	8(4)	7(3)	8(3)	9(3)	9(3)	7(4)	10(3)	13(3)	8(5)
NE	9(4)	8(4)	7(4)	10(3)	7(3)	7(4)	7(3)	8(3)	8(5)
E	17(4)	25(3)	10(4)	17(4)	10(3)	12(4)	12(3)	6(3)	12(4)
SE	10(3)	17(4)	13(4)	10(3)	8(2)	15(4)	12(3)	8(3)	17(4)
S	7(3)	6(3)	12(3)	9(3)	9(2)	15(4)	16(3)	10(3)	20(4)
SW	11(3)	6(3)	20(4)	12(4)	12(3)	17(4)	12(4)	12(4)	17(4)
W	19(4)	13(3)	15(4)	18(4)	23(3)	15(4)	17(4)	22(4)	16(4)
NW	13(4)	9(2)	12(4)	10(5)	16(4)	10(4)	14(4)	20(4)	9(5)
Calm	6	9	3	5	6	2	5	7	1
Strong winds	10	7	16	12	9	22	20	12	20

Fog is limited mainly to November to May, i.e. overlapping slightly into the early sailing season. There tends to be less fog in the southern part of the area towards the Kieler Bucht.

Number of days with fog and rain

		Apr	*May*	*Jun*	*Jul*	*Aug*	*Sep*	*Oct*
Kiel	***Fog***	2	½	½	½	1	2	3
	Rain	13	12	14	15	15	15	17
Bornholm	***Fog***	6	5	2	2	1	2	3
	Rain	10	9	9	10	11	12	14
Skagen	***Fog***	6	5	3	2	1	2	2
	Rain	8	8	6	7	8	8	9

Icing of harbours occurs in about five out of every ten winters in the region and even less frequently, nearer three in ten, on the German Baltic coast. Late December/early January is the earliest observed date for ice, and mid-April the latest date. In recent years winters have been warm, but there is no reason why this should continue, and if you are leaving your boat in the area it is advisable to lay it up ashore.

Mean air and water temperature (°C)

		Apr	*May*	*Jun*	*Jul*	*Aug*	*Sept*	*Oct*
Kiel	***Water***	5·5	9·5	14·0	16·5	17·0	15·0	11·5
	Air max	11·0	15·5	19·5	21·5	21·0	18·0	12·5
	Air min	3·5	7·0	10·5	13·0	13·0	10·5	6·5
København	***Water***	4·5	8·0	13·0	16·0	17·0	14·5	11·5
	Air max	10·5	16·0	19·5	22·5	21·0	17·5	12·0
	Air min	3·0	7·5	11·0	13·5	13·5	10·5	7·0
Bornholm	***Water***	4·0	7·0	2·5	16·0	17·0	14·5	11·5
	Air max	8·5	15·5	17·5	20·5	20·0	16·5	12·0
	Air min	2·5	6·0	11·0	14·5	14·5	12·0	8·0
Århus	***Water***	4·5	9·0	14·5	16·5	17·5	15·0	11·5
	Air max	10·5	16·0	20·0	21·0	20·0	16·0	12·0
	Air min	3·0	7·0	11·5	13·5	12·5	10·0	7·0

3–10·5°C (37–51°F) compared with Felixstowe's 6–12°C (43–54°F). May is very little different from eastern England: Århus 7–16°C (45–61°F) and Felixstowe 8–15°C (46–59°F). June, July and August give very similar average temperatures to eastern England's, i.e. 11–21°C (52–70°F), but September and October tend to deteriorate a little more rapidly than in England, with Århus temperatures 7–16°C (45–61°F), some 2–3°C (3·5–5·5°F) lower.

LIGHTS AND BUOYS

On Germany's North Sea coast 2m of water is often enough for pilotage and the daily rhythm of the tides is critical to passage-making, particularly behind the Frisian islands. In the Baltic the trick is to stay in deep water if possible and watch the wind direction like a hawk, since the hilly land makes it erratic and it is the wind which drives the currents.

The main objective is to keep outside the 5m contour, except in a limited number of protected fjord and island shoal areas. The position of the 5m contour is particularly important around the many headlands, since inside this limit there are often isolated rocks dangerous to surface navigation. Even in some of the anchorages, care is needed to avoid rocks and stones where depths are under 4m.

The cardinal buoys marking the headlands tend to be placed on the 10m contour well offshore, and they are somewhat spindly and difficult to sight, in contrast with the abundant, sun and light reflecting, red and green lateral buoys and beacons, often of spar type, in the fjords and channels. The single and double conical topmarks of the green and the cardinal buoys are usually made of triangular coloured besoms, and the red buoys have square besoms for their topmarks. In these nontidal waters the buoyage direction should always be checked out from the chart.

Because of the multitude of islands, headlands, rocks and shoals the major lights in the area are prolific in number but limited in range. The main problem in night sailing is to interpret correctly the many lights which can be seen at any one time. The widest straits in much of this area are 15–20M at most, except in the two approach areas of the Kattegat and the Swedish-German entrance: the former is 30–70M across and the latter about 40M.

In the area covered in this chapter there are over 1,300 lights. On average, in terms of the straightest cruising distances available, there are one to two for every mile cruised. Over 1,200 of the lights are of less than 15M range, and only about 90 have a range of 15M or more, of which about 30 are of over 20M range.

SW Baltic numbers of lights (approximate)

	15–20M range	*Over 20M range*	*All lights*	*Cruising distance*
Danish Kattegat	7	4	70	100
Lille Bælt to Kiel	16	2	200	130
Store Bælt	5	3	300	80
The Sound	17	9	300	90
S Swedish coast/ Bornholm	2	1	130	120
N German coast/ Kiel-Rügen	12	11	330	200
Total	59	30	1,330	720

FISHING STAKES AND BUOYS

It is always necessary to watch out for fishing buoys with flags, and above all for fishing stakes and net traps. These sometimes stretch out several hundred metres from the banks and headlands, but, fortunately, are usually well above the water level and highly visible – well and good in good visibility in the daytime, but in fog and at night beware! Fishing, according to a Danish friend, provides a major supplement to the diet of Denmark's pensioners.

MARINE AND AERO RDF BEACONS

Radio-wave reception is somewhat erratic in the Baltic due to the scattering of islands and the fjords, particularly in Jutland. This applies to RDF, Decca, Navtex and coastal radio.

Marine radiobeacons in the area transmit under the system established on 1 April 1992, i.e. the RDF set's beat-frequency oscillator (BFO) must always be used and each station broadcasts individually and continuously (not as a member of a group), giving the identification signal at least twice for approximately 13 seconds followed by a long dash for approximately 47 seconds. Problems can be encountered from interference overlap between neighbouring (and sometimes distant) beacons on frequencies which are close together.

Name	*Freq. (kHz)*	*Ident.*	*Range (miles)*	*Position*
Denmark				
Skagen W Lt	298·5	SW	50	57°45'·0N 10°35'·8E
Frederikshavn (NE Bkwtr Lt)	414	FK	10	57°26'·0N 10°33'·4E
Hals Barre Lt	299	HB	50	56°57'·3N 10°25'·6E
Sjællands Rev N Lt	310·5	SG	50	56°06'·1N 11°12'·2E
Nakkehoved Lt	306·5	NA	50	56°07'·2N 12°20'·8E
København (Calib Stn)	309	MU	10	55°42'·8N 12°35'·4E
Stevns Klint Lt	290	ST	50	55°17'·5N 12°27'·5E
Gedser Lt	303·5	GR	50	54°33'·9N 11°57'·9E
Rønne, Fauna (Aero)	334	FAU	50	55°01'·7N 14°54'·1E
Hammerodde Lt (Bornholm)	289.5	MN	50	55°18'·0N 14°46'·4E
Germany				
Kiel Lt	310	KI	20	54°30'·0N 10°16'·5E
Friedrichsort Lt (Calib Stn)	312.6	FB		54°23'·5N 10°11'·7E
Fehmarnbelt Lanby	304	FE	10	54°36'·0N 11°09'·0E
Travemünde Lt (Calib Stn)	312.6	UB		53°57'·8N 10°53'·0E
Timmendorf Lt (Calib Stn)	311		02	53°59'·6N 11°22'·7E
Warnemünde (Calib Stn)	311	LHD		54°10'·7N 12°05'·9E
Sassnitz (Calib Stn)	311	SAZ		54°30'·7N 13°38'·7E
Sweden				
Falsterborev Lt	303	FV	40	55°18'·5N 12°39'·5E
Kullen High Lt	294	KUL	70	56°18'·1N 12°27'·4E

DECCA COVERAGE

The whole of this area is covered by the excellently positioned Danish Decca Chain 7B; the master station is in a central position on Samsø island, with a slave at each end of Jutland and one in the SE of the Sjælland archipelago. However, on my cruises the Decca set was often showing uncertain reception from one or more of the slave stations when near the heads of the fjords and in the shadows of islands. This is no problem when you can see the prominent landmarks round these places, but could be a problem in poor visibility. With Navtex, too, reception was sporadic in the same places.

Danish Decca Chain 7B

Station	***Place***	
Master	Samsø	(55°57'N 10°35'E)
Red slave	Møen	(54°57'N 12°28'E)
Green slave	Eøjer	(55°01'N 8°42'E)
Purple slave	Hjorring	(57°27'N 10°03'E)

COAST RADIO STATIONS, WEATHER FORECASTS, NAVTEX

See chart page 74 for coast radio coverage.

The chart shows the positions and channel numbers of the area's VHF coast radio stations. Skagen, Lyngby and Göteborg Radios are also the area's MF radio stations. For further information (frequencies, traffic lists etc.) see Admiralty *List of Radio Signals.*

I would strongly recommend yachtsmen who cannot speak a Scandinavian language to use Navtex for the twice-daily weather forecast (0600 and 1800) from the Stockholm station (J). (As with Decca, however, reception can be somewhat variable with the lie of the land). These give a brief synopsis and forecast for a number of sea areas. The sea area mainly covered in this chapter is called 'The Sound and the Belts' and extends from Eckenförde in the S to Århus Bucht in the N and eastwards to the Sound. N of this (to a line from Skagen to Göteburg) the area is 'Kattegat', and SE of this (to a line from Rügen in Germany to Skanär in Sweden) is 'Western Baltic'. Wind speeds in these forecasts can be confusing, since they are given in metres per second (m/sec); a gale is 17·2–20·7 m/sec (34–40kn), a force 6 is 10·8–13·8 m/sec (22–27kn). If you haven't got Navtex, these forecasts are available in English on Stockholm Radio VHF Channels 24 and 28 at 1033, 1433, 1833 and 2233 local time. In summer this is UT plus 2 hours (BST + 1 hour).

As always, one cannot recommend enough the use of yacht clubs and local harbourmasters for up-to-date weather forecasts.

Finally, a skipper from the British Kiel Yacht Club kindly passed on to me a most useful telephone number: that of the Danish weather service, 97 10 17 95. If you call them in the morning before sailing (like many Danes they speak good English) and tell them where you are sailing, they will provide the latest forecast of wind speeds and directions.

LIFEBOAT STATIONS

This is a well covered search and rescue area given the short distances from land, and VHF Ch 16 is the customary distress frequency. There are 24 motor life vessels located along the coastlines of this area, of which 11 are based in Denmark, 10 in Germany (including eastern Germany, which is not far from route 7 in this book) and 3 on the Swedish coast of the Sound. Rescue is also carried out by coastal helicopter services, particularly in Danish waters.

Station	*Position*
Denmark	
Skagen Havn	57°44'N 10°38'E
Sæby	57°20'N 10°33'E
Hals	57°00'N 10°19'E
Grenå	56°23'N 10°56'E
Vesterø	57°18'N 10°55'E
Österby	57°19'N 11°07'E
Anholt	56°43'N 11°41'E
Odden Havn	55°58'N 11°22'E
Hundested	55°58'N 11°51'E
Klintholm Havn	54°57'N 12°28'E
Gedser Odde	54°34'N 11°58'E
Germany	
Maasholm	54°41'N 10°00'E
Laboe	54°24'N 10°13'E
Weissenhaus	54°19'N 10°46'E
Burgstaaken	54°25'N 11°11'E
Travemünde	53°58'N 10°53'E
Timmendorf	54°00'N 11°22'E
Warnemünde	54°11'N 12°05'E
Wustrow	54°21'N 12°23'E
Prerow	54°27'N 12°34'E
Barhöft	54°26'N 13°02'E
Sweden	
Helsingborg	56°03'N 12°41'E
Barsebäck	55°45'N 12°54'E
Malmö	55°36'N 13°00'E

6. The Jutland east coast and the Lille Bælt

Route 4
Kiel to the Limfjord entrance via the Lille Bælt

Commentary

The SW Baltic is one of the world's outstanding family cruising areas. This is particularly true of the islands and fjords along the east coast of Jutland, from Germany's Kieler fjord in the S to Denmark's Limfjord at the northern end of the peninsula. There are around 40 yacht harbours with over 200 moorings each, as well as several much larger ones in the south of the area. Passages are never far from a lee from the land, and the many harbours and anchorages are within easy distance of each other. Frequent anchoring makes cruising economical, and mooring, boat-handling and storage charges are cheap by British standards, as are buses and trains, which are also frequent and reliable.

Part of this area is known as the Lille Bælt. It is a relatively narrow channel, protected from the weather, between the concave east coast of mainland Jutland and the convex west coast of Denmark's second-largest island, Fyn (Fünen in German). A multitude of fjords cut deeply into the coasts on each side of the channel, which is scattered with smaller islands. This is an area of rolling, wooded hills and fields, with houses and country mansions peeping through the trees, low sand cliffs and narrow beaches. In the variable weather of a typical Baltic summer, the sky is a moving kaleidoscope of fascinating cloud formations above distant coastal perspectives of the delicate greens, greys and blues of overlapping headlands and islands.

No two fjords are the same. There are wide variations in their length, width and scenery. Haderslev is narrow and riverlike, with trees close to the banks and a similarly narrow town harbour with posts and platform moorings on each side. There are also many tiny, lakelike fjords, while Flensburger, Åbenra, Vejle and Horsens fjords are wider, with rolling hills and woods, and purpose-built yacht harbours on one or both sides of the outer approaches to the main town harbour. At Vejle a high bridge sweeps across the head of the fjord. The islands of Samsø and Tunø also have their distinct personalities, with tiny, well protected harbours and hilly country inland. On Samsø there is plenty of room for a long cycle ride inland to the main town, Tranebjerg, or across to the other harbour, Ballen.

At the head of each main fjord is a no-nonsense working town, the approach to which is usually heralded by a distant silo. These places are a mixture of ancient and modern, with blocks of flats, pedestrian shopping precincts, factories, slaughterhouses and silos cheek by jowl with gabled, half-timbered houses in varied pastel colours, churches and cathedral spires. The architecture is reminiscent of both East Anglia and the Netherlands. In Denmark, however, in contrast to the Netherlands, the rolling scenery is more eye-catching than the architecture. The similarities of the area to East Anglia are no coincidence. At the southern end, on the peninsula between the Schlei and the Flensburger fjord, is a region with highly English scenery and villages called Angeln, home of the 5th-century invaders of the English east coast, the Angles.

The head of the Schlei fjord is of particular historical interest as well as having fine scenery. It is easy to visit by train from any of the fjord towns as well as by cruising down the Schlei. Though now in Germany, Haitabu (or Haddeby), across the ferry from Schleswig's spire, is the site of the Viking trading capital of the eighth and ninth centuries. From here the ancient Dänevirke, marking the old boundary of Denmark, stretches southwestwards. At Haitabu is a fascinating museum devoted to the Vikings, overlooking the picturesque and peaceful Haddebyer Noor (lake), where it is not difficult to picture the long black ships anchored. Schleswig itself is a fascinating medieval city, and Schloss Gottorf is a major attraction; its museum has a macabre display of 2,000-year-old 'Moorleichen', the peat-bog corpses with skins tanned like leather.

Flensburger fjord is the boundary between Denmark and Germany (Flensburg city is in Germany), so customs launches patrol this area, although the relaxed single-market regime makes life much easier for EU yachts.

Close N of Flensburg fjord, Sönderburg on Als island and the Dybbøl hill on the mainland opposite were the scene of a major battle in the Prusso-Danish War of 1864, and for this reason were an objective of Davies' pilgrimage to the Baltic in Erskine Childers' *The Riddle of the Sands*. The

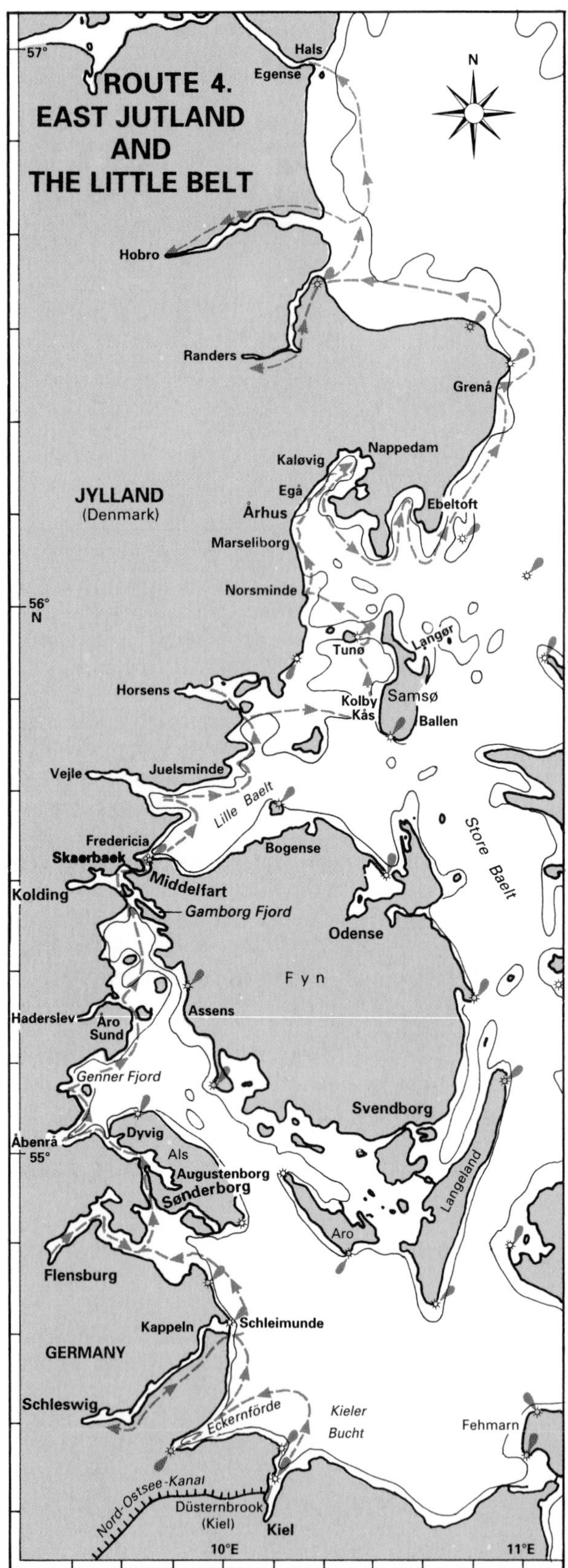

Danes can certainly recreate historical atmosphere, and the museums at both places are well worth visiting.

Yet further N at Kolding is Koldindinghus Slot (castle), a classic of ultramodern Danish restoration. Last burnt out in 1808, it has been constantly under reconstruction since the 1890s until today its interior is a phantasmagorical Gothic, yet modern, dream of delicate soaring wooden pillars, steel suspension bridges, spiral staircases, a chapel and a dungeon.

The series of Z-bends forming the Snaevringen narrows is particularly interesting, with their high rail and road bridges to Fyn (neither of the bridges requires lowering masts), sand cliffs, woods, the old town of Middelfart on the S bank and the industrial tanks and chimneys of Fredericia at the northern entrance.

Århus is Denmark's second-largest city, with a cathedral, restaurants and the Søndergade, a pedestrian shopping precinct with street musicians. It is a lively place, and in September holds a cultural festival similar to that of Edinburgh.

A relaxed approach to cruising in the area is to take 20 or 30-mile morning trips, usually running or reaching out of a fjord and along the coast and tacking or motoring into the next one, hopefully early enough to obtain mooring space. While all the main harbours have port radio stations, the yacht harbours do not listen out, so be prepared to motor out of a harbour if your test foray finds it full, as often happens in summer. However, there is no need to press on to the point of exhaustion to the next harbour, since anchorages are plentiful.

Indeed, on any passage if wind and current are adverse it is advisable to seek out the nearest protected anchorage. In Flensburger fjord there is an almost perfectly protected anchorage between the small twin Okseør (Denmark) islands. Dyvig, a tiny 'lake' in the northern end of Als island, approached by an extremely narrow but (as always) well buoyed channel, is another classic anchorage. The Genner Fjord, a short westerly-trending indentation on the Jutland coast N of Åbenrå Fjord, and Sandbjerg Vig, a tiny bay N of the Veijle Fjord, are yet other examples. The northern end of Århus Bucht itself is surrounded by anchoring possibilities, and we found ourselves, as in many other places, alone at the southern end of the virtually landlocked Knebel Vig. For the really penny-pinching yachtsman it is even possible to avoid all mooring charges by anchoring at night, visiting the nearest harbour at around midday when the crowd has left. Indeed, in the crowded midseason, even if you are anxious to support the local economy by paying mooring fees, anchoring can often prove to be the only option.

If you wish to leave your vessel anywhere in the area it is advisable to do so at a secure marina, and I have found this relatively inexpensive. Transport to and from most main harbours is cheap and easy, with plenty of buses and railway stations. The two best ways of getting there from the UK are by air to

Hamburg, or by ferry from Harwich (Parkeston Quay) to either Hamburg or Esbjerg. There is a spinal railway line from Hamburg along the eastern side of the peninsula to Ålborg, with stations at each of the main fjord towns and a connection across the peninsula from Fredericia to Esbjerg on the west coast and eastwards across the bridge to Fyn, Sjaelland and København.

Most of the moorings available in this area are the usual 'boxes' with posts at the stern. However, in some smaller harbours such as Anholt posts are lacking, so boats lie to a kedge anchor at the stern with bow to the jetty.

Distances

615M, excluding the suggested diversions which are described en route (return mileage from passage route in brackets):

Gamborg Fjord (4M)
East coast of Samsø (40M continuing round to Tunø)
Anholt (54M return from Grenå)
Læso (60M return from Limfjord entrance)

Depths/water levels

See also Appendix IV

Open-sea pilotage in this area tends to be outside the 10m contour and the major seamarks. The remaining pilotage is generally in depths of over 3m, often in buoyed channels in the fjords and across the wide shoal-scattered areas W and N of Fyn and on the shores of Ålborg Bugt, where it is essential to keep an eye on the wind and its effect on water levels (see below).

As for all of these routes in the relatively tideless SW Baltic, do not assume that the charted dredged depths of any of the shallower *rende* channels are accurate at time of sailing – actual depths are often less.

Most of the yacht harbours and landing stages on this route have depths of at least 1·5m and many have up to 3m. There are a few shallower ones in some of the fjords. Having said this, it is essential to keep an eye on fluctuations in water levels (see Appendix IV, Route 4. Water levels). These fluctuations are due to two factors:

Tidal range, from MHW to MLW, varies from negligible in the Kieler Bucht to 0·6m in some of the outlying harbours of the Kattegat and Århus Bucht. It can also be up to 1·4m in the constricted necks and at the heads of some fjords and bays.

Wind Strong and/or persistent winds from a particular direction can raise or lower water levels in some of the harbours by up to 1·6m in addition to the tidal range, and in exceptional circumstances by even more. This is mainly in the German fjords, e.g. 2m either way at Flensburg, and up to a 3·5m rise in NE–ENE gales at Schleimunde. In the southern fjords as far N as the Snævringen, easterlies (NE–E–SE, i.e. blowing onshore into the Kieler Bucht) tend to raise the water level in the harbours, and westerlies (SW–W–NW) to lower it, but to a lesser extent than the easterly wind-induced rise. In the northern fjords as far N as Mariager, northerlies (NW–N–NE, i.e. blowing down the Kattegat) increase the water level and southerlies (SE–S–SW) lower it, but again to a lesser extent.

It is difficult to avoid taking the ground accidentally somewhere, at some time, hopefully for only a brief period. Two examples from Appendix IV, Route 4: Egå Marina (Århus Bucht; one of the largest in the area) has MSL depths of 2·2–2·7m, so a persistent SE gale could reduce the MLW depth by 0·75m, giving an actual depth range in the harbour of 1·4–1·9m. Årø yacht harbour (Årøsund) has an MSL range of 2–2·5m, and a NW wind could reduce this to 1–1·5m. Always check your depth sounder from time to time in harbour. It is also essential to avoid navigating shallow channels in uncertain weather and depth conditions.

Bridges

5 opening bridges and 3 fixed bridges (33m, 44m, 40m clearance).

Charts

Note Soundings and heights on all the charts are based on mean sea level (MSL).

German hydrographic *15, 16, 17, 18, 19, 20, 21, 24, 25, 26, 27, 30, 62, 78.*

NV *Sportschiffahrtskarten Series 1* and ***3*** (plus ***Die Schlei***).

Note Significant depth contours are at 2m, 4m, 6m, 10m and 20m. Many of the buoys off headlands are on the 10m contour. These charts are often a little small in scale, and it is essential to have the pilot books, *Der Grosse NV Hafen Lotse, Bands 1* and *3*, which accompany the chart sets for pilotage in the harbour entrances.

Danish hydrographic *24, 26, 30, 100, 101, 106, 110, 111, 112, 114, 122, 124, 128, 141, 151, 152.*

Danish *Søportskort Serie 1* (part of series only) and ***Serie 2*** (122S only).

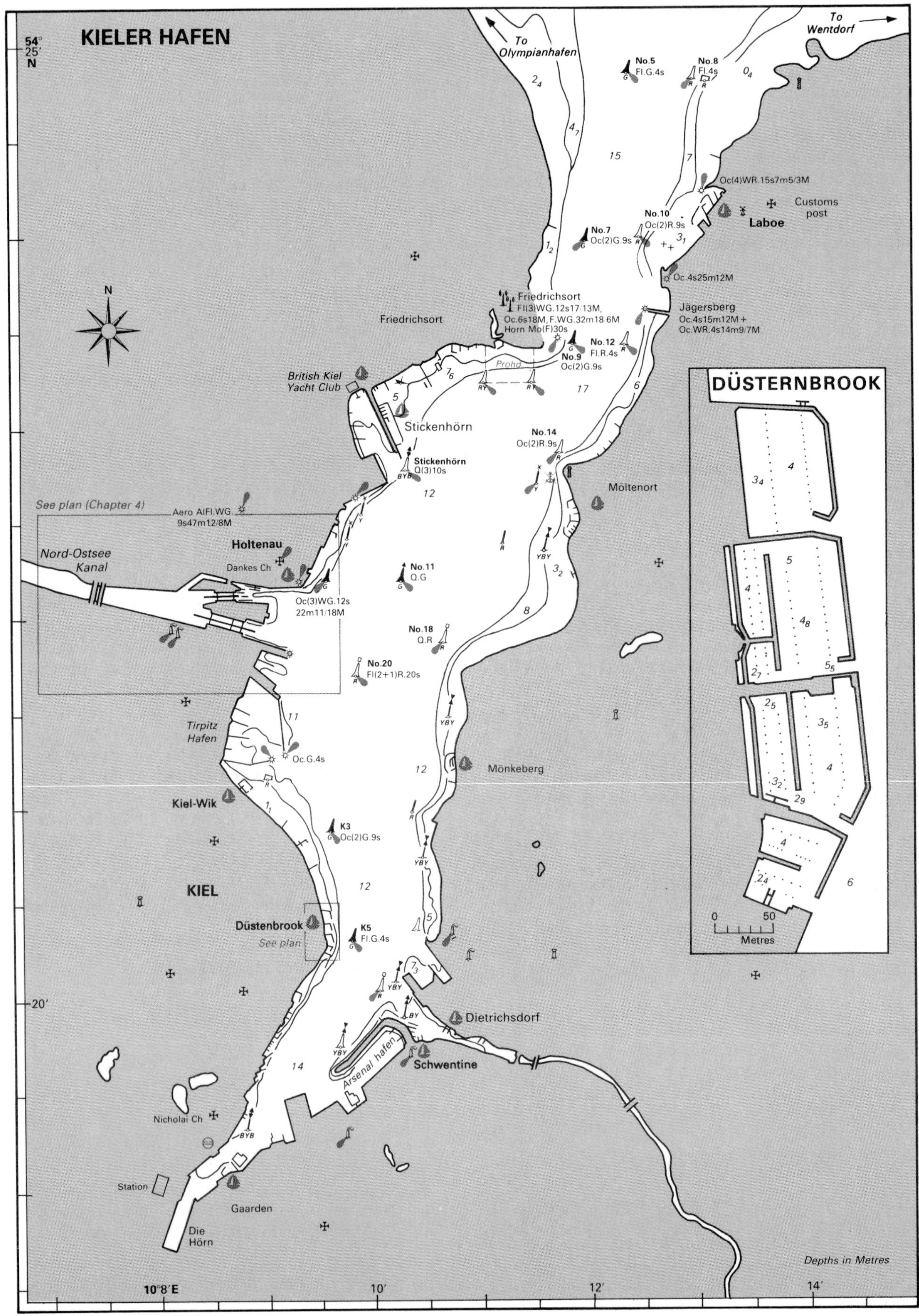
KIELER HAFEN
DÜSTERNBROOK
To Olympianhafen
To Wentdorf
Laboe
Customs post
Friedrichsort
Jägersberg
British Kiel Yacht Club
Stickenhörn
Möltenort
See plan (Chapter 4)
Holtenau
Dankes Ch
Nord-Ostsee Kanal
Tirpitz Hafen
Mönkeberg
Kiel-Wik
KIEL
Düstenbrook
See plan
Dietrichsdorf
Arsenal hafen
Schwentine
Nicholai Ch
Station
Gaarden
Die Hörn
Depths in Metres
Metres
10°8'E
10'
12'
14'
20'

Route description

KIEL DÜSTERNBROOK

This complex of four yacht basins is the home of the *Gorch Foch* training ship and of the Kieler yacht club – a meal in their impressive restaurant is a must. Unlit entrance, but green lit offing buoy nearby. Harbourmaster's office is on the central jetty between the two pairs of basins. There were no fuelling facilities at the time of our visit. Kiel and its railway station are about a 3km taxi drive S.

KIELER FÖRDE

There is sometimes a weak current in the fjord in strong winds: outgoing with S and W and ingoing with N and E winds, particularly in the Friedrichsort narrows. Gales/prevailing winds from SW and NE can respectively reduce or increase the average water level by up to 2m.

Winds tend to be funnelled along the fjord, with crosswinds less frequent.

Basin II of Düsternbrook yacht harbour, home of the Kieler Yacht Club.

→ Channel buoyed and lit, with several major lights at the points and at the entrance to Nord-Ostsee Kanal. Deep water (mainly 12m plus), but extremely busy with shipping for the Kanal and military ships, including submarines, so keep out of the main fairway.

There are at least a dozen yacht havens on the fjord, all easy to enter in daylight from deep water and most with good facilities. **Stickenhörn** (4–7m in main harbour, PD*), 1M N of the Holtenau entrance of the canal, is a military base, home of the British Kiel Yacht Club, and a favourite call for British yachts, although it is advisable to call Sailtrain on VHF Ch 67 in advance. The other 11 harbours are: (E bank, S to N) **Düsternbrook** (2–4m*), **Kiel-Wik** (3m plus PD), **Holtenau** (by the lock entrance is a simple landing stage; PD), **Olympiahafen Schilksee** (3–4m, PD*) and nearby **Strande** (3–4m, PD*); (W bank, S to N) **Schwentine** and **Dietrichsdorf**, on each side of the river Schwentine (each 4m plus), **Mönkeberg** (2–8m, D), **Möltenort** (2–3m), **Laboe** (2–3m, PD) and **Wendtorf** (2–2·5m*). Of these harbours, only Wendtorf, at the N end of the fjord, has a marked entrance channel, with lights in line across a 3–5m shoal patch and a withy-marked channel from the root of the breakwater to the landing stages.

Kieler Förde. German U-boat war memorial at Möltenort. Masts of yacht harbour just beyond this.

There is a prominent U-boat memorial at Möltendort and a naval memorial N of Laboe, both on the eastern shore. N of the Friedrichsort narrows the fjord widens out, with rocky shoals on each side. Keep clear of these near the main fairway and round Kleverberg point shoals outside their E cardinal lit marker buoy and well inside the 14M-range Kiel light tower (white round tower, red gallery and base).

ECKERNFÖRDER BUCHT

Currents in Eckenförder Bucht are weak, rarely exceeding 1kn, and are usually wind driven.

W As in Kieler Förde, winds from the NE quadrant tend to be funnelled along this fjord. (It is much more open to NE-quadrant winds).

→ Channel buoyed, many lit. Much of the route depth plus. Head northwestwards outside the 10m contour, along the edge of the marked Stollergrundrinne channel between the Stollergrund and Kleverberg shoals, to the buoyed (some lit) fairway S of Mittelgrund and thus to the head of the fjord.

23M
ECKERNFÖRDE

Eckenförde (2–3m*) is approached from the S and is close E of the built-up area. Keep nearer to the Marinehafen wall (to starboard, where it is deeper) before swinging to port into the yacht-haven entrance. There is an ancient town centre, with a church and a museum in the Rathaus, as well as holiday-resort facilities nearby

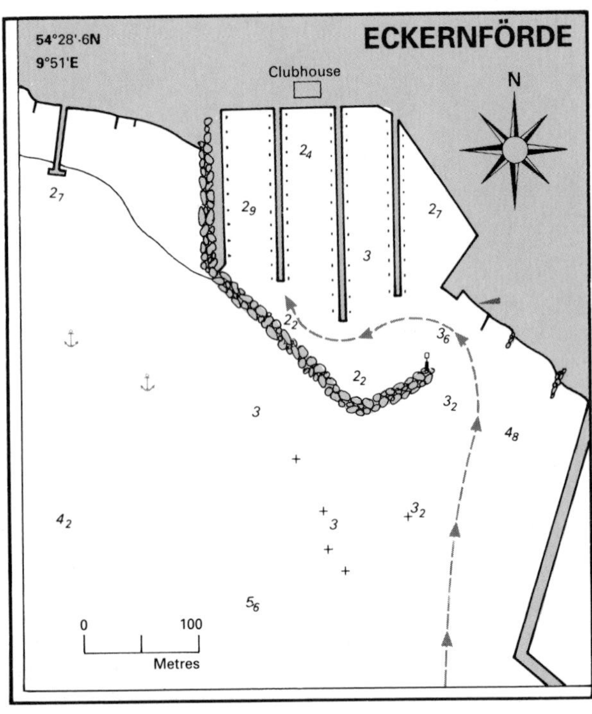

Eckernförde yacht harbour looking back to the entrance.

→ Leave the fjord following the N shore outside the 10m contour, then go northwards, heading offshore at the entrance to the Kieler Bucht. Keep offshore of the northern channel buoys, a small buoyed prohibited area, two major offshore platforms and a large rectangular prohibited area marked by yellow buoys S of the Schleimünde approach. Here mining practice and explosives dumping occur; the area is usually patrolled by launches.

Damp 2000 (2–3m, PD*) can be approached directly from offshore between the prohibited areas of the two platforms and through its SE-trending entrance, doglegging carefully round its northern breakwater.

SCHLEIMÜNDE

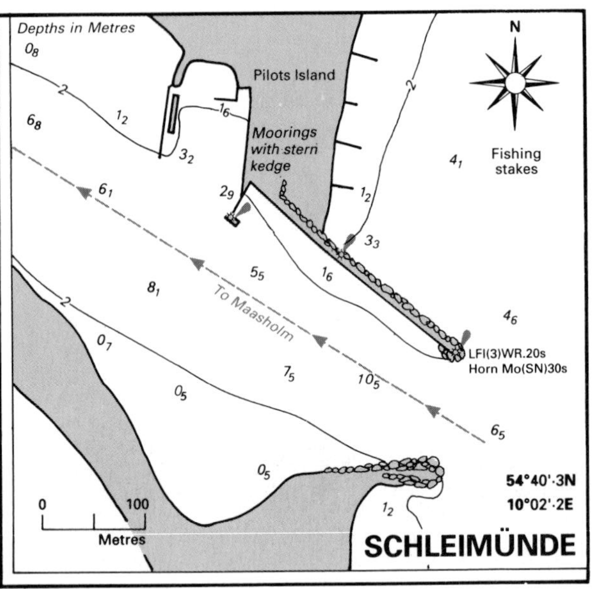

Approach

The end of the N breakwater of Schleimünde entrance has a prominent light tower (white with B band) with a sector light, and 800m NW of this a prominent white house, the 'pilot' house. It is approached by a buoyed (some lit) channel. Watch out for the Kappeln ferry in either direction and if necessary wait until it has negotiated this very narrow entrance.

→ From inside the entrance, looking back astern to the entrance along the channel, the light sector is obscured. It is replaced by occulting lights in line on the northern breakwater leading along the first stretch of fairway, which is well buoyed with lateral withy-topmarked but unlit buoys. There are two more sets of isophase and one of occulting lights in line leading along the buoyed fairway and to the N approach to Kappeln.

Schleimünde entrance with an outgoing ferry.

Schleimünde's mini-light.

DIE SCHLEI

Currents in the Schlei generally run outwards. They can be strengthened by steady SW–W winds, particularly in the narrows, where up to 4kn is possible, and an ingoing current is sometimes induced by N–NE winds. Water levels in the entrance can be raised by up to 3m in persistent NE–ENE gales and fall by up to 2m in WSW–W gales.

W Although quite sheltered, this NE–SW-trending fjord tends to funnel winds from these quadrants.

→ There is a good laterally buoyed fairway throughout the Schlei, but this is for daylight travel only as the buoys are unlit. The fairway is 6m and more deep as far as Arnis, and is narrow and close to the bank at Kappeln. Below Kappeln the Schlei has varying depths, which change with current silting, so it is essential to keep to the buoyed channel, particularly below the Arnis narrows, where depths fall to below 4m, and take the deepest routes across the lakes when there are few buoys.

Maasholm (2·5–3·5m, D*) is just N, off the entrance channel, and easily approached in 3m-plus depths.

⚓ In the wider reaches near the entrance, in the two wide reaches along the fjord and in the Grosse Breite and Kleine Breite near Schleswig there are plenty of opportunities carefully to choose and sound out a safe anchorage away from the busy fairway in 2–4m of water, although in passage-making it is best to keep to the buoyed channel. Some of the wide bights in the banks, such as Gunnerbyer Noor and Missender Noor, are possibilities, with landing places nearby.

KAPPELN

Kappeln-Grauhöft (2m plus), 0·5M N of Kappeln bridge. A somewhat long walk to the town. Mooring also possible at **town quay** near the silo (PD), but keep well clear of fishing boats and ferries. 300m S of the bridge mooring is possible, but shallow, at the landing stages of **Arnisser Segelclubs** (ASC). Kappeln has a pleasant traditional old town centre with an interesting church and good shopping facilities.

The railway swing bridge (3m clearance closed) opens on the hour from one hour before sunrise to one hour after sunset, i.e. basically in daylight hours. It has traffic lights. Yachts wait at least 200m off and usually go through in convoy, giving precedence to commercial shipping.

Continuing southwards, there are several small yacht havens or simple landing stages, all with limited facilities. These include (from N to S): **Marina Kappeln** (W bank), **Kopperby** (2·5m, E bank), **Arnis** (2·1m-dredged entrance channel, 1·4–2·2m in harbour, W bank), **Karschau** (landing stage), **Siesby** (landing stage), **Lindaunis** (3·5m, W bank just before railway bridge).

Kappeln-Grauhöft. Yacht harbour north of Kappeln.

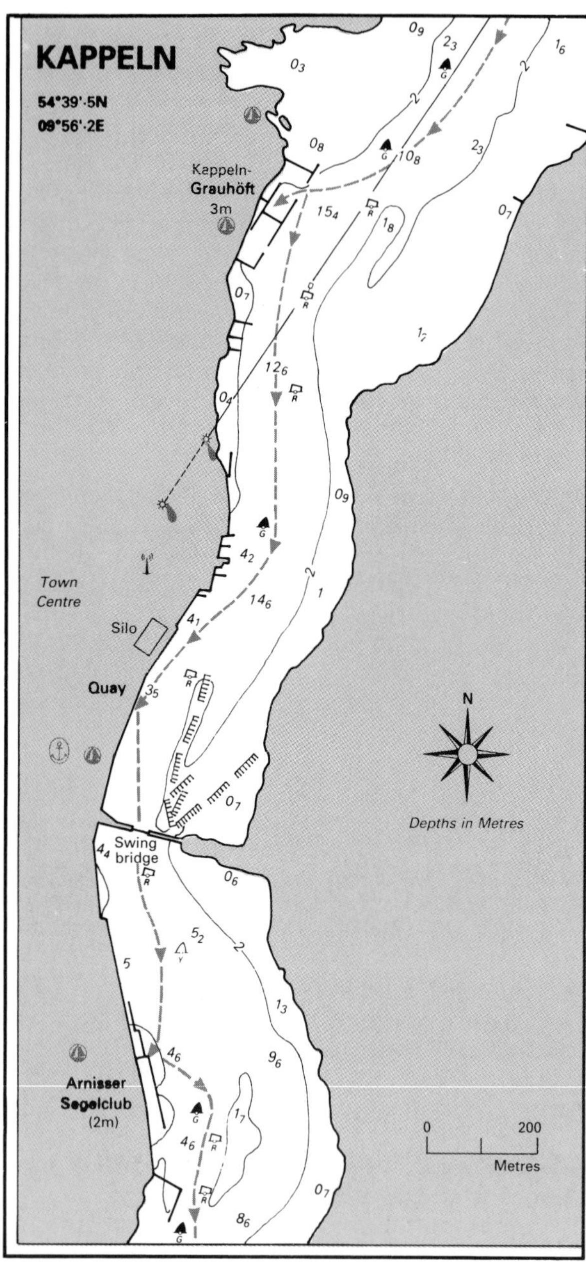

Railway bascule bridge (clearance 3·85m MLW) with some swinging moorings above and below the bridge for small vessels to wait at; otherwise instructions are as for the Kappeln swing bridge except that openings are 15 minutes before the hour.

There are at least ten yacht havens or simple landing stages on the way to the head of the navigable fjord at Schleswig. Many are shallow and small with limited facilities. In the Arnis to Missunder stretch (from N to S) are: **Bohnert Hülsen** (1·5–2m, S bank), **Missunder Yachtclub** (2–3m, W bank), and the nearby **Marina Brodersby** (W bank, shallow, PD).

→ In the Grosse Breite a direct course across the deepest parts of the lake leads to **Fleckeby** (1·3–2·4m, with a buoyed approach channel, S bank) and further W **Borgwedel** (1·7–2·5m, S bank). **Stexwig** (0·6–1·5m, S bank) is only for extremely shoal-draught vessels; it is near the narrow, closely buoyed channel past Stexwiger Enge.

→ In the Kleine Breite a buoyed channel continues NW to the sugar factory. The route to Schleswig Häfen, however, follows the S shore, picking up another buoyed channel with shoals on each side, into the final lake.

22M (Wiking Jachthafen)

SCHLESWIG

At the eastern end of the lake, **Fahrdorf** (1·2–1·9m, S bank) is almost as difficult as Stexwig, while **Haddeby** (2·5m, S bank, near the Wikinger Museum Haithabu) is only a little deeper. **Wiking Jachthafen** (1·9–2·6m*) is the largest marina in the area; its entrance is to the W of the prominent Wiking Tower at the W end of the lake and near Schloss Gottorf museum, with a buoyed channel right across the lake. **Schleswiger Jachthafen** (0·8–2·7m, PD), at the W end of the Altstadt, is next largest. Its entrance, to the W of the cathedral spire, is convenient for the *dom* (cathedral). It is approached from the last two channel-marker buoys across a 2–3m patch, with a final close turn round the end of its central landing stage.

The E end of the Altstadt can also be approached from the SE along another buoyed channel across the lake, but the limited facilities in **Schleswiger Holm** are mainly used by local fishermen and small craft, although large yachts sometimes lie in 2·5–3m alongside the quay. A river-bus ferry service runs from the Holm in the season around the three western yacht havens, including Haddeby.

22M (Schleimunde)

→ Return by same route to fjord entrance at Schleimunde.

Stand well offshore along the approach channel before turning NE along the 10m contour in order to avoid the rocky shoals of the Schleisand.

Schleswig cathedral across the lake from Haddeby yacht harbour.

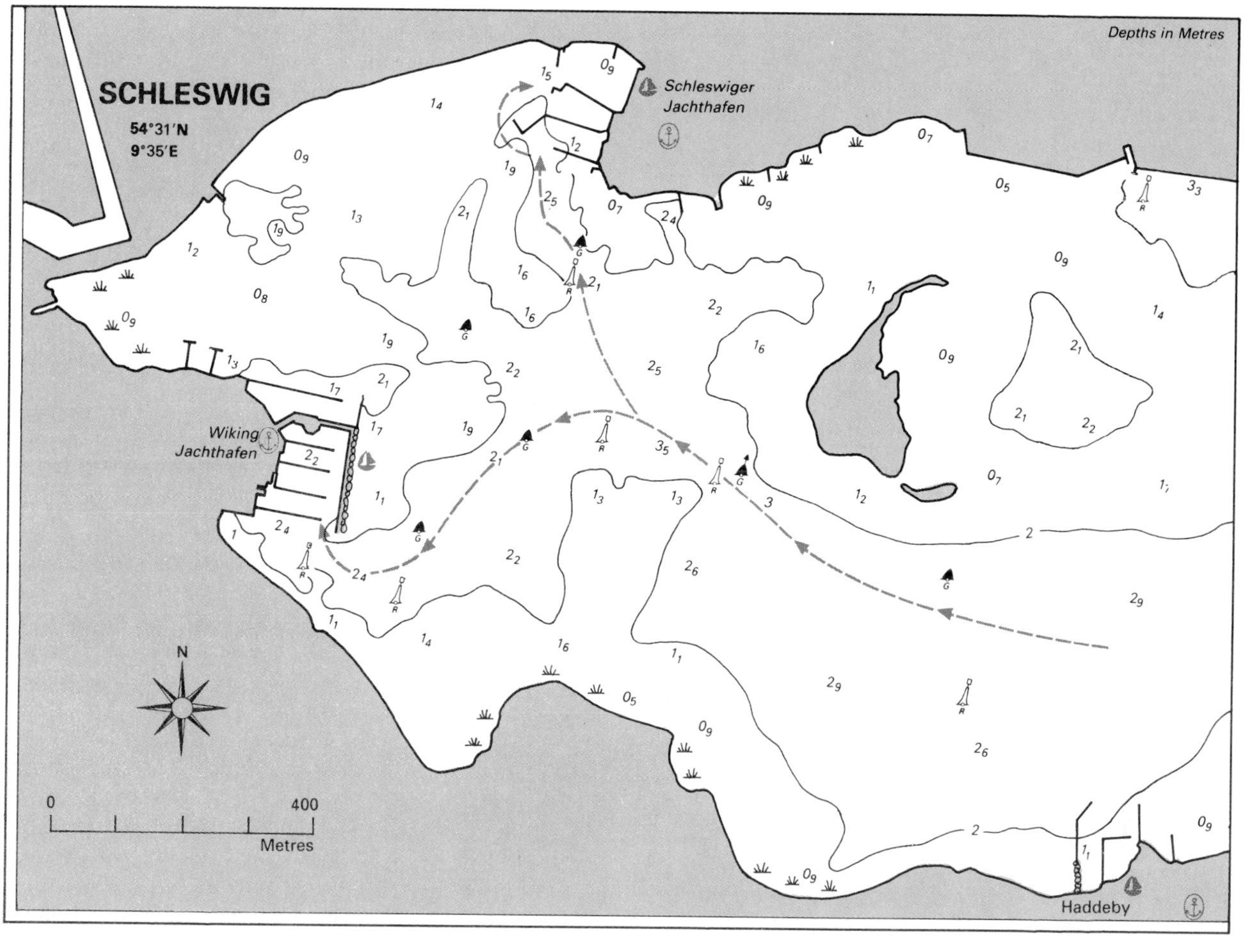

SCHLESWIG
54°31′N
9°35′E
Depths in Metres
Schleswiger Jachthafen
Wiking Jachthafen
Haddeby
0
400
Metres
N

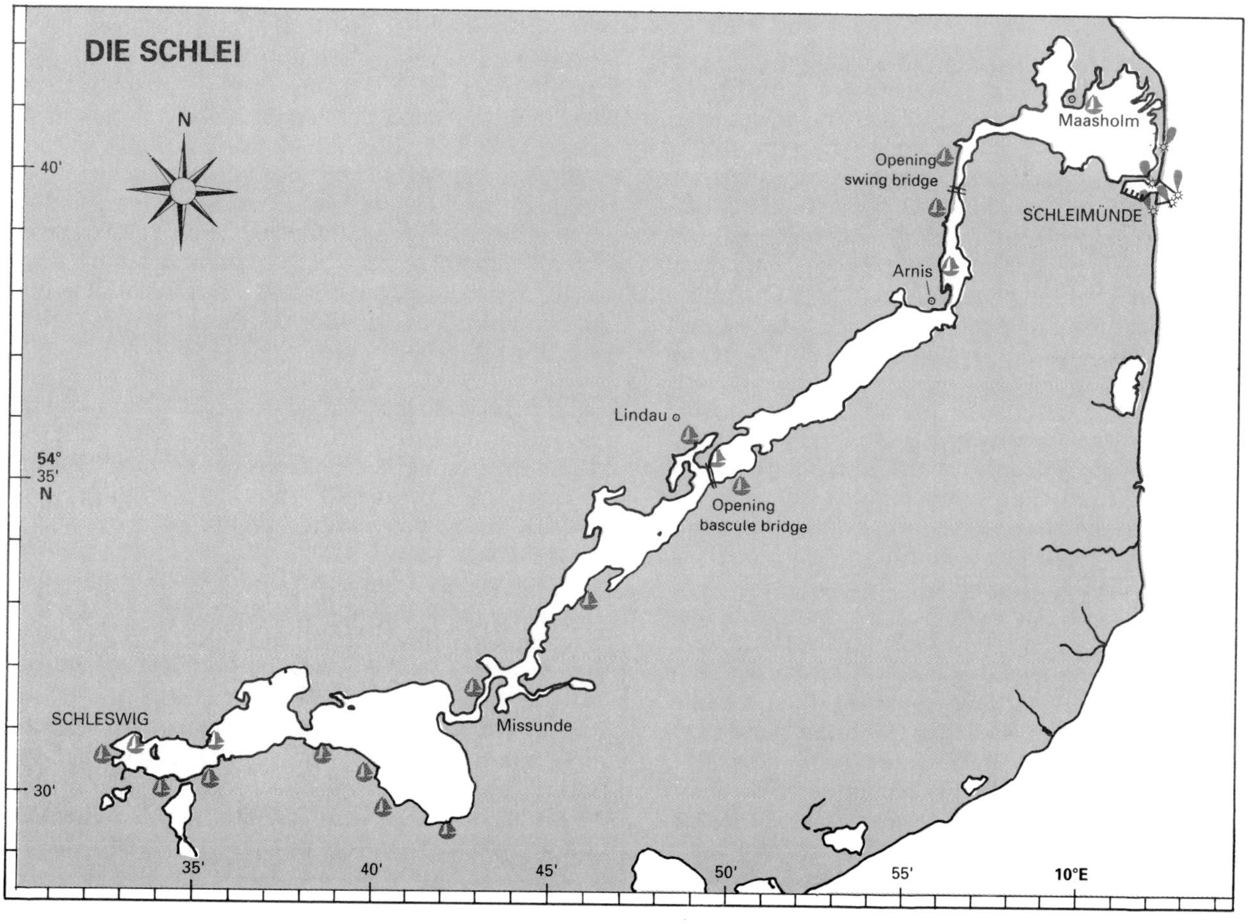

DIE SCHLEI
N
Maasholm
Opening swing bridge
SCHLEIMÜNDE
Arnis
Lindau
Opening bascule bridge
Missunde
SCHLESWIG
40′
54° 35′ N
30′
35′
40′
45′
50′
55′
10°E

*14M (*Kalkgrund)
FLENSBURGER FÖRDE
(Danish: **FLENSBORG FJORD**)

Currents driven by strong winds can occur in the fjord, particularly in the Holnis narrows, where in W–NW gales water levels may fall by up to 2·5m. At the head of the fjord at Flensburg, water levels may rise by up to 3m in E winds and be lowered by up to 2m in W winds.

This is another W and SW-trending fjord which funnels the winds from the eastern quadrants.

→ A straightforward deep-water (20m-plus near the entrance and 10m-plus beyond), wide but winding fjord, the frontier between Germany and Denmark. It is well buoyed and lit. In most wind conditions the fjord provides a cruising passage yacht with a variety of points of sailing. It is surrounded by a rolling, hilly country of fields, meadows and woodlands.

The entrance is to port round a 2M-long spit, keeping well clear of its marker, Kalkgrund light tower (red round tower, 2 white bands), which is sometimes difficult to round in strong westerlies. Gammel Pøl (white column, red band) and Kegnæs (yellow round tower) light towers provide good landmarks to the N of the entrance in Denmark. A direct course westwards across the N side of Geltinger Bucht leads to the fjord's first channel buoys.

There is another light tower at Neukirchen on the S bank, and lit buoys and a prominent light tower (red with white band) at the critical Holnis narrows.

NW from Kalkgrund, across the entrance on Denmark's Als island, is the entrance to the highly sheltered **Hørup Hav**, which can be approached from either side of the Middelgrund (marked by buoys). Its marina, on the northern bend of the Als shore, has good facilities (1–3m, PD★). Continuing on along the dogleg, there is a good anchorage just beyond the 6m contour near Gåsevig (mud, clay, rocks, weed). Another anchorage, also in Denmark and depending on wind direction, is tucked well into the bay at Vemmingbund due W of the entrance to Sønderborg.

There are three other good anchoring possibilities, all on the Danish shore. The Nybøl Nor bay is entered from the Holnis narrows from the SE along a buoyed channel (some lit) with F.R lights in line, passing through Egernsund bascule bridge (opens 0600–2400, signal with N flag, VHF Ch 16, or one long and one short blast on horn). Continue along buoyed channel past Gråsten, keep away from the W bank shoals and anchor off Adsbøl village in the NW (3m, sand, clay, some weed). Stranderød Bucht (anchor in 3–4m, sand) is on the N shore SW of Holnis narrows, but beware the Munkemølle Grund rocks to the W. 1·5M further SW on the Danish shore, approach the anchorage between the two Okseør islands from the NE, being very careful to avoid the northern and eastern shoals surrounding the larger island and heading towards Sønderhav before rounding S into the gap between the islands and anchoring in 3–4m (sand). Landing on the smaller island is prohibited.

Flensborg Fjord, Okseør Islands. The anchorage is in the gap between, and is approached from the other side of the islands.

(Danish shore). There are four: **Marina Minde** (2–6m, PD★), easily approached in over 6m of water, in the Holnis narrows (entrance W of the forest of masts); **Egernsund** and **Gråsten**, 2M away; and **Yachtzentrum Nord**, 2M beyond on the S side of the Nybøl Nor. The three last are initially approached through Egernsund opening bridge (see above for Nybøl Nor anchorage). The harbour at Egernsund (2m) is then entered close by to port; alternatively, head 345° for the first of the Gråsten channel buoys and to starboard for Fisknæs landing stage (1–2·5m). Neither of these is likely to have spaces in season, so you may have to anchor if you wish to visit Gråsten and its castle, the summer home of the Queen of Denmark. Yachtzentrum Nord (landing stage, 3·5m) is approached by heading along the buoyed channel into Nybøl Nor, NE to the green buoy off Bosbåk shoals and SE to the landing stages.

(German shore). There are at least ten harbours or landing stages. Excluding the three in Flensburg, these are (from E to W): **Gelting** (2–3·5m★, ferry to Fåborg on Fyn island) and **Wackerballig** (2·5–2·7m), near the entrance and approached via a buoyed channel and lights in line to avoid a middle-ground shoal; **Langballigau** (1·5–2m), also with occulting lights in line; **Schausende** (2–2·5m), with an approach channel marked by green and red top-marked posts and fixed lights in line; **Glücksburg** (1·5–2·8m), with a green buoy, guarding the W-side shoal, to round in order to reach the entrance; **Farensort** (2–3·5m), with an easy approach; and **Harrisleer Segelclubs**, 1M NW of Flensburger shipyard on the W bank (2–3·5m), with an offshore baffle wall to round in order to reach the landing stage.

Holga Danske in Helsingør. Brooding while he waits to save Denmark

Ship model at Nederby church (Fur)

Bremerhaven's historic ships collection from Columbus Centre

Ven Island. Bicycle overkill prepares for visitors

Fåborg. Long ship monument

The Danish flag on a boom end

A colourful street in Aerøskøbing

The frigate *Jylland* at Ebeltoft

Danish weather is variable

Kattegat. High pressure island clouds

Helgoland at dusk

Jutland fjord vista

Skagen. Grenen peninsula – the extreme northern point of Denmark

Inner entrance to Neuharlingersiel

Danish yacht harbours are often surrounded by boulders as here at Horsens

Fehmarnsund bridge on the German Baltic coast. 22m clearance

22M (Gästehafen)
FLENSBURG

Approach

Flensburg's inner fjord is easily navigable deep water, mainly over 6m, with two sets of lights in line and two lit buoys in the approach.

All the yacht landing stages are easily approached. **Flensburger Yachtservice,** at the head of Industriehafen (3–4m*), is the first, but a long way from town if you want a short visit. **Niro Petersen** (guest landing stage W shore, S of the shipyard, 8m) is similarly a little remote. **Flensburg Gästehafen** (3–7m), at the head of the fjord, is convenient for a short stay in this pleasant city with its spired churches, historic merchants' warehouses, pedestrian precincts and good restaurants.

Flensburg spires from the Gästehafen.

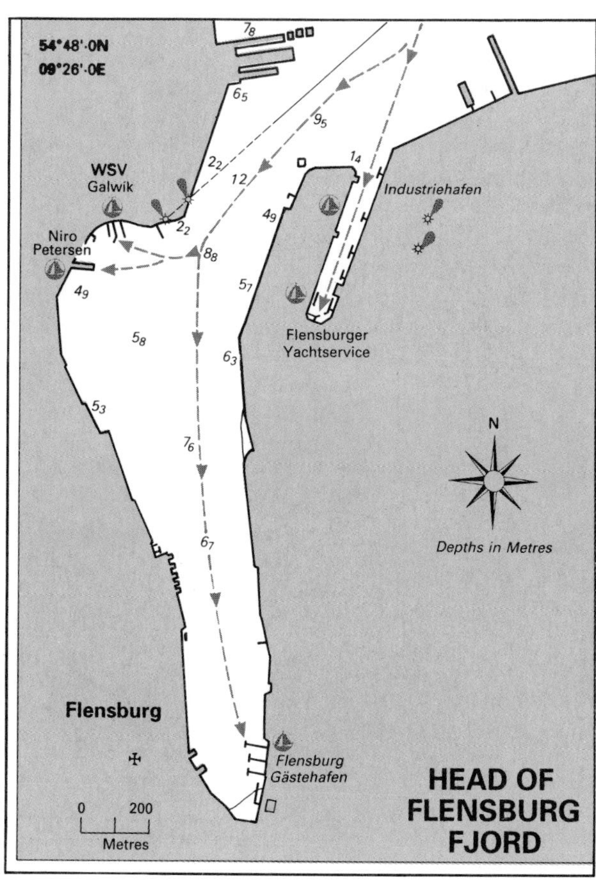

Flensburg Gästehafen and its restaurant.

→ Return by the same route to Borreshoved point, near the entrance to the fjord, and round the Helts Banke buoy in 10m plus, heading northwards for Sønderborg's entrance buoys.

24M (quay)
SØNDERBORG

Approach

No problem crossing Sønderborg Bugt, with the long hill sloping up to the Dybbøl windmill and war monument to the left of the entrance. Dogleg round a W cardinal and a red buoy to avoid the E and W shoals at the entrance.

Sønderborg Yachthafen (3m, D*) is to starboard before the red buoy, with an easy right-hand turn entrance just N of centre of its cluster of masts. **Sønderborg quay** landing stage is inside the entrance on the E side before the bridge and the ferry wharf. It is convenient for a visit to the town, the castle or Dybbøl (across the bridge), or for waiting for the bridge to open.

ALS SUND

The current through Als Sund, usually N-going, can be 2kn or more, so the opening bridge should be navigated with care.

Als Sund, Augustenborg Fjord and Dyvig are a sheltered cruising area.

→ Buoyed channel, many (not all) lit, particularly at N end near the two northern exit spits and Sottrupskov sector light (also lights on opening bridge). Depths in main fairway well over 10m. Generally relatively steep-to, with some shallow bights off for anchoring.

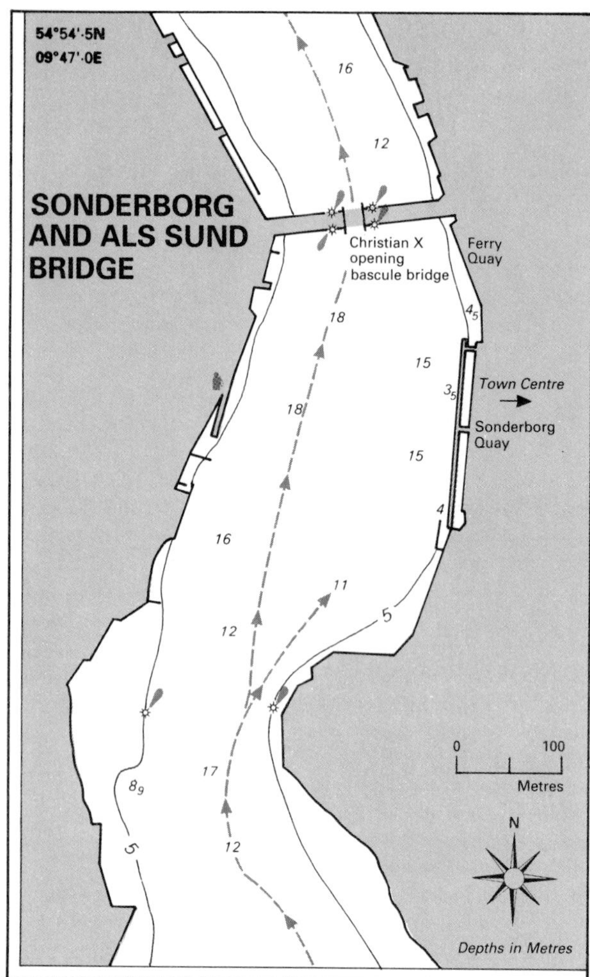

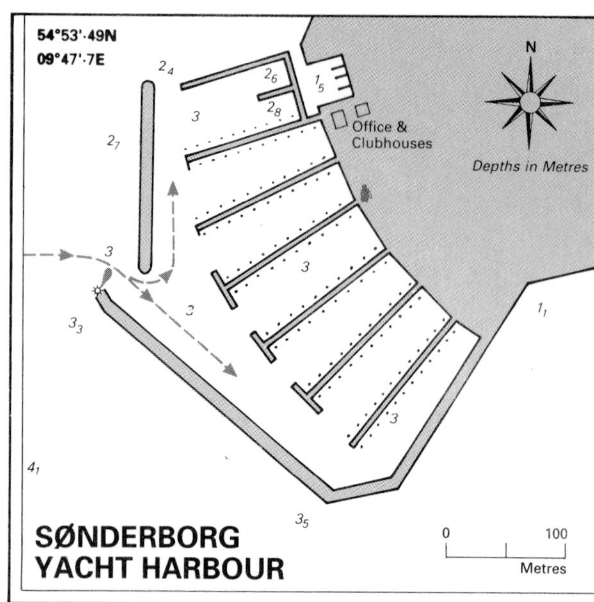

Christian X bascule bridge usually opens every hour, but rail and road traffic sometimes creates longer delays. Contact on VHF Ch 16, and/or fly the N flag. Convoys of yachts usually form. Just under 1M along the sound is Als Sund road bridge with 33m clearance.

Sønderborg. Approaching the town quay northern end with mooring for visitors.

Als Sund. Sønderborg's Christian X bascule bridge.

Sønderborg. Town quay northern end ferry terminal.

Als Sound is narrow and tree-lined, with **Sottrupskov landing stage** (1·5–2·5m, PD) on the W bank at the N end and a possible anchorage under Arnskilhuk near the E bank in E winds.

There are at least two other possible anchorages (sand and weed) in westerlies: Møllebugt (just after bridge on W bank) and Marens Gaf near the W bank 300m S of the headland S of Sottrupskov landing stage.

AUGUSTENBORG FJORD

➜ Wide, somewhat tricky, shallow fjord demanding careful compass navigation. Buoyed, but unlit. First 1·5M has depths of 10m plus, then last 3M drops until there is a 4m-dredged channel across a shoal area less than 3m in depth.

Sea level can rise by 1·2m in persistent strong northwesterlies and fall by 1·2m in northeasterlies.

10M (Augustenborg yacht haven)
AUGUSTENBORG

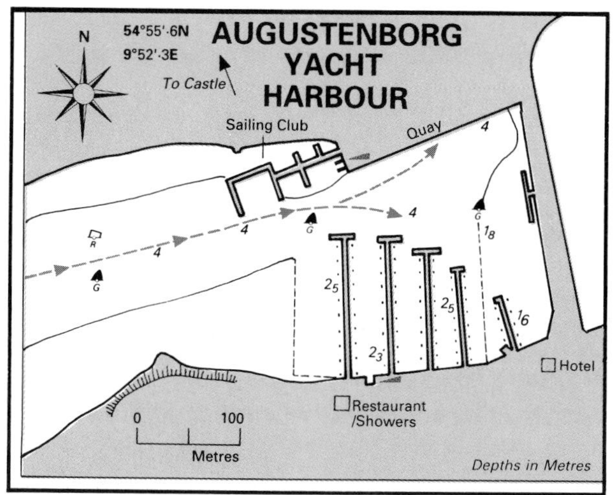

Dyvig. The narrow buoyed entrance channel, heading eastwards.

Approach

Leaving Als Sund, round and keep well clear of Arnskilsøre point, which is unmarked. 1·5M to the first green buoy off Ulkebølskov point, then 1·5M to first of closely spaced channel buoys (all unlit). Keep in the channel until the final green buoy is rounded to starboard into the yacht haven. The impressive castle, now a nursing home, is across the bridge, NW of the harbour.

⛵ Augustenborg (2–2·5m, PD*). Return by same route to entrance.

ALS FJORD

➜ Wide, deep (10m to over 30m), with a few unlit buoys on extreme edges.

⚓ (W side) Arnkil Fred (2–3m, mud), just below Arnkilsore point in the lee of a wood. (E side) Ketting Nor (3–4m, weed), SE of Katholm island and in lee of Sebbelov Skov woods. Sandvig bay (3–4m, sand and stones), off Stevning Skov.

⛵ ⚓ Dyvig, a bay cutting deeply into Als island to starboard, is entered along the very narrow, closely buoyed channel Dyvig, minimum depth 3·5m. Head NE across the lake and round Hesnæs point to the **yacht haven** (2·5–3m, PD), with its Dyvig Kro inn. There is an anchorage on the opposite side of the bay W of Hesnæs, and another opposite the yacht haven, but weed is a problem in these sheltered waters.

ÅBENRÅ FJORD

☂ This fjord is wide open to NE-quadrant winds.

➜ Wide and mostly over-deep. Vårnås Hage shoals to the S of the entrance are unmarked, so give a wide berth to the point as you turn to port and head for the first channel markers (unlit) into Åbenrå.

⛵ ⚓ **Varnæs Vig** (2·5m, landing stage) is tucked round the point to its S, and there is an anchorage off this to the E.

18M (Åbenrå yacht haven)
ÅBENRÅ

Approach

Two sets of isophase lights in line. The first marks the buoyed channel to the main recommended yacht haven (straightforward entry to port). The second continues on to the commercial harbour, but large yachts could turn to port and use the Sydhavn (4m deep).

⛵ Åbenrå (Apenrade) (2·5m, PD*). The buildings of the old trading town are a short walk N.

12M (Kalvø yacht haven)
GENNER FJORD

☂ This is an extremely well sheltered fjord.

➜ Small but generally deep (10–15m) fjord, with some patches less than 6m. Tricky entrance. From Åbenrå Fjord, Starbåk Grund (unlit buoy off) and Knudsgrund spits to port must be given a wide berth, entering the fjord close to the steep-to Barsø

Åbenrå. The approach.

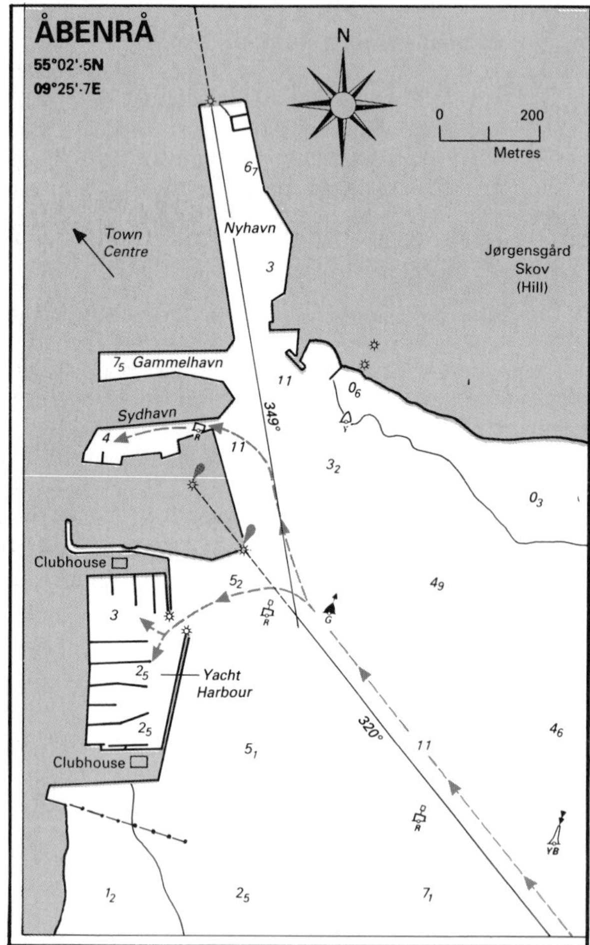

island. Then head for the N side of the fjord, Sønderballe Hoved, but watch out for the fish traps. Continue directly to the yacht haven just N of the peninsula, or to an anchorage.

⚓ **Kalvø** yacht haven (0·9–1·8m) is small and shallow. There are at least three possible anchorages (2–4m, sand, mud and weed), depending on wind: in the N bight of the fjord not far from the landing stage, and in either of the two southern bights, again near a landing stage.

→ If you wish to take the N exit from the fjord, beware: you must cross two firing-practice ranges NE of Barsø. A signal mast on Barsø's N hill shows two balls when there is firing on the larger range and one ball if it is on the smaller. If you use this route, make sure you are closer to Barsø island, to avoid the Sønderbolle Hoved spit on the mainland to the W (depth plus). Then head NE from Barsø close past the buoyed (unlit) Schønheyder Banke (in the green sector of Nordborg light on the N shore of Als), and go northwards (in white sector of Årø light) to the first channel buoys (unlit) of Årø-sund. If you take the S exit from the fjord, keep close to the island and follow outside the line of yellow buoys, marking the larger firing range as well as the S edge of Barsø Grund shoals and the Holst Banke, before heading N to Årøsund.

⚓ There is a good anchorage (sand, 2–4m) close inshore in Sandvig W of the headland off a sandy beach, but again here you have to cross the firing range.

15M (Årø yacht haven)
ÅRØSUND

↳ The current in the Sound varies in strength and direction. Easterlies/southerlies (NE–E–S) produce N-going currents, and westerlies/northerlies (SW–W–N) S-going ones.

Except in a southerly wind in the approaches, both Årøsund and Haderslev Fjord are protected from weather. Most of the cruising grounds to the N as far as Fredericia on the Snævringen narrows are similarly protected.

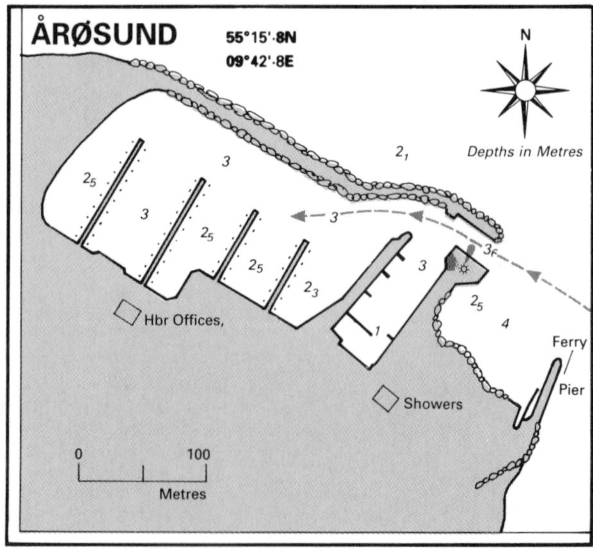

→ Narrow fairway (watch out for ferries between the two harbours) over 10m deep, with S entrance spits on each side. Well buoyed, but unlit, with two sector lights for both N and S approaches.

Årøsund yacht harbour entrance.

Approaching Haderslev.

ÅRØSUND yacht haven

Approach

Åro light (white round tower, red band) is prominent; the island is low, with few clumps of trees. Follow channel buoys, then go directly starboard or port into yacht havens on each side of the Sund.

⛵ ⚓ To port, **Årøsund** harbour (2·5–3m, D) is entered in 3·5m through a narrow entrance under the N mole, with Årøsund light (white round tower) on the S mole and ferry (local) wharf 100m SE of this. **Årø** harbour (2·5m), on the E side of the Sound to starboard, has a somewhat wider entrance below its N mole.

HADERSLEV FJORD

→ Narrow 7M-long fjord winding through hilly meadows and woods, mainly less than 2m deep except in 6m-dredged fairway, closely marked by lateral spar buoys, unlit. Maximum speed 6kn in fjord, with merchant ships sometimes forcing small craft to move outside the buoys.

From Årøsund, continue along the 10m-plus channel northwestwards between the Ørby and Knude Grund shoals to the final S cardinal buoy, then carefully follow the port and starboard spar channel buoys, keeping clear of the many fish traps on each side of the channel. This wide entrance involves the most difficult pilotage, since the channel winds across the flats and the spars are difficult to see, so reasonable visibility is necessary for a visitor.

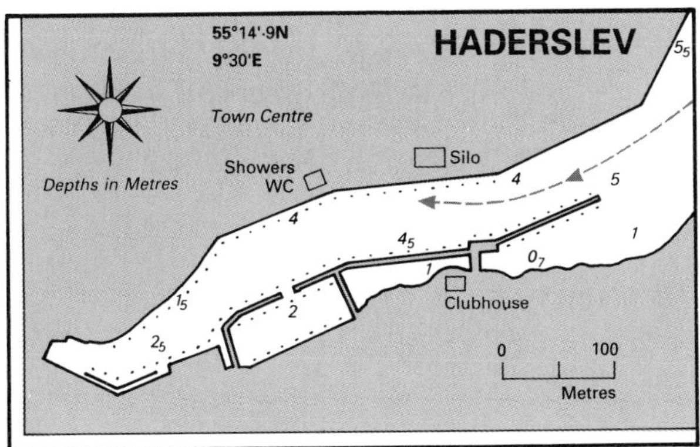

Haderslev. Head of the fjord.

⚓ Anchoring is difficult except for shallow-draught vessels, but is feasible N of the channel at Ørby Hage (2·5m) near the entrance, where there is also a shallow (0·5–1·9m) landing stage at Stagodde on the S bank.

10M

HADERSLEV

⚓ ⛵ Yachts moor head-to along each side past the silo at Haderslev (1·5–4·5m, D*). Shops, cathedral and open-air museum (in N of town, with farms, windmill, excavation etc.) are all convenient.

W The SW approaches to Bågo Sund tend to funnel winds from this quadrant, but from here northwards to Fredericia are the most sheltered reaches of the Lille Bælt.

→ Return to W cardinal buoy at S entrance to Årøsund. Turn to port, following round the 10m contour, and go NE along the buoyed (some lit) channel, Bågø Sund (10–35m deep), towards Tvingsbjerg light (white sector). Double back to starboard round the last red buoy before the light and head southwards along the 7m-dredged channel to Assens (isophase lights in line), with its Q.Fl.G light on the W mole, and prominent silos to the E of the harbour.

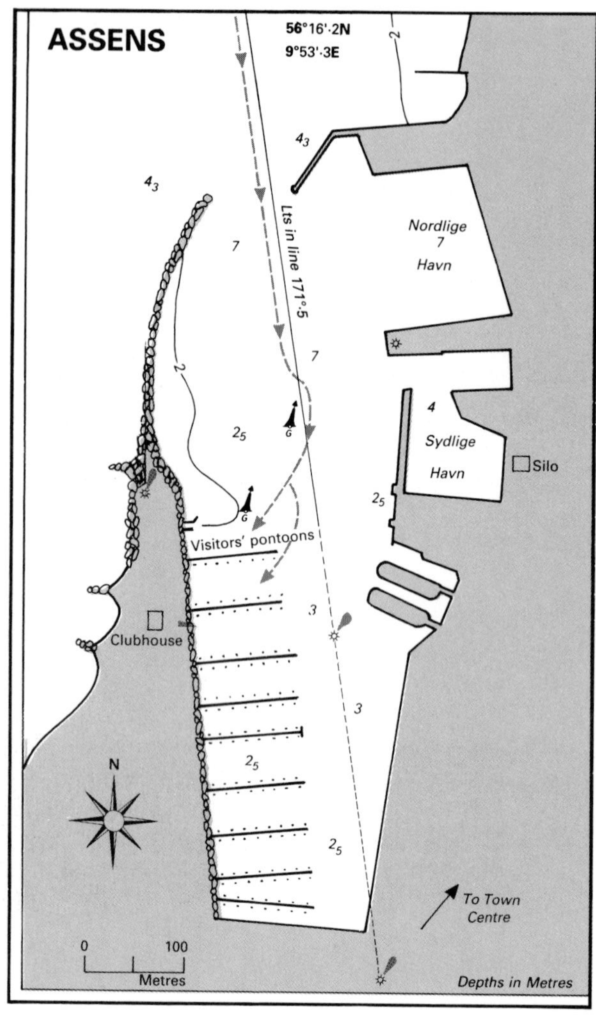

ASSENS (FYN)

Easy direct entrance to Assens, with its large yacht haven (2–3m, PD★). Church and half-timbered houses are of interest.

⚓ S of Assens a 6–10m-deep channel, Torø Red, separates Torø island from Fyn. Approached from the NW from the main deep-water offshore channel W of Asnås Rev, the easiest anchorage (sand) is just off the NE coast of the island.

Assens. Guest pontoon.

BÅGØ SUND(N) AND BREDNINGEN

The wind-generated currents in Bredningen are moderate, being strongest at the northern outlet and the southern main outlet between Bågø and Fænø. To the W of Brandsø a strange phenomenon occurs: the stream is always S-going, since a back-eddy from the main N-going Bredningen stream produces an anticlockwise stream round the island.

→ Much of this wide area of the Lille Bælt is 15m or more in depth. There is a buoyed (unlit) channel round Bågø island's shoals. From a point midway between the low wooded Brandsø island and the buoy off Wedellsborg Hoved, the course leads along the white sector of Fånø light, past the E cardinal buoy off Flåkojet shoal, to the buoy off Stenderup Hage at the entrance to Snævringen fairway.

Both mooring possibilities in the area are limited. **Bågø** (2–3m) is a small harbour approached in daylight directly on a 300° course from the end of Assens fairway across a shoal patch with just less than 3m soundings. **Heijlsminde** landing stage (2–2·5m) is approached across Heijlsminde Bucht through two channel buoys, with a sharp turn to starboard to the posts, making sure you do not run onto the S shoal. Strong NW winds can cause this corner of the bay to dry out, and it is much easier to anchor off in deeper water.

⚓ Many possibilities in most wind directions, in sand and mud in 2–4m close inshore and often in the lee of trees near sandy beaches, but watch out for the shoals and fish traps off the headlands. (E coast): Tybrand Vig (under the S or the N-shore woods); Føns Vig (head of the bay near Føns). (W coast): Mosvig (E of Skamlingsbanken hill).

DIVERSION TO GAMBORG FJORD (FYN)

(not included in total mileage)

→ Most of this fjord is well under 10m deep and unmarked; enter very carefully to avoid Fønsskov Rev to starboard. This is just below the surface, stretching 350m NE, so head NE midway between Fåno and the headland and continue well onwards towards the Fyn shore before turning to starboard.

⚓ There are several anchorages in most wind directions, but as well as a mud bottom there is some weed inshore in these sheltered waters. Three of the easier examples: close S of each of the two headlands on the SW side, and Ellebåk Vig, on the NE shore, nearer the main island than Svinø. Continuing on into the Vig along the 1·2m fairway to the landing stage (1–1·2m) is only possible for shoal-draught boats.

16M (Russelbåk)

FÆNØ SUND

→ Clear deep (10–26m) fairway, unmarked, with steep wooded shores.

⚓ Lænkevig is the bay close W of Nordkajshoved on Fænø. There is a 4m shelf here with a steep slope offshore.

MIDDELFART SPORTBOOTHAFEN

⛵ The large Middelfart Sportboothafen (Russelbåk) (3m, D*) is easily entered NE of Lænkevig, keeping closer to the S mole (F.G light) when entering. Although it is a moderate walk from Middelfart, with its castle and church, this yacht haven is more comfortable than the more commercial Gammelhavn, on the N side of the peninsula.

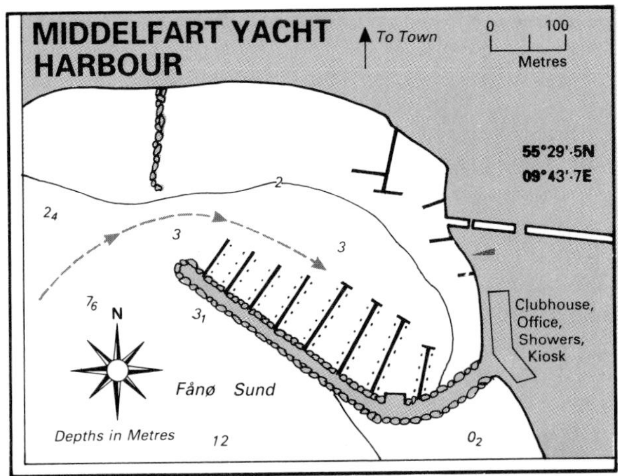

Middelfart. Gammelhavn (commercial harbour).

➜ Return to the S entrance of Fænø Sund and then go to starboard. Round the S shoals of the island, giving them a wide berth, and continue NW along Snævringen's SW shore.

SNÆVRINGEN

↘ Normally currents do not exceed 1kn. They generally set N in spring and S in autumn, and in summer depend on the overall weather pattern in the North Sea and Baltic (N-going stream in ENE–E–S–SSW winds, S-going in SW–W–N–NNE winds). They can, however, reach 3–5kn in persistent strong winds.

Snævringen road bridge. 44m clearance.

Snævringen railway bridge. 33m clearance.

➜ From Fænø to Fredericia these narrows are deep (22–79m in main fairway) with steep-to sides, except at the N entrance.

KOLDING FJORD

W This is another well sheltered fjord, with some tendency to funnel prevailing winds.

➜ Entrance over 10m deep but with wide shoals to N and S, followed by a buoyed (some lit) channel dredged to 6·9m, but with wide shoals of less than 3m on each side. The main hazard is the dogleg S round Drejensodde with its sector light, with the choice of cutting off part of the bend by using the dredged channel. Most of this area is over 3m deep and well suited to anchoring (see below).

SKÆRBÆK YACHT HAVEN

⛵ Skærbæk yacht haven (2–2·5m, D) and its close neighbour, the fishing harbour to its E, are at the extreme eastern entrance of Kolding Fjord on the N side, just W of the headland. Approach is from the S across a 3–4m shoal. Entrance unlit (but F.G light on E mole of fishing harbour next door).

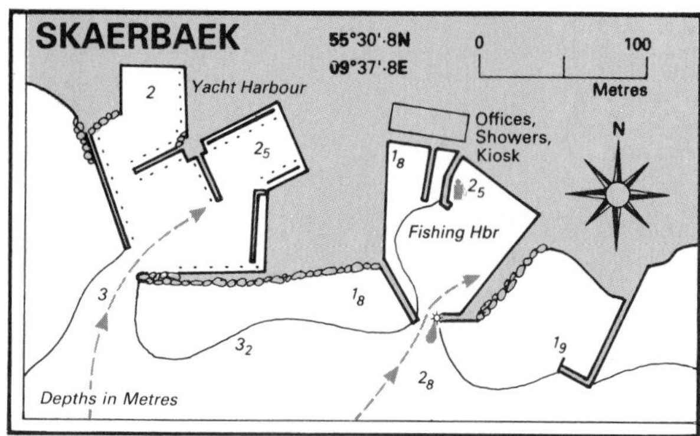

Kolding. The final approaches.

⚓ Depending on wind, the best anchorages (sand, 2–4m) are: directly E of Drejensodde, or on the S bank on either side of Agtrup Vig bay, which is due S of Drejensodde. Further E there is another possibility on the E side of Skarreodde point, although it is shallower here.

10M
KOLDING

There is a large yacht haven (around 500 places in each) on each side of the head of the dredged channel at the entrance to the Industriehafen. There are F.R lights in line into the Industriehafen. Entering the northern yacht haven (3m, PD★) involves a straightforward starboard turn at the entrance round its Fl green light. The southern yacht haven (2·5m, PD★) is entered by following a buoyed (unlit) channel off to port just before the entrance, with lights in line and a F.G light at the head of its S breakwater. About 1M walk from either harbour into the town, with its castle museum, town hall and half-timbered buildings.

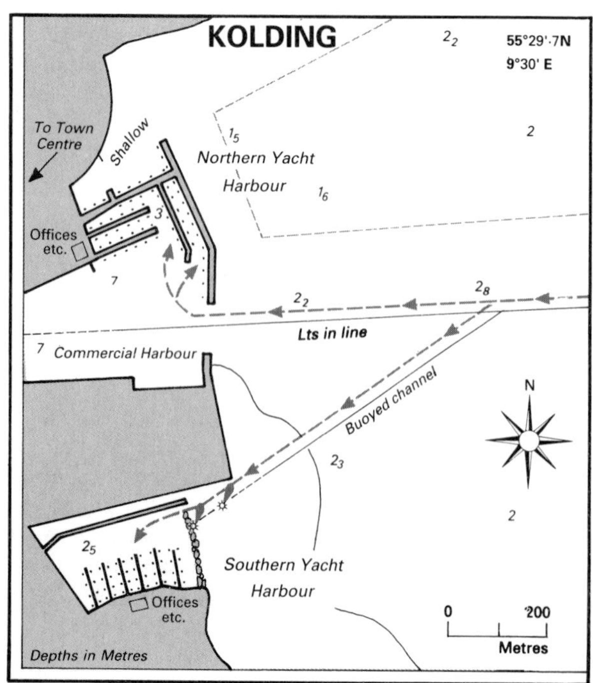

→ Return to fjord entrance. Turn to port into Snævringen.

SNÆVRINGEN

→ There are four sets of narrow-sector lights at Børup on the northern bend, a pair in each direction; the E-directed pair leads under the railway bridge. There are wider-sector lights at the Strib and Fredericia points at the northern outlet from the narrows.

The first (fixed railway) bridge has 33m clearance, and the next (road, suspension) bridge 44m clearance.

The small harbours on the S/E bank are, in succession, **Kongebro** (2·5m), **Middelfart Gammelhavn** (3–4·5m, for commercial vessels and deeper-draught yachts) and **Strib** (4–5m). All permit straightforward, direct entry, and the first two have an entrance light, but the stream can run strongly across all of them in strong winds. Middelfart has a 12th-century church, a museum and the 18th-century Hindsgavl mansion, on the site of a former castle.

12M
FREDERICIA SPORTBOOTHAVN

Fredericia Sportboothafen (1·5–3m, PD★). The buildings and oil tanks of Fredericia to the N provide a major landmark in both directions from Skanseodde point, and there are two lit approach buoys. The stream off Fredericia's harbour almost always sets E, i.e. in the expected direction, during the N-going stream, but continues in the same direction during the S-going stream, from which there is a back-eddy. The views from the ramparts of the old fortifications of this historic defence stronghold are good, if you are prepared to walk.

TRAGTEN AND BÅRING VIG

Winds from the NE quadrant have a long fetch to this funnel-shaped entrance to the Lille Bælt.

Departure from Fredericia, out through Tragten Vig past the offlying Skanseodde light on its green metal mast, is no problem. However, a triangular firing area extends from the N shore at Hyby

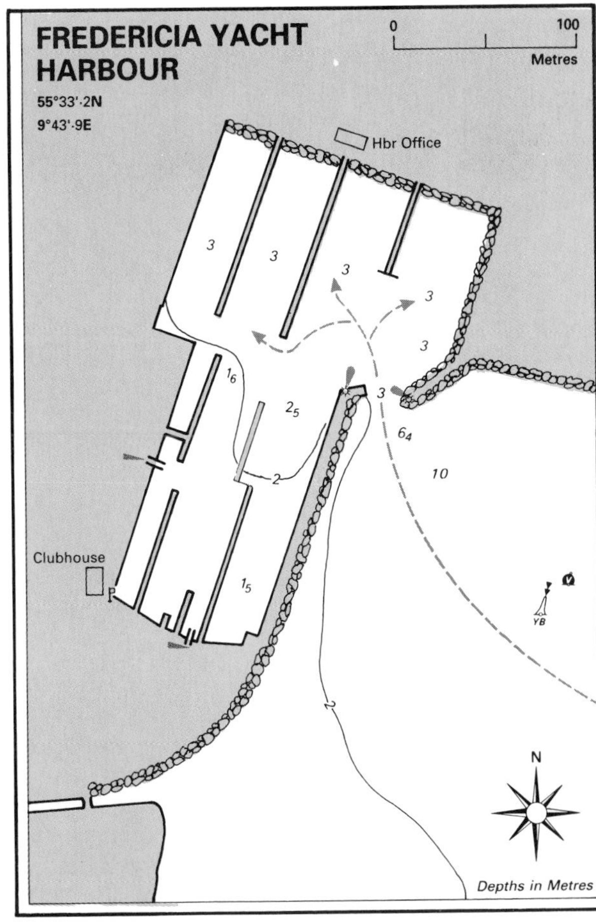

Fredericia. Entrance to yacht harbour.

Fælled, marked by yellow buoys. When firing is in progress balls are hoisted on signal masts ashore.

Before turning E across Båring Vig it is best to go out to the first yellow (lit) buoy in order to clear Stavrshoved point's shoals. Heading for Bogense, it is also advisable to work N to the 55°35'N parallel and follow this to pick up the outer green buoy (lit) of the channel markers.

12M
BOGENSE

Approach

The short white tower of Bogense sector light among the cluster of masts is a good landmark at the end of the E breakwater of the harbour. Approach from the N is best, having picked up the outer lit green buoy N of the entrance. Follow the buoys closely southwards, doglegging round the two green (keep them to starboard) and single red (keep to port).

Once through the entrance, the large (600 moorings) Bogense yacht haven is ahead (2–2·5m, PD*), with the fishing harbour to port. The town, which has several historic buildings, is a short walk E.

→ From the outer channel buoys, a course slightly NE of Kasserodde Flak cardinal buoy (unlit) will clear the shoals and allow direct entrance into Veijle fjord to port.

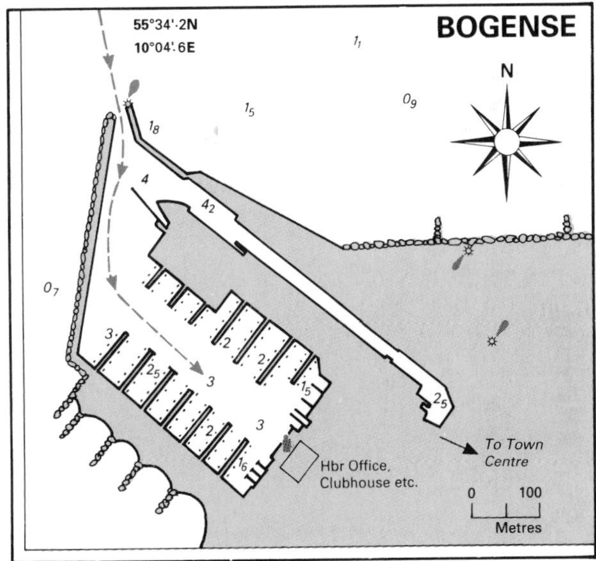

VEJLE FJORD

In strong E winds there can be a strong ingoing current in the fjord's dredged channel.

Except at the entrance, this is a well sheltered fjord, with several headlands and bends.

→ A wide fjord with high wooded shores. There is an outer deep area (10–17m depth), with shelf areas on each side, an inner part, reducing to 6–10m, and finally a 2M-long straight dredged (to 7m) channel leading under a prominent road bridge (clearance 40m) directly to the harbour. The inner part of the fjord and the dredged channel are buoyed/lit and have red isophase lights in line. The outer approach to the fjord, if made from the S, requires doubling round Kasserodde point, which is tricky: the point has a major sector light (Trelde Næs), but a 2M spit trails off NE, marked only by an unlit cardinal buoy. There are lit buoys off the two headlands on the N shore of the fjord.

⚓ There are possibilities in most winds. Kulvig (clay, 2·5m) is the bay close W of Kasserodde point, but keep outside the 2m contour (stones). Andkær Vig (2–3m, sand, weed), in the inner fjord, is also on the S bank, close W of Holtserhage point (but make sure you clear the point round the offlying buoy); there are some landing stages nearby. Due N of the point, there is also a bay on the N shore with anchoring possibilities.

⛵ ⚓ There are two small harbours, one on each side of the outer fjord, with unlit but straightforward entrances in 3m depths: **Rosenvold** (2m), **Brejning** (1–2m, E side deepest).

21M
VEJLE

⛵ The large (650 places) yacht haven is directly off the N side of the entrance channel beyond a series of unlit channel buoys leading to the shallower E side of the harbour (1–1·7m); the deep water is on the W side (1–2·5m, PD*). A longish walk into this interesting old town, with its Gothic church, two museums and excellent views over the fjord and town from the surrounding wooded hills, as well as archaeological sites and restaurants. Legoland Park is at Billund, about 30km W of Vejle.

Vejle road bridge. 40m clearance.

Vejle. Looking across to the inevitable silo from the yacht harbour.

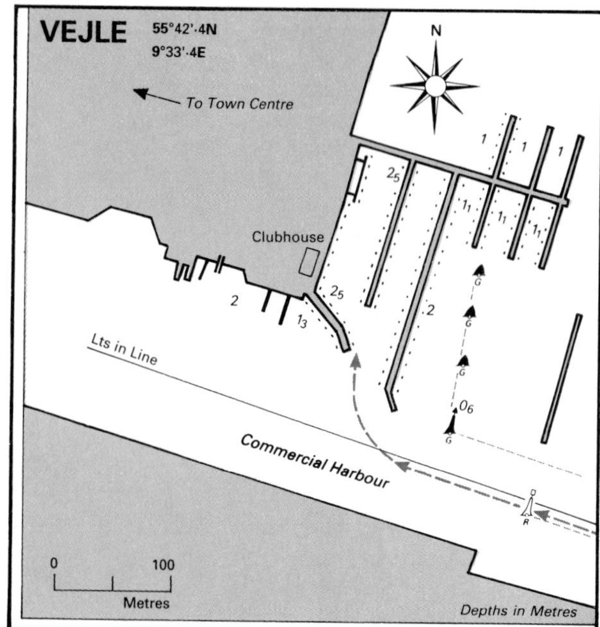

→ Return to the fjord entrance, then go NE, rounding the S cardinal buoy (unlit) marking the southern edge of the extensive outer shoals of Bjørnsknude point, which also has a N cardinal buoy (unlit) on its northern side and a shoal area, Bjørnsknude Flak, in between the buoys. This last should be given a wide berth, using the echo sounder to clear it, before heading W past the N cardinal buoy towards Juilsminde's offlying red buoy (unlit).

Bjørnsknude peninsula and spit are very exposed in winds from NE, SE and SW quadrants, but Sandbjerg Vig, and particularly Juelsminde harbour, are well sheltered from most winds. Asvig, further N, is more exposed to easterlies.

23M
JUELSMINDE

⛵ Juilsminde's two harbours are approached in a southerly direction from the W side of the offlying red buoy. The entrances are on each side of the Parkplatz; that of the old harbour (1·3–3·8m, PD) is to the E, marked by a Fl.R light on the E mole, and that of the new marina (2·5m*) is hard to starboard round the W mole (unlit). There is a long ferry pier 0·4M westwards along the coast, so watch out for the large ferry (to Kalundborg on Fyn), which is frequently manoeuvring past the harbour entrance.

⚓ In the NW corner of Sandbjerg Vig off the woods (3–4m, sand, weed).

Continuing northwards, the next hazard is Bogehoved point, followed by the wooded Ashoved Flak headland with its offlying shoal and cardinal marker, so it is best to work out well offshore when leaving Sandbjerg Vig anchorage.

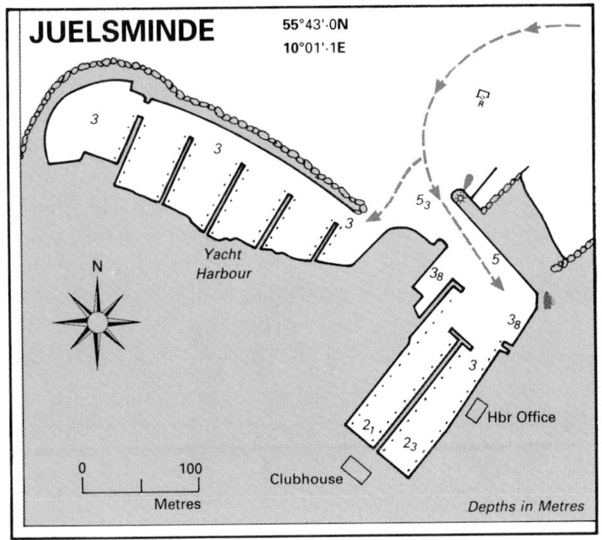

⚓ In Asvig off Kirkholm or NE of Sonderby woods (3–4m, sand, weed).

HJARNØ SUND AND DRAGET

There are normally weak (up to 1kn) six-hourly tidal streams in this channel, but strong winds can disrupt this regime, increasing rates to 2·5/3kn and causing streams to persist for up to 12 hours in the same direction.

Only in SE-quadrant winds is the channel exposed to a wind-funnelling effect; otherwise it and Horsens Fjord beyond are well protected waterways.

→ This channel between the low, partly wooded Hjarnø and Alrø islands and the mainland is deep (12–22m) and buoyed at each end (lit beacon at the S end, lit buoy at N end), and there are two sets of lights in line.

Snaptun yacht haven (2–2·5m) is a tiny harbour on the W side of the channel, with direct entry under the N mole, taking care to keep clear of the ferries (to Hjarnø and Endelave) which tie up on the N side of the central mole. The old harbour (2–3m, PD) is entered S of this central mole. Neither entrance is lit. **Hjarnø** (2·5m at end), on the E side of the channel on the island, has a possible mooring on the outside of the main pier, but keep away from the ferry which ties up on the S side of the N mole.

⚓ Borresknob (sand, 2·5m), on the E side of the Borre peninsula just off the Draget.

HORSENS FJORD

There are weak (up to 1kn) six-hourly tidal streams in the fjord, but strong winds disrupt and vary their strength and timing.

→ A wide, shallow fjord, particularly in the E, with wooded hills to its N and S and the town of Horsens on the low-lying land at its head. There is a 4M-long 6·9m-dredged buoyed (lit) channel with lights in line into the harbour. To reach this channel from the Draget it is necessary to round the red light buoy off the Salgrund shoal N of Borre and then go southwestwards to the first lit channel buoy (there are also lights in line along this stretch as you head towards the shore). There is plenty of elbow-room for sailing in the outer fjord, where depths are over 4m, but less in the shallower inner fjord.

16M

HORSENS

The yacht haven is on the N side immediately outside the commercial harbour. Entry to Horsens yacht haven (560 places, 1–2·5m, PD*) is virtually a repeat of that at Vejle, i.e. hard to starboard round a green buoy and starboard again directly into the entrance (F.G light on E mole). The town is a short walk to the W; it is somewhat industrial, but has some interesting restored old buildings, including churches.

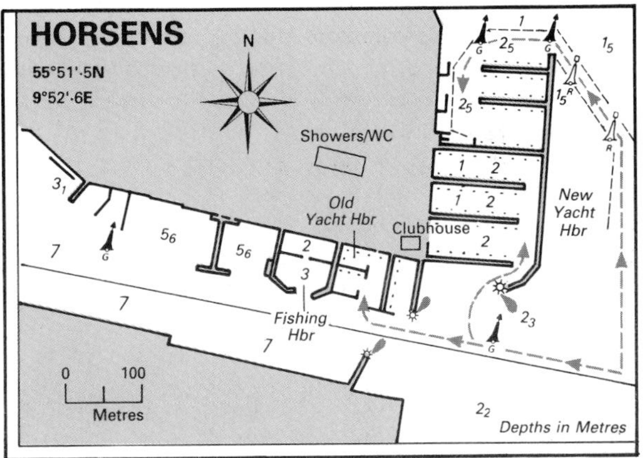

Horsens. Another large yacht harbour at the head of a fjord.

→ Return to the entrance of Hjarnø Sund at the Søndergrund buoy.

SVANE GRUND AND ENDELAVE SHOALS

The initial part of this route, across the shoals, is well sheltered, but in the deep approaches to Kolby Kås there is a long fetch for winds from approximately SW through S to SE.

→ There is an extensive shoal area from the Horsens approaches and Endelave island in the S to the southern end of Århus Bugt in the N, with depths less than 10m and below 5m in many places. It is advisable to navigate across this in fine to moderate weather conditions when sea levels are relatively stable, in daylight and following the buoys (mainly unlit). From Søndergrund eastwards to Samsø there is a deeper area (mainly over 5m), with two (unlit) cardinal marks at the entrance and a N cardinal (unlit) SW of Svane island. This is the trickiest part; a course southeastwards from this buoy, constantly sounding of course, leads across a 3·5–6m patch between Svane and Endelave, but beware of the long, shallow spit S of the buoy, trailing out from Endelave. This route leads into deep water, and when the 10m contour is reached course can be altered eastwards to head for Kolby Kås.

Endelave (2·5m) is a tiny harbour (around 200m long) at the end of a pier on the N shore of the island, but it is not for newcomers, since approach is from a RW buoy heading E of S across a very tricky shoal area which requires local knowledge.

25M

SAMSØ/KOLBY KÅS

Kolby Kås (2–4m, PD) has entrance lights. It is mainly a commercial and ferry (to Kalundborg, Sjælland) harbour, with room on the landing stages only for small yachts. Most visitors lie against the W wall, if there is room amongst the shipping.

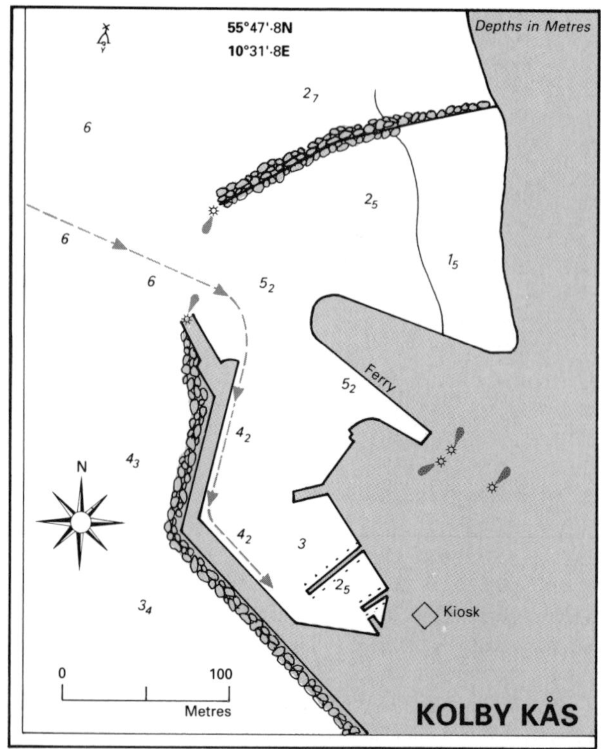

Kolby Kås, Samsø Island. Alongside the southwest quay.

Kolby Kås, Samsø Island. Approaching the entrance.

DIVERSION TO SAMSØ'S EAST COAST

(not included in total mileage)

Ballen (2·5–4m, PD), on the E coast of Samsø, is a 10–12M detour in deep water around the S coast, keeping well off the shoal areas (there are two lights and four lit buoys off the S coast). It is a picturesque little harbour, with most facilities and a lit entrance. Bicycles or some other form of transport are needed for a tour of the island, or to reach its inland capital, Tranebjerg, and the surrounding villages.

Langør (2·2–2·5m, PD), another tiny harbour on the E side of the island's northern Nordby peninsula, is an even more difficult diversion (10M from

Ballen. Tiny harbour on east coast of Samsø.

Ballen and also not included in total mileage) and is a daylight route. Continue N from Ballen, keeping outside the 10m contour; there is a buoyed (unlit) channel, Lindholm Lob, across the Kyholm shoals to the red buoy (unlit) S of Kyholm island. Here course is altered westwards and round the N side of a white dolphin (leave it about 100m away), then southwestwards to an unlit green buoy (keep the buoy to your starboard) off the Lilleøre peninsula, and to another green buoy (unlit, also keep to your starboard) 100m before the harbour entrance (unlit); head W, being careful not to turn N into another tiny shallow dock before the entrance.

⚓ There is an anchorage in the bay to the N of this last green buoy (2–6m, sand). Langør was an important naval port in the Anglo-Danish war at the beginning of the 19th century, and also in Viking times, when the Kanhave canal was dug across the narrow part of the peninsula to allow escape from attack in either direction.

MÅRUP VIG

From Kolby Kås northwards the whole of Århus Bugt, with its coves and scattered shoals, provides one of the most sheltered cruising grounds in the SW Baltic; a yacht is never far from a lee or an anchorage in any weather.

→ From Kolby Kås, follow the deep-water (20m-plus) buoyed channel towards Tunø, taking care to clear Ringebjerg Sand to starboard.

Mårup (1·2–2·4m) is a tiny harbour on the S shore of Nordby Land at the N end of Samsø, approached along a buoyed channel (2·4m) from the SE. There is a ferry from Sælvig, further S, to Hov on the mainland.

10M

TUNØ

⚓ Tunø island's harbour (2–2·5m) is another small (100m long) one, approached from ENE along a buoyed (unlit) 3·4m-deep channel, and with a F.R light on the S mole. Tunø sector light is on the white church tower amongst the trees behind the harbour.

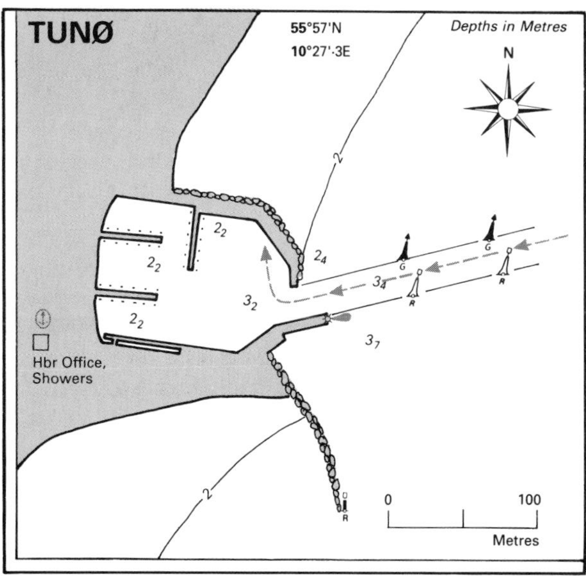

Tunø light is on the church tower (under repair at this time).

Tunø entrance.

ÅRHUS BUGT

Currents are relatively weak and mainly N-going in the Bugt, but NE gales can reverse this direction. The N-going current turns E near Århus towards Mols Hoved point and then runs S to Helgenæs, where it meets the current from Samsø; both are diverted E towards Hjelm.

Passages in this area are never far from a lee from the land. The middle of the bay eastwards of Århus has the longest fetches for seas to build up.

→ N of Tunø, Århus Bugt is mainly over 20m in depth, but there are scattered shoals, particularly off Norsminde. From Tunø the route sweeps widely round the E side of the island around the buoys to avoid the shoals, then WNW to Norsminde's offlying small N cardinal buoy (unlit). This route just cuts across the 5–6m patches at the S end of the offlying shoals.

Norsminde (1·4–2·2m, D) is another small harbour. Approach from N of the offlying cardinal buoy, between a N mole and a line of red buoys parallel with it, marking the opposite side of the channel. Soundings should be made in the initial approach when leaving the cardinal buoy in order to make sure that you stay to the NE side of the approach route, thus keeping clear of the shoal area and stones on the SE side. There are sometimes fishing stakes near these shoals.

Norsminde's narrow entrance channel, between the wall and the red buoys.

7M S of Norsminde (and not included in this route plan and distance), **Hov** (2·2–3·2m, PD) is another harbour on the more direct route from the Søndergrund buoy at the S entrance to Hjarnø Sund. This route heads northwards from the buoy across a 3m patch between the cardinal buoys W of Svane. It continues northwards to pick up the buoyed channel (unlit, green to port going N) past Hov, turning hard to port just N of the harbour and then heading southwestwards along the buoyed channel (two Q.G beacons to starboard), past the ferry (to Sæby, Samsø island) harbour and into the small yacht haven to starboard (F.R light on W mole). Hov's major sector light, on the E mole of the ferry harbour, can be of assistance in finding the outer buoys at the N and S ends of the main offshore channel. From Hov northwards to Norsminde, following the deepest water (around 10m at most) is tricky. Keep about half a mile offshore (somewhat more than this at Dyngby Hoved) and then head directly across the bay to the Norsminde offing buoy, giving a wide berth to Kysing Næs shoals SE of Norsminde harbour.

→ Return to Norsminde's cardinal buoy, then round the green buoy off Hesbjerg Grund shoals and follow the coast (deep water, 13m) northwards.

MARSELISBORG

The large (450 places) harbour of Marselisborg (2·5–3m, D*) permits easy direct entry from the S. It has a F.G light on the E mole and F lights on the middle and W moles. The harbour is about 4km S of the centre of Århus. Marselisborg castle, nearby, is the summer residence of the Queen of Denmark.

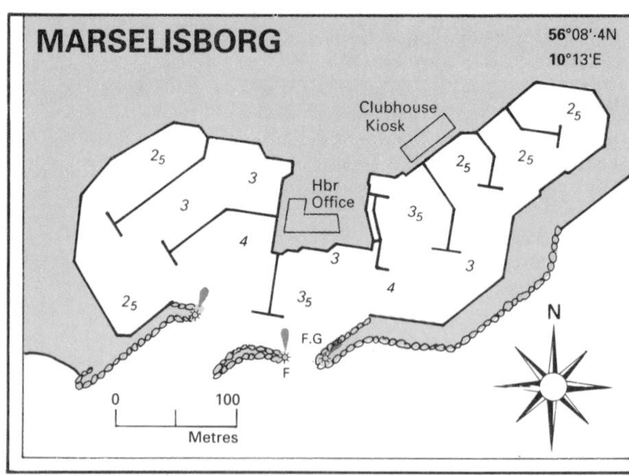

→ Continue N, keeping well outside the harbour walls and buoyed approaches to Århus' major container terminal. Take care to give way to commercial shipping.

Marselisborg. A highly modern marina.

23M
ÅRHUS

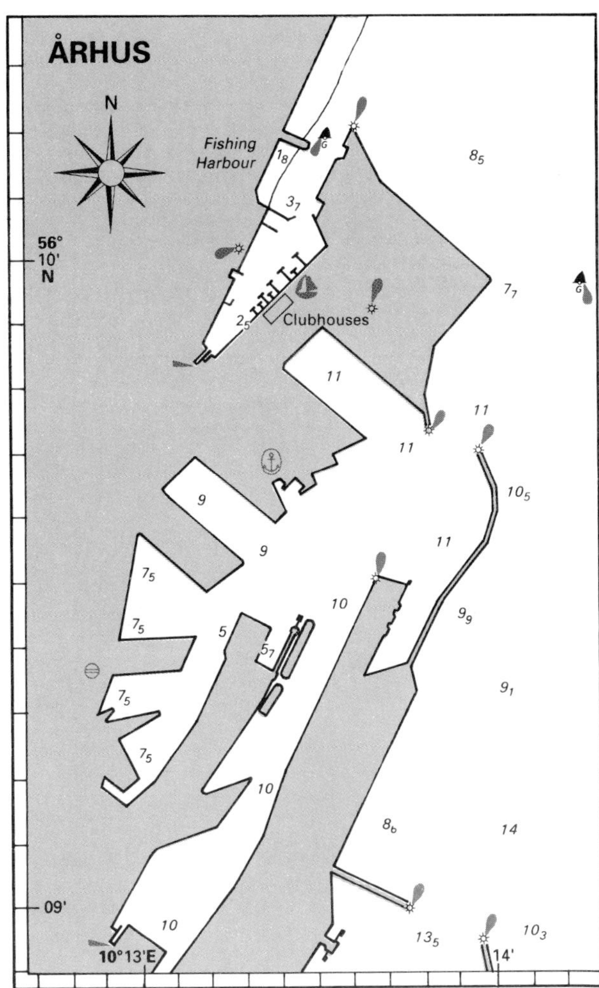

⛵ Lystbåde-Fiskerihavn (2–4m, D★), with about 500 pleasure-craft spaces, is the northernmost harbour in Århus, approached from the E along and slightly N of the 56°10'N parallel (Ryes Flak, a 3·4m shoal, lies to the N). The isophase lights in line from offshore lead to the wall of the container terminal S of the Lystbådehavn entrance. The NE-facing yacht-haven entrance has a F.R light on the E mole (a conspicuous round red-and-white-banded tower); the moorings are on the E dockside. The city centre is close by, with restaurants, museums, theatres, cathedral, and bus and railway stations. There is a ferry from Århus harbour to Kalundborg on Fyn island.

→ For the newcomer, the route northwards which provides peace of mind lies eastwards from the entrance outside Ryes Flak, following the lit buoys northwards in the deep water midway between Skødshoved point and the mainland.

EGÅ MARINA

⛵ The entrance to Egå Marina's (2·2–2·7m, PD★) forest of masts (600 places) is slightly N of centre in its outer wall. There are a F.G and a F.R light on the W and E sides respectively of this north-facing entrance, which is also N of a conspicuous triangular building on the outer mole. It is approached directly from S of a yellow (unlit) buoy SE of the entrance in 3m (plus) of water, turning hard to port to enter.

→ The yellow buoy SE of Egå entrance is the SW marker of a number of yellow buoys which mark the corner of a rectangular prohibited area right across the deep part (10–24m) of the entrance to Kalø Vig. Many local yachts and fishing boats appear to ignore this prohibition, but it is necessary to warn visitors. This was, unfortunately in such a scenic area, a Second World War explosives-dumping ground. Under engine, by careful compass work and sounding, small vessels can enter the bay by keeping

Århus. Looking across to the yacht harbour from the fishing harbour.

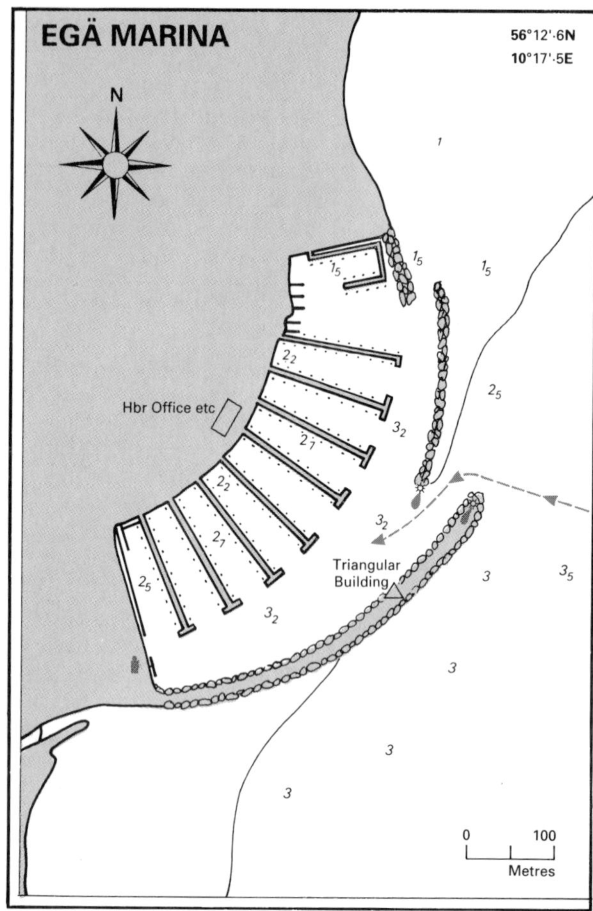

Egå marina. *Kylora* beneath the demasting facilities.

just outside the two NE-trending lines of yellow buoys on either side of the area in around 3–4m of water. Skødshoved Flak at the NE end is tricky, but there is a green as well as a yellow buoy here. There is a similarly tricky spit from the W shore at the northern end, but again there is a red (lit) buoy to mark this. From this buoy the deep water can be followed and Kaløvig yacht haven entered from the E.

KALØVIG

⛵ Kaløvig (2·5–3m, PD*) is another marina (500 spaces) with a north-facing entrance and lights on each mole, approached in 3m (plus) of water. There are prominent chimneys close N of the harbour.

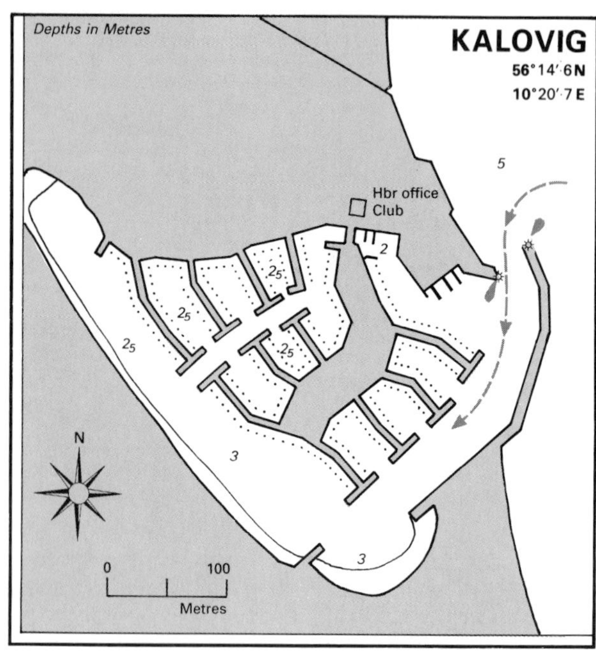

→ A Kalø Vig bay is virtually landlocked, with rolling, protective wooded hills. It has wide shoal areas around it, including several subsidiary coves, in most of which there are many good anchoring possibilities in 2–4m on a bottom varying from sand to mud and clay. The water in the area is surprisingly clear. The main anchorages are at Løgten Bugt in the N of the bay, in Egens Vig just S of the yacht haven at Nappedam (see approach to Nappedam below), and on the S shores of Knebel Vig. The last-named cove has a narrow, slightly tricky entrance with a small green buoy (keep to starboard entering), and has to be approached from north-eastwards, sounding to stay in the deep water (over 6m) between the shoal patches on each side. There is a landing stage in the SE of the bay with pleasant walks around it.

13M

NAPPEDAM

⛵ Nappedam (1–3m, D*) is a medium-sized yacht haven in Egens Vig. It must be approached through the S entrance to the cove, close past the Fl.R light on the red dolphin (leave to port) in the narrow approach channel. Continue NNE directly to the east-facing harbour entrance (F.R light on S mole).

In heading S out of Kalø Vig, the prohibited area has to be negotiated, again close to the green (unlit) buoy off Skødshoved point shoals. Continue to the green (lit) buoy in deep water E of Ryes Flak.

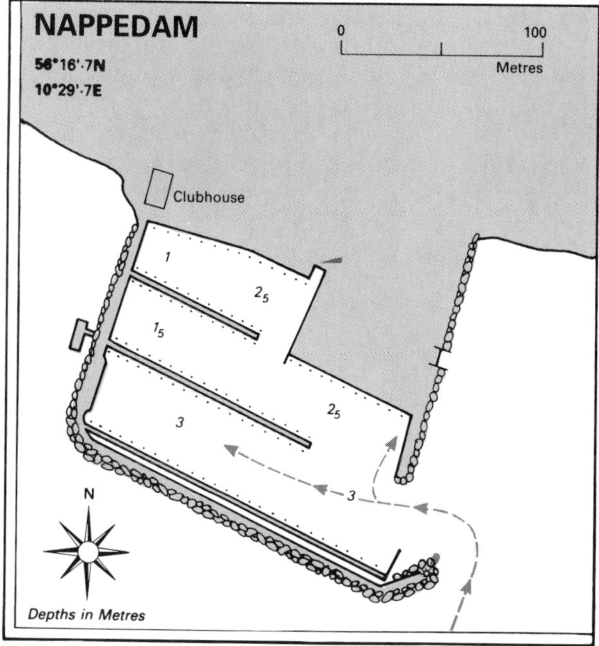

⛵ **Skødshoved** (1·2–1·5m) is a small, shallow harbour mainly for shoal-draught boats, with only 1·5m in the entrance. It is approached from the SW, taking frequent soundings to avoid the outlier of Skødshoved shoal to port. There is a hill on Skødshoved headland.

BEGTRUP VIG AND EBELTOFT VIG

Anchoring and fishing are banned in two areas well offshore on each side of Mols Hoved point. The latter is backed by 79m-high ground. There is a shoal (5·6m) in the middle of Begtrup Vig. Mols Hoved point should be rounded about 0·8M off.

⚓ In Begtrup Vig in a natural harbour NE of the tiny Rønnen island, or alternatively in the NW corner of Begtrup Vig (both sand, 3–4m depths, but watch out for stones and rocks close inshore at Rønnen).

→ The route then leads round the Helgenæs peninsula, which is fairly steep-to. From the W, the church and mill and Sletterhage sector light (round white tower) are the most prominent landmarks in the peninsula. Ebeltoft Vig is then entered through the narrow channel between Helgenæs and the Skadegrund shoal (2 offlying cardinal buoys), and course is set for the anchorages or either of the two yacht harbours. Ebeltoft Vig light, at the head of the bay, has narrow sectors, useful for approach at night from either side of Skadegrund, with the central red sector covering most of this shoal and several different-coloured sectors on each side to help clear the two shoal areas, on each shore of the bay. Approach Ebeltoft yacht haven round the green (unlit) buoy marking the NW corner of the Sandhagen shoal, off Ahlhage point with its grove of trees.

⚓ On the W coast of Ebeltoft Vig there are several anchorages, but N of Bogens Hoved is the most convenient for shore expeditions to the Mols hills (3–4m, sand, watch out for stones inshore along this stretch of coast).

32M

EBELTOFT

⛵ Ebeltoft yacht haven (2–3m, PD*) is S of both the commercial harbour and the tiny fishing harbour. There are two possible approaches: a southern route with red lights in line (104°) towards the fishing harbour entrance; and a northern route with green lights in line (143°) towards the commercial harbour entrance. In each case pleasure craft wishing to enter the yacht harbour, which is at the southern end of this group of three harbours, must turn southwards about 150m off either the commercial or the fishing harbour entrances and follow the harbour wall, keeping about 150m offshore in 2–3m, doglegging northwards round into the (lit) yacht harbour entrance.

Ebeltoft is a small, extremely attractive, mainly half-timbered medieval town with a tiny 16th-century town hall. In the harbour the 19th-century auxiliary-engined sailing frigate *Jylland* is being reconstructed; it is well worth visiting. Near the ferry terminal close along the coast is a 'windmill park' of modern wind generators. The ferry goes to Sjællands Odde on the NW extremity of Sjælland.

Southernmost approach I would not recommend this (red lights in line) approach to the newcomer – this is only for the locals. The first part of this route is from the W, keeping close N of the two offlying G (unlit) buoys marking the N edge of Sandhagen shoals, and at the second of these buoys keeping a 104° course along the line of the F.R lights leading to the fishing harbour entrance – but we found that although this misses the Sandhagen shoals to the south, it leads directly across a 1·8m shoal patch with fishing stakes and flagged fishing buoys obstructing the route and diverting vessels off the leading line into shallow water.

Northernmost approach This route (green lights final approach) would seem to be much better for a new visitor. The approach starts from 8 cables NE of the first Sandhagen shoal buoy, then heads on 115° towards the red and green unlit buoys marking the outer end of the entrance channel to the commercial harbour. In this NE corner of the bay there are four named shoal patches and this recommended approach is approximately between the two southernmost (unmarked) shoals, Pikkelgrund (2·5m depth) and Pilken (5·6m depth), keeping just north of the latter. At the two commercial harbour channel buoys turn into the channel directly towards the commercial harbour entrance (143° green lights in line), and finally turn southwards about 150m off the entrance to follow the harbour wall past the fishing harbour entrance and down to the yacht harbour entrance.

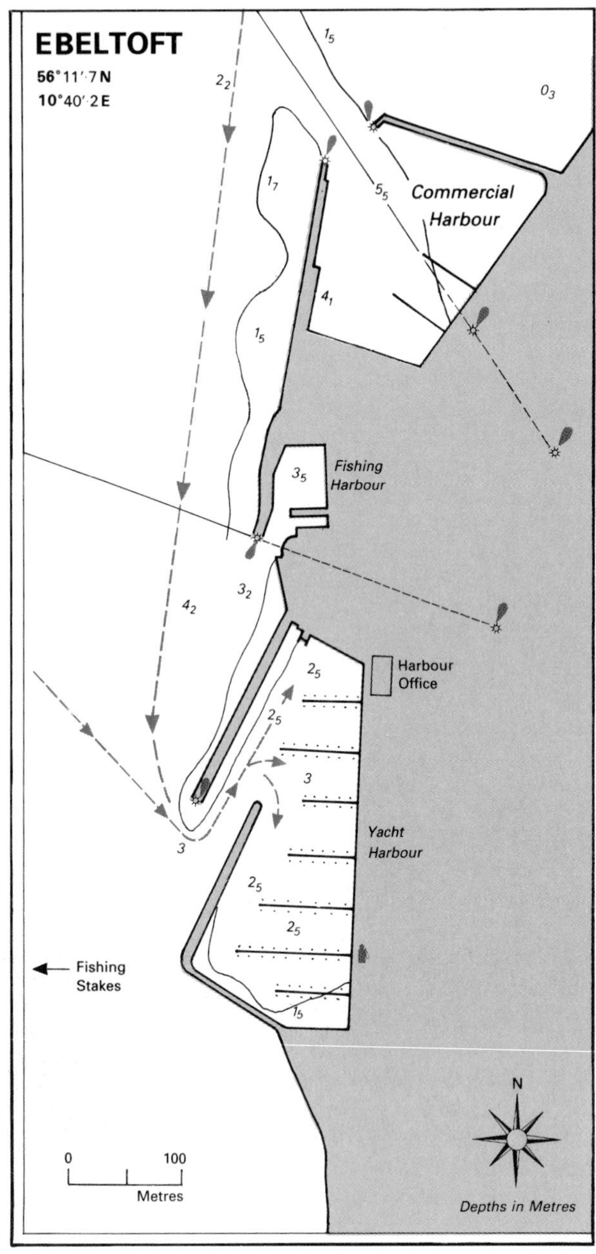

Hjelm Island.

→ Leave Ebeltoft round the outside of the Sandhage green buoys. Round the ferry harbour and the Gåsehage peninsula at about 0·8M offshore, inside the Øreflak shoal (4·3–6m), but heading S of and giving a wide berth to the small isolated Klokkegrund shoal (2·3m) to the SE of the Hasenør point, marked by an unlit green buoy on its E side. Take a northerly course along Hjelm Dyb in deep water (20m plus). At night a narrow-sectored light on Hjelm island (small, conspicuous, partly wooded, with the light's white tower on top, very useful for daylight pilotage as well) can be used to navigate between Gåsehage and the Øreflak, or to take the route round outside the Øreflak, where there is a lit buoy.

Before leaving Ebeltoft Vig the highly modern Øer yacht haven (1·5–3·5m, D★) can be approached from a RW offing buoy (unlit) along a 600m-long buoyed (unlit) 3·5m-deep channel (3kn maximum speed). This is E of the large ferry harbour, so beware of the ferries. Entrance, in daytime only in summer, is via a 200m canal and a lock by the harbourmaster's office, where a signal mast displays 3 black balls or 3 red lights when approach to the canal is prohibited (vessels already in the canal when the signal is given are allowed through). Contact can be made with the harbourmaster on VHF Ch 16.

DJURSLAND PENINSULA COAST

The current offshore is predominantly northerly except in strong westerly winds, when it can be reversed.

This is an extremely exposed coast in weather from the two eastern quadrants, and through into part of the SW and NW quadrants at the southern and northern ends where the coast turns. The windfetch across the Kattegat from Sweden and Sjælland is 20–30M.

→ The 20M passage from Gåsehage to Grenå should be made well offshore of the hilly coast in deep water (20m plus), keeping inshore of the 2 red (lit) buoys marking the outlying shoals of the Hjelm Banke and offshore of the unlit buoys marking the mainland shoals of Jessens Grund and Haveknude. From the last of these a course along the 10m contour picks up the offing buoy E of the yacht haven at Grenå. Be sure to keep clear of the Naveren shoal (1·3m) protruding eastwards from shore 1,500m S of the yacht haven.

29M
GRENÅ HAVN

Grenå Sportboothafen (2–3·2m, PD★) entrance is 1,200m S of the main harbour entrance, facing NE with lights on each side (3·5m deep in entrance but around 2·5m just outside). It is best approached from the NE, i.e. from N of the offing buoy. Grenå Havn sector lights are on the ends of the E and W

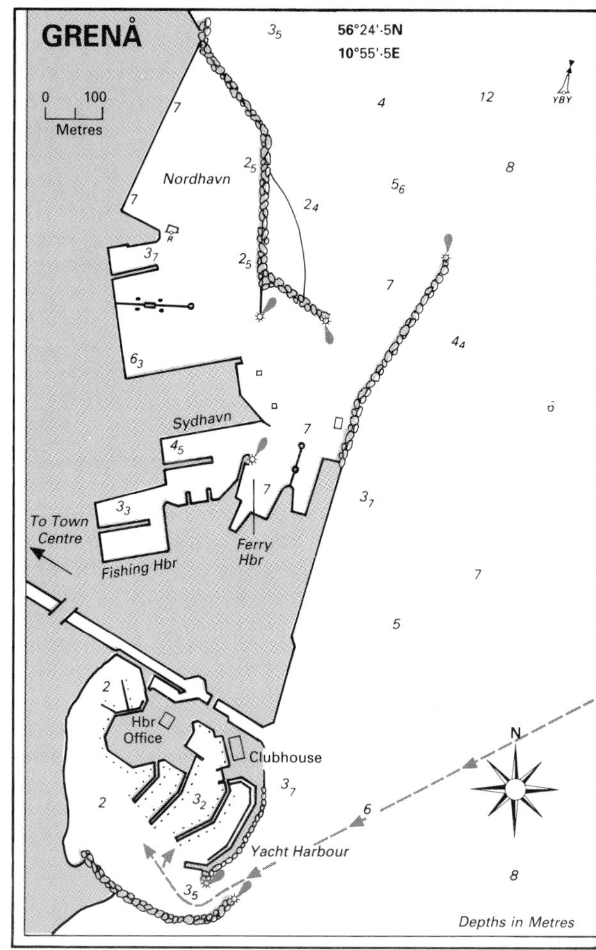

Grenå yacht harbour entrance.

moles of the commercial harbour; the white, red, green and red sectors of the E light are crossed in sequence when approaching the yacht-haven entrance. Fornæs light (23M range, round stone tower) is on the prominent headland some 2M N of the harbour. The yacht haven's entrance is well S of all the chimneys and has squat GW and RW entrance towers, not to be confused with the similar towers of the main harbour entrance to the N.

Grenå is a pleasant historic ferry town and holiday resort, with half-timbered houses, a museum and a good shopping centre, but all at some distance from the marina. However, there is a bus service from the harbour as well as a useful free municipal bicycle-lending service, whereby these (green) machines can be collected from and left at a wide range of places in open racks (including one near the marina), with no need to return them to the original pick-up point. The ferry harbour is not far from the yacht haven; there are ferries to Anholt island, to Hundested at the entrance to the Isefjord on Sjælland, and to Halmstad and Varberg in Sweden.

DIVERSION TO ANHOLT ISLAND

Anholt island, in its nodal position in the centre of the Kattegat, is an interesting diversion from the route. It was captured and occupied by the British in 1809–11 and, in one of the island's leafy lanes, there is a memorial to the Danish fallen. Although the heavy pine forests of the early 19th century have disappeared, there are still many delightful mixed woodland areas as well as dazzling sandy beaches to be visited on bicycles hired at the harbour. Nordbjerg, the hill behind the harbour, is well worth climbing for its view.

Anholt harbour from the Nordbjerg.

Anholt harbour. Its radar tower can be seen a long way offshore.

Anholt harbour (1·5–3·7m, PD*) has about 250 places, but without stern posts, so lying to kedge anchors is encouraged, although rafting out occurs to a lesser extent with the larger vessels. It has an easy (in moderate winds) SW-facing entrance, approached in 5m of water from the W. A white radar pillar on the hill behind can be seen from well offshore, and there is a round red light tower with a sector light on the end of the N mole. It is a straightforward 27M NE of Grenå entrance (not included in the overall route distance in the commentary at the beginning of this chapter).

However, a warning – in anything from Force 5 upwards onshore winds can make the 5m approach across the underwater 'plateau' surrounding the island very uncomfortable indeed, and on our visit a crowd of Swedish, Norwegian, German and Danish yachts from all corners of the Kattegat were pinned in the harbour for two days by strong westerlies. The blood sport of the less intrepid yachtsmen was to line the inner harbour wall and watch the occasional intrepid yacht plunging into the short steep seas and taking the shortest possible route out to the 6m contour.

→ Return to the offing buoy, then head northwards in deep water round Fornæs point. From this headland to Bønnerup harbour there are extensive shoals with irregular depths (5·3–7·7m), extending out from Gjerrild's Flak, with a sector light (11M range) on Knudshoved point. There are also many fish traps inshore. In onshore winds this is an extremely uncomfortable sea area, and even in offshore winds there can be considerable swell. A 2·5M offing just outside the 6m contour is about right in good weather conditions; close in to 1M approaching Bønnerup, after rounding the buoy marking the N edge of Stavnshoved Rev.

The tiny fishing harbour of **Bønnerup** (2·8– 4m, PD) has a lit outer entrance, facing due N, which is approached in 3m depth from the N. In strong onshore winds it should be avoided; there are rocks and stones in the shallows to the W of the harbour. There is a second inner entrance, from which additional port and starboard entrances open up into the E and W basins. Visitors' moorings (2·8m) are in the SW basin (the Gæstehavn); larger yachts can arrange deeper berths elsewhere with the harbourmaster.

ÅLBORG BUGT

The underlying currents in Ålborg Bugt are weak and tidal, setting S with the flood and N with the ebb, but winds distort this regime. The predominant current is westerly along the N coast of Djursland and northerly in the Bugt, and only in strong westerly winds are these directions reversed.

The southern bight into which the Mariager and Randers fjords debouch is exposed to the NE wind quadrant but is otherwise well protected. Both fjords are extremely well sheltered inland.

The coast further N is exposed to both NE and SE quadrants as far as the approaches to Læso, whose extensive shoals give some easterly protection. Strong easterlies can create a dangerous swell over the extensive area of less-than-10m soundings in the southern approaches to the Limfjord entrance.

→ The route to the Randers Fjord RW (lit) offing buoy is protected by the Tangen bank (buoyed, unlit on its S side, and as little as 2·3m in places) and Boels Plade bank (5m) to the N, and by the Djursland coast to the S. Passage should be made in 7–8m of water. The narrow coloured sectors of Udbyhøj light (on the gable of a white building) make pilotage towards the buoy and keeping off the shoals easier. The main hazard is a visible wreck about 1M W of Bønnerup near the 4m contour so make a good offing on leaving the harbour. There is a triangular firing range, Hevring Flak, to the S of the Randers approach, marked by yellow buoys, but the approach route should easily avoid this.

*32M (*Udbyhøj Nord)

RANDERS FJORD

→ The fjord is 15M long, extremely shallow (less than 1m in many places outside the main channel), and a minimum of 22m wide. It winds through reed-edged fields, and contains a multitude of fishing stakes, in many places outside but close to the channel, which is dredged (7m) and closely buoyed (some lit), beaconed and withied along the whole route to Randers. This is a motoring run for most cruising yachts, and a reliable engine and a motoring cone (when under sail) are essential. Pleasure craft should give way and if necessary stop to let commercial vessels by in this narrow channel. There is little space in any of the small harbours and no large marina.

The entrance to the fjord is in the dip between the gentle slopes of Udbyhøj and Sødring hills. Entrance or departure can be extremely uncomfortable in strong easterly winds across the 6–7m approach shoals. Because of the commercial shipping and the associated careful dredging, the directional lighting of this entrance channel, which loops in a U-bend round Udbyhøj point, is complicated. At night the lights can be extremely confusing, so read your chart carefully. In daylight follow the buoys carefully.

From the offing buoy there is a closely buoyed (unlit) dredged (7m) offshore channel S of westwards, with isophase lights in line. The Melbank light (Fl(2)R) is on a post at the end of this fetch. Make a slight turn to N of westwards into the entrance, with isophase red lights in line both astern and ahead and another light on a post (Fl(2)G, the Mellempolde), then a further slight adjustment northwards along the eastern white sector of the coloured-sector light close W of the northern fishing harbour. Turn round the U-bend to head southwestwards close W of the fishing harbour, following the narrow western white sector of the same light, and carry on southwards along several series of leading lights, including a canalised section, along the channel as far as Uggelhuse. The leading red triangle marks of all the lights in line are extremely large and easy to see in daylight (in good visibility) along all these stretches.

Pleasure craft can bypass the canal to its W, starting at a GRG post just off the N end of the canal and continuing along a narrow but very easy to follow 2·2–3·6m-deep channel marked by pairs of tiny yellow port and starboard can and cone buoys. From Uggelhuse westwards the main channel is narrow and the buoys (many lit) are close to the land. This stretch of fjord is surrounded by reeds and is reminiscent of the Norfolk Broads.

In calm weather there is a six-hourly ebb (up to 4kn) and flood (up to 2·5kn) in the entrance, disrupted by bad weather. In the fjord proper there is a prevailing stream, strongest in the fairway. Strong northerlies increase the water level at Randers by up to 1·5m and southerlies reduce it by up to 0·9m.

⛵ All of the harbours are small and (apart from two) entered directly from the fairway. The fishing harbour on the N side of the entrance, **Udbyhøj Nord** (1·5–2·2m, D), has a lit entrance but very limited space, and is shallow at the landing stages (1·5–1·7m). The yacht haven, **Udbyhøj Syd** (2m), has an unlit entrance and also very limited space. **Mellerup** (1·5–2m, PD), at the end of the canal on the W bank, has a few more spaces, a 2m-deep lateral system, a post-marked approach channel and a lit entrance. **Voer** (4·5m landing wharf), with very few spaces, is a little further S on the opposite bank; a ferry plies to Mellerup from the S side of this wharf. **Uggelhuse** (2m, P), on the S bank at the S bend, is unlit and a little smaller than Udbyhøj Sud. **Dronningborg** (2·3m, unlit entrance), on the N bank just before Randers, is the largest yacht haven in the fjord and has a 3m-deep withied approach channel.

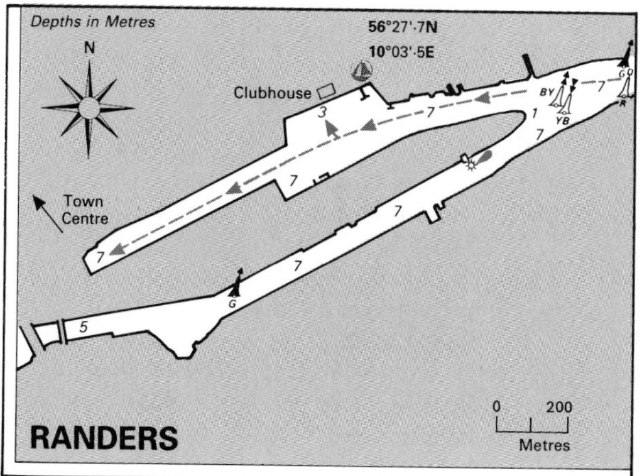

Hobro Sejlklubs Havn. Head of Mariager Fjord.

⚓ The only place one can anchor inside the fjord is on either side of the Raden channel (2–3m), W of the 1·1M-long canalised section, marked by yellow buoys in summer (1 April to 15 November). Keep well clear of the Mellerup ferry crossing in the S.

15M
RANDERS

⛵ Randers yacht haven (2m, PD), on the N side of the dredged (7m) harbour, is somewhat smaller than Dronningborg. Large yachts can lie in deeper water near the head of the commercial harbour close to town (small yachts could risk this too). Though industrial close to the harbour wharves, the nearby town has an elegant town hall, old buildings, precinct shopping and squares, a 15th-century church and a museum – we were there in May for the town's 'Clown Fest', a cheerful romp dating from medieval times. A historic railway runs to Mariager.

→ Return by the same route to the entrance offing buoy. A northeasterly course from here, over or round the end of Boels Plade and E of the cardinal-marked (unlit) Boels Rev, leads to the outermost green (lit) buoy of four leading to the Mariager entrance channel.

15M (Als Odde)
MARIAGER FJORD

↳ Inside the entrance in calm weather there are ebb and flood streams which can reach 3–4kn, but further inland there is little or no tidal effect.

→ One of Jutland's most picturesque fjords, Mariager is around 21M long, with Norfolk Broads scenery near the entrance but beautiful rolling wooded hills beyond. Like the Randers entrance, possibly more so since it is shallower, Mariager's entrance channel can be extremely rough to negotiate in either direction in strong easterlies (on one departure I made, the combination of adverse wind, current and short steep waves cut down my motoring speed with a 50hp engine in a 10m boat to around 1·5kn). The largest harbour in the fjord has only about 150 boxes, so you should be prepared to anchor if necessary, or moor in the commercial harbour at the head.

Fishing stakes and traps abound, particularly near Hadsund.

From the northernmost green (lit) buoy (3M offshore) of a group of four offshore buoys, the channel is buoyed (unlit), with sets of lights in line throughout the fjord to Hobro, lit beacons in some places and very clear leading red triangle marks. As in Randers, pleasure craft should keep out of the way of commercial vessels.

⚓ From the entrance to about 3M above Hadsund the channel winds amongst wide sandflats and drying areas, with a few possibilities for (but little appeal in) anchoring. Below this there are around 7M of deeper (10m plus) water, with plenty of 2–4m anchoring possibilities in the many bays, mainly over mud. A few examples: Ovegarde bay, SW of Dania cement works; Hollet, N or W of Langsodde point (NW of Mariager); the bay S of Bramslev 2M below Hobro.

✎ Hadsund railway bridge opens from sunrise to sunset plus half an hour during the week, but at weekends there are occasional periods of an hour when the bridge does not open, and it is always advisable to telephone on approach. There are traffic lights. The signal to request passage is the N flag, or use VHF Ch 16 (12 and 13 working).

Als Odde is a small landing stage (2m) on the N bank at the entrance. **Hadsund Fiskerihavn** (1·5m, PD) is below the bridge on the N bank, and a deeper mooring is beyond the bridge at **Hadsund yacht haven** (1·8–2·5m, PD*). Hadsund is a small industrial town with good shopping facilities.

Kongsdal (2m) is a small yacht haven on the S bank E of the Dania cement works, with an outstanding turf cutout of a yacht on the hill behind and a buoyed entrance channel. Vive, on the N bank opposite the Dania cement works, is a tiny shallow harbour (1m inside, 1·2–1·8m on outer wall). Yet further down on the N bank beyond the anchorage (see above), **Høllet's** landing stage has 2–2·5m depth.

Mariager is a small yacht haven (1–2m, PD) on the S bank, approached from between a red and a green buoy. There is a F.G light on the N mole, but depths are below 2m at the S end of the harbour. The old yacht haven to the S (east-facing entrance) has 3·7m depth but very little space. This small town is noted for its roses and half-timbered buildings as well as for its museum.

21M

HOBRO

→ A 33m-clearance overhead cable crosses the fjord 2·7M below Hobro. Visitors are advised to keep in or near to the buoyed channel in these final reaches. Hobro Sejlklub Havn (1·8–3·5m, PD), on

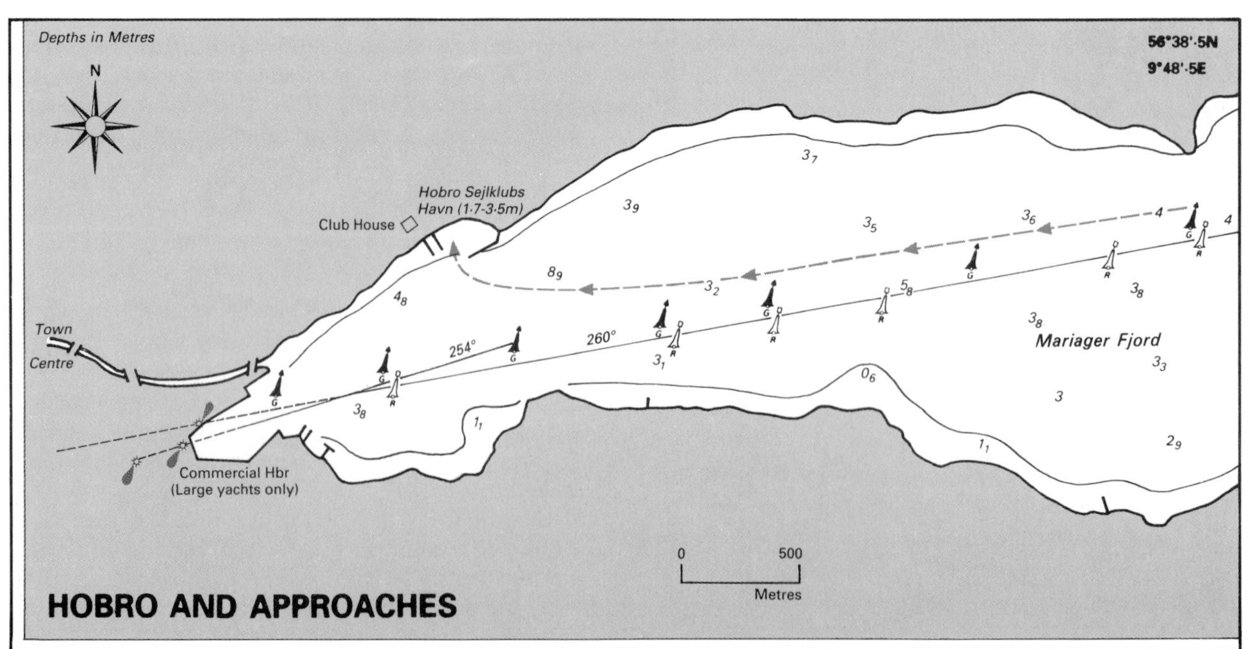

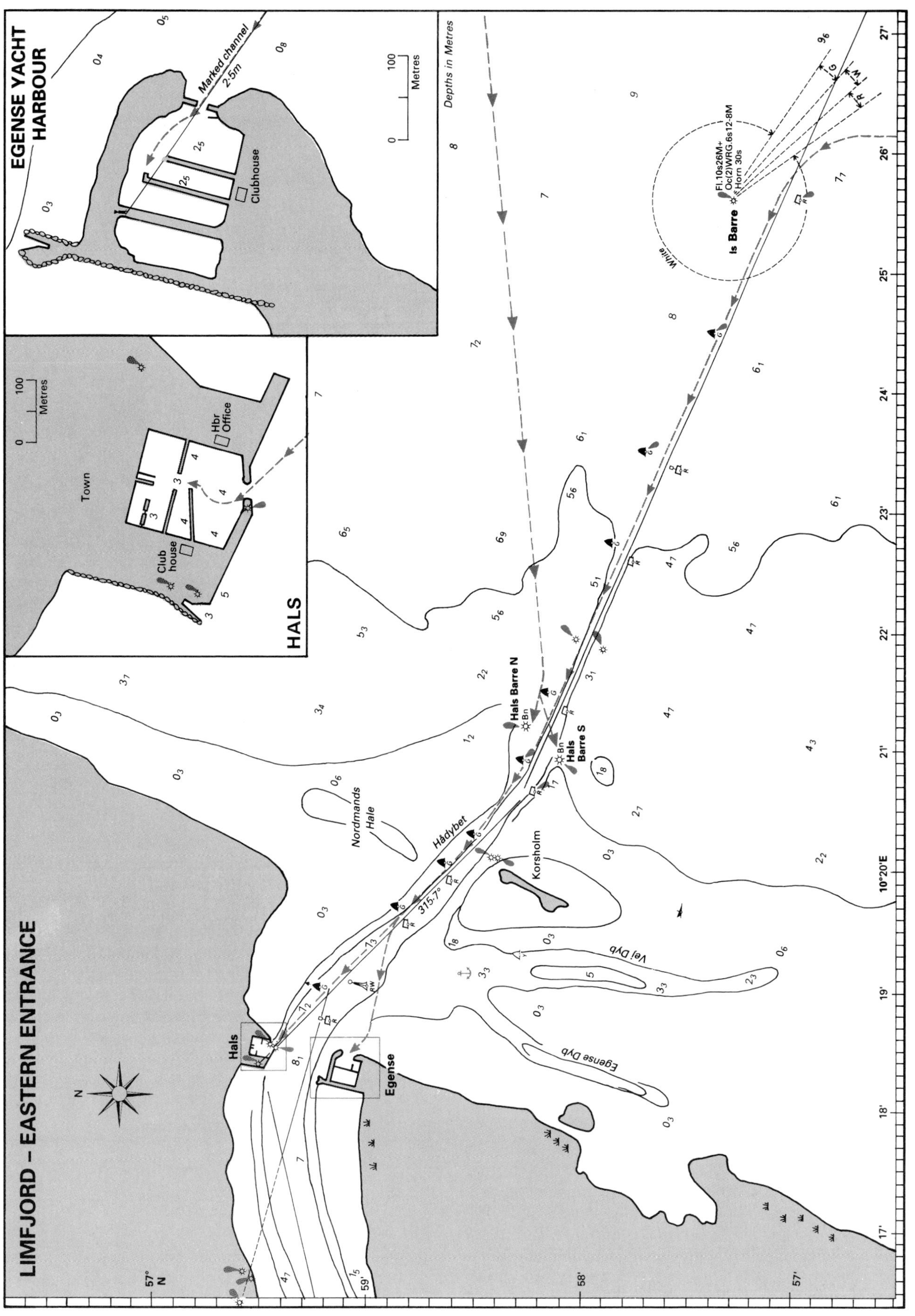
LIMFJORD – EASTERN ENTRANCE
EGENSE YACHT HARBOUR
Marked channel 2·5m
Clubhouse
Metres
HALS
Town
Hbr Office
Club house
Depths in Metres
Is Barre
Fl.10s26M+
Oc(2)WRG.6s12-8M
Horn 30s
White
Hals Barre N
Hals Barre S
Hådybet
Nordmands Hale
Korsholm
315·7°
Vej Dyb
Egense Dyb
Hals
Egense

the N bank just before the head of the fjord, is easily approached in 4m and more from the fairway, but the entrance is unlit. Large yachts can continue on and tie alongside in deep water in the Handelshafen with the agreement of the harbourmaster.

Hobro town has an impressive 19th-century church and a museum with finds from Fyrkat, a circular Viking stronghold whose remains are 2M to the SW. There are fine views down the hill from the railway station.

Return by same route to the entrance and carry on out to the green (lit) offing buoy.

Entrance to Hals. Eastern end of Limfjord.

ÅLBORG BUGT

W In strong easterlies on an open reach or a run this 7m-deep offshore passage can be extremely uncomfortable, and it is definitely to be avoided in force 6 or more winds.

→ The course is virtually due N, in about 7m of water throughout, to the conspicuous Hals Barre light (26M range, red tower with white band, floodlit). To the E of this approach route there is a lit, buoyed channel from Svitringen Rende S light to Hals Barre light, so watch out for commercial shipping.

Hals Barre light tower, Limfjord eastern approach, 26M range.

⛵ There is one small fishing harbour on this coast, at **Øster Hurup** (2–2·8m, PD, lit), about 6M N of Mariager entrance. Its east-facing entrance is entered directly from offshore.

58M
LIMFJORD ENTRANCE

Approach

The lit buoyed channel, with two sets of lights in line leading into the entrance, starts 1M SE of Hals Barre light. Small vessels can keep just outside this channel until they reach the entrance buoys just E of the Hals Barre N (green) and Hals Barre S (red) towers, where the dredged channel (10·1–10·4m) cuts through the shoals screening the entrance. From here it is necessary to keep inside the channel (Hådybet) between the Nordmans Hage and Korsholm drying patches.

⚓ There is a well sheltered anchorage over sand in about 4m to the W of Korsholm and S of the main channel in Vejdyb (N of the main channel is a drying area).

⛵ **Egense yacht haven** (2·5m, D*), on the S side of the entrance, is approached along a withied channel (2·5m), the outside end of which has (from 1 April to 15 November) a red and a green buoy and beyond these a RW offing buoy at the edge of the main channel. The entrance is unlit and the harbour is remote from any town, but it has more spaces than Hals. **Hals** (3–4m, PD), the fishing harbour on the N side of the entrance, has somewhat less space, but has a directly entered lit entrance, as well as an interesting town with ruined fortifications, including a magazine and arsenal. There is a ferry between the two harbours.

DIVERSION TO LÆSO ISLAND

The harbour of Vesterø (2·9m, PD, with something under 200 spaces; not included in total distance in this passage), on the island of Læso, is just over 30M from the Limfjord entrance via the Læso Rende channel and round the Læso reef at the W end of the island. A more direct approach route is from Frederikshavn Seesporthafen, a mere 15M to the NW of Vesterø, or from Sæby, only 13M westwards. As at Anholt, approach to this entrance in strong onshore winds is to be avoided. There is a ferry from Frederikshavn to Vesterø.

HARBOURS NORTH FROM LIMFJORD ENTRANCE

In addition to Læso Island, there are nine other harbours on Jutland's east coast. All are directly entered from the sea and any pilotage problems stem from weather conditions rather than tricky navigation: the offshore ground is undulating between 2m and 10m with buoys near shallows; some harbours are shallow in approach and very difficult in lee-shore conditions. In succession northwards along the 50M of coastline from the Limfjord entrance their main features are listed below, with five clustered around the largest town, Frederikshavn.

Hou. Tiny fishing/pleasure boat harbour, 1·8m at lit entrance, 2m inside.

Aså. In addition to fishing harbour there is a small yacht harbour, 2·5m depth, 2m lit and buoyed approach.

Sæby. Fishing and yacht harbour with 200 berths, 2·5m, lit entrance, 4m approach.

Frederikshavn. Large commercial and ferry harbour not recommended for yachts. Frederikshavn Seesporthavn, with 350 yacht berths, 1–2m depths and a 2m approach, is close S of the commercial harbour, at Stadtrand.

Rønnerhavnen. 500-berth recently built marina, lit entrance, 2·5m depths, but 1·5–2m approach.

Strandby. Large fishing harbour but with few visitors berths, 3·5–4m, lit entrance, 4m approach.

Hirsholm (island). Good for easterly conditions. West-facing small fishing harbour on a 3·5M-long picturesque nature reserve island. 22M light, 3m approach, lit entrance and 2–3m depths but very few berths at a pontoon behind N mole.

Albæk. Tiny fishing/pleasure boat harbour, lit entrance, only 1·5m depth and 1·8m approach.

Skagen. Major fishing/commercial harbour. Depths and approach 4–6m, succession of three lit entrances, two major lights on the peninsula to the north. Yacht facilities west of Gamle pier. Good base for North Sea or Kattegat crossing.

7. The Limfjord

Route 5
A cruise round the Limfjord

Commentary

According to the Admiralty *Pilot*, 'W of Ålborg the Limfjord is not suitable for navigation by ocean-going vessels'. This is due to depths of as little as 4m in parts of the main fairway.

This fjord is therefore a peaceful as well as a sheltered and varied pleasure-craft cruising ground, with its labyrinth of islands, broads, fjords, heathlands, rolling farmland, woods, sand cliffs and beaches, many places of geological and historic interest, with accompanying museums, and at least 30 yacht harbours (at last count!), of which six have more than 200 spaces each.

There are countless anchoring possibilities, mainly in the middle reaches between Løgstør and the Oddesund and usually in 2–4m depths over sand, mud or clay. Vessels should be aware of wildlife when passing through the nature reserves, and try to avoid anchoring there (they are marked *Vildtreservat* in green and sometimes have green pecked lines around them on the Danish charts).

Wind generators (marked by a small circle on a post on the Danish charts) provide so many long-distance landmarks in the Limfjord that the route description below mentions them only occasionally, but it is useful to note them from the chart during passage, although new ones are springing up so frequently that many may not yet have been charted.

Throughout the area, watch out for fishing stakes near the headlands and shoals.

As in much of the rest of Denmark, some entrance-channel buoys for the smaller yacht harbours and most of the Dansk Sejlunion mooring buoys in recommended anchorages are laid only in the season (usually 4 April-15 November); the positions and dates of these buoys are marked on the charts.

Although many of the smaller harbours have limited numbers of spare boxes for visitors, it is often possible to raft out on the walls of fishing harbours, or of course to anchor off or not far away from harbours and landing places. Even the smallest of yacht harbours has a 'kiosk' where milk and food can be obtained. We found several of the larger marinas half-empty during our 1993 visit, since Denmark, like many other EU countries, was in recession. 'There is no money in Denmark', said one Dane. These spacious marinas can therefore usually look after a boat for a month or two in summer or over winter at reasonable rates.

Distance

Hals and return 283M.
Hals-Thyborøn 176M outwards via southern fjords.

Depths/water levels

See also Appendix IV

The maximum draught I would recommend for visiting most places in the area is about 1·5m, although 1·3–1·4m is more comfortable in some of the smaller harbours and channels. These are sometimes only 1·5 to 2m deep, and even this often depends on frequency of dredging. The tidal range, though small, can be significant in such places. Watch out for shallow and drying patches in the harbours, particularly on the inshore sides. Wind conditions can also, of course, cause vessels to ground in some harbours. A final warning: as for all of these routes in the SW Baltic, do not assume that the charted dredged depths of any of the shallower *rende* channels are accurate at time of sailing – actual depths are often less.

The Danish charts with their 2/4/6/10m contours (below mean sea level) show depths of between 6m and 10m over much of the through route in this area. In the eastern part of this main fairway, however, there is a 4m-dredged marked channel across Løgstør Grunde which is liable to silting. In the western part there is a 4–6m patch S of Jegindø island, and beyond this in Nissum Bredning there is another 4m-dredged channel, Sælhundeholm Løb, approaching Thybøren from the S, which is also liable to silting.

Tidal range is small and wind effect upon water levels is important (*see also Appendix IV, Route 5*):

Tidal range At Thyborøn the mean tidal range is 0·5m and at the Ålborg end of the fjord it is 0·3m. Some of the harbours in the southern offshoots of the fjord have tidal ranges of just over 1m.

Wind In mainly (not entirely) NW–SW-quadrant winds water levels can be raised by up to 0·5 to 1·9m, and in NE–SE-quadrant (again not entirely) winds they can be lowered by 0·5m to 1·5m, often completely overriding the tidal effect.

Currents

There are noticeable six-hourly tidal streams in the Thyborøn Kanal (up to 2·5kn) and near Ålborg (up to 2kn), but not in the wide bays and broads of the central fjord. Winds are the prime current generators, and even at each of the entrances persistent winds in one direction can override the tidal stream

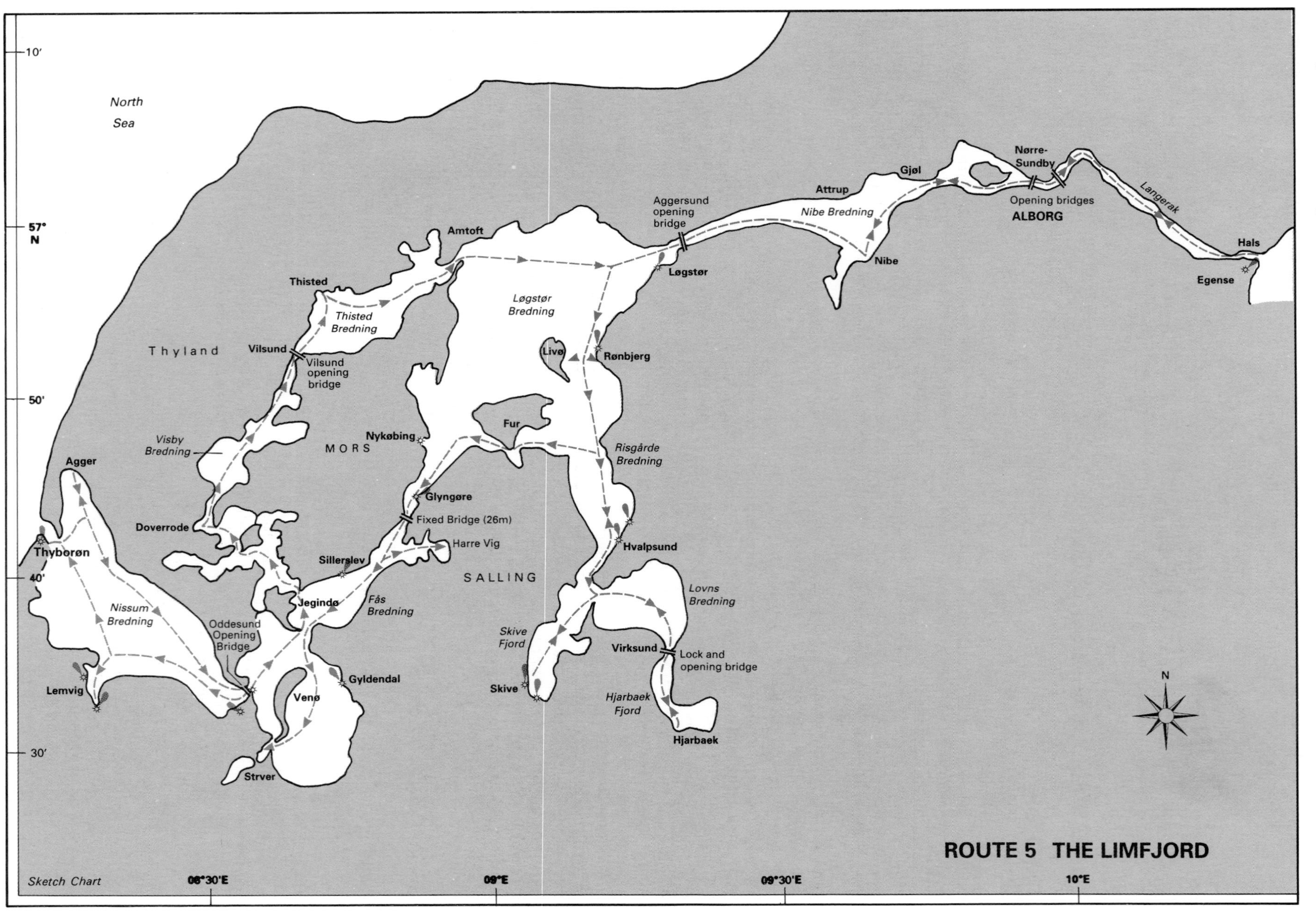
ROUTE 5 THE LIMFJORD
Sketch Chart
N
North Sea
Thyland
MORS
SALLING
Hals
Egense
Langerak
Nørre-Sundby
Opening bridges
ALBORG
Gjøl
Nibe
Attrup
Nibe Bredning
Aggersund opening bridge
Løgstør
Rønbjerg
Livø
Løgstør Bredning
Risgårde Bredning
Hvalpsund
Lovns Bredning
Virksund
Lock and opening bridge
Hjarbaek
Hjarbaek Fjord
Fur
Skive
Skive Fjord
Amtoft
Glyngøre
Fixed Bridge (26m)
Harre Vig
Nykøbing
Thisted
Thisted Bredning
Vilsund
Vilsund opening bridge
Fås Bredning
Sillerslev
Jegindø
Gyldendal
Venø
Strver
Oddesund Opening Bridge
Visby Bredning
Doverrode
Nissum Bredning
Agger
Thyborøn
Lemvig
10'
57° N
50'
40'
30'
10°E
09°30'E
09°E
08°30'E

for several days. Currents in the various narrows can be up to 2kn, and even 3kn through the Oddesund bridge.

Weather

The complex of channels and broads trends in a westerly to southwesterly direction from Hals to Oddesund, so the prevailing summer winds from the two westerly quadrants tend to be funnelled along it, while in spring winds from the NE quadrant are funnelled in the opposite direction. However, in the middle and southern reaches, which are more broken up by islands, there is plenty of shelter; the most exposed areas are at each end of the complex in the wider Nissum Bredning and Løgstør Bredning.

Bridges

There are five opening bascule bridges in the area: two near Ålborg (one a railway bridge), and three at Aggersund, Vilsund and Oddesund (railway and road bridge). There is one fixed bridge (26m clearance), at Salling Sund near Nykøbing. The N flag at the crosstrees or a call on Channel 16 (also working channels 12 and 13 at time of writing) obtains passage. All the bridges are open at least in normal daylight hours. The rail bridges close 15 minutes before a train is due; the Limfjord road bridge at Ålborg is a little more restrictive, being closed for a number of set periods (usually half-hours) during the day but prepared to open at other times.

Charts

Note Soundings and heights on all the charts are based on mean sea level (MSL).
German hydrographic *80, 81.*
Danish hydrographic *105, 106, 108, 109.*
Danish *Søsportskort Serie 1* *105S, 106S, 108S, 109S.*

Route description

LIMFJORD BALTIC ENTRANCE

See Chapter 6

LANGERAK

Persistent westerly winds (more frequent in autumn and winter) can override the six-hourly tidal flow, creating a persistent E-going stream of up to 4kn, and persistent easterlies (more frequent in spring and summer) can produce a somewhat lesser W-going stream, so a reliable engine is essential on this part of the passage. Big ships use this channel, so pleasure craft should keep just outside the fairway. It is difficult and unwise to anchor in these busy reaches. The eastern reaches are pretty, rolling farmland, but the approaches to Ålborg are industrial and dockland areas.

Winds tend to be funnelled along all of the reaches to Løgstør in either direction, and if they are against you the passage can be a hard push, particularly if the current is in the same direction.

→ In the 16M between Hals and Ålborg the deep-water fairway is over 10m deep in the middle, but has steep-sided, wide shelves of less than 2m on each side. However, it is well buoyed throughout, with lit buoys (green on the N side of the channel in the direction of flood westwards as far as Ålborg, where the buoyage direction changes) and lights in line on all reaches. The fjord here runs through a low-lying land of churches and farmhouses.

There are two small yacht havens on this stretch. **Mou** (2·5m, unlit) is 2·6M from Hals on the S bank, with about half as many places, and is approached directly between two entrance-channel buoys in 2·5m. It is about 1·5km from a village. **Nørre Uttrup** (1·7–2·8m, unlit), also tiny, is just before the tunnel on the W bank. It is approached via a 2m seasonally marked channel, and is 3km from the bridge into Ålborg.

16M (Limfjord road bridge)
ALBORG

The Limfjord road bridge (central double bascule, 9·75m clearance closed) and the Jernbanbro rail bridge (central single bascule, 4·4m clearance closed), on the second northern meander of the fjord at Ålborg, are opened on request from 0500–2100, but the road bridge is closed for around half an hour at approximately hourly intervals and the rail bridge is closed for 15 minutes before a train crosses. Each bridge opening span has red (S side) and green (N side) lights.

There are four main mooring possibilities, all approached from deep water. From E to W: **Nørre Sundby Bådehavn** (1·5m, unlit, PD) is on the N bank immediately W of the road bridge. **Vestre Bådehavn** (2·5–3·5m, PD), on the S bank, is one of the two largest, but has an unlit entrance. Also on the S bank, **Skudehavnen** (6m at the S quay for visitors, PD) has leading lights, but make sure that you keep the green buoys inside the entrance to starboard as you enter, as there is a shallow patch behind them. Finally, also on the S bank is **Marina Fjordparken**, also called Marina Strandpark (2–3m in harbour, 3m approach, PD*). This marina has at least 350 berths, and is the only large harbour with a lit entrance.

Ålborg's old town centre, with its castle, museum, theatre, town hall, and beautifully restored Gothic, Renaissance, classical and 19th-century buildings and churches, is S and E of the road bridge and centres upon Budolfi square. On the N edge of Nørre Sundby 1M from the N bank is the Lindholm Høje, an Iron Age and Viking cemetery; its settlement is to the N. Both have now been excavated and many of the finds are in Ålborg's history museum.

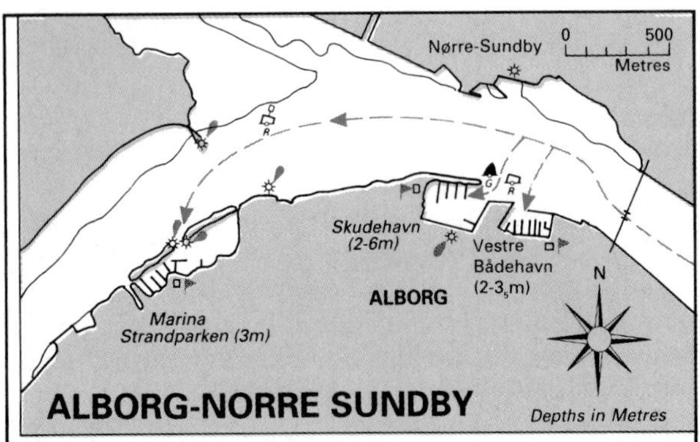

Ålborg. Skudehavn entrance.

Ålborg bascule road bridge from the E.

GJOL BREDNING AND NIBE BREDNING

The 25M-long channel continuing on to Løgstør has a minimum depth of 4m, is buoyed but unlit, and winds tortuously between soundings which are often less than 1m, so it should only be followed in daylight by visitors. From Ålborg westwards the direction of the buoyage changes, with the flood direction from Thyborøn to Ålborg now assumed to be eastwards. The green buoys are therefore now on the S side of the channel. A tidal and wind-driven current system similar to that described for the Langerak (above) applies. These reaches to Løgstør are generally aligned with the prevailing winds, so shelter is sparse. If you must anchor make sure you pick the occasional areas of deeper water, well away from the buoyed channel.

Gjøl (2·5m, PD) is a small fishing and pleasure harbour on the island of the same name, approached directly from the red buoy on the N side of the Hummerbaken channel; it is 0·65M across a 1·9–3m patch to the short, marked entrance channel. The village has a 12th-century church.

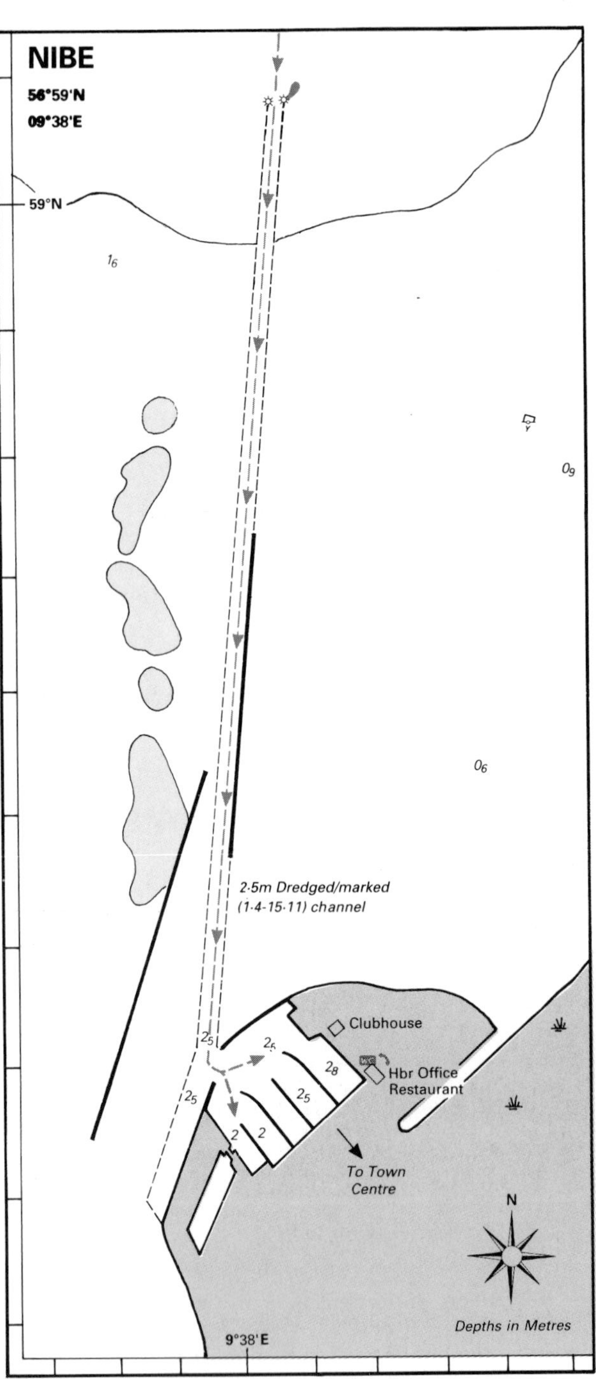

13M
NIBE

Nibe (at least 300 moorings, 2·5m, PD★) is approached from the E cardinal buoy at the extreme eastern end of the Draget channel off the wood on Klitgård Hage, following a line of seasonal (1 April to 11 November) RW pillar buoys across a 2·5–3m patch. On first leaving the main channel watch out, as there are patches of less than 2m on each side of the subsidiary channel. Red and green Fl beacons mark the beginning of the marked 2·5m-dredged channel southwards to the harbour entrance, which is not lit. On our visit we found depths of as little as 1·8m in this channel during a high-pressure spell. Nibe itself is a picturesque village, a short walk from the harbour across a main road.

HAGEDYB, BEJSTRUP LØB AND AGGERSUND

→ Return to the Draget channel by the same route and follow the buoyed channel carefully, as there are some longish gaps between marks.

Attrup (2m on W side, D), on the N bank, has a difficult and unlit approach. Leave the main buoyed channel N of Marbjerge Tunge and head north-westwards across Attrup Lo, then double back down the Brovst Løb buoyed channel, following the northern bank to the harbour entrance. There are some charted patches of less than 2m to avoid in leaving the main channel and crossing to the first two buoys of the Brovst Løb.

13·5M

Aggersund road bridge (double-leaf bascule, clearance 5·4m closed) opens from sunrise to 30 minutes after sunset on request. From here the channel narrows, with steep-to sides. Follow it carefully to Løgstør, where it runs directly adjacent to the main harbour and canal entrance.

Aggersund road bridge, E of Løgstør.

2·5M

Løgstør (1·5–3·5m) has a small, easily negotiated but unlit entrance E of the canal entrance on the S bank; both entrances are approached in about 3m. Most visitors moor in the canal (3m, D), but silting on each side of its entrance means that you must enter carefully between the two small marker buoys. The canal has most facilities, including electricity and a kiosk.

→ The straight 4m-dredged channel (liable to silting) across Løstør Grunde narrows to around 100m in width. The 1m contour, particularly on the N

Løgstør canal entrance. Yacht leaving between the two small entrance buoys.

side, is not far from the buoys, so the channel must be followed religiously. There are a sector light and a lit buoy at the Løgstør end of the channel, and another lit buoy at the deep-water end just over 3M from the harbour.

LØGSTØR BREDNING

A course southwards from the Løgstør Grunde lit offing buoy, keeping outside the 5m-depth contour, leads to the approach to Rønbjerg.

7·5M

RØNBJERG HAVN

Rønbjerg Havn (1m southern part to 2·5m northern part, D) has an easy deep-water approach, with a lit entrance and a buoy at the end of the spit extending out from the northern wall.

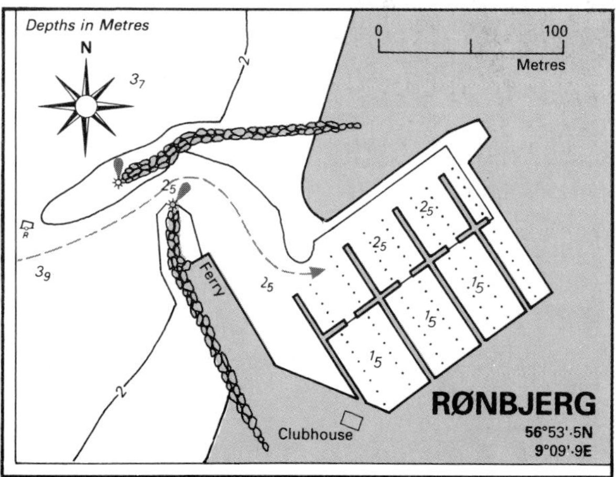

Livø (2m) is a harbour with two L-shaped basins on the island opposite, approached across 2m from the E. Take care to avoid the nature reserve, marked by yellow pillar buoys, on the southern spit of the island. Livø island is one of the most interesting in the Limfjord, with mature woodlands in the N, sandy beaches, and heathland and seal colonies at the S end.

⚓ Livø island provides anchorages in appropriate winds in 2–3m on its E side (seasonal mooring buoy), off the harbour, and also off the wood on its NW coast.

BJORNSHOLM BUGT AND RISGÅRDE BREDNING

➜ The winding route S from Rønbjerg to Hvalpsund is definitely a daylight passage for a visitor; there are several hazards to avoid on both sides in order to keep in a minimum 5m depth and avoid any risk of grounding. Many of these are marked, but with unlit buoys, and the buoyage can be a little confusing, as S of Bjornsholm Bugt the tide is assumed to be rising southwards towards Skive and Hjarbæk, with green buoys on the W side. From N to S the dangers are: Rønbjerg Hage shoals (E side of route, marked by unlit green buoy); the end of Livø Sandrev spit (W side, marked by unlit cardinal buoy); Ertebølle Høved point (E side, marked by unlit red buoy); Junget Øre point (W side, unmarked, but with a wood on the point); Rind Grund shoals (E side, marked by unlit cardinal buoy); Rotholm Rev and its two islands (W side, marked by unlit cardinal buoy at N end and unlit green buoy on E side); and finally, just beyond Hvalpsund Marina and opposite the fishing harbour, Sundsøre point (W side, marked by a green unlit buoy).

⚓ On the W side of the entrance to Risgårde Bredning, SE of Junget Øre point, by the wood (sand, 3–4m).

12·5M

HVALPSUND MARINA

⛵ Hvalpsund Marina (around 250 moorings, 2·4m plus, D*), 0·5M N of the fishing harbour, has a straightforward approach from the W in 3m and has a Fl red light on the N wall. There is a ferry to Salling island from the fishing harbour, and Hessel Agricultural Museum is in a thatched manor house nearby.

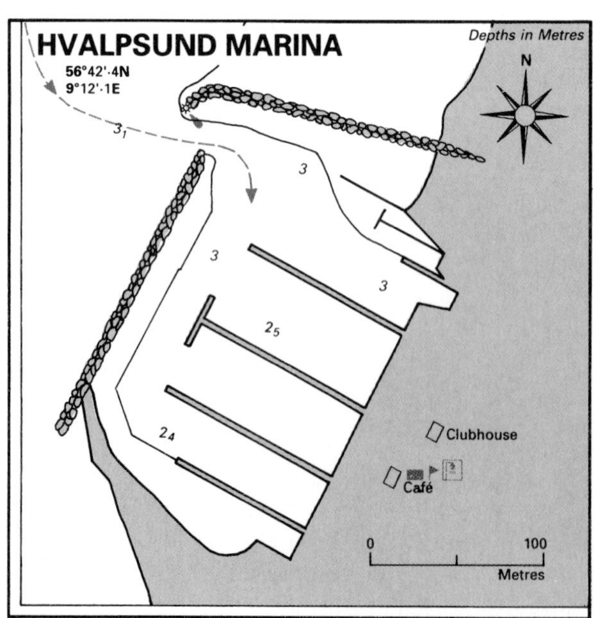

Hvalpsund marina. S end of Risgårde Bredning.

Sundsøre spit. W side of Hvalpsund. Photograph from *Kylora* in 20m of water a few metres from the green buoy.

⚓ At the head of the bay S of and behind Sundsøre spit (3–5m, mud).

LOVNS BREDNING

➜ The winding route to Virksund continues to be marked, but with unlit buoys. To enter Lovns Bredning the visitor must first round two red buoys on the E side of the route off Bregnsø Hage and Knudshoved points. Keep well offshore of Melbjerg Hoved in between, and sound continually, taking care also to keep off Jelse Odde point, to the S of the entrance, marked by a cardinal buoy. Jelse Odde is a dangerous ¾-mile-long winding spit, barely above the watermark, but often marked in parts by roosting sea birds – be sure that you sight the spindly cardinal buoy. Inside, the *bredning* is wide and generally 5–6m deep. Two green buoys (unlit) must be rounded to avoid the Trangmanden shoal to the S before heading into the entrance to Virk Sund. This shoal is a wide one, and again the green buoys are easy to miss.

⚓ On either side of the Lovn Bredning entrance in around 2–3m, i.e. in Lundø Bugt to the S and on the E side of Knudshoved point to the N.

10M
VIRKSUND

⛵ Virksund harbour (2–2·5m, D), on the W side of Virk Sund, is approached between two buoys and the entrance lights along a short 2m-dredged channel.

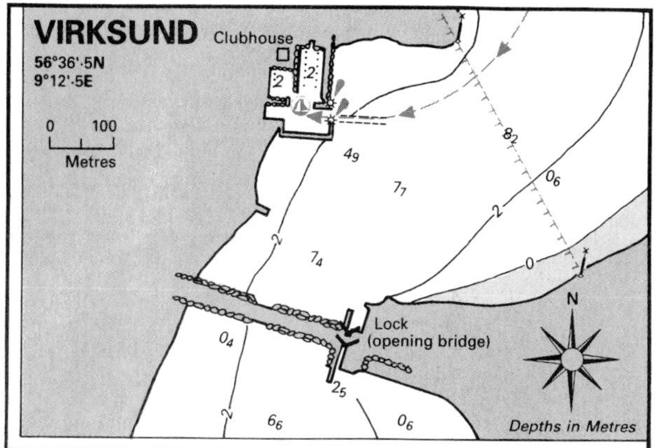

Virksund lock from Hjarbæk fjord. Small lock with rising gates.

5M (harbour)
HJARBÆK FJORD

Vessels wishing to continue on to Hjarbæk Fjord and Hjarbæk harbour (2·5m, D) must pass through Virksund lock and opening bridge (VHF Ch 16, on request during most daylight hours), in the embankment which crosses the narrows. The lock has guillotine rising gates, so vessels must wait for the green light showing that the guillotine is completely retracted, making particularly sure to remember this before rushing to leave the lock.

Hjarbæk Fjord, which is fresh water, is shallow, with a (2–3m) tricky approach to the harbour, assisted by a few unlit buoys towards its head, including two pairs near the entrance. Spotting the green buoy against the green hill to the N of the harbour is the main problem, but the channel up to that point is a wide one. This is a heavily fished area, so watch out for stakes and buoys. Hjarbæk is a picturesque village.

⚓ The whole fjord is a nature reserve in a magnificent setting, and while the W side is too shallow for anchoring there are plenty of anchorages over mud on the steep-to E side.

Hjarbæk entrance. Tricky, 2m approach channel (red can-topped perches).

Hjarbæk. A small and pretty harbour.

→ ⚓ Return to Jelse Odde point by the same route, round the point to port and head southwards. The two points on the opposite E bank – Per Færgemande (marked by a wood) and Grønning Øre (a sharp promontory) – are both steep-to but unmarked. There is a good anchorage round the edges of Astrup Vig bay between these headlands in 3m over mud/sand.

19M (yacht haven)
SKIVE FJORD

Continuing S in 4–5m, the major hazard is Lundø Hage shoals, just to the E of the line of the first set of leading lights into Skive, and marked by an unlit red buoy.

⛵ Skive has three basins, approached along a closely buoyed (two lit; there are also two sets of lights in line) channel directly to the two southern entrances, the southernmost of which (Sydhavn) is lit. Visitors should use the large Søsportshavn (around 400 berths, 2·5m at main pontoons but shallow elsewhere, PD*), which is through the northernmost of the three entrances (unlit); leave the main buoyed channel just before its end, approaching the SE-facing entrance across 2–3m

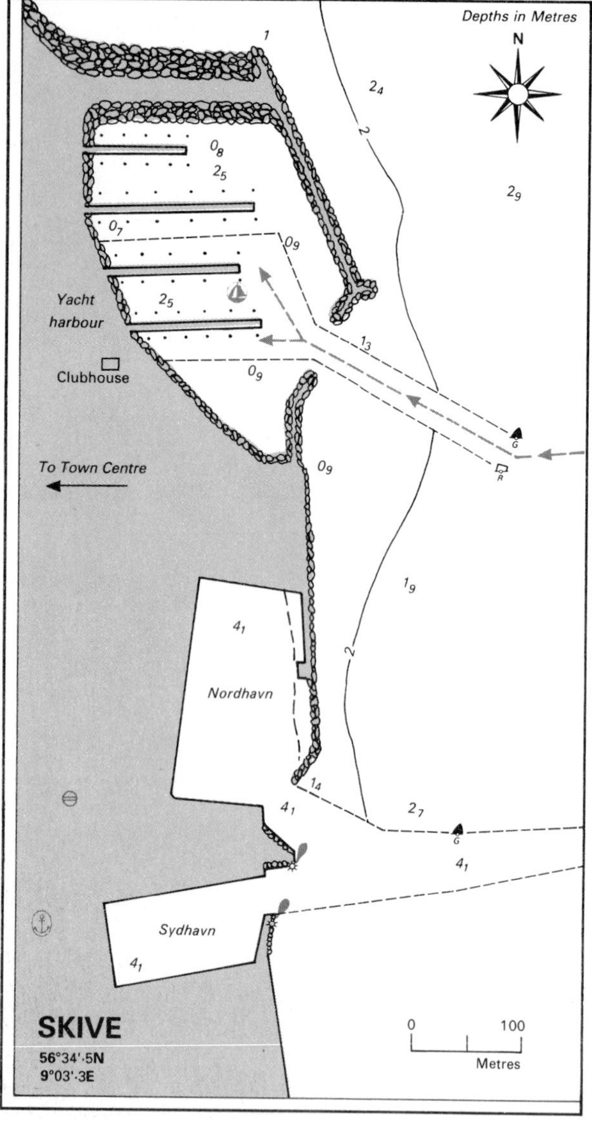

soundings and then between two unlit buoys. Alternatively, visitors can use the middle basin (entrance unlit), confusingly called Nordhavn (4m).

Skive, whose precinct shopping centre is about a mile away from the harbour, is an important nodal communication centre and has a Romanesque church, a museum focusing on Greenland, and Frøken Michelson's *Mindestuer* ('Miss Michelson's Memorial Rooms'), with a collection of objects from the travels of a local shopkeeper.

→ Return by the same route to the entrance to Risgårde Bredning, near the unmarked but steep-to Junget Øre point. After passing the point, continue sounding in order to stay in 6m-plus depths, curving only gradually to port in order to give a wide berth to the shoals to the S on the Salling shore. Finally, head for the N side of the Middelgrund buoys (green plus a cardinal; keep both to port) at the entrance to Fur Sund.

⚓ Close N of the approach course, Færker Vig (over sand, 3–4m, or on seasonal mooring buoys) on Fur's E coast is another woodland-surrounded anchorage.

19M (harbour)

FUR SUND

Fur (2·8m, PD) is a small harbour with a lit SE-facing entrance, easily entered from deep water. Fur is a fascinating small island with a wide variety of scenery, ranging from strange hills, rift valleys and woods in the N to flatlands in the S. Fifty-million-year-old deposits of molar clay, a whitish substance used for bricks, are quarried in the N, in which thousands of fossils of animals, fish, birds and insects have been and continue to be discovered.

Skive approach. Yacht harbour to the right, commercial harbour ahead.

Fur approach. Harbour entrance is at extreme left-hand edge of photograph along the harbour wall.

Skive. Buoyed approach to yacht harbour entrance.

Fur harbour entrance.

Some of these are exhibited in the Fur museum at Nederby, N of the harbour. The deposits form spectacular cliffs on the N side of the island.

⚓ Pulse Vig (2–3m close inshore, clay/mud), immediately W of the harbour, provides an alternative anchorage.

→ The dogleg exit from Fur Sund to the S of the harbour is difficult to see in daylight as well as in darkness, and the visitor may need his compass to pick out the green buoy (unlit) marking its S side. Depart from Fur Sund between Odde point and this buoy to its SW, turning northwestwards to round the second unlit green buoy off Sæbygårds Hage, and head into Salling Sund, once again giving the shoals to the S a wide berth by sounding and keeping in at least 6m.

SALLING SUND

→ Salling Sund is part of the main Limfjord through fairway, which has sector lights of moderate range (varying from 7–14M) throughout.

Salling Sund road bridge. 26m clearance.

Glyngøre harbour. Light nearer to right-hand side, and entrance through wall nearer to left-hand side of photograph.

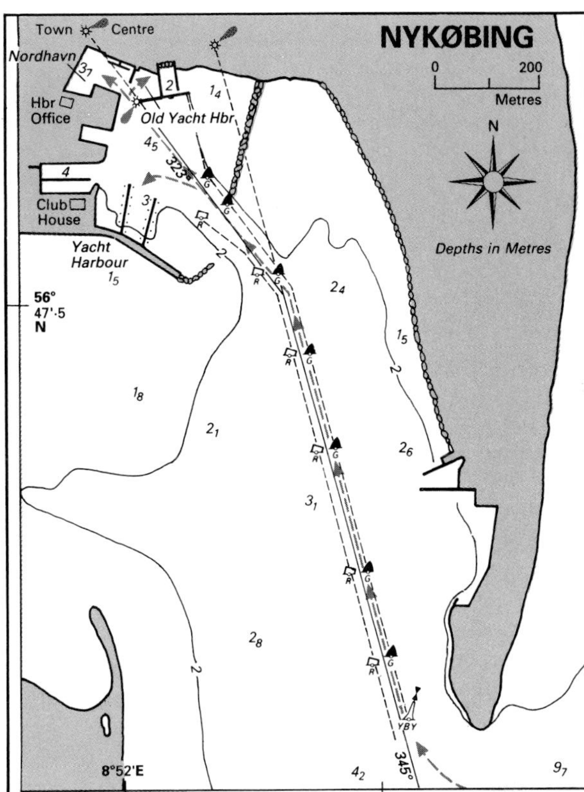

Nykøbing approach from halfway along the entrance channel.

Nykøbing approaches from the cardinal buoy at the entrance.

6M (harbour)

NYKOBING (MORS)

⛵ Nykøbing harbour (around 350 berths, 2·5–3·7m, PD*) complex on Mors island is approached from deep water after passing the steep-to Ørodde peninsula and rounding the cardinal buoy (less than 3m of water between the point and the buoy). Head along the NNW-trending 4·5m-dredged channel to the harbour, which is buoyed (unlit) and has two sets of leading lights. Visitors can head NW after passing through the outer entrance and use the Nordhavn, W of its single entrance light, or the old yacht haven, to the N of this light. They could also peel off earlier to use the marina W of the outer entrance, taking care to round the buoy and avoid the shallows surrounding the marina (these are less than 2m directly E of the marina, so watch out). The town is an old oyster-and-herring-fishery centre, and has many museums: Morslands historical museum, in a medieval building, an iron-foundry museum, a museum of archaeology and geology, and a museum of bottles.

Further S, on the E bank of Salling Sund, **Glyngøre** (3m, D) is a tiny fishing and pleasure harbour with a tiny lighthouse on the W wall of the entrance as well as a sector light on the point. There are a limited number of moorings in the SE basin.

→ Continuing southwards, Glyngøre point is steep-to. Sallinge Sund road bridge has a clearance of 26m, with navigation in opposite directions through two adjacent bridge sections (lit, with a siren) and with middle-ground and channel-marking buoys on each side of the bridge.

Further S, Sillerslev Øre (unmarked, W shore) is low-lying but has no offlying shoal, and the Nymølle Sand, opposite on the E bank, is marked by an unlit green buoy.

⚓ Immediately S of the bridge on the W bank, the bay N of Gammelør Odde point provides holding in 2–3m over mud, with a sand beach nearby. On the E bank further S, Lysen Bredning leads to the superb natural harbour of Harre Vig and its triangular N offshoot Harre Nor, with anchorages anywhere round the edges of the *vig* in 2–3m over mud, often within 100m of the shore. There are some sand and gravel beaches, backed by rolling farmland, round the bay. However, the approaches are tricky: the entrance to Lysen Bredning is flat and low-lying, and compass and echo sounder will be needed constantly. A compass course must be steered from the middle of this entrance to the Harre Vig entrance to avoid the Hjertholm shoal to the S. Harre Vig entrance is between Sester Odde and Hjerk Berg, two unmistakable sandstone cliffs, and requires a dead-centre passage, immediately skirting N round the shoal extending outwards from the S bank.

KÅS BREDNING

→ Continuing S through Kås Bredning, the three buoys marking the S exit from the bay are unlit (two mark the Kås Sand on the E, and one the Jegind Tap spit on the W), but the lights in line from Sillerslev astern mark the passage into Venø Sund.

⚓ **Sillerslev** (2·5m, D) is a tiny harbour on the N bank of Kås Bredning, entered in 2·5m from between two buoys, with a single red light on its W mole. **Jegindø** (1–2·5m, D) is a small fishing harbour on the island of the same name further down on the W side of Kås Bredning, also entered in 2·5m from between 2 buoys. A small yacht-haven extension has now been built E of the old entrance. The harbour is the auction centre for the Limfjord's eel-fishing industry. There is an anchorage in the little bay immediately S of the harbour over mud in 2–3m, but it is some distance from the sandy beach.

VENØ BUGT

→ From the Jegind Tap buoy the course leads southeastwards through the entrance of Venø Bugt (the shoals on each side are marked by unlit buoys) and from the second green buoy to starboard (marking Venø Tap) southwestwards round the steep-to and unmarked Venø Odde point into Struer Bugt.

Ferry crossing the 200m-wide channel at Venø Sund Snævring.

Venø island. Entrance to the tiny harbour.

After passing Hvidsens Hage point (red buoy) at the entrance to the Bugt, taking care to avoid its shallows, **Gyldendal** (1·5–2·5m), a small fishing and yacht harbour on the NE side of Venø Bugt, is approached from south-southwestwards (lights in line; seasonally buoyed channel near the entrance), finally rounding the F.R light to port on the western mole.

21M
STRUER

Holsterbro-Struer (1–4·4m, PD*) is a complex of basins with two entrances (the outer western mole of the W entrance had not been completed at time of writing). It is one of the largest yacht havens in the Limfjord (around 560 places), with moorings in the W harbour and on the E side of the eastern harbour. A buoyed (unlit) channel with lights in line leads southwards into the E entrance. However, it is essential when approaching the first outer-channel

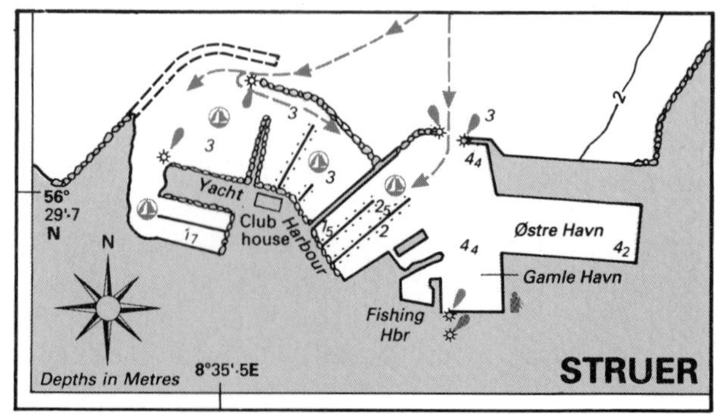

buoys from Struer Bugt to keep away from the Vralde Odde shoals, E of the entrance and marked to their N by a cardinal buoy. The W side and the approaches to the W yacht haven are 3–3·5m deep and no problem. The town of Holsterbro, the cultural centre of West Jutland, with museums, art galleries and street sculptures, is 7 miles S of Struer. Struer itself is a small town, with another local-history museum which has a collection of model ships.

VENØ NARROWS AND VENØ SUND

→ Return N along the entrance channel, but this time head for Venø Sund Snævring, the narrows between the island and the mainland, only 100m wide, but 14–17m deep between the green buoy (keep to port going N) and the steep-to Venø Odde. Course can then be set directly for Grisetåodde point in the Odde Sund.

Venø (1·8m only in the channel and basin, D), on the E side of Venø Sund, is a tiny fishing harbour approached from the SW (occasional lights in line) between two entrance buoys. Venø island is well worth a visit; hire a bicycle from the harbourmaster and visit Denmark's tiniest church. **Oddesund** (mainly 2–3m, PD), on the N side and W of the bridge, also has a small fishing basin, with an even smaller private harbour to its E.

⚓ Although there is not much space in the nearby harbours, there are anchoring possibilities (depending on the wind) all round Venø island in 2–3m, usually just over 200m offshore over mud and clay. The best scenery is near the sandy beaches and hills on the W coast. Odby Bugt lies immediately N of the Oddesund bridge; anchoring is possible all round the bay over mud in 2–3m.

6M

ODDESUND NARROWS

Oddesund road and rail bridge (single lifting span between pillars 6 and 7, clearance 3·5–5m) opens 24 hours a day on request but closes 15 minutes before a train is due. Make sure you have enough power if you are pushing the current. There are almost too many navigational aids on the bridge: lights in line in both directions, a sector light on its S side, traffic lights on each approach side, and on each side of the bridge Denmark's largest 'park' of wind generators, visible for many miles.

→ Two buoys mark the edge of the shoals on the W side of the bridge exit channel. Dogleg southwards then northwestwards into Nissan Bredning, where another sector light on the peninsula behind (Toftum) makes it easier to find the Lem Vig offing buoy on the S shore, and both the approach to Thyborøn and the southerly approach to Krik Vig at the western end of the bay.

Odde Sund bascule bridge closes behind us. (S side).

NISSUM BREDNING

→ The wide shoal along the S coast necessitates keeping about 0·8M offshore, staying in over 5m of water, before picking up the lit Lemvig offing buoy and the first channel-marker buoys near the extensive Rønnen shoal, an area to be carefully avoided. If you are heading for Thyborøn directly from Oddesund, however, a lit green buoy marks the extreme N edge of the shoals.

11·5M (main harbour)

LEMVIG

Lemvig is approached from the Nissum Bredning from a lit offing buoy and between two buoys marking the gap in the Rønnen shoals. Continue down the Lem Vig (cove) along a 4m-dredged buoyed (unlit) channel which requires two sets of lights in line because of the sharp port-hand bend. The red triangular leading marks are extremely easy to see in daylight. Lemvig Marina (2–3m, with a lit entrance) is a medium-sized yacht haven on the W side of Lem Vig, entered across 3m from halfway down the second reach of the main channel. If he requires fuel and proximity to the town and shops, the visitor can continue along the channel, which eventually curves across to Lemvig (2·8–3·7m, lit entrance, PD), on the E side of the bay, and moor either on the N or W walls of the western fishing basin or in the eastern Gammelhavn. The town has an eye-catching church, with an onion dome, and a 'life-saving at sea' museum. It is possible to obtain diesel fuel from the N quay of the Østre Havn if the pump in the main harbour is not in operation.

⚓ Lem Vig, in the bay at the entrance immediately S of Follup Odde over sand in 2–3m.

→ Depths over the Rønnen are marginal. It is better to be safe than sorry: follow the channel back out to the offing buoy, then go N to the green lit buoy before heading for the Sælhundeholm Løb channel to Thyborøn. In settled conditions, however, it is possible to cut across the Rønnen shoal in 2–2·5m close to the green unlit buoy, which is N of the first few approach-channel buoys.

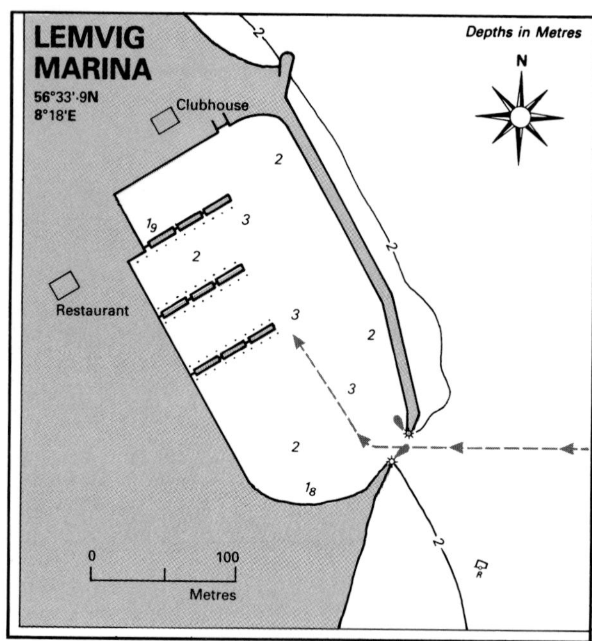

13M (main harbour)

THYBORØN

See Chapter 3 for chart and description of sea approaches

→Two cardinal buoys (one lit) mark the beginning of the lit buoyed channel, Sælhundeholm Løb, which curves northwards to Thyborøn and is dredged to 4m but is liable to silting.

There is a small yacht haven at the end of this channel (dredged to 2m in the NW corner of **Søndre Arbejdshavn**) where it enters Søndre Dyb, the deep-water channel off Thyborøn main harbour complex. This harbour is not recommended for visitors – its marked approach across the wide shallow basin is difficult and it is a long way from town (it is S of and not included on the chart in Chapter 3).

Thyborøn (3·5m plus, PD) harbour complex proper opens off one lit entrance to port further N in the Søndre Dyb. Visitors should thread their way through to the extreme northern basin, Nordre Inderhavn, for a mooring, and make their peace with the harbourmaster, whose office is almost opposite the main harbour entrance. Thyborøn is a fishing town, with a 15-minute ferry crossing to the dyked Agger Tange peninsula and its nearby holiday area.

Lemvig commercial harbour approach. A better way of seeing the town than the marina.

Lemvig marina entrance from the channel buoys.

Thyborøn harbour. Nordre Inderhavn.

Søndre Arbejdshavn. Small yacht harbour at S end of Thyborøn complex.

Agger (1·5–3m, unlit entrance), a tiny fishing harbour, is another possibility for a visit by water at the N end of Krig Vig. It is about 8M from Thyborøn along a winding buoyed channel (unlit, except at the Søndre Dyb entrance opposite the S end of Thyborøn). Before it silted, Krikdyb, leading to the harbour, was a link with the North Sea, used by Viking bands to launch their raids on western Europe. The easiest approach to Krikdyb, however, is from the S (I came from Lemvig on my visit), picking up the first red buoy close under the steep green cliffs of Kobberø past Røjensø Odde point. The channel, close inshore of the line of red buoys, has depths of as little as 3m; closely spaced port and starboard buoys mark the final approach. Agger is a somewhat stark fishing harbour with few pleasure-craft boxes but (on our visit) plenty of room round the fish-dock wharves, providing you do not mind cleaning your decks afterwards.

⚓ Krig Vig (2–3m, mud), near Gramstrup, but keep out of the Krikdyb channel and use an anchor light.

→ Return to Kås Bredning via Nissum Bredning, Odde Sund and Jegind Tap/Kås Hoved narrows (reverse of the route above).

23M (Bøløre Odde)

BØLØRE HAGE NARROWS TO NEES SUND

→ The narrows between Bolore Odde and Hestor Odde are marked by a buoy to the S and two buoys to the N (all unlit). From here the route is a winding one, round a series of islands in a flat marshy landscape, in 4–6m soundings, but with some 8–9m deeps W of Agerø. The few unlit buoys marking the sharp bends and shoals must be carefully followed.

⚓ Several, but take care to sound into the coves and avoid the shallows. Tambosund (northern part), W of Jegindø, has many mud/sand anchorages, but keep to the middle of the Sound before nosing in. Other possibilities are Glomstrup Vig (2–3m sand/mud), between Agerø and Mors islands, Skibsted Fjord (2–3m, sand and mud), 300m offshore W of Katholm Odde (but the fjord further W demands very tricky navigation), and the W side of Nees Vig (2–3m, mud), N of the buoyed channel beyond Agerø island. The scenery in the last two anchorages is flat and less picturesque than that in the other two.

Doverodde (0·7m inner, 2·5m outer pontoon, D) is a small unlit open harbour entered from W of the Dove Mulle Grund cardinal buoy at the dogleg bend into Ness Sund. It is in a delightful setting of trees and there is room to anchor off if the outer pontoon is overcrowded.

7M (Dover Mølle Grund)

VISBY BREDNING

→ The main hazard travelling N in this wide bay is Visby Grund, a circular shoal (1·9m) which obstructs the exit to Dragstrup Vig. The widest passage is on the W side, keeping close outside the cardinal buoy. On the E side two buoys mark the narrow passage between Visby Grund and the E coast shoal, Ørndrup Hage.

⚓ Karby Odde (2–3m, sand, wide beach), on the E side of Visby Bredning.

DRAGSTRUP VIG

A There are at least three anchorages (2–3m, sand) in Dragstrup Vig: Magerodde, S of the entrance; inshore of the Dansk Sejlunion buoy E of Gudnæs Hage and N of the entrance; and, best of all, near Dragstrup at the E head of the bay under the wood.

VILSUND

→ The sides of the channel are steep-to and navigation is no problem, providing the bays on each side (see below anchorages) are given a wide berth.

⚓ Rov Vig (2–3m), a perfectly protected cove on the E bank, and Fævig (4m close inshore), on the W bank just before the bridge, both over mud. Both are near rolling farmland.

12M

Vilsundbroen is a road bridge (lit) with a single-leaf bascule (4m clearance closed), opening on request (VHF Ch 16, working channels 12, 13) from sunrise to 30 minutes after sunset. **Vilsund Vest** (2·5m, lit entrance, PD) is a small yacht haven close to the SW side of the bridge, entered directly (east-facing entrance) from Vilsund.

Vilsund bridge.

THISTED BREDNING

→ Another wide lake, 9–14m deep at the W end but shoaling in the E. Heading across to Thisted the only hazards are Sundby Stengrund to the S, marked by an unlit green buoy, and Silstrup Hoved, a steep unmarked point to the W.

5M
THISTED

Thisted harbour (2·4m plus, PD) has an easy lit entrance from deep water. The silo and chimneys of the town can be seen from a long way off. The yacht basin is to port of the entrance and is approached around the N end of its E wall, but it has little spare mooring space. Visitors, and particularly deeper-draught vessels, can use the Trafikhavn quays at the N end of the harbour complex. The Annekshavn, 0·8M E of Thisted, is not for use by visitors. Thisted is the main town of Thy, with a precinct shopping centre, a Gothic church and a regional museum containing objects associated with the 19th-century poet Jans P. Jacobsen and the teacher Kristen Kold, as well as Bronze Age artefacts.

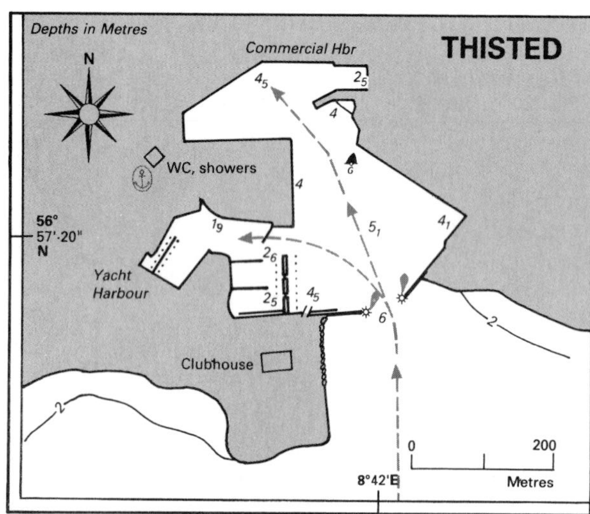

⚓ Hovsør Havn (2–3m, sand and mud) is a superb, protected natural harbour on the N coast E of Thisted before the entrance to Feggesund, with hills and woods to the W and marshes to the E. The most convenient spot is on the SW side near the woods.

→ The E end of Thisted Bredning narrows and shallows rapidly, with a deep (8–17m) narrow exit channel with steep-to sides through Feggesund. Watch out for the Feggesund ferry across the narrower part of the channel. This channel from Skarrehage point (S danger with a cardinal buoy) is buoyed (unlit), but there are two sets of leading lights (behind the vessel going in this direction), leading to and then through the channel. Three buoys and a sector light behind on the mainland mark the eastwards turn into Løgstør Bredning and the dangerous shoals to the S at the end of Feggerøn spit. **Amtoft** (2·5m, lit entrance, PD) is a tiny yacht haven on the mainland due N of the green buoys at the end of Feggerøn spit, directly entered (east-facing entrance) across 3–4m and with 2·5m in the entrance.

Approaching Thisted.

Amtoft. Leaving the entrance of this small yacht harbour on the N shore of Løgstør Bredning.

Thisted entrance.

→ Another spit, Holmtange Hage, impinges southwards from the N shore of Løgstør Bredning, marked by a cardinal buoy on the 6m contour. It must be given a wide berth when heading for the Løgstør Grunde entrance-channel offing buoy.

19·5M
LØGSTØR
41M (Hals)

→ Return to Ålborg and Hals from Løgstør by reversing the route described at the beginning of this chapter.

HALS
See Chapter 6

8. South Fyn and the Store Bælt

Route 6
Kiel to Odense via South Fyn and the Store Bælt

This route covers the delightful islands and S coast of Fyn, together with the winding and wooded Svendborg Sund, the 'Danish Riviera', with its long history of wooden-sailing-ship building. The route then zigzags northwards up the Store Bælt and through the major bridge and tunnel works which in 1996 will revolutionise Denmark's communications network. In practice, however, you may prefer to vary the suggested itinerary, keeping to the E side of the Bælt via the Vesterrenden and returning down the W side via the Østerrenden TSS. This part of the route allows visits to all of the historic Store Bælt ports; the mid-17th century was a period of war with Sweden, and this is reflected in the museums of these ports, as well as in the nearby fortified houses and castles. Finally it winds through the Odense Fjord and canal to end up in Odense, the country's third-largest city and the birthplace of Hans Christian Andersen.

There are about a dozen yacht harbours with over 200 moorings, four of them with 400 or more. There are also a large number of tiny harbours and single wooden jetties en route, typically with 20 to 40 mooring spaces and sometimes with room to raft up or lie head-to with a stern kedge. Most of these can only be approached in daylight in good visibility.

Mooring in the Odense area is a problem, so you may prefer to take a train from Nyborg or a bus from Kerteminde on the E coast of Fyn to the city and cut out the final visit to Odense Fjord.

Fishing stakes abound on this route, particularly in S Fyn and the islands, in Odense Fjord, and in or near the fjords and inlets en route.

Distance

257M, excluding the following suggested diversions (return mileage from passage route in brackets):

Strynø and Ristinge (18M)
Drejø (10M)
Otterup and Bregnør (9M)
Reersø, Mullerup and Musholm (48M)

Depths/water levels *(see also Appendix IV)*

There is a mix of open-sea (Kieler Bucht and Store Bælt) and shallow-water (South Fyn and Skælskor and Odense Fjords) pilotage on this route. As for all of these routes in the SW Baltic, do not assume that the charted dredged depths of any of the shallower *rende* channels are accurate at time of sailing – actual depths are often less. Keep an eye on the fluctuations of water levels from the MSL soundings on the charts.

Tidal range The MHW–MLW range is least in the South Fyn area (nil to 0·3m in most places, but more on exposed islands) and greatest in the constricted sea passages and fjords of Svendborg Sund, the Store Bælt and Odense (from 0·3m to 0·7m).

Wind In the southern part of this passage area strong winds mainly (not entirely) from E to NE tend to raise water levels by about 0·6m to 2·0m (the latter at Ærøskøbing), while in the Store Bælt strong winds from the northerly quadrant from NW to NE tend to do this. More importantly for shallow-water pilotage, in the southern part of the area strong winds mainly (not entirely) from the SW quadrant can reduce water levels by 0·5m to 1·6m, and in the Store Bælt SE-quadrant winds can reduce levels by 0·6 to 0·9m.

Bridges

There are two fixed bridges en route, with clearances of 33m (Svendborg) and 26m (Rudkøbing). The 18m Vesterrenden (Store Bælt) is bypassed via the Østerrenden; when this latter bridge is completed in 1996 it will have 65m clearance.

Charts

Note Soundings and heights on all the charts are based on mean sea level (MSL).

German hydrographic *11, 13, 14, 15, 18, 21, 30.*

NV *Sportschiffahrtskarten Series 1* and ***2*** (Chart 17 only). Note that significant depth contours are at 2m, 4m, 6m, 10m and 20m. Many of the buoys off headlands are on the 10m contour. These charts are often a little small in scale, and it is essential to have the pilot books, *Der Grosse NV Hafen Lotse, Bands 1* and *2*, which accompany the chart sets for pilotage in the harbour entrances.

Danish hydrographic *114, 152, 170, 141, 142.*

Danish *Søportskort Serie 1* (part of series only).

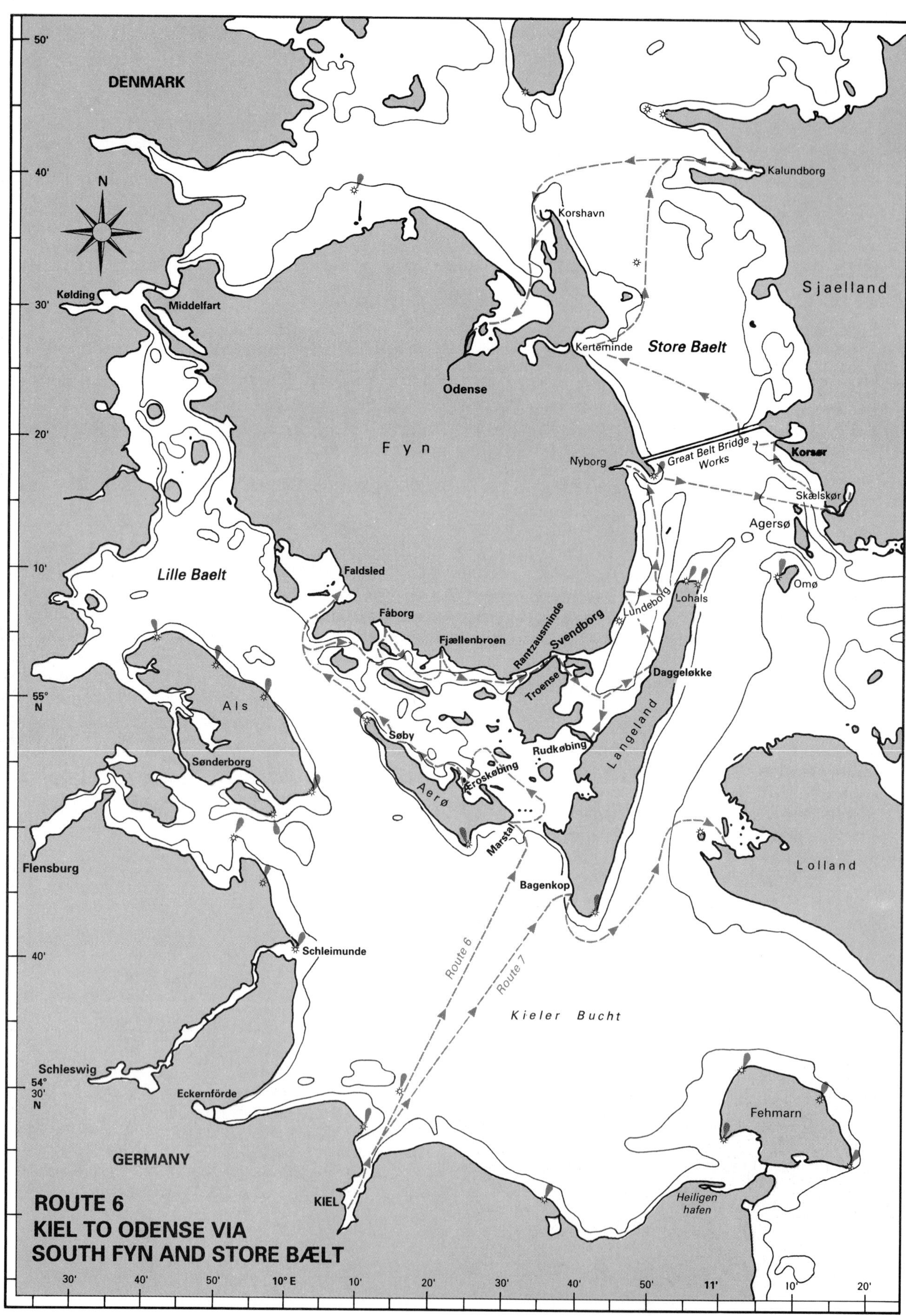

DENMARK
N
Kølding
Middelfart
Korshavn
Kalundborg
Sjaelland
Kerteminde
Store Baelt
Odense
Fyn
Nyborg
Great Belt Bridge Works
Korsør
Skælskør
Agersø
Omø
Lille Baelt
Faldsled
Fåborg
Fjællenbroen
Rantzausminde
Svendborg
Lundeborg
Lohals
Daggeløkke
Troense
Als
Søby
Rudkøbing
Langeland
Sønderborg
Ærøskøbing
Aerø
Marstal
Flensburg
Bagenkop
Lolland
Schleimunde
Route 6
Route 7
Kieler Bucht
Schleswig
Eckernförde
Fehmarn
GERMANY
KIEL
Heiligen hafen
ROUTE 6
KIEL TO ODENSE VIA
SOUTH FYN AND STORE BÆLT
50'
40'
30'
20'
10'
55° N
54° 30' N
10° E
11'

Route description

KIEL AND KIELER FÖRDE

See Chapter 6

KIELER BUCHT

Currents are relatively weak (1–2kn) and cross-track here: SE-going in winds from WSW–W–N and NW-going in winds from NE–E–SSW. However, the W-going stream can be extremely strong close to Ærø. In settled weather there are weak tidal streams.

Prevailing winds tend to be cross-track on this passage.

→ The route follows the E side of the buoyed channel out of Kieler Förde, then leads directly across Kieler Bucht to the approaches to the Marstal offing buoy (unlit) off the E end of Ærø island. Depths are good: 10–25m, reducing to 6m near the buoy.

The main hazard is the Traffic Separation Scheme close SE of Kiel light tower (white round tower, red gallery and base), where a number of shipping routes into Kiel converge. Keep to its periphery before striking across the bay.

Vejsnæs Nakke sector light (grey framework, 7–14M range), on the southern point of Ærø, is useful at night. The offing buoy (unlit) is approached from 2M away along the line of its leading lights, approximately northwestwards. This avoids the 3·7m spit extending southeastwards from the E corner of the island.

36M

MARSTAL (ÆRØ)

From the offing buoy, the buoyed Klørdyb channel (unlit but with lights in line, 4·5m deep but liable to silting) leads directly to the harbour entrance. Enter in an acute turn to port (there is a light on W mole to starboard). The yacht-haven pontoons (800 moorings, 1·6–2·7m, PD★) are on the starboard side at the southern end of the harbour's long narrow basin.

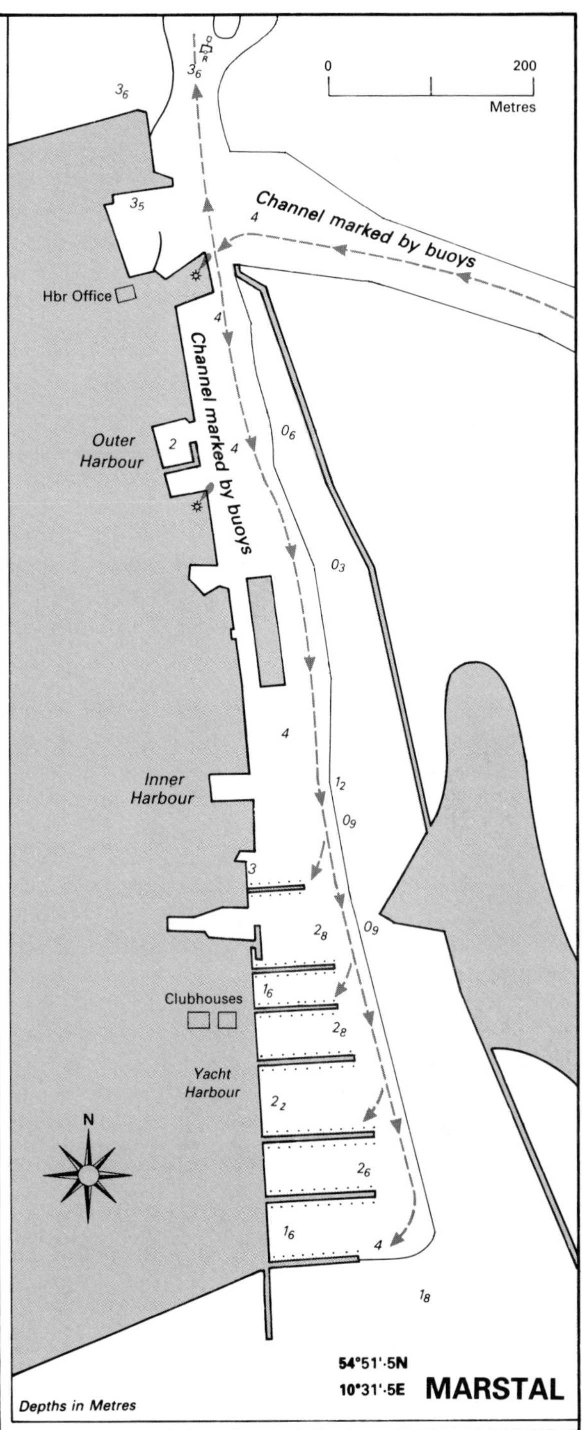

Marstal. Old lime kiln on outer wall.

This ancient seaport is the largest town on the island, with a ferry to Rudkøbing. A maritime museum with many model ships and mementoes of sailors' voyages, several historic sea captains' houses and the 150-year-old breakwater with its ancient lime kiln are the main points of interest.

DIVERSION TO STRYNØ AND RISTINGE

(not included in total mileage)

A possible one-day round trip from Marstal (about 18M) involves visiting first the low-lying island of **Strynø**, with its tiny harbour on the S side of the end of a sea wall (2m, PD, sector light on N mole), then **Ristinge** on Langeland (2m, D, unlit entrance). Both are fishing and holiday centres; the route is protected by the surrounding shoals. Another option for visiting these two harbours, covering a similar distance, is from Rudkøbing (see later in this route).

The route follows the buoyed channel (an extension of Klørdyb) due N from Marstal in over 2m, turns east-northeastwards from the cardinal buoy along another buoyed (unlit, 3·5m) channel, and then rounds a green light buoy at the southern end of Strynø, following just outside the 4m contour northeastwards. It then approaches Strynø entrance from the SE – there is 2·5m in the entrance, but only 1·7m close S of this. The ferry ties up on the N side of the wall outside the harbour; the village is 1km away.

Leaving Strynø, give about 0·5M clearance southeastwards to the harbour entrance before turning southwards across a 4–5m area of soundings to pick up the Ristinge offing buoy and follow the buoyed (unlit) channel. There is a dogleg turn to starboard and then port (keeping the green buoys to starboard) into the harbour, which is very small; it is often better to lie or raft to another boat on either side of the northwards-pointing outer mole (2·5m). The route back to Marstal returns northwards until well across the 4m contour again, then heads northwestwards to pick up the outermost RW buoy (unlit) of the two buoyed channels described above, and finally retracks west-southwestwards and southwards along these two channels to Marstal entrance.

MÖRKEDYB AND MÖLLEGAB CHANNELS

With the exception of Svendborg Sund, most of the area within the triangle of the South Fyn coast, Æro and Langeland has relatively weak currents. It is also protected from weather, except northwesterlies, which can funnel down the deeper bight N of Æro.

The route to Ærøskøbing describes a wide loop from Marstal. It first heads northwards and east-northeastwards along the two buoyed (unlit) channels (which are the extension of Klørdyb) to the RW buoy, and then turns northwestwards along the buoyed (unlit) Mørkedyb, past another tiny harbour on 1M-long **Birkholm** island (2m, unlit entrance approached northwards along a short buoyed 2m channel from a red buoy in the main channel). At the end of the channel the route rounds the cardinal buoy off Egholm Flak, keeping in over 5m, and then heads south-southwestwards to pick up the offing buoy and follow the Møllegab approach channel (unlit buoys, lights in line, light beacon on E side near northern end) to Ærøskøbing.

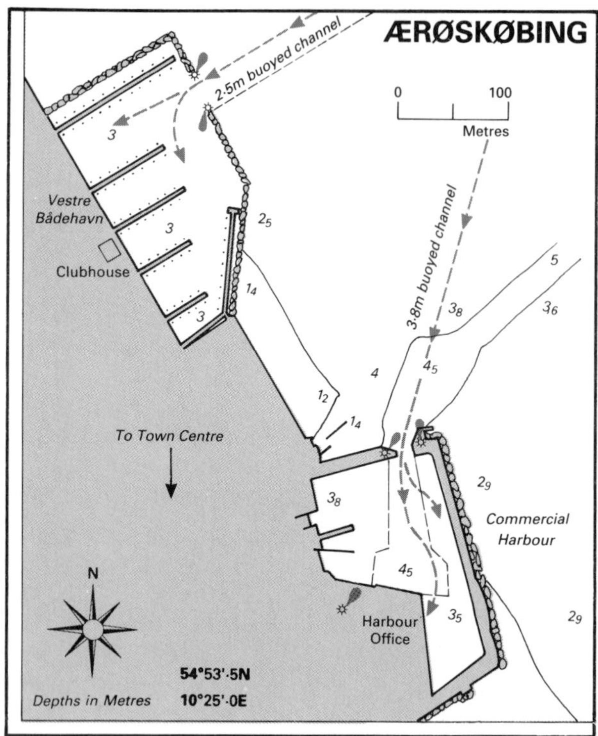

12M

ÆRØSKØBING (ÆRØ)

The Møllegab leads directly to Ærøskøbing's commercial harbour (3·8m, PD, VHF Ch 16, 13, 6), where larger yachts can also moor (keep clear of the ferry wharf and the boatyard). Some 0·6M from the entrance to the commercial harbour, a buoyed 2·5m channel leads southwestwards to the Vestre Bådehavn yacht haven (lit entrance, 2·5m, PD*).

This is a delightful market town, with some restored merchants' houses from the 17th and 18th centuries, and a 1749 post office (Denmark's oldest). There are a town museum and a shipping museum, and a ferry to Svendborg.

There is a very good anchorage in 3–4m E of the commercial harbour wall. There is a second anchorage, also nearby, over mud in 2–3m at the SE side

Ærøskøbing. Entrance to the Trafikhavn.

of Dejrø island. A third is some 2·5M southeastwards in 2m over mud in Kløven bay (keep in the middle of this unbuoyed 2–3m channel between the stone markers). Here there is also a landing stage (2m, unlit), where you can lie to a stern kedge or raft up and visit Ommel, a village with several thatched cottages.

DIVERSION TO DREJØ
(not included in total mileage)

4·5M N of Ærøskøbing, the low-lying Drejø island is worth visiting, taking the Møllegab channel and continuing northwards between the cardinal buoys into the 1M-wide 'broad' in between this island and Hjortø to the E. Approached across deep water, **Drejø pier**, on the SE coast of the island, has a right-angled endpiece with 2·5m on the outside of its SE side (inside this it is shallow, and the ferry is on the NE side of the jetty). You can also anchor in 2–3m further SW along the coast; the village is about 1km inland. Alternatively, in winds from the two N quadrants you can anchor (2–3m, sand) at the top of Skovens Vig, the deep bay some 2M W of this, but first you must negotiate the spit extending SE from the island and marked by a S cardinal buoy (unlit) (or approach directly from Møllegab). The tiny **Drejø harbour** on the N coast (1–1·2m basin, 1·1m marked channel, unlit entrance) has too shallow an approach to be recommended to visitors.

There is a short cut to Svendborg Sund along Højestene Løb (3·5m-deep channel, unlit buoys and lit beacons), which leads northeastwards from between Drejø and Hjortø. Hjortø fishing harbour (1·8m, unlit), on the N side of the island of that name, requires a difficult unlit approach southeastwards from Højestene Løb and is not recommended to newcomers.

NORTH COAST OF ÆRØ

→ The next route follows Møllegab, then heads northwestwards, keeping in over 10m. It then follows the Urehoved peninsula and rounds it at about 0·6M (its spit is unmarked) to head west-northwestwards for the headland E of Søby. This headland has another unmarked offlying shoal, so it must be rounded about 0·5M off and the harbour approached southwards from deep water. Most of this N coast is moderately high land. En route there are good anchorages (3–4m, mainly sand, some mud) round Revkrog bay with its sandy beaches, especially S of Urevohed point and at the S end of the bay; only in N to northwesterlies is the area exposed.

7M

SØBY (ÆRØ)

The entrance (sector light on E mole) is approached directly. The yacht haven (2·5–3m, D*) is to port after entry; it is about the same size as Æroskøbing yacht haven. The town nearby has no outstanding features. There are ferries to Fåborg and Mommark (on Als).

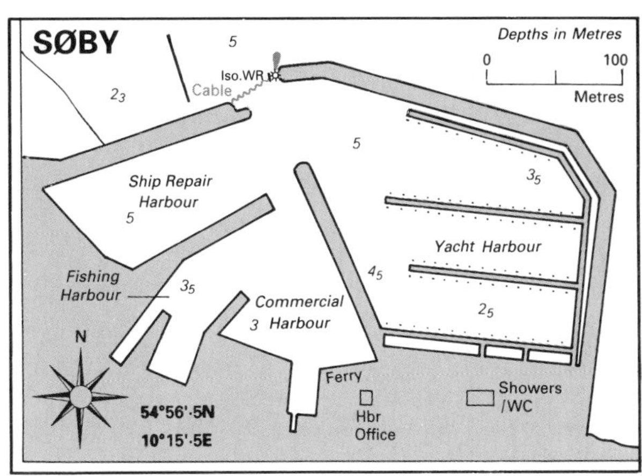

LILLE BÆLT, HELNÆS BUGT

There can be strong currents along this side of the Lille Bælt. In spring the stream is usually N-going; in autumn, S-going. In summer the overall North Sea/Baltic weather pattern determines the direction: ENE–E–S–SW winds create a N-going current and winds from other directions a S-going current. Helnæs Bugt is virtually landlocked.

Winds tend to be funnelled along this part of the Lille Bælt, whereas Helnæs Bugt is protected.

→ The route continues in deep water northwestwards, sounding round another unmarked spit, Næbbet, and passing Skjoldnæs light (round stone tower, 20M range). It then passes W of the cardinal buoy marking Lyø W Flak, on Lyø island (SE part is hilly – up to 24m), and heads for the entrance to Helnæs Bugt, past Hornenæs peninsula with its steep cliffs.

Helnæs Bugt is divided by a string of islands into a northern and a southern fjord, Nørre Fjord and Sønder Fjord. At each end of the islands is an unlit buoyed channel; there is also an unlit buoyed channel along the inner part of Sønder Fjord to Faldsled (see below). This channel is reached by following the steep W side of Hornenæs (Helnæshoved Flak shoal is to the W of this approach) and carefully passing the ferry entrance (lit). Sound round yet another unmarked reef, Kalvøre Rev, then head northwards past two green buoys (to starboard) towards the eastern end of Illumø island, where the buoys and topmarked withies of the channel to the harbour begin.

Before reaching the harbour there are several anchoring possibilities (watch out for fishing stakes). It is possible to pass through the two E entrance buoys (unlit) to Nørre Fjord, sound carefully northwestwards to avoid the shallows, and anchor in 2–3m over mud off the wood on the E side of Helnæs island (good for a stroll ashore to see the village, the Helnæs lighthouse and the extensive W-coast beaches). It is also possible to anchor in 2–3m over mud close N of Vesterhoved, the extreme W point of Illumø island, or to continue sounding carefully northwards and anchor in 3m over sand off the N end of Helnæs E coast, under the 30m Galgebakke hill. Finally, it is possible to continue yet further N and sound even more carefully into the inlet NE of Agernæs, anchoring over mud and weed in 2–3m.

⛵ **Bøjden pier** is an unlit landing stage (1·2–2m) with a side jetty for pleasure craft, 0·5m E of Bøjden ferry harbour (prohibited to pleasure craft). The approach, from the NNE after rounding two green buoys N of Kalvore Rev, is difficult, and there is little space for visitors. The ferry goes to Fynshav, on Als island.

18M
FALDSLED

⛵ ⚓ The marked channel to the entrance has about 2m. The harbour (1–2·5m, P*) has a NW-facing lit entrance. Visitors are better off staying in the deeper outer harbour, although anchoring, less nerve-wracking for a first visit, is possible SE of the harbour. This is a an old fishing village with an inn dating back to 1744.

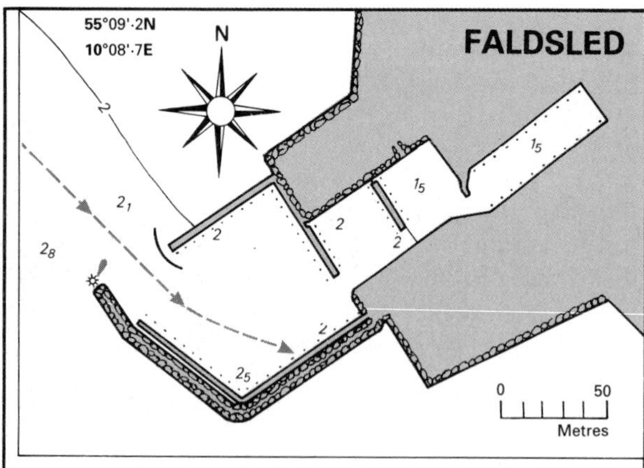

LYØ KROG AND FÅBORG FJORD

From this point for the rest of the route to Svendborg these are well sheltered waters.

→ ⚓ Return by the same route, then round Hornenæs peninsula into the deep (20m and more) Lyø Krog. Round the N point of Lyø (Lyø Rev and Lyø Trille headland, with its light beacon and unlit green buoy). Head south-southeastwards and finally approach the unlit harbour entrance from its N, in 3m and over. On the approach, there is an anchorage (including two yellow buoys) on the W side of the bay in 3–4m, 300–500m offshore over sand and weed.

⛵ **Lyø** (2–3m, unlit entrance) is entered directly; watch out for the ferries which dock at the end of the E mole. The harbour is small. The island is farmland, surrounded by a narrow beach; the ancient village centre is 1km from the harbour.

→ ⛵ ⚓ Return to the deep water N of Lyø harbour and continue eastwards round Lyø Sand, with its cardinal buoy. Round the buoys marking the ends of Knastegrund (lit) and Lillegrund (Bjørno sector light, 7–10M range, white hut with red band, leads through this passage at night). Head along the buoyed (two lit, mainly 10m-plus) channel to enter the small harbour of **Dyreborg** (0·5–2·5m, lit entrance, D), another picturesque main-island fishing village. There is a useful optional anchorage in 3–4m over sand about 200m S of the entrance. En route to Dyreborg, in good weather there is room for around three or more (if rafted) yachts at the northern end of the quayside at **Avernakø mole**, on the NW end of Avernakø island, in 3m (the ferry to Fåborg and Lyø docks on SW-facing wall).

→ From Dyreborg the route returns to the main buoyed (2 lit, plus lights in line at Østerhede) channel northeastwards round Bjørnø, then turns northwestwards at a red light buoy and heads directly along the leading line (lights in line) to Fåborg's lit commercial-harbour entrance in mainly 5m.

18M
FÅBORG

⛵ The W side of the commercial harbour (3·2–5·4m, PD) is the best and most convenient place for visitors to lie. There is also a yacht haven (2·5m*) about 0·4M NW of the commercial harbour, with a northeast-facing entrance (unlit), which is entered in 2·8m by following the wall round and doubling in.

Fåborg is an extremely attractive seaport with two museums and a long history. Its architectural features include a 13th-century church belfry tower, a medieval town gate and many handsome buildings from the 19th century, when it was an agricultural trading port. There is a ferry from the harbour to Gelting in Germany as well as local services to nearby islands.

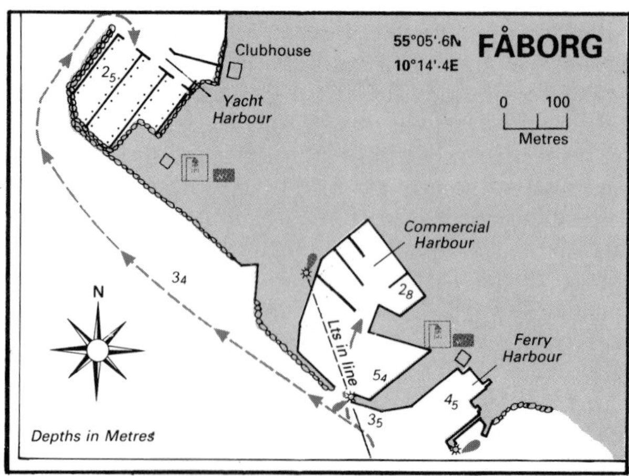

Fåborg. A traditional commercial harbour.

FÅBORG FJORD, GRYDELØB AND HANSE BUGT

→ The route outwards returns along the leading line, then continues southeastwards to Grydeløb, the 3·4m-deep buoyed gap in the reef between Bjørnø and the mainland. It then heads southwards in deep water (10–15m) past the buoyed (unlit) end of Bjørnø Holm spit. En route, there is a possible mooring along either side of **Bjørnø jetty** (2·2–2·3m), about halfway along the NE side of Bjørnø island, reached directly in over 2m from the NE.

NAKKEBØLLE FJORD AND APPROACHES

→ From Bjørnø Holm spit the route continues south and eastwards along the buoyed main channel to a red unlit buoy (keep to port) at the entrance to Nakkebølle Fjord. Finally, the route leads along the channel northwards and northwestwards to Fjællebroen harbour; it is marked with buoys (unlit) and topmarked perches.

⚓ Before turning N into Nakkebolle Fjord there are three possible anchorages. The first is on the steep E side of Svelmo island, N of the red main-channel buoy, in 3m over sand very close inshore. It is also possible to anchor in 3m over sand about 200m NE of **Korshavn pier** at the head/centre of the deep bay at the SE end of Avernakø island, or alternatively at the pier itself (1·5–2·5m, unlit; deepest water at the end). Finally, it is possible to anchor over sand in 2–4m in Revkrog bay (yellow Danske Sejlunion buoys), at the SE end of Avernakø, taking care to sound round the shoals S of Nakkeodde point and E of the Ravnebjerg hill (32m).

10M

FJÆLLEBROEN

⚓ The harbour (2·1m in main harbour, unlit entrance, PD) is approached from the SW along the buoyed channel, turning to port between the red (to port) and green buoys into the southeast-facing entrance. Apart from a kiosk there is little of interest nearby.

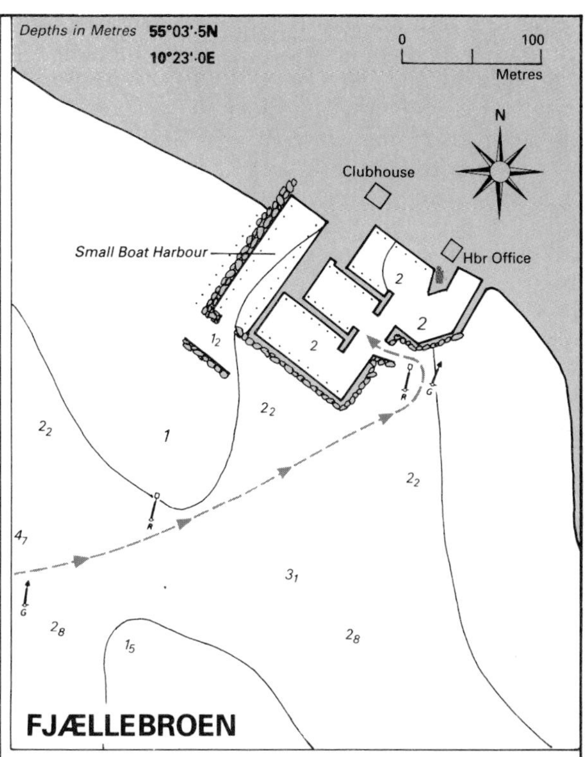

Fjællebroen yacht harbour. Looking out of the entrance.

APPROACHES TO SVENDBORG SUND (WEST)

The current in Svendborg Sund and approaches is erratic. In calm weather there is a 6–hourly tidal flow. This is overridden, however, by strong winds: northwesterlies create an E-going current and lower water levels by up to 1·2m, and easterlies create a W-going current and raise water levels by a similar amount. The current averages a significant 2/3kn in moderate but persistent winds, and can reach 6kn in gales in the narrower reaches.

The most uncomfortable conditions to be experienced in these sheltered waters are after a wind shifts to blow against the current direction, particularly in the funnel-shaped eastern approach when a southwesterly is blowing against an outgoing current.

→ Return to the entrance of Nakkebølle Fjord, past the S cardinal buoy marking the eastern shoals, then follow the main deep channel (10–19m) eastwards to Svendborg Sund. Skarø Rev, to the S of the course, is marked by a green buoy (unlit). Svendborg Sund's deep-water channel (mainly over 10m in the initial reaches) is on the N side, with extensive shoals on the S side. It is marked by (1) unlit buoys (red to port, green to starboard as far as the main Svendborg commercial harbour), (2) two directional sector lights, Bækkehave (white hut, red band, 8–12M range) and St Jorgens (white hut, red band, on piles, 7–10M range), and (3) a series of lights in line. The fixed Svendborg bridge has 33m clearance, with lights on each side of the navigable span (red to port, green to starboard in this direction).

En route from Nakkebølle entrance to the bridge, there are three possible mooring places. **Ballen** (1·5–2m, lit east-facing entrance) is a small shallow yacht haven on the mainland which is directly entered across 3m. To the S of the route, **Skarø**, on the island of that name, is an even smaller yacht haven (2–2·5m, light on end of N mole near where the Svendborg ferry docks) which is approached southwestwards from the main channel and past the RW offing buoy. **Rantzausminde** (1·5–2·5m, lit east-facing entrance) is a small yacht haven where, if you are lucky, you may find room on the deeper S and E sides of the harbour. A good anchorage on the S side of the route, albeit suffering some swell from distant passing vessels, is in 3m over sand and weed in the small bay between Vornæs point and Bækkehoved sector light.

10·5M (Svendborg yacht haven)

SVENDBORG SUND

→ Svendborg Sund is often nicknamed 'the Danish Riviera'. It winds between tree-clad slopes with scattered villas. The most built-over parts are at the western end and in Svendborg on the N bank. The buoyed channel E of Ranzausminde is mostly over 6m deep.

Svendborg yacht haven, a medium-sized marina on the N bank (1–3m, unlit entrance, PD*), has little spare space. **Vindeby yacht haven** (2·5–3m, lit entrance), opposite on the S bank, is worth a try, but could also be full. Visitors are probably better off (and are certainly more conveniently placed for the town) continuing on along the Sund to the **commercial harbour**. On the extreme northern bend, turn to port into the harbour's Østhavn entrance (lit on S corner), then pass through the next unlit inner entrance into the Nordhavn and head for the yacht pontoons (over 4m of water*) on the W side of the basin. On the SE side of the harbour are repair yards for vintage square riggers.

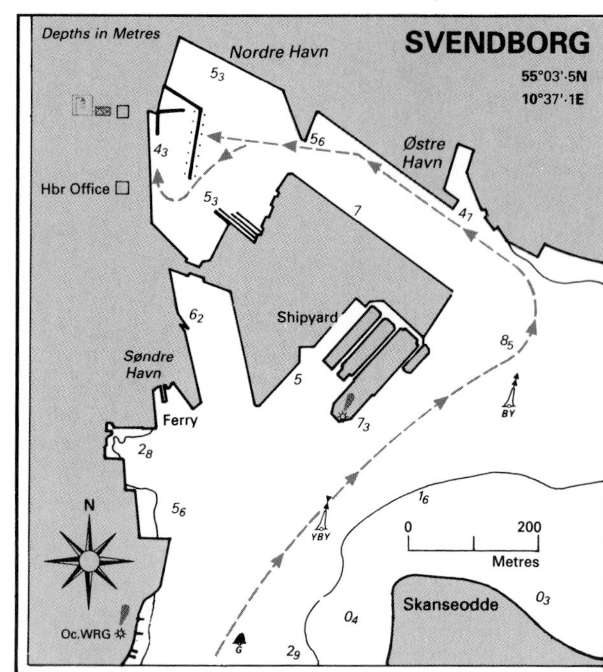

Troense on Tåsinge island in Svendborg Sund. Picturesque harbour which attracts the square riggers.

Svendborg yacht haven. This circular marina is not to be confused with Svendborg Sund Marina further E.

Svendborg is a large sprawling town with a zoological museum and a number of old buildings, including a 13th-century church (Skt Nicolai) and a museum in a 16th-century half-timbered building. For a busman's holiday you can choose from several boat trips touring the Sound and outlying areas. There are also several local ferry services to the islands, with connections to Sjælland and Jutland.

SVENDBORG SUND (EAST), THURØ BUND AND RUDKØBING LØB

(*See above for Svendborg Sund*). In Rudkøbing Løb the tidal current reverses every 6 hours in calm weather and runs at 1–2kn. In strong westerlies, however, the current runs southwards, and in easterlies northwards, when it can reach as much as 4–5kn.

Outside the protection of Svendborg Sund, Rudkøbing Løb is aligned in a northeasterly direction, and winds from the NW quadrant in particular tend to be funnelled along it.

→ The route from Svendborg's commercial harbour follows the remaining part of the Sund and crosses the bay to the S to join Rudkøbing Løb.

From the first red buoy on the northern extremity of the bend E of the commercial harbour, the buoyage (all unlit) direction changes, with the flood assumed to be coming from the E and with red buoys now to starboard in this direction. There are four directional sector lights in this and the following winding reaches. Gasværk light (4–6M range) beams northeastwards past the commercial harbour. Kristiansminde light (red post, white bands, 8–12M range) leads westwards along the northern bend and is also the front one of a pair of leading lights directed southwards down the next reach. Mårodde light (white column, red band, 10M range) leads south-southeastwards. Troense light (also white column, red band, 8–10M range). Finally, three more sets of lights in line zigzag down the channel between the unlit buoys and out to the N of the E cardinal buoy marking the end of Slotshage and Middelgrund shoals.

⚓ **Svendborg Sund Marina** is a series of boxes (0·8–3m) 0·8M E of the commercial harbour along the N bank, and near the entrance to Scårupøre Sund.

Troense on Tåsinge island is a small picturesque yacht haven below a hill (1–1·6m on inner and 2–6m on outer pontoons). If it is crowded, there is an anchorage in Pilekrog, about 300m NW of the yacht haven under Bregninge Skov beech woods, in 2–3m over weed (unfortunately), or you might pick up a nearby mooring. Troense was once a traditional sailing-ship mooring place, and the Troense maritime collection, in the old village school, is well worth a visit. Close S of the village is Valdemar's Slot, a mid-18th-century mansion with a lake, gardens and two superb gatehouses at the end of a lovely avenue of limes.

Vindeby yacht harbour. Entrance on S side Svendborg Sund.

Gambøt (1·5–2·5m, D) is a somewhat larger yacht haven, NE of Troense and N of Kidholm Flak shoals (marked by W cardinal buoy), with pontoons and boxes along the N bank of Thurø Bund. The traditional shipyards (including Gambøt) on this N bank built many sailing ships in the late 19th century. Kidholm shoals protect the entrance to Thurø Bund. Eastwards of both the yacht haven and the underwater cable there are good anchorages in 2–4m over mud and clay below the woods and farmland all round the bay, with a small private yacht harbour on the S side.

Typical Danish beach, south coast of Thurø Island.

→ ⛴ The course from Slotshage cardinal buoy leads southeastwards past Stehodde point (unlit cardinal buoy) to the RW offing buoy of Rudkøbing Løb buoyed channel (unlit, red to port with the flood, 5m deep). There are three sets of lights in line along a shallow Z-bend, the last set leading to Rudkøbing commercial harbour. The channel is crossed by a fixed road bridge, Langelandsbroen (26m clearance, red lights on E side of navigable span and green lights on W side), from Siø island to Langeland.

⚓ On leaving Svendborg Fjord, there are at least two peaceful anchorages (depending on wind direction) well to the W of this well beaten track in the Lunkebugt, a bay which digs deep into the E side of Tåsinge island. Both are in 2–3m over sand and weed; one is on the W side (yellow Danske Seijlunion buoy) of the bay near the woods of Pederskov, the other in the SE corner off the Venmenæs peninsula.

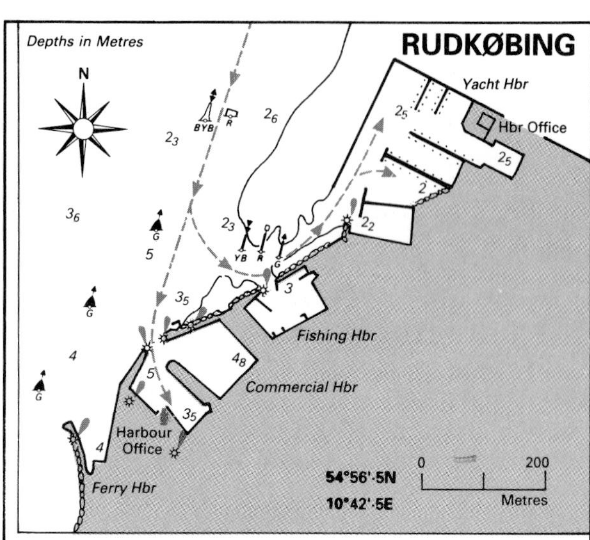

9·5M

RUDKØBING (LANGELAND)

⛵ Rudkøbing has four harbours (PD), which are, from N to S:

i. A well equipped yacht haven (2·2–2·5m*) with a lit WSW-facing entrance and a long 1·4m shoal extending southwestwards from the northern mole, so that it is approached in 2m or more water in a loop eastwards from the main channel, doubling northeastwards between a red buoy and a green buoy into the lit entrance.
ii. A fishing harbour (2·5–3·1m; not for pleasure craft) with a lit northeast-facing entrance entered directly S of the above red and green buoys.
iii. A commercial harbour (3·5–5m, lit entrance), entered directly, where large yachts can use the S basin.
iv. A ferry harbour which is to be avoided.

Langelands Bridge (26m clearance) from Rudkøbing yacht harbour.

Langeland is a holiday island, popular for its beaches and lovely beech woods. Rudkøbing, the largest town, is an interesting old place, with meandering streets, old merchants' houses, a 12th-century church, an apothecary's-shop museum (the birthplace of Hans Christian Ørsted, who established the theory of electromagnetism), and the Langeland museum, with exhibits of Viking weapons and armour, and of underwater archaeological research.

CHANNEL BETWEEN FYN AND LANGELAND

↳ Currents are mainly wind-driven: N-going with SE-quadrant winds, S-going with NW-quadrant winds (strongest towards the westerly side of the quadrant). In some conditions the current can set in opposite directions on each side of the Vresen bank at the N end of the channel.

The channel is most exposed to the NE wind quadrant. As in Svendborg Sund, the most uncomfortable conditions are when wind is against current after a wind change.

→ ⚓ ⛵ The route retraces itself back along Rudkøbing Løb, at the end of which a course (in 6m increasing to 13m) is set directly for the two cardinal buoys (unlit) marking the gap in the reefs (Snøde Rev to the N, Egeløkke Rev to the S) opposite Dagelokke on Langeland. There is a popular anchorage in the middle of the E coast of Thurø, off the woods and with a sandy beach, in 2–3m.

The whole of the W coast of Langeland is hilly and wooded. The lights-in-line course leads directly between the cardinal buoys to two more spar buoys (red and green, unlit), through which the W-facing entrance (lit, 2·8m) is approached. S of the entrance is a westwards-pointing breakwater and S of this are rocks and shallows. **Daggeløkke yacht haven**

(1·7–2·6m, D) is an old fishing harbour converted into a small marina, with a modern holiday resort nearby; it is often full in season, so could call only for a lunchtime stop.

→ ⚓ ⛵ From the outer buoys on the reef the course (13–14m decreasing to 4–5m) leads directly north-northwestwards, correcting for crosscurrent as necessary, across the channel to a point about 2 cables E of Lundeborg. The E coast of Fyn as far as Nyborg rises inland and appears generally wooded, but more thickly so in places, particularly near Lundeborg. To port of the course, Elsehoved sector light (short red round tower, white bands, range 8–12M) is on the headland. There is an anchorage under the woods close S of Elsehoved point near Tiseholt in 2–4m. **Lundeborg** is a small fishing harbour (3m, D), often full in season, whose lit S-facing entrance (2·5m) must be approached from due E across a 4·7m patch (a dangerous rock is charted to the SE of this on a 4·3m patch), since there are shoals about 80m S of the entrance.

→⛵ The course (mainly in 14m) next leads from Lundeborg entrance directly to the red offing buoy of Smørstakke Løb, the channel across the banks (Smørstakken to the N, Rødgrund to the S) opposite Lohals, and again may require a cross-current correction. The course lies N of the two red buoys and S of the lit green buoy, along the white sector of Lohals Havn light (short white square tower, 8–12M range, close S of the harbour). There are two harbours at **Lohals**, both with S-facing entrances which must be doglegged into from the W, and both of which visitors can use – so you may be able to find a space! From N to S these are:

i. A fishing harbour (2·2–3·7m, D, lit entrance. Keep clear of the ferry quay to starboard in the entrance.
ii. A small modern yacht haven (2–2·5m, unlit entrance). Watch out for the large ferry ships using the northern entrance.

Tom Kundsen's Safari Museum, in the E of the village, is the main point of interest. There are some excellent walks in the woodland and coastal scenery N of the village in the Hov peninsula area, or bicycles can be hired near the harbour. There is a ferry service from Lohals to Korsør on Sjælland.

→ The course returns to the offing buoy outside the outer shoals and then leads directly northwards to the lit RW buoy in the entrance to Nyborg Fjord. The depths are 8–20m, but keep sounding to avoid the Vresen reef, E of and parallel with the course. W of the course, Stokkebæk Flak shoal is marked by an E cardinal. E of the course is Frankeklint sector light (gable of white house, 7M range), on the end of Hov.

An optional route, depending on wind conditions, leads northwards from the harbour on the E side of the Vresen and then westwards through the bank via the 4·3m Kobberdyb channel (unlit cardinal buoys) to join the main channel northwards to Nyborg.

Lohals, Langeland. The northern fishing harbour.

Lohals, Langeland. The southern yacht harbour.

Knudshoved sector light (white square tower, 11–16M range) is on the point northwards of the RW lit buoy in Nyborg Fjord entrance. The course then leads northwestwards, keeping in the deep water of the main buoyed channel (some lit, light beacons, a set of lights in line followed by a second set of lights in line combined with a directional sector light – keep to starboard side of channel). There are extensive shoals on each side of the channel, and wooded slopes on the W side and the flat Østerø point to the E. Holckenhavn castle is a prominent square tower to the W of the channel, on the S side of the entrance to Holckenhavn Fjord. There is a windmill near the first set of leading lights. The final directional sector light is the front one of a second pair of leading lights, and is on the E mole of Nyborg yacht haven basin entrance. Watch out for the huge ferries which berth on the E side of the harbour opposite the yacht haven basin.

25M
NYBORG

At the end of the buoyed channel the large modern yacht haven (400 boxes, 1–2·7m, PD*) is hard to port. It occupies the southern end of the basin; the fishing harbour (2·5–3m) is N of this. Large yachts can lie in 5·5m in the Østrehavn, a basin at the N end of the harbour complex outside the yacht haven. The yacht haven is in somewhat stark, industrial surroundings, but the town is a picturesque one.

Nyborg was the site of the Danehof, the Danish parliament of the middle ages. As at Helsingør in the Sund, in the 16th to 19th centuries the town's guard ship collected tolls from ships using the Store Bælt. There are many preserved buildings, including the remains of a 12th-century castle built to dominate the Store Bælt, a 15th-century merchant's house converted to a museum, a 14th-century church, and the remains of 17th-century town ramparts with a gate and a tower. This is the main train/car ferry port connecting Fyn and Jutland with Sjælland.

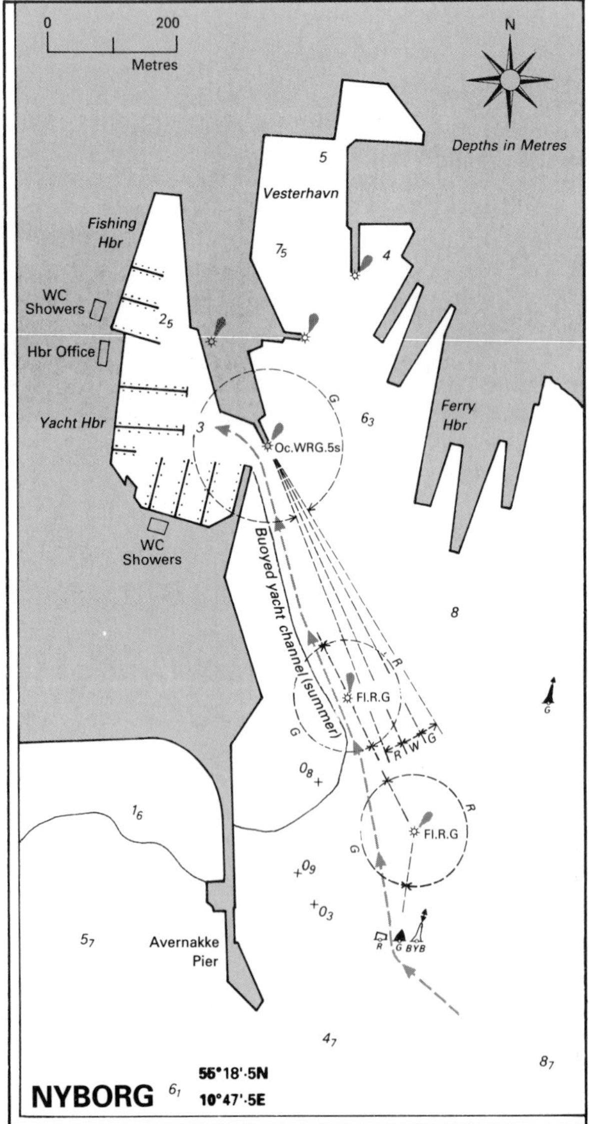

Nyborg's yacht harbour, E Fyn. Looking out to the entrance towards industrial ferry harbour.

If you are worried about visiting Odense by water because of its lack of mooring space, here is the place from which to take a train.

STORE BÆLT, AGERSØ SUND AND SKÆLSKØR FJORD

The overall North Sea/Baltic weather pattern determines the direction of currents in the Store Bælt. NNE–E–S–SSW winds create a N-going current and winds from other directions a S-going current.

The Store Bælt has a long fetch to the N, and winds from the NW quadrant create the worst conditions. Strong SE-quadrant winds also create progressively more uncomfortable conditions further N. The Bælt is a wide stretch of water, so when winds move easterly or westerly the bights on either side can become lee-shore embayments for a small vessel.

→ The course returns to the fjord entrance, sounding eastwards round Knudshoved Flak (S cardinal buoy). Continue across the Store Bælt, passing well to the N of the W and E Puller shoals (mainly in 10–30m of water), then carry on, keeping in the white sector of Knudshoved light, towards the first

Agersø. Harbour entrance. Not included in this route but picturesque alternative to Skælskør, a short distance down Agersø Sund.

unlit green entrance buoy of Agersø Sund. This course crosses both the current and the two traffic routes towards the bridge-building area, but the longest distance between visible buoys is about 6M.

The route continues southeastwards to the third green buoy (two, including this one, are lit; on this reach there are lights in line on Gedehave point). It then leaves the main channel and heads (in 6–10m) SE for the RW unlit offing buoy of Skælskør Fjord, following the spar-buoyed channel (also lights in line) south-southeastwards into the entrance, where the winding spar buoys to the head of the fjord must be followed religiously. It is easy to stray from this channel, and although it is theoretically dredged to 4·5m, many parts of it are nearer to 2·5m.

19M

SKÆLSKØR (SJÆLLAND)

There is a mole with about 4·5m at its head on the N bank at the fjord entrance at Vasebro. Skælskør yacht haven (2·5m, unlit entrance W of channel*) is usually pretty crowded, and you may have to pick up a buoy, or continue on and raft alongside in the outer harbour (3–4·5m), just N of the fishing harbour (not for pleasure craft). The northern inner harbour has an extremely strong current from the narrows under the bridge.

Skælskør yacht harbour from the hill above.

The town is attractive, with a hill on each side down to the harbour, timber-framed houses and shops, a small museum and a 13th-century church and tithe barn. 2km S is Borreby manor, a beautifully preserved 16th-century fortified country house.

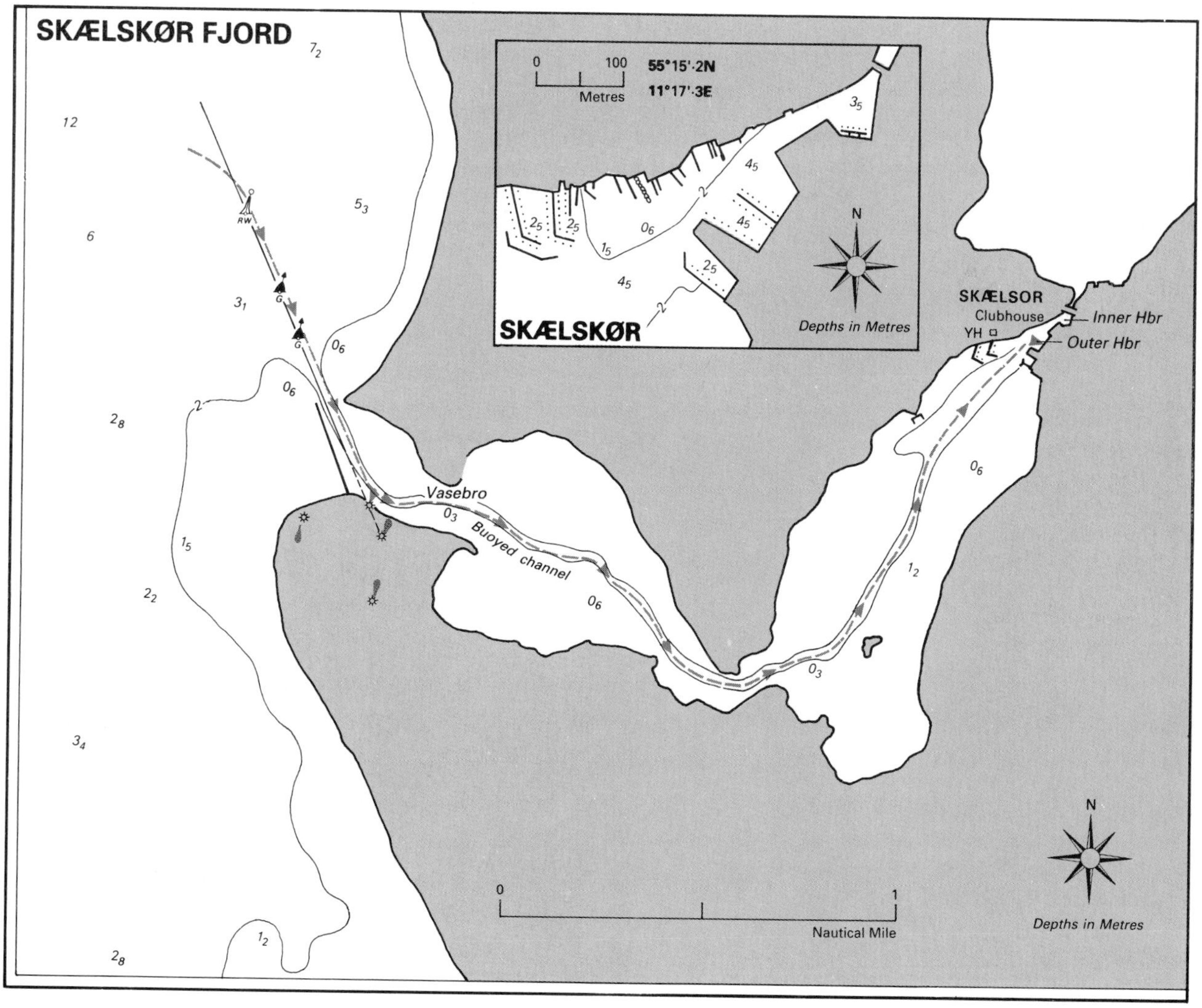

SKÆLSKØR FJORD

SKÆLSKØR

0 100 Metres

55°15'·2N 11°17'·3E

Depths in Metres

SKÆLSOR

Clubhouse

YH

Inner Hbr

Outer Hbr

Vasebro

Buoyed channel

0 1 Nautical Mile

Depths in Metres

9·5M (yacht harbour)
STORE BÆLT AND KORSØR ANSTEURUNG (SJÆLLAND)

→ A The route returns to the unlit green buoy at the outer end of Agersø Sund. It continues northwestwards outside the 10m contour to the unlit W cardinal buoy off Badstue Rev shoal, then heads northeastwards, rounding the two green buoys (keep to starboard) marking the Blinde Badstue shoal. Finally, it turns to port into the lit S-facing **Korsør** yacht haven entrance in 2·6m. Korsør sector light (red framework tower, white base, 10–14M range) is close N in the final approaches. This light is only 0·6M SE of Halskov sector light, in the train-ferry harbour approaches to the N. En route there are good anchorages to the E of the course in sand and clay in 2–4m, close inshore in Skælskor Reede and under the woods in the wide bay to the N of Lindeskov Flak.

⛵ Korsør has a large yacht haven (450 spaces, 2·4–2·9m, lit entrance with sector light on W mole, PD*), with a restaurant and some limited repair facilities.

Korsør has been a market and ferry town for nearly 800 years, but really came into its own in 1856, when the railway to København was completed, since ships from Kiel now docked here and transshipped their goods by rail instead of continuing round to the capital. As well as some interesting half-timbered buildings near the 19th-century church, there are the ramparts and tower of a 14th-century fortress overlooking the harbour, together with a building housing the town museum, with extensive exhibits from the history of the ferry service. In the harbour complex there are a naval basin and control tower, and during our visit the peace of each morning and evening in the yacht haven was shattered by a cannon shot as the ensign was raised and lowered on the nearby wall.

Nowadays there are ferry services from Korsør to Nyborg on Fyn island and Lohals on Langeland, backed up by a ferry from nearby Halsskov to Knudshoved on Fyn. The trains to Nyborg are now shunted onto the ferries, after which the passengers can leave their seats to enjoy the sea passage before rejoining the train and travelling directly to mainland Europe.

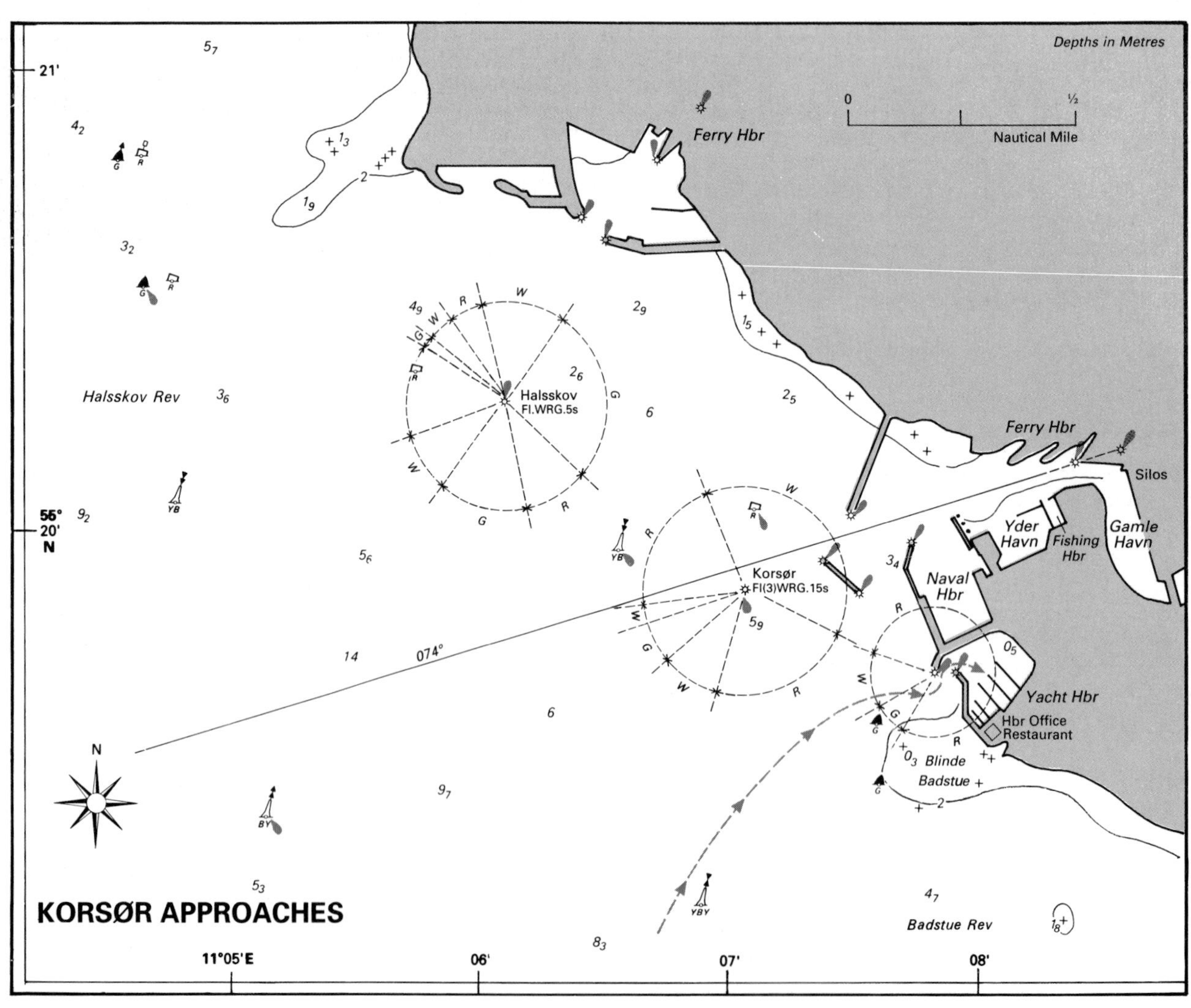

Store Bælt bridge and tunnel works

All this will change in 1996, when the Store Bælt motorway bridge and railway tunnel are scheduled to be completed. The multi-piered rail and road bridge from the Nyborg side to Sprogø island across the Vesterrenden was the first section to be completed, and the second stage, a rail tunnel and a high motorway suspension bridge across the Østerrenden to Hallsskov, was well under way in 1994. When completed, the suspension bridge will have a clearance of 65m.

There is a buoyed channel through the Vesterrenden (some lit buoys, green to port going N), with 70m width in each of the two (N-going and S-going) span passages and a maximum clearance of 18m. There is a traffic-separation scheme through the Østerrenden. In this channel going N the lit buoys are red to starboard, RW buoys mark the central separation boundary and green buoys mark the W side of the S-going lane. There are sector lights on each side of the TSS: at the SE end Halsskov Rev S (yellow tower, range 5–6M), on the NW side Sprogø NE (green tower, white lantern, floodlit, range 5–6M).

It is not compulsory, but traffic control prefer small vessels to use the Vesterrenden channel. If you do use the Østerrenden, keep to the extreme starboard edge of the channel. All vessels should keep a listening watch on VHF Ch 16 (working channel and information: VHF Ch 11), and while small craft are not required to request passage by radio, large vessels have special radio reporting points at which they report their progress. It is always advisable to have an up-to-date chart when piloting this area.

ØSTERRENDEN, STORE BÆLT CROSSING AND KERTEMINDE BUGT

See above.

See above.

→ The route leads due W from the yacht-haven entrance to the Østerrenden TSS, then turns northwards, following the extreme eastern edge of the buoyed (lit) N-going lane. Beyond the end of the channel it turns at right angles across the TSS, and finally heads directly northwestwards to the green and red (unlit) buoys at Kerteminde entrance. On this last 15M stretch a cross-track correction for current and repeated Decca/GPS checking will probably be necessary, since there are no intervening marks.

18·5M

KERTEMINDE (FYN)

A The yacht-haven entrance, with a F green light at the end of the N mole, is behind an offshore baffle wall with a Q.R light at each end. After passing the unlit green buoy (leave to starboard) in the approaches, a dogleg turn is needed to enter the large yacht haven (over 600 berths, 1·5–2·5m, PD★). Visitors can also lie alongside the N quay (4·9m)

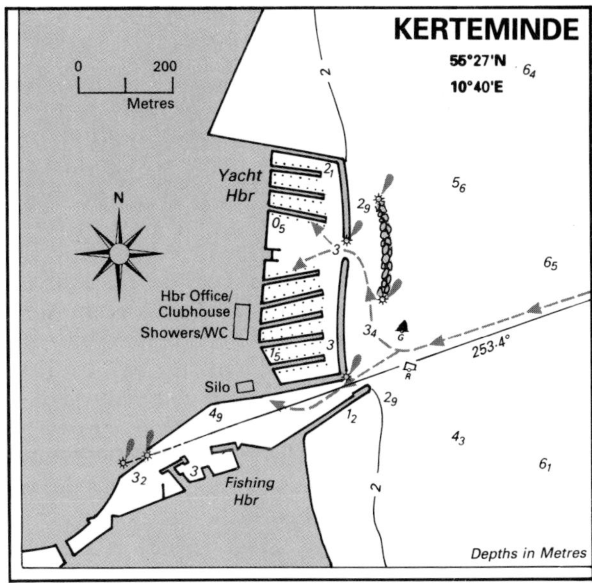

Kerteminde yacht harbour.

near the silo in the commercial harbour, which is through a lit entrance to the S of the yacht haven and has a lights-in-line approach. Good inshore anchorages over clay and mud can be found round the wooded edges of Kerteminde Bugt and near the harbour.

This is a fishing town founded in the Middle Ages, with a 13th-century church housing relics of the late 16th-century Swedish War, a 15th-century custom house with a local-art exhibition, a town museum, half-timbered houses and a reconstructed shop from the turn of our century in an 18th-century building. About 2km W of the town, on a commanding site overlooking the Kertinge Nor lake to the N of Ladby village, is the grave of a Viking chief, buried in his ship with his horses and hunting dogs and now preserved in a chamber inside the mound.

Like Nyborg, Kerteminde is within easy reach of Odense, but this time by bus.

KERTEMINDE BUGT, STORE BÆLT CROSSING AND KALUNDBORG FJORD

(*See also above.*) Currents within Kerteminde Bugt are weak and mainly tidal, but wind can produce 3kn currents in the narrow Kerteminde Havn.

(*See also above.*) Strong easterlies create the worst conditions.

→A From the entrance buoys the route leads northeastwards; keep in 7–17m and sound round the wooded Stavreshoved point, inshore of the Møllegrund shoal (5·6–9m), to the E cardinal marking the eastern end of Romsø Pullar shoals. There are three possible inshore anchorages round the low wooded Romsø island: on its eastern coast, N and S of the old lighthouse, and just NE of the western peninsula of the island after sounding round the N and W coasts. As the island is a nature reserve, landing during the summer season is permitted only during daylight hours.

From Romsø E cardinal buoy the course continues directly across the Store Bælt to round Sjælland's Asnæs peninsula outside its two offlying cardinal buoys. This part of the course passes Romsø Tue sector light (green tower, 5–8M range); a cross-course correction for current will probably be necessary. The course then leads east-southeastwards down Kalundborg Fjord directly to the harbour entrance.

The N side of the fjord is high rolling farmland and the S side is low and wooded. There are a sector light and an all-round light on Rosnæs spit and peninsula to the N, and an all-round light on Asnæs peninsula to the S, as follows: Rosnæs Puller (round red tower, granite base, 5–8M range); Rosnæs (white square tower on headland, 20M range); Asnæs (white pedestal, red band, 4M range). There is a directional sector light, Kalundborg Fjord (orange metal framework, 10–14M range), with a white approach sector along the fjord. There is an inshore anchorage, protected mainly from the two southern quadrants and from the W, in Havnemark Vig, E of Havnemark village on the N side of the Asnæs peninsula.

26M

KALUNDBORG (SJÆLLAND)

Unlit red buoys mark the northern shoals of the approach channel, which follows the first set of lights in line past a red unlit buoy (to port) and the two lights on the N and S moles, then heads north-northeastwards along another buoyed (unlit) chan-

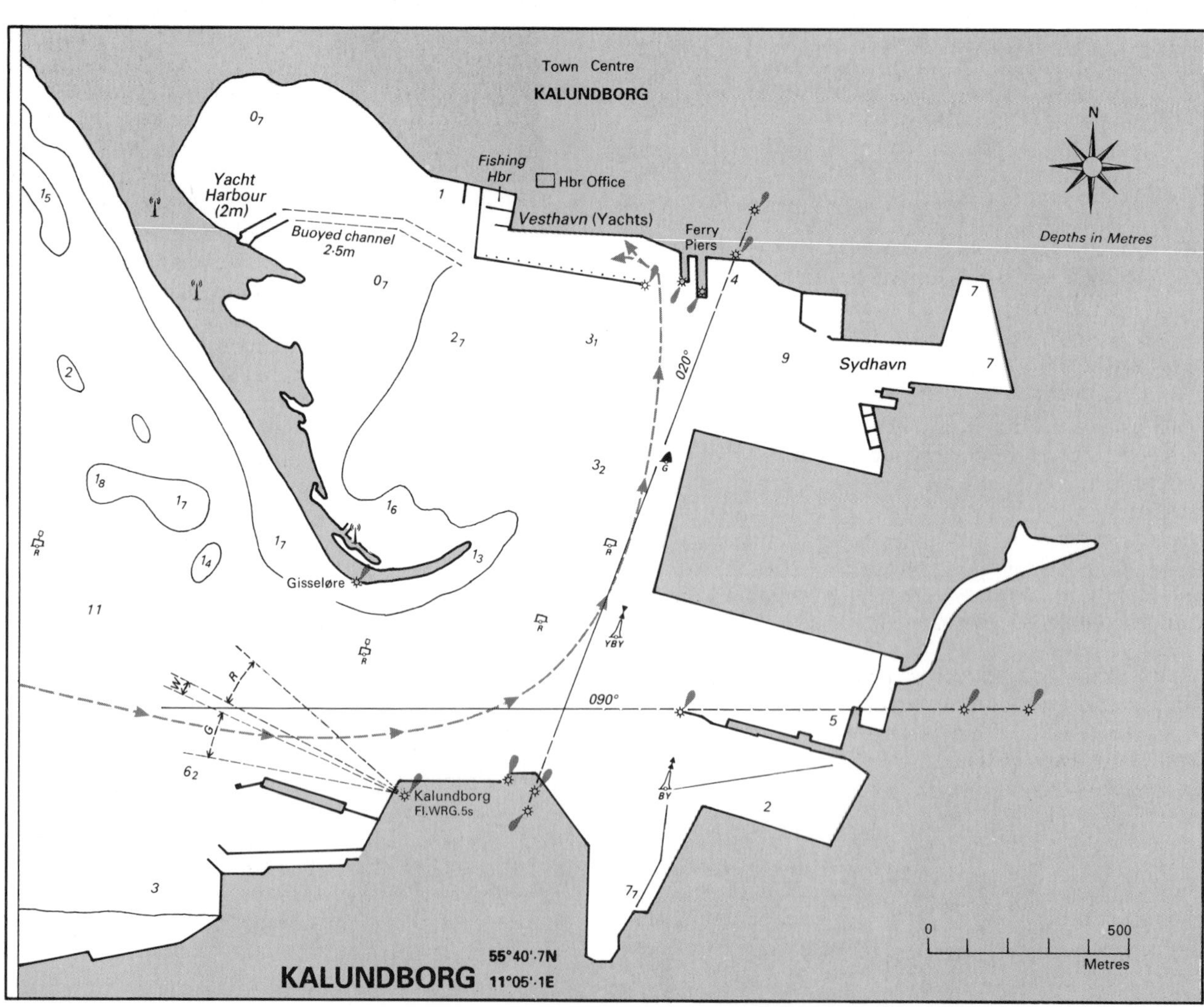

nel with lights in line. The Vesthavn yacht haven (3m, PD) is entered from its E end; its boxes are along the N side of a long pontoon, and there may also be room alongside on the commercial quayside to the N. There is an alternative, 2m-deep, smaller and usually full yacht haven on the Gisseløre peninsula, which forms the W side of this natural harbour. This is entered along a buoyed channel W of Vesthavn, and is approached along the S side of the main yacht-haven pontoon.

The main feature of this town is its wonderful 12th-century church with five towers, in a carefully preserved medieval quarter of the town. Nearby is the museum, in a half-timbered 16th-century mansion. There are ferries to Juelsminde and Århus on the main Jutland peninsula.

DIVERSION TO REERSØ, MULLERUP AND MUSHOLM

(not included in total mileage)

→ ⛵ ⚓ A possible excursion from here leads southwards for about 20M and round two headlands to **Reersø** harbour (2–2·5m, lit entrance, PD), on the E side of the peninsula of that name. Reersø is a fishing village with thatched cottages, one of which has been restored and furnished as a farm labourer's cottage of the 18th century. There is an anchorage nearby to the NE. Just over 2M SE is **Mullerup**, a small commercial harbour converted into a yacht haven (2·3–3·8m but now tending to silt up, lit entrance, PD). About 2·5M SW of Reersø is Musholm Havn, a tiny natural harbour on the E side of the island of that name, in which it is possible to anchor.

KALUNDBORG FJORD, STORE BÆLT CROSSING AND ODENSE FJORD APPROACHES

↪ *(See above.)* The northern approaches to Odense Fjord tend to experience currents which are weaker than those in the Store Bælt, tending more northeastwards with the N-going current in the Store Bælt and more southwestwards with the S-going current.

☂ *(See above.)* Kalundborg Fjord is exposed to winds from NW to W, while the northern approaches to Odense Fjord are exposed to winds from the whole NW quadrant.

→ This tricky navigational passage requires good weather and visibility, preferably in daylight. Return to the unlit N cardinal buoy off Asnæs NW Flak, then head west-southwestwards across the Store Bælt directly to the lit N cardinal buoy off Lillegrund, the very shallow northern end (1·3m with rocks) of the northerly spit of Fyns Hoved, at the northern end of Fyn. This 10M run is crosscurrent, with only the 4M Asnæs light and the Lillegrund cardinal light buoy to help at night. There is a RW light buoy about halfway, but well to the S of the course, so you probably won't see this, and in any case will need to keep checking the Decca/GPS position. In daylight, if you are bold and conditions are ideal, you could try the 5m buoyed channel through the bank 8 cables S of the light buoy.

Either way you must next sound round the W side of the Fyns Hoved and Bæsbanke shoals, keeping in over 10m offshore, and then head southwards (the underwater contours here are steep) to the red and green unlit entrance buoys of Korshavn's natural harbour. Fyns Hoved cliffs are backed by the 25m Bæs Banke hill. Korsøre, S of this, is a flat sandy headland.

23M (Korshavn)

ODENSE FJORD AND KANAL

→ ⛵ ⚓ From between the red and green buoys, the white sector of Korsøre light (and in daytime the triangular marks of the lights in line) leads northeastwards to Korsøre headland, which should be rounded about 80–100m off. Continue northwards to the T-shaped landing stage (2·9m), which, even with stern kedge anchors out, is usually full. The anchorage, in 3–4m in the middle of Korshavn cove, is over sand and eelgrass, so make sure your anchor bites. Hotel and shop nearby.

→ The route continues from the entrance buoys southwestwards to the RW lit fjord offing buoy (you can cut the corner across the 7m eastern shoal in good conditions). Head for the E cardinal N of the entrance, then along the buoyed Gabet channel (red to port, some lit), winding between the rocky Skoven and low-lying Hals peninsulas. The approach from the N is made easier at night by two sector lights: Skoven (framework, 3–5M range) and Enebærodde (white tower, 8–11M range).

The fjord is shallow and the marked channels must be followed. Several sets of lights in line and beacons and buoys (red to port), many of which are lit, take the winding main channel (dredged to an unreliable 7·5m) southwards into the 4M-long Odense Kanal.

⚓ Three possible anchorages, depending on wind direction, are: in Dalby Bugt, the bay E of Skoven outside the entrance; on the E side of the Hals peninsula; inside the entrance just behind the Hals headland.

DIVERSION TO OTTERUP AND BREGNØR

(not included in total mileage)

⛵ ⚓ **Otterup** (2–2·5m, sector light E side of entrance) is a small yacht haven, usually with very few spare boxes, approached along the spar-buoyed (unlit) Egense Dyb channel, which leads northwestwards from the main channel 1M SW of the Gabet entrance. It is entered from the NE along the last reach of the buoyed channel. There is a good anchorage in mud and clay towards the top of the channel near the yacht haven, but try to keep just outside the fairway.

Bregnør is an even tinier yacht haven (2m) with an E-facing entrance (light on N mole). It has a tricky unmarked approach southeastwards from the main channel 1M SW of Gabet entrance, requiring the chart and sounding to avoid stones and sandbanks on either side of the approach. Visitors lie on the W wall.

Klintebjerg can only be described as a mini yacht haven (0·4–1m inside; 2m on the outside of the outer pontoon, but there is swell from passing vessels). It is on the N side of the main channel 4M SW of Enebærodde.

15M (excluding visits above to Otterup and Bregnør)

ODENSE (FYN)

Stige is a yacht haven (3–3·5m, unlit entrance) with about 150 places, halfway along the Odense Kanal in the northern suburbs of Odense, entered directly on the E bank. The southern part of the entrance is the deepest (3m); on the northern side is a spit which may have been dredged since this book was written. A little further S on the opposite bank is a small 1m-deep boat harbour.

Near the head of the Kanal on the W side is a small **Motorboathavn** (2–2·5m deep) entered through a 3·5m-high tunnel. On the N side of the next bend in the Kanal, just before the basin at the head, are several **yacht pontoons**, pleasantly located by the woodlands of Næsbyhoved Skov and with a restaurant nearby, but these moorings are usually full. A better possibility is to raft up on the E side (2–4·5m) of **No. 2 basin**, the middle one of the three southwards-pointing commercial basins at the head of the navigation. This area is N of and within walking distance of central Odense.

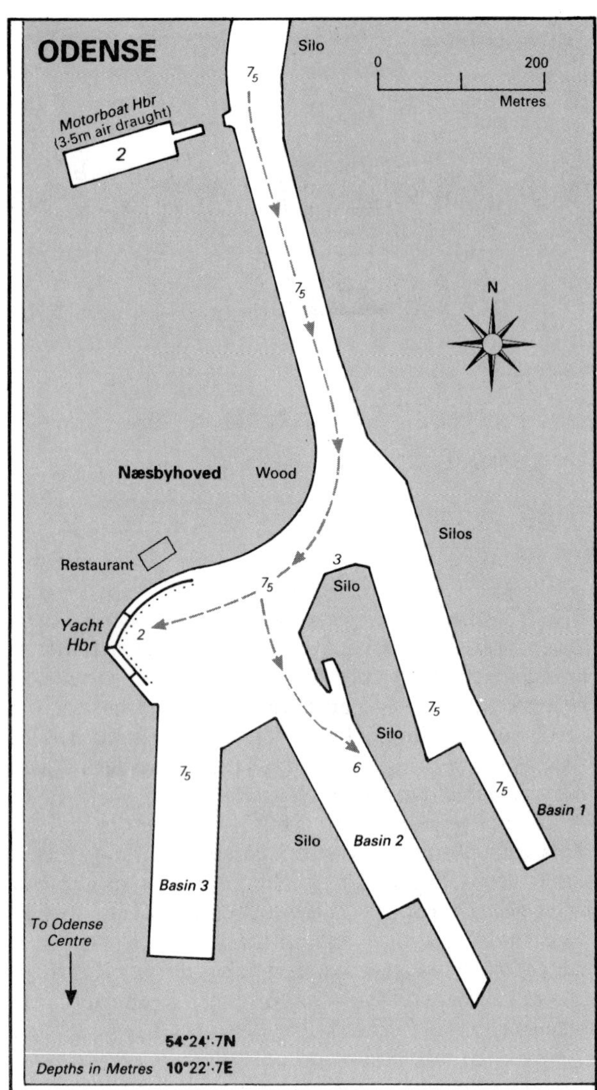

Odense is Denmark's third-largest city. Although it has preserved its ancient layout, with a maze of winding streets and pedestrian precincts, there are few buildings built before the late 18th century. The shopping, nightlife and restaurants are good. In the crypt of Odense's Gothic cathedral, Skt Knud's Kirke, is the shrine of the murdered King, now Saint, Canute. The town is the birthplace of Hans Christian Andersen (1805–75), although his guiding principle, 'To travel is to live', meant that he rarely returned here after his early 'teens. His supposed birthplace is now part of a much-extended museum in Hans Jensens Stræde. There are several other museums, including the Falcke (rescue corps) museum, the major DSB railway museum, and Møntergården, a collection of refurbished 16th and 17th-century houses. There are no major ferry services from Odense.

Odense. The pontoons under Næsbyhoved woods.

9. South Sjælland and the Sound

Route 7
Kiel to Roskilde via Smålands Farvandet and the Sound

Commentary

In choosing the first part of the passage route from Kiel to the Sound, the major decision is whether to take the simplest and deepest, but most exposed, route southwards round Lolland, Falster and Mon, or to take the shorter, more complicated but scenic route via Smålands Farvandet between these three islands and Sjælland. I have chosen the latter route, but have been highly selective in considering the many possible overnight stops.

The passage crosses Smålands Farvandet via Vejrø island, missing out five small islands to the N and S (Omø, Agersø, Fejø, Femø and Askø). All of these have harbours. Two other possible passage routes would lead to either the N or the S of my selected route before heading towards Vordingborg. I have bypassed the channels between and the harbours on E Lolland, Falster and Møn islands. However, in a number of places I have suggested diversions to places off the passage route, and in particular a few short passages to Sweden. In strong westerlies Smålands Farvandet can be a very uncomfortable cruising ground.

The route is scenic, with many beautiful anchorages, picturesque fishing villages and places of interest, including the ancient towns of Vordingborg and Køge. It offers a bewildering variety of things to see and do in København and a visit to Shakespeare's 'Elsinore' before culminating in a stop at the historic town of Roskilde, with its Viking-ship museum, and the tombs of the kings and queens of Denmark in its cathedral.

This area has one of the greatest concentrations of yacht moorings in Europe, so you should have no difficulty in finding a berth at night, or in leaving your boat for the winter. There are at least 30 yacht harbours with at least 200 moorings each, and about half of these have over 400 berths. The Køge Bugt Strandparken Marinas alone have around 2,500 moorings, and Helsingør has 1,000, while the three Swedish marinas covered probably have over 1,500 berths.

Many of the smaller harbours do not supply fuel, so make sure you stock up with this as well as with better provisions at the larger harbours. Most of the moorings available en route are the usual 'boxes' with posts at the stern. However, in the small harbours such as those on Ven posts are lacking, so boats lie to a kedge anchor at the stern with bow to the jetty.

The head of Roskilde Fjord demands shallow, tricky pilotage, so deeper-draught yachts may prefer to visit Isefjord instead.

Distance

312M, excluding the suggested diversions which are described en route (return mileage from passage route in brackets):

Femø, Fejø and Askø (25M)
Næstved (Smålands Farvandet) (36M)
København Sydhavn (14M)
Malmø/Limhamn (18M)
Flakfortet (8M)
Ven (9M)
Råå (14M)
Isefjord/Holbæk (30M)

Depths/water levels (*see also Appendix IV*)

There is not much deep-water, open-sea pilotage on this route, except in the initial crossing of the Kieler Bucht and Langelands Bælt to Nakskov.

In the shallow-water areas, as for all of these routes in the SW Baltic, do not assume that the charted dredged depths of any of the shallower *rende* channels are accurate at time of sailing – actual depths are often less. Smålands Farvandet, the Bøgestrom and Praesto Fjord at one end of the passage and Roskilde Fjord at the other demand shallow-water navigation; there can be as little as 2m in the channel, and even less if you wander slightly away from the perches or spar buoys. The route in between is mainly coast-hopping, keeping generally in at least 6m, although the entrance approaches to many of the yacht harbours are often as little as 2m.

There are a number of deep (2–3m) marinas, particularly on the approaches to and in København, but there are also many fishing/pleasure-craft harbours with depths of as little as 1·5m in places, and a few of less than this. As usual, it is advisable to keep an eye on the fluctuating water levels from the MSL of the charts (see Appendix IV, Route 7. Water levels).

Tidal range From MHW to MLW this varies from negligible at Roskilde and 0·2m in Nakskov and in København's harbours, through 0·4–0·6m in

ROUTE 7
KIEL TO ROSKILDE
VIA SMÅLANDS
FARVANDET AND
THE SOUND
Hesselø
Gilleleje
Sund
Helsingør
Hälsingborg
Råå
Hundested
Lynaes
Frederiksvaerk
Nivå
Rungsted
Ven
Isefjord
Roskilde Fjord
Frederikssund
Vedbæk
SWEDEN
Skovshoved
Jyllinge
Holbaek
Sund
Kalundborg
KØBENHAVN
København
South
Kastrup
Strandpark
Roskilde
Amager
MALMÖ
Limmhamm
Køge
Bugt
Dragør
Sjaelland
Køge
Støre
Baelt
Korsor
Stevns
Klint
FYN
Karre baeksminde
Naestved
Praesto
Vejrø
Vordingborg
Kalvehave
MØN
Femø
Fejø
Askø
LANGELAND
Nakskov
FALSTER
LOLLAND
Bagenkop
N
To Kieler
Förde
Fehmarn
Mecklenburger Bucht
GERMANY
56°N
55°N
11°E
12°
13°

Smålands Farvandet and on the W coast of the Sound, to 1m at Helsingør in the narrows.

Wind In the southern part of the passage area strong northerly to easterly winds raise water levels by around 0·6–1·6m, whereas from København northwards it is northerly to westerly winds which do this. More critically for soundings, in the southern part of the passage area winds from the SW quadrant can reduce water levels by around 0·3–1·5m. In the northern part of the passage area winds from the SE quadrant can do the same.

Bridges

2 opening bridges, 2 fixed (20m and 26·5m clearance), and 1 fixed (only 16m) on the diversion to København Sydhavnen.

Charts

Note Soundings and heights on all the charts are based on mean sea level (MSL).
German hydrographic *12, 15, 20, 22, 23, 24, 30, 40, 289, 328, 329, 477, 478, 479, 480.*
NV *Sportschiffahrtskarten Series 1, 3,* and ***4***. Note that significant depth contours on these charts are at 2m, 4m, 6m, 10m and 20m. Many of the buoys off headlands are on the 10m contour. These charts are often a little small in scale, and it is essential to have the pilot books, *Der Grosse NV Hafen Lotse, Bands 1, 3* and *4,* which accompany the chart sets for pilotage in the harbour entrances.
Danish hydrographic *116, 117, 118, 129, 131, 132, 133, 142, 160, 161, 162, 187, 190.*
Danish *Søportskort Serie 1* (part of series only).

Route description

KIEL AND KIELER FÖRDE

See Chapter 6

KIELER BUCHT

Currents are relatively weak (1–2kn) and cross-track in the Kieler Bucht: SE-going in winds from WSW–W–N and NW-going in winds from NE–E–SSW. However, the W-going stream becomes much stronger as Langeland is approached. In settled weather there are weak tidal streams.

Winds in spring and summer also tend to be cross-track, funnelled by the land, but they tend to be on either bow or quarter rather than abeam until the approach to the Store Bælt.

→ The route follows the E side of the buoyed channel out of Kieler Förde, then leads directly across Kieler Bucht to the Bagenkop offing buoy on the W side of the S end of Langeland island. Depths are good: 10–25m. Main hazard is the traffic-separation scheme close SE of Kiel light tower (white round tower, red gallery and base), where a number of shipping routes into Kiel converge; keep to its periphery before striking across the bay.

Keldsnor light, 25M range, white tower, extreme S end of Langeland.

32M

BAGENKOP (LANGELAND)

Keldsnor light (prominent white tower, 25M range), on the SE side of the peninsula, is soon obscured after passing Gulstav point. Keeping outside the 10m contour along the hilly and wooded W side of the Gulstav peninsula, Bagenkop harbour (3m, PD) is approached from close S of the offing buoy (red lit). Continue east-southeastwards along

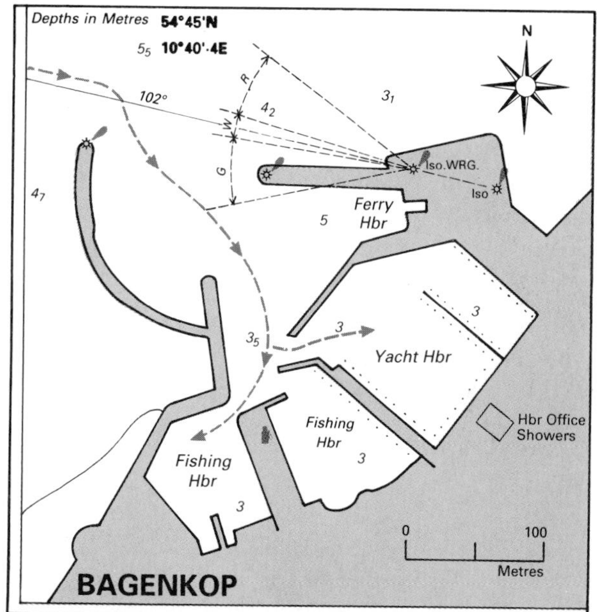

Bagenkop entrance. Yacht harbour is to left behind the square rigger.

the leading line (lights in line on the E mole) in depths of 4m or more to the harbour's north-facing outer entrance (lit on each side). Watch out for fishing buoys and stakes. The small yacht haven is in the NE basin through the inner entrance; the southern basin is an overspill area for visitors. Watch out for ferries on rounding the outer mole, since close E of this is the ferry harbour for Kiel. This end of Langeland is another scenic one for walking or cycling.

STORE BÆLT CROSSING

↰ Depending on wind strength, the cross-track currents in the Store Bælt can be extremely strong (up to 3kn or more): S-going in winds from W–N–NE (particularly NW) and N-going in winds from NNE–E–WSW.

☂ In strong winds from the NW quadrant the approaches and channel to Nakskov across the outer grounds can be rough.

→ Having broken the crossing conveniently at Langeland, the next stage to Lolland is short, but you need to keep a good lookout for the frequent shipping which uses this entrance to the Store Bælt (Langeland Bælt). From Bagenkop offing buoy the route leads southwards round Gulstav to Keldsnor light, keeping outside the 6m contour. It continues directly across the Bælt to the offing buoy (red lit) at the head of the Nakskov channel, northwestwards of Albuen island, which has a sector light (8–11M range, white round tower). The land around is low-lying, but the houses and the light tower on Albuen are conspicuous. Turn eastwards about 0·5M S of the offing buoy to pick up the first of the buoys in the channel to Nakskov. Depths in the Store Bælt are 10–30m, falling to 6–10m W of Albuen.

NAKSKOV FJORD

→⛵⚓ The 6·3m-dredged channel to Nakskov is closely buoyed and beaconed (lit) throughout. Additionally, four sets of lights in line lead to the southern end of Enehøje island, off which there is a sector light (Ramsø) aimed along the next 2M of the channel, and a final set of lights in line leads to the outskirts of the town. S of Enehøje a buoyed (unlit) channel, with lights in line and dredged to 3·1m, leads off the main channel to the tiny fishing harbour of **Langø** (2·8m, PD).

⚓ Albuen (sand, 2–2·5m) is another of Denmark's superb natural harbours, but only for vessels of 1·5m maximum draught. It is a nesting area for birds. S of the low grassy headland of the same name, the approach is initially made from the first of the Nakskov channel buoys directly towards the Albuen light. Follow the Albuen coast eastwards about 0·5M offshore, doubling back closely round the buoy off the Sandodde spit, and anchor halfway between this point and Horsnæs Hage in 2·5m – further along towards the two landing stages at the head of the bay it is somewhat shallower.

A buoyed channel (unlit, but this was the main channel at the beginning of the century) leads in a huge loop from the main channel near the S cardinal buoy off Enerhøje island, round Slotø island and back into the main channel near Kuddeholm. There are several anchoring possibilities off this channel in 2–3m sand. The best is on the W side outside the channel about 500m from the southern end of Enorhøje island (in easterlies the steep and wooded W coast is another anchoring possibility). Continue along the marked channel to the wooded N point of Slotø island, where you can anchor offshore of the landing stage and visit the remains of what was until the beginning of the 17th century Denmark's largest naval shipyard.

23M

NAKSKOV (LOLLAND)

⛵ **Hestehoved yacht haven** (3m), about 1M from the town (its unlit entrance is easily entered N of the channel), has few visitors' places. **Nakskov yacht haven** (2m, PD) is similarly short of space. Visitors can usually moor or raft alongside in 4·5m near the showers on the N quay of the **commercial harbour**, towards the head of the navigation; this is also convenient for the town.

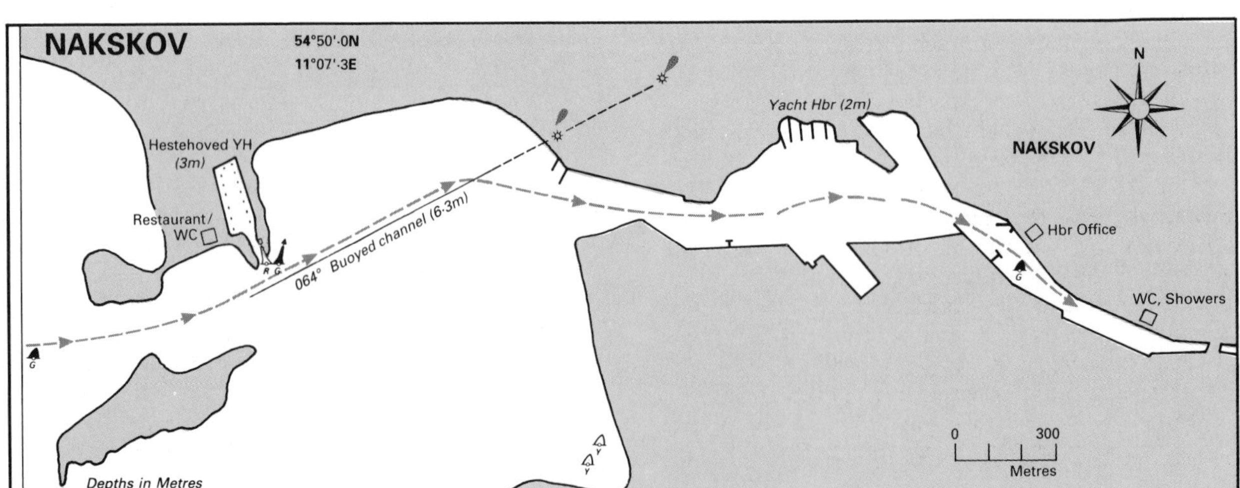

Although it boasts Denmark's largest sugar-beet refinery, Nakskov is also an interesting medieval town, with many half-timbered buildings and a museum near the Skt Nicolai Kirke with its spire.

→⛵ Return to the offing buoy, head northwards and round Lolland, keeping about 3m offshore to avoid its wide shoals and sounding to keep in 10m. Several inland churches are conspicuous from offshore. **Onsevig** (2m) is a tiny fishing harbour at the entrance to a bay surrounded by woods. It is at the end of a causeway on the N coast of Lolland, approached along a buoyed channel with lights in line and a single light at the entrance. There is little visiting space, but, depending on weather, somewhat exposed anchorage is possible in about 2·5m some 50–100m W of the entrance.

SMÅLANDS FARVANDET

In calm weather there are light E and W-going tidal streams, but in stronger wind conditions E and S winds create a W-going current and N and W winds an E-going current, both of which may reach 3kn to 4kn in the narrow channels in the E but only 1kn in the western channels S of Omø.

Because of its shape, Smålands Farvandet tends to funnel the winds in the quadrant from NW through to SW, and if these are strong the strait can be extremely rough, particularly in areas where the sea bed is uneven, for example across the entrance and at the head towards Masned Sund.

→ The buoyage in the Smålands Farvandet as far as Kalvehave bridge E of Vordingborg assumes the rising tide to be coming from the W, with red buoys generally on the N side. Approaching Vejrø island from the W is only advisable in daylight. The island is low and wooded with some scattered buildings, and the Lolland coast to the SW is also low-lying and wooded. Vejrø sector light (white hexagonal tower, 19m high) has an all-round 12–16M range, and is only useful as a long-range mark or in an approach to the harbour from northwards – it was also surrounded by trees when we visited, which could have obscured it from some directions. From a position about 1M NW of the N cardinal buoy at the end of Onsevig's approach channel, the buoyage (mainly cardinals) must be strictly followed in order to avoid the extensive Vesterflak shoals and rocks W of the island. Vejrø yacht haven is on the E side of the island. The course initially leads east-northeastwards, S of Stålgrunde shoal and its S cardinal buoy, to the RW (lit) buoy at the head of the Stål Dyb channel. From this position the shortest, but shallowest (3·5m minimum depth), route to Vejrø is round the S side of the island between two successive pairs of cardinal buoys (unlit): firstly southeastwards between a W cardinal and a N cardinal, then northeastwards between a S cardinal and a N cardinal. Depths on this part of the route are 6–12m, falling to 3–4m near Vejrø.

29M

VEJRØ

⛵ Vejrø yacht haven (1·6–2·5m, PD) has around 140 berths. Its entrance (unlit) is approached from the SE in 3m. The harbour has limited facilities, apart from a nearby 'taverna' where bicycles can be hired, since the island's original development plan as a holiday resort has been delayed (there is even an airstrip). The northern basin is the deeper; the southern one tends to silt up.

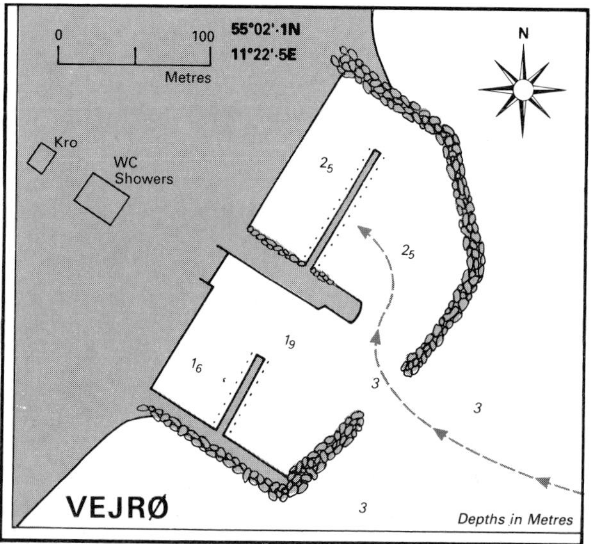

⚓ This is one of the prettiest islands in the Smålands channel, with somewhat sad derelict old farmhouses and a secluded graveyard from the days when there was a modest population of smallholders. The island is mainly tree-clad, with a narrow sandy beach surrounding it. There is an anchorage in 3m over sand on the SW coast, and there are possibilities on the NW coast (take care to sound round the extensive northern shoals of the island).

DIVERSION TO FEMØ, FEJØ, KRAGENÆS AND ASKØ

(not included in total mileage)

⛵⚓ The islands and harbours on the N side of the Smålands entrance are all over 10M away from this section of the passage, but the three islands to the SE are within 5–10M and only an hour or two's sail from Vejrø. All require careful pilotage round the buoys to avoid shoal patches and all have fewer mooring boxes than Vejrø. **Femø**'s harbour (1·5–3m, D) is the nearest (6M) and largest, with lights in line on the approach; the island is hilly. Fejø is another low island, like Vejrø, but with three harbours. **Dybvig** (Fejø Havn) is the largest (2–3·1m, D), with a lights-in-line approach. **Vesterby** (1·2–2·7m, PD) is a small ferry and fishing harbour entered directly from the main Stål Dyb channel, and **Skalø** (1·2m) is tiny. Virtually 'next door' to Vesterby on the Lolland coast is the yacht haven of **Kragenæs** (2–3·5m, lit), which is even bigger than

Vejrø, with a buoyed and lights-in-line approach. The harbour on the low-lying island of **Askø** (2–3m) is small and over 10M away from Vejrø, off the channel leading to **Sakskøbing** (2·5–4·4m, PD), a small industrial harbour about 19M away in Lolland. There are many possible anchorages near the islands, mainly over sand in 2–3m, for example off the W and E coasts of Femø and the W side of Skalø.

SMÅLANDS FARVANDET AND MASNED SUND

There is normally a six-hourly tidal current of up to 3/4kn in Masned Sund and 1–2kn in the wider Storstrøm to the S. However, strong winds from W to NW create an E-going current and winds from E to SE a W-going current, either of which may persist for over 6 hours and reach up to 6kn.

→ The route from Vejrø eastwards to Masned Sund and Vordingborg is simpler. After crossing the 6m contour SE of the harbour, the course leads east-northeastwards, rounding the Ydergrund N of its cardinal buoy. It continues eastwards, rounding Mellumgrund N of its cardinal buoy, and carries on S of Knudsskov Rev's cardinal and red buoys and the wooded peninsula of Knudsskov to the green buoy at the entrance to Masned Sund. To the N and E of Vordingborg can be seen the hilly ground which culminates in the 107m-high Kulsbjerg.

DIVERSION TO KARREBÆKSMINDE AND NÆSTVED

(not included in total mileage)

Should you require the facilities of a medium-sized harbour en route, **Karrebæksminde** (2–2·5m, D*), with over 200 spaces in two yacht havens, is about 13M from Vejrø, N of the passage described here (not included in the distance). It has an easy lit entrance. Between the inner and outer yacht havens there is an opening bridge, requiring the usual signals. In the fjord beyond, a 5M-long dredged (to 6m) buoyed channel and canal lead to the industrial harbour of **Næstved**, with a small yacht haven (1·5m) in its southern suburbs and another, **Pouls Vig** (1·5m), just E of the SW entrance to the harbour canal. There is also a T-shaped pier, with head and stern moorings in 1·8m at the outer end, at **Hvide Svaner**, about halfway along the W side of the buoyed channel WSW of Pouls Vig.

Up to this point none of the buoys are lit, but from now on lights in line lead to the buoyed (some lit) channel (red to port) to the Masnedsund road and railway bridge (single lifting span lit at night, 4·8–5·4m clearance when closed. 1 red light: passage forbidden, 2 red lights: vessels from the E can pass through, 3 red lights: vessels from the W can pass through). The N flag at the crosstrees, or a call on VHF Ch 16, or a long blast and a short blast on the horn, obtains passage, but officially vessels of less than 2 tons cannot obtain special passage, i.e. they need to wait for others going through. However, there is an optional route which it is always recommended that you use if your draught permits. This is under the Storstrøm bridge (26m clearance) S of the main channel and S of the flat Masnedø island, although it means crossing the Middlegrund (2·5m) to get back into the main channel.

Storstrom bridge (26m clearance). Approaching the port and starboard-hand pillars from the E.

→ From the bridge the passage follows the channel buoys, doubling back round the Trellegrund E cardinal buoy and heading along the 2·5m-dredged, buoyed (unlit, red to port) channel with lights in line to Vordingborg Nordhavn.

21M

VORDINGBORG

At Vordingborg **Nordhavn** visitors can use the N quay W of the boatyard (1·7–2m, PD) if they cannot find a box E of the boatyard (2m). The modern town centre with all facilities is close by.

Vordingborg was an important medieval ferry town. There is a castle near the harbour built by Valdemar the Great, of which only the curtain walls and the 'Goose Tower' (26m high, surmounted by a gilded goose and with panoramic views) remain. The woods and open spaces around the castle ruins are a delight, with peacocks, a herd of deer and many wild duck. A museum, botanic garden, 15th-century church, and 18th and 19th-century houses are also of interest.

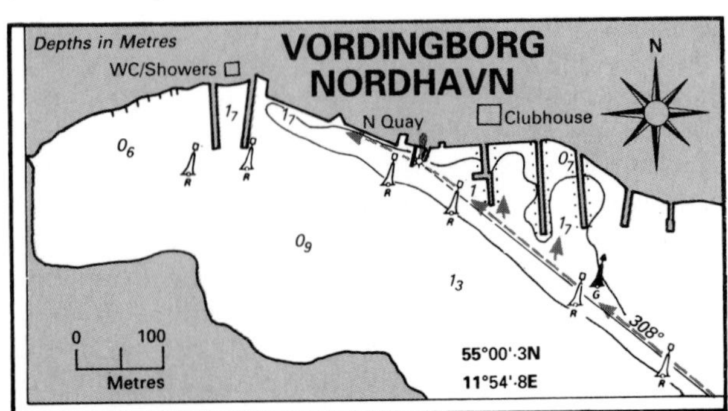

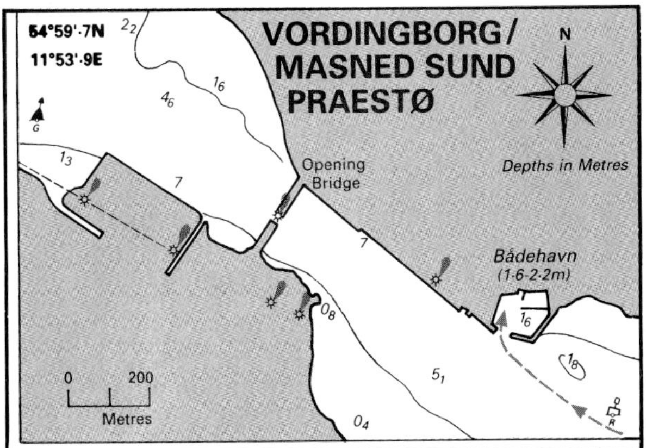

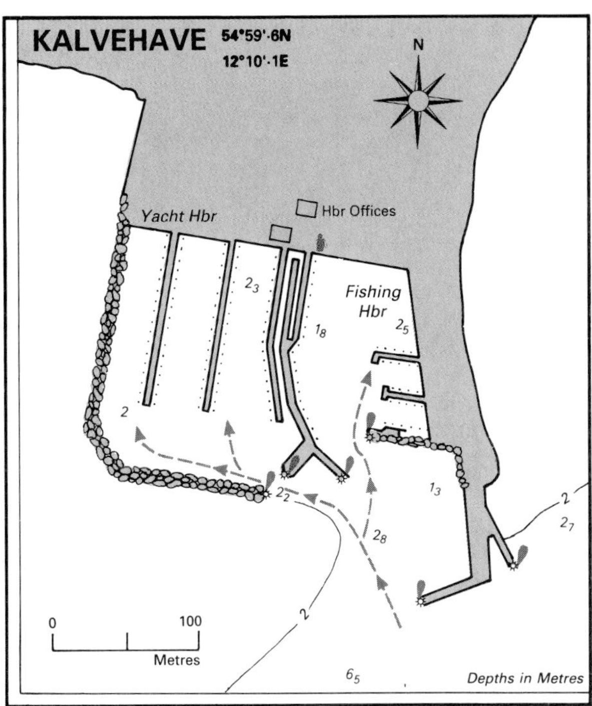

Another option is the small **Vordingborg Bådehavn** (2m, unlit), close SE of the Masnedsund opening bridge. This is entered directly from the main Masnesund channel, which is also reached by doubling back after crossing the Middelgrund, but this time keeping S of the Trellegrund in the Færgestrøm channel and heading back towards the opening bridge.

FÆRGESTRØM AND ULVSUND CHANNELS

→ After leaving the Vordingborg approach channel and entering the main channel at the red buoy at Kirkegrund, the channel is buoyed (unlit, red to port) all the way to Kalvehave yacht haven, with minimum depths of about 4m at two closely buoyed double bends at Ny Farvand and Langø Vrid. There are several stretches of woodland on the N bank. There are two fixed road bridges, the first at Fredskov (20m clearance) and the second at Kalvehave (25·6m clearance); both are lit at night. The buoyage direction in the channel changes after the latter bridge, with green now to port and the rising tide assumed to be coming from the E.

Although they are not strictly on this route, there are three other yacht havens within visiting distance to the S on the Grønsund route between Mons and Falster. **Gåbense** is a tiny harbour (1– 2m, unlit) at the end of a mole on Falster, to the E of the southern end of the Størstrom bridge. It is approached from the main channel to the N along a 2·6m buoyed (unlit) channel. **Stubbekøbing** (yacht haven 1·5–2·7m, PD, unlit, but lit approach channel), also on Falster, is a respectably sized yacht haven further down Grønsund through the Farø fixed bridge (25·5m clearance, lit). It is approached from the main channel to the N along a 5·5m buoyed (unlit) channel. Finally, yet further along the Grønsund, but this time on Møn island, is another tiny yacht haven, **Hårbølle** (2·5m, D, lit), approached directly in 3m.

11M
KALVEHAVE

Kalvehave yacht haven (1·9–2·3m, PD*) has a lit entrance approached directly from the main channel in 2·2–2·8m (deeper if entered from nearer to the SE outer mole). The yacht-haven entrance is W of the fishing-harbour entrance. With over 300 spaces, this is the largest yacht haven in this area.

⚓ There is a good anchorage (mud, 2–3m) about 2M N of Kalvehave harbour (continuing on along the buoyed channel), 200m offshore under the wood at Viemose Skov. Watch out for fishing stakes.

Kalvehave bridge (25·6m clearance) from Stege Bugt.

STEGE BUCHT AND BØGESTRØM

There are no prevailing currents in Stege Bugt – westerly winds create a N-going current and easterlies a S-going one. Depths on this route are critical and the depth gauge (to MSL) near the end of the Bøgestrøm is not much help to vessels entering from the S. In the Bøgestrøm easterly winds at first raise water levels and westerlies initially reduce them, but over a long period of persistent winds the overall Baltic weather pattern dominates, with easterlies reducing and westerlies raising water levels. In spring depths tend to be low. It is helpful to check soundings against charted depths in known positions on the edges of the shallow patches, particularly in extreme conditions.

While Stege Bugt is protected from weather, the Bøgstrøm is open from N through to E, and winds from this quadrant can produce rough conditions across the shallow outer grounds.

→ The route from Kalvehave is a daylight one, following a very shallow marked channel (unlit, red buoys to starboard on this outward route). Cardinal buoys mark some of the shallower patches and should be carefully interpreted, particularly in the wide area of Stege Bugt. There is also as little as 2·3m charted depth in the closely marked outer Bøgestrøm channel, but depths can be less than this, depending on dredging (we found 2·1m on our visit). The church at Nyord is a conspicuous landmark. The channel is protected except at the NE outward end, between Stenhage and Sandhage flats out to the Bøgestrøm offing buoy (lit); this end is to be avoided in strong northeasterlies.

There are four small harbours off the channel in its early reaches: **Stege** (PD, 4M detour to 4·2m-deep Nordhavn, lit entrance approached along an unlit buoyed dredged (4·1m) channel with a directional sector light; **Nyord** (2m, direct, unlit); **Sandvig** (1·7m in S basin, lights in line); **Stavreby** (1·2m, 1·5m buoyed approach channel, lights in line, very small).

⚓ If the harbours are crowded there are many anchoring possibilities in 2–3m over sand and clay (watch out for fishing stakes). For example: the small bays N and S of Sandvig; off the steeply shelving W coast of Nyord near the harbour; 0·5M offshore in the bay, S of the low-lying wooded Jungshoved point and just off the S end of the Bøgestrøm.

FAKSE BUGT AND PRÆSTO FJORD

→ From the Bøgestrøm offing buoy (lit) the 6m contour leads northwestwards to Normandshage shoals at the deep (over 10m) outer entrance to Præsto Fjord. These shoals should be given a wide rounding berth at their northern end, from which two sets of lights in line lead round a N cardinal buoy (unlit) to the first of the buoys which mark the extremely tortuous 3·3–3·5m-dredged channel (we found less water nearer Præsto) heading westwards to Præsto. The spar buoys must be carefully spotted and the cardinals interpreted. There are fishing stakes and flags in many places to complicate the issue further.

Winds from NE through to SW are funnelled into the Præsto approaches, but S of the N cardinal buoy Normandshage provides a lee on the approach.

23M

PRÆSTØ

Præsto (2–4m, PD*) has a commercial basin (single red light on E molehead), in which visitors are advised to lie, as well as pleasure-craft landing stages and boxes open to the fjord.

Præsto is a delightful fishing harbour with cobbled streets, a fire-service museum and a museum of dolls. Close N at Nysø is a 17th-century baroque mansion with a small museum and sculptures by Bertel Thorvaldsen.

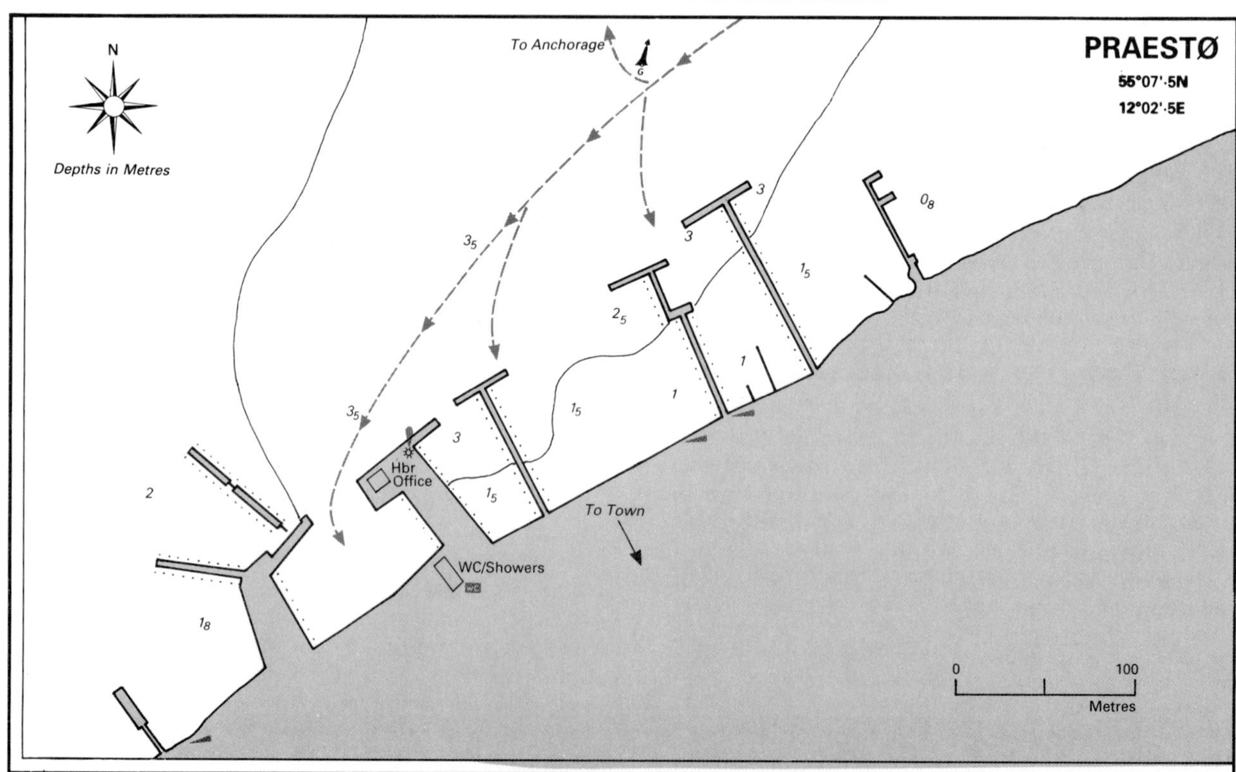

⚓ Anchorages abound in the virtual lake of Præsto Fjord. These are over mud and weed, and involve the problem of getting ashore across wide shoals. The three places where the contours come closest to the shore are the NE (the best, with a nearby landing stage) and W 'corners' of the fjord's quadrilateral, and the W side of Feddet. However, getting to this inner fjord is a delicate operation; there are two alternatives. From the E cardinal buoy at the S end of Feddet a sparsely buoyed channel (3 buoys only) with somewhat less than 2m of water leads northwestwards into the inner fjord. Alternatively, from the green buoy at Praesto harbour entrance a 1·6m-dredged channel (we found that this was very true on our visit, with swans sunning themselves on isolated exposed boulders close to the fairway) marked by a series of unlit spar buoys leads northwards into the fjord.

→ Return by the same route to the cardinal buoy off Normandshage shoal.

THE SOUTHERN SOUND, FAKSE BUGT AND KØGE BUGT

↪ In Fakse Bugt currents are generally light, flowing outwards in strong westerlies and inwards in strong easterlies. In Køge Bugt with a southerly stream in the Sound, i.e. usually in strong westerlies, the current runs clockwise (northwards and northeastwards round the bay and southwards and southwestwards offshore) and in very strong westerlies S and southeastwards. More often the stream in the Sound is N-going while that in Køge Bugt sweeps northwards round the bay. The strongest currents are between Stevns Klint and Falsterbo Rev on the Swedish coast.

Stevns Klint headland is to be given a wide berth in strong winds from both eastern quadrants. Here wind as well as current is funnelled between this headland and the Swedish coast 15M to the NE. Køge Bugt S of Amager island is exposed to winds from the SE quadrant, and the shallower final approaches to Køge yacht haven are to be treated with caution in these conditions.

→ The route round Stevns Klint to Køge is straightforward. Keep just outside the 10m contour, which leads past all the hazards: Fallesskov Rev (cardinal buoy); Stevns light (white round tower on a vertical chalk cliff, range 26m); Kalkgrund, to clear which it is wise to keep well outside the 10m contour and if necessary take back-bearings on the Stevns light; and finally Køge's offing buoy (lit), to be approached from well offshore. Fishing stakes abound throughout most of the inshore areas on this passage, and on our visit we found them extending as much as 1·5M offshore W of Fællesskov Rev in a series of clusters joined together by flagged or pink buoys.

The land behind Fakse Ladeplads is high, with lower-lying woodlands to the E. From Rødvig round Stevns Klint to near Bøgeskov there are white cliffs, while the rest of Køge Bugt is mainly low-lying, with woods to the S of Køge.

There are three small, directly entered fishing/pleasure harbours en route: **Fakse Ladeplads** (2·5–3m, D, lights in line and lit entrance), **Rødvig** (2·3–3·5m in main basins, PD, lit entrance), and the tiny **Bøgeskov** (2–2·2m, D, unlit entrance but lights in line). A historic railway, still in operation, runs from Rødvig to Køge. Rødvig, a popular holiday village, houses a marine-engine museum and a flint-oven museum.

⚓ There are several possibilities, in 2–4m over sand, chalk mud or clay. On leaving the fjord, the E coast of Feddet, with its woods and sandy beach, provides two, at the N and S ends of the peninsula. Other possibilities are between Rødvig harbour and Falleskov Rev, close E of Højerup church (14th century) S of Stevns light, between Mandehoved point and Stevns light, and under the woods SE of Køge Sønakke point. The cliff anchorages are for short stays only, watching out for possibly strong N-going currents and wind gusts caused by the cliffs.

35M

KØGE

With a direct, lit entrance (2·5–3m, PD*) and a sector approach light, this 600-mooring marina is the first of five large marinas in the southern approaches to København which provide over 3,000 yacht berths. From a distance the upturned-champagne-glass shape of the water tower behind the harbour is highly conspicuous, as is a radio mast further N.

The town is half an hour's walk from the yacht haven, or a short bus ride – or hire bicycles. Køge was a medieval market town founded on the herring

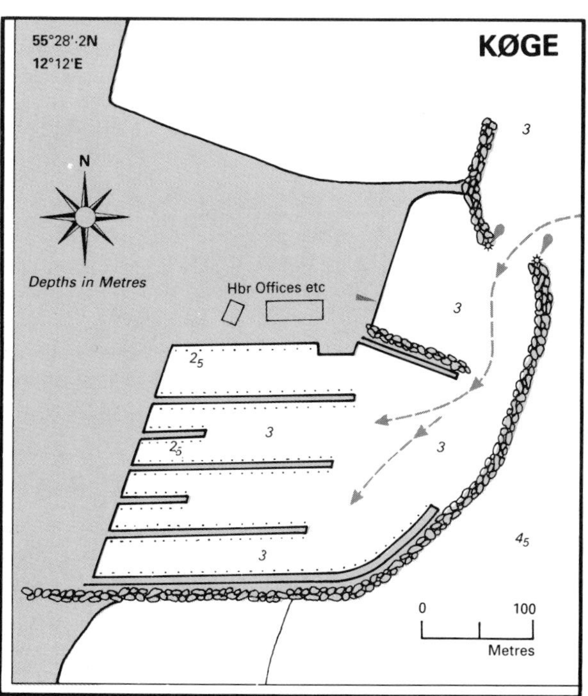

Køge harbour entrance.

fisheries. There are many timber-framed 16th and 17th-century buildings, a 15th-century church and several museums.

→ From Køge's offing buoy a course should be set for the two pairs of buoys and the single buoy off Hundige, which provide a marked channel to the harbour between the charted fishing areas.

Mosede (2–2·3m, PD) is a small fishing/pleasure-craft harbour 2·5M SW of Hundige, approached from the SE to avoid the fishing areas.

11M
HUNDIGE

Enter (the entrance is lit) directly from the SE. This huge marina (2·4–2·5m, PD*), with all facilities, has two 'islands', Mågen (the northern one, with 300 places) and Hejren (the southern one, with 600 places). The harbour together with the two described below, Ishøj and Brøndy, forms what is known as the Køge Bugt Strandparken. The development of these marinas, started in the late 1980s, has been retarded by economic recession. Their island layouts are an interesting alternative to the longer, somewhat boring pontoons of most modern marinas.

2M
ISHØJ

The approach from Hundige to the W requires sounding to keep in at least 3m depth before rounding and doubling back into the lit entrance. The harbour (2·5–4m, PD*) has two island complexes, Ishøj (600 spaces at last count, now possibly more) and Vallensbæk (400 places).

⚓ It is possible to anchor over sand in 2–3m S of Ishøj harbour entrance.

1·5M
BRØNDBY

Easily entered lit entrance opposite the Ishøj entrance. The harbour (2–3m, D*) has around 500 places.

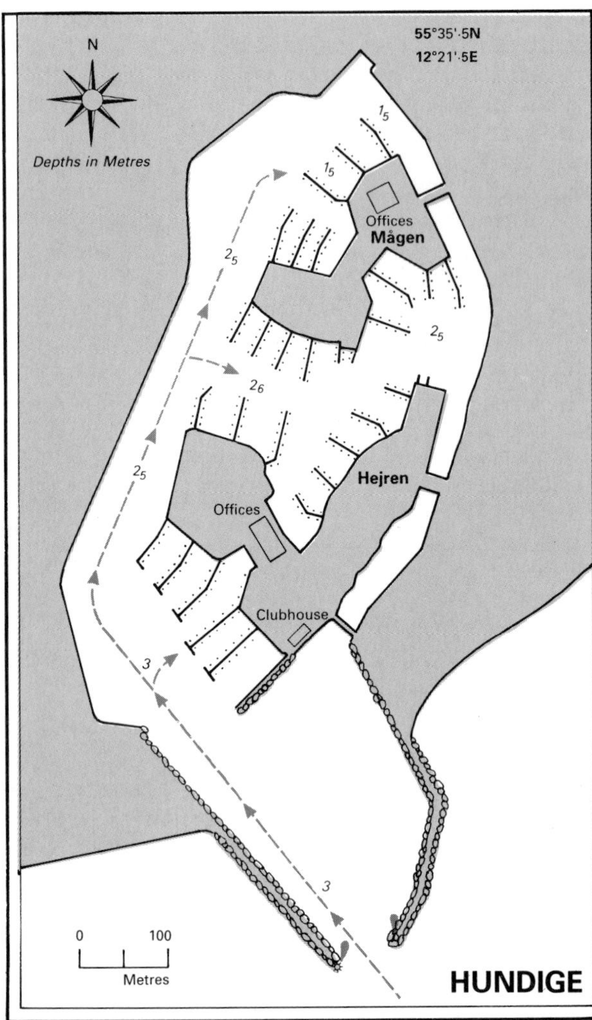

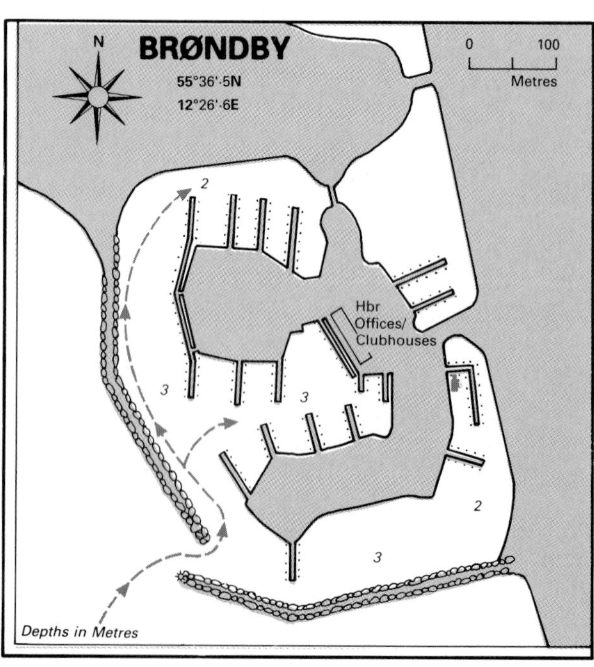

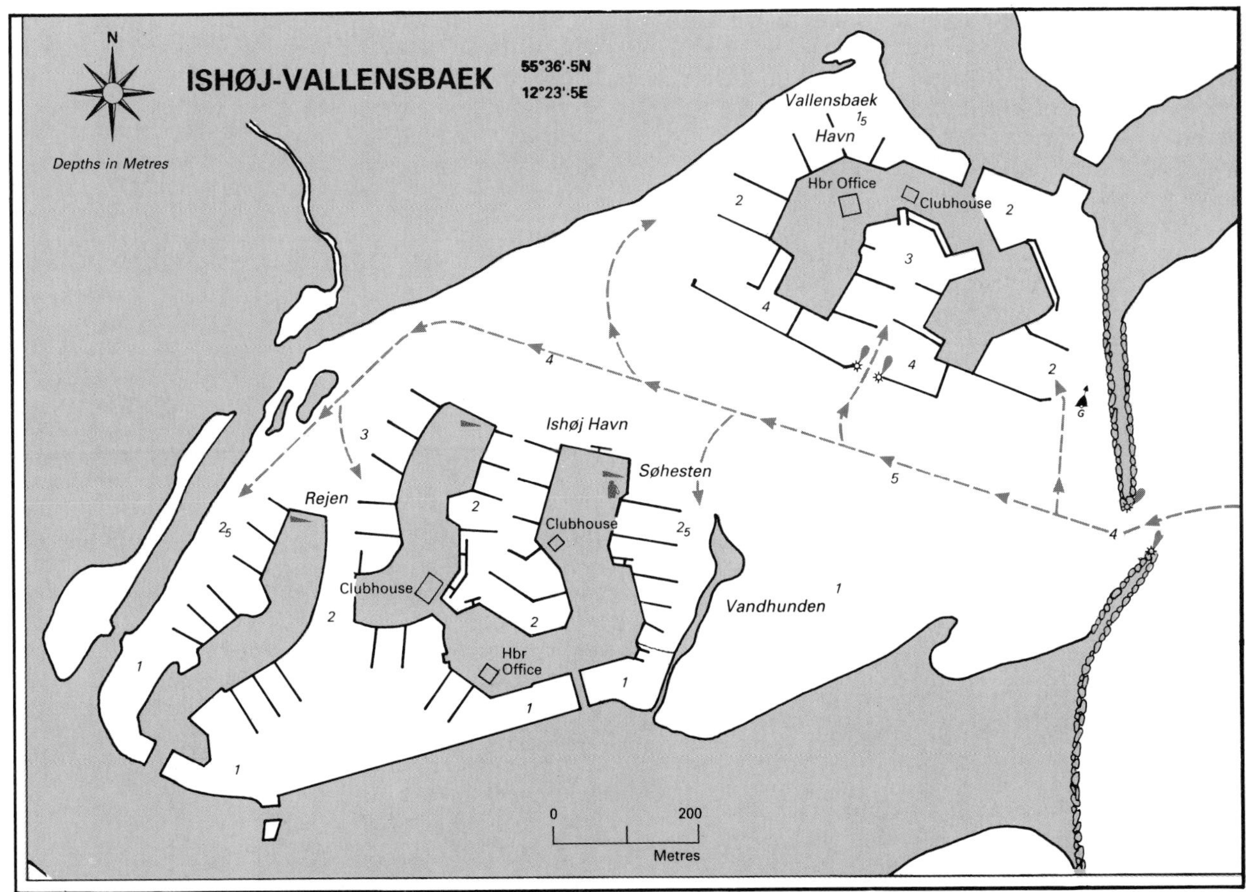

DIVERSION TO KØBENHAVN SYDHAVNEN

(not included in total mileage)

→ For those wishing to avoid large marina complexes and the city's main centre, København's Sydhavnen are an easy diversion. Once you have skirted round the fishing area E of Brondby (buoyed), two lit buoys as well as lights in line lead approximately just E of northwards along a buoyed (unlit) channel, through a motorway bridge (clearance only 16m, so make sure you know your air draught), to the marked and dredged (to 2·5m) Søndre Løb channel, or alternatively the channel along the eastern wall of Amager, the Kalvebod Løb (3·7m).

As in the Sound (see below), a N-going stream tends to predominate between Sjælland and Amager, controlled at Sluseholm.

0·6M N of the first fixed bridge and to port of the Søndre Løb is the long narrow **Hvidovre** yacht haven (2m, PD*), with easy if unlit entrance. Both Søndre Løb and Kalvebod Løb lead to a short stretch of canal. Visitors can moor on the port side near the head of this canal, which is 2M N of the fixed bridge, on the landing stages of **Kalvebod-erne** (3m plus), or continue round to port into the **Fiskerihavn** (3m, PD). A swing bridge (Sjællandsbro), followed by a dam with a lock and sluices (Sluseholm), at the head of this canal is as far as pleasure craft are allowed to navigate.

THE MIDDLE AND NORTHERN SOUND

In strong winds from SW–W–NW a S-going current prevails in these reaches of the Sound. A N-going current prevails in calm weather or in winds from other points of the compass (NNW–E–SSW). The S-going current tends to prevail in summer from July to October. The strongest streams, in both directions, occur in the narrows off Helsingør along the Swedish side, particularly off Malmø and in the nearby Flintrånnan channel, and in the Drogden channel between Amager and Saltholm on the Danish side. The lighter streams, sometimes with clockwise eddies in the S-going stream, occur in the Danish bay S of Helsingør. In fine weather the N-going stream is 1–1·5kn, but in the narrower parts changes in the water levels and strong winds can push rates up to as much as 5kn. In certain wind conditions, the N-going current on the Danish side opposes a S-going current on the Swedish side.

THE MIDDLE SOUND – DROGDEN

Amager island is heavily built up. The route round it to København is buoyed (cardinal, yellow and lateral). It is essential to keep outside these buoys to avoid (a) the charted fishing area, (b) the Aflangshage firing range (two flag signal staffs ashore and yellow buoys offshore), and (c) Dragør Sand Rev (S cardinal). From this last the route follows but keeps outside the buoyed (lit) Drogden channel (green to port), sounding to keep in 6m or more, before turning to starboard into either of Dragør's harbours.

A major problem at night in this area is the plethora of lights. As well as the lit Drogden channel buoys, there are three sector lights on the Danish side of this part of the Sound: Drogden light (white square tower, red bands, grey base, range 13–18M) to the S, Dragør Fort (grey beacon, 10–14M range) to the S of the yacht haven, and Nordre Rose (round granite tower, 13–18M range). On the Swedish side, only 5–8M to the E, there are several 9–16M-range sector lights.

It is in this area that the tunnel and bridge across the Øresund will be built.

Nordre Rose

16M
DRAGØR

There are two options to port, both with lit entrances and buoyed approaches. The **new yacht haven** (1·3–2·1m, D★) is entered to the N of the sector light; depths are less on the inner sides of the pontoons and near the outer wall. The **old harbour** (2–3·5m, D★, lights in line) is entered just N of the ferry harbour (so look out carefully). The ferry harbour and the fishing basin at the SW corner of the old harbour complex are both out of bounds to pleasure craft.

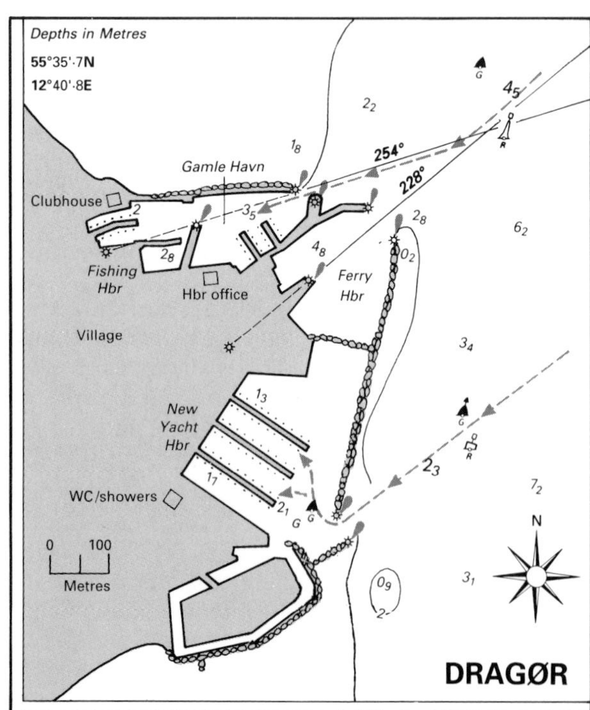

Dragør is a former medieval fishing village with cottages, cobbled and flower-fringed alleyways and a maritime museum. There is a ferry service (55 minutes) to Limhamn in Sweden.

DIVERSION TO MALMØ (SWEDEN)

(not included in total mileage)

→ From Dragør it is only 9M (not included in the overall mileage for this passage) to the two yacht havens at Limhamn, on the western outskirts of Malmø (Malmø itself is closed to visiting pleasure craft). The passage is across the two very busy southern shipping channels into the Sound, so demands considerable caution. From Dragør, the passage crosses the main Drogden, rounding the low-lying Saltholm island well to its S just outside the 6m contour, crosses Flint Rånnan channel S of Oskarsgrundet SV sector light (white tower, red bands, grey base, range 12–16M), and then follows the Trindel Rånnan channel (two cardinal buoys) northeastwards about 1M off this industrial coast with its chimneys and oil tanks. Watch out for a strong crosscurrent when turning to starboard and approaching either of the yacht havens.

LIMHAMN-WEST AND LAGUNEN (SWEDEN)

Limhamn-West yacht haven (2–3·2m, PD★, unlit entrance, lights in line) is the more southerly and larger of the two yacht havens, with over 700 moorings. The S-facing entrance is approached from its NW to avoid a 1·2–1·5m shoal close S of the entrance. The final approach from about 0·3M W of the entrance is made eastwards along the leading line just N of two green buoys, doubling N into the harbour. About 1·5M further N, beyond the commercial harbours of Limhamn Södra and Centralhavn, Limhamn-North/Lagunen yacht haven (probably over 500 moorings, 3m, PD★, unlit north-facing entrance) is approached from the NW directly from a RW (lit) offing buoy and finally across 3m between two pairs of entrance buoys. Keep out of the way of the shipping which enters Centralhavn's entrance (also north-facing) to the W. There is a ferry to Dragør on Amager island in Denmark.

Malmø is Sweden's third-largest city, with extensive shipyards. It is the proposed terminus of a tunnel to Denmark.

→ A passage back to Denmark from Limhamn to København Nord can be either S of Saltholm again or N of Saltholm and the tiny offlying Flakfort-island, depending on the current direction and rate. Saltholm is a low island with a few scattered houses and temporary moorings at a tiny pier (2m) at **Barakkebro** on its NW corner. This is approached along lights in line close N of a rocky shoal.

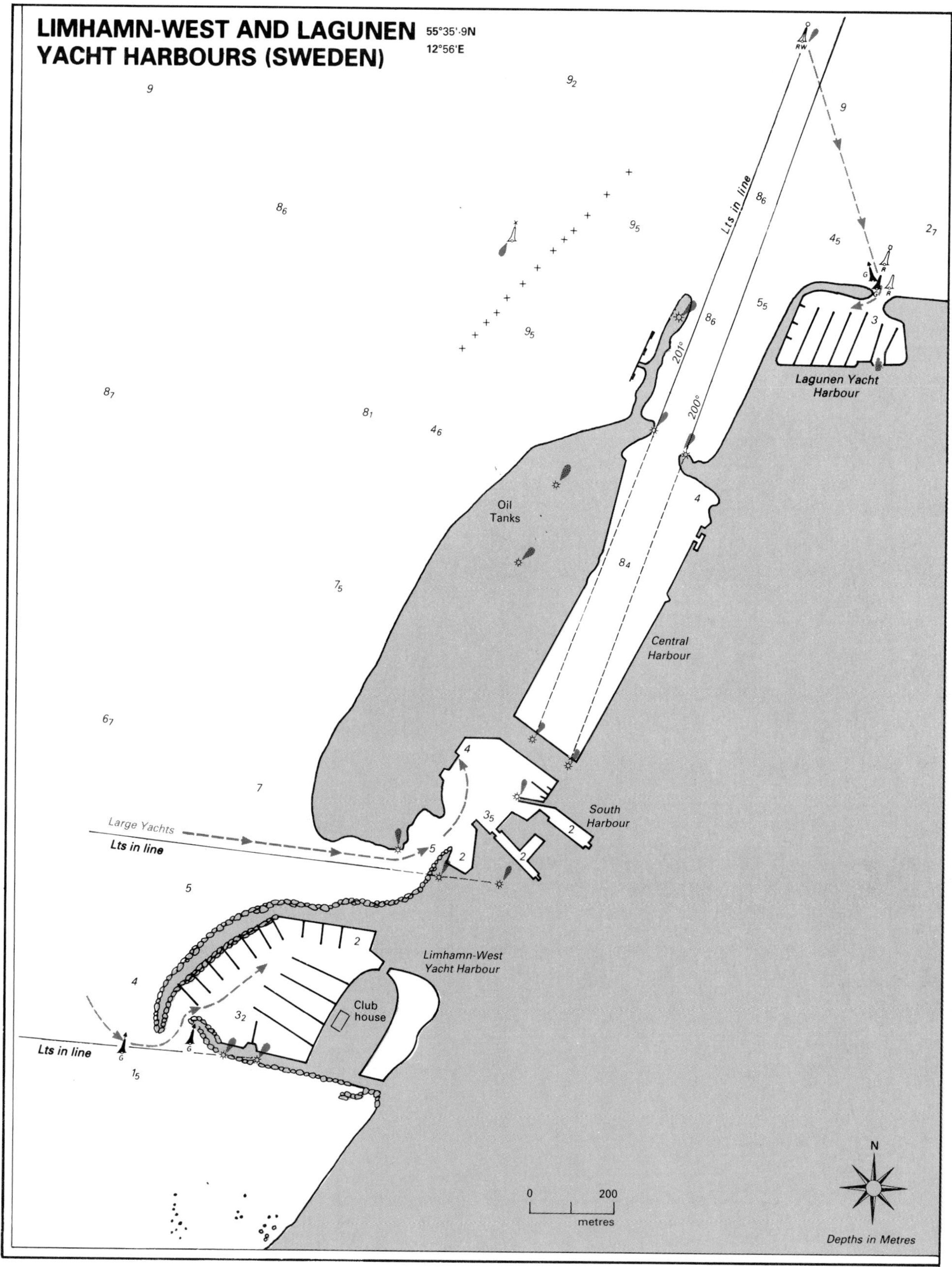
LIMHAMN-WEST AND LAGUNEN YACHT HARBOURS (SWEDEN)
55°35'·9N
12°56'E
Lts in line
201°
200°
Lagunen Yacht Harbour
Oil Tanks
Central Harbour
South Harbour
Large Yachts
Lts in line
Limhamn-West Yacht Harbour
Club house
Lts in line
0
200
metres
N
Depths in Metres

DROGDEN

→ The route from Dragør follows the 6m contour, just outside the channel buoys (green on port-hand side of channel) and outside Nordre Rose sector light (a conspicuous round granite tower on a flat island base, 13–18M range). København's airport at Kastrup and a complex of chimneys and chemicals tanks are the most significant marks on Amager's W coast. **Kastrup yacht haven** (1·7–2m) entrance, close S of the commercial harbour (prohibited to pleasure craft), approached via a 2m-deep buoyed channel, is lit, but there is little room for visitors.

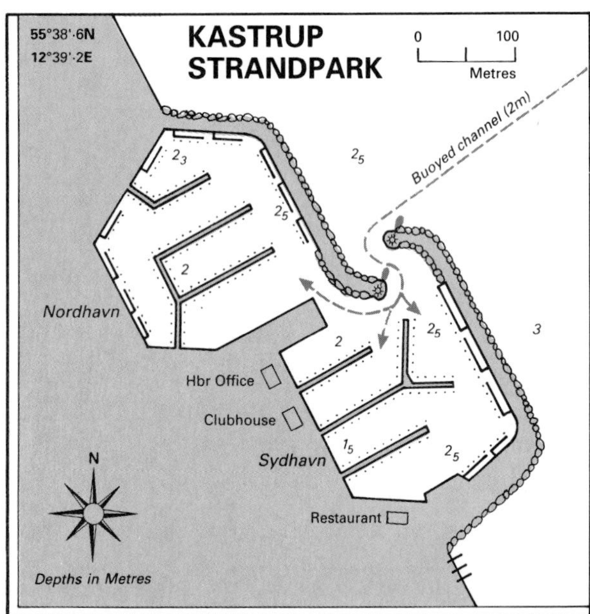

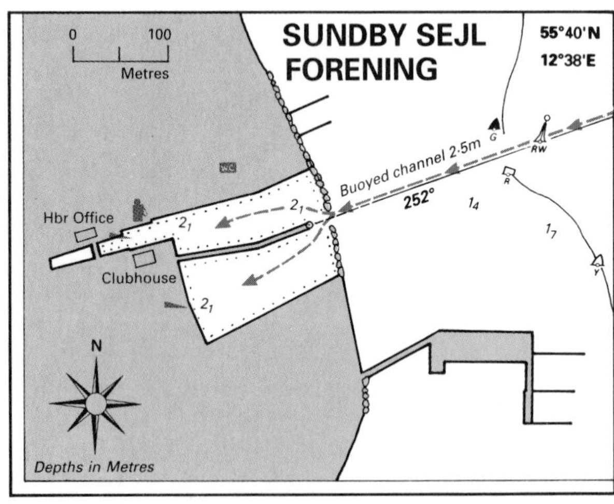

4M

KASTRUP STRANDPARK

Another large marina, with over 700 moorings in two basins, Kastrup Strandpark (1·5–2·5m, PD*, lit entrance) is approached via another 2m-deep buoyed channel and entered in a sharp dogleg round the E mole.

3M

SUNDBY SEJL FORENING

Sundby yacht haven (2·1m, PD*) is yet a third harbour approached in a similar direction via a 2m-deep buoyed channel, this time with lights in line. On entering, a yacht has to peel off to port or starboard round the front leading light, on the end of a middle wall dividing the harbour into two small basins.

DIVERSION TO FLAKFORTET

(not included in total mileage)

→ Since it is only four miles off the passage route, you may have time for a morning visit to this former offshore fort protecting København's approaches. Both Flakfortet and Middelgrunds fort, some 2·5M to the NE, are conspicuous landmarks in the N approaches to København, as is the city itself. Flakfortet's entrance is approached from the W from the Hollånderdybe channel in over 4m depth, doglegging S round the W mole. Moorings (4·8–5m, no fuel) are on the southern wall and under the fort buildings on the northern side of the harbour. The moat behind the fort is out of bounds. There are a restaurant and a kiosk shop on the island. On the N side of the island is a 7M-range all-round white light on a tripod.

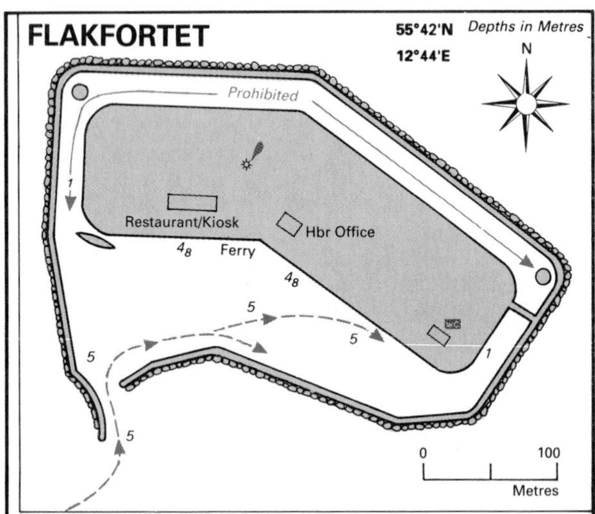

KONGE DYB

→ From Sundby green (unlit) offing buoy the deep (11–16m) buoyed Konge Dyb channel leads north-westwards. The many spires, chimneys, tanks and cranes of Amager island and København can be seen to port. Some 1·5M NW the channel buoys leading to Margretheholm open off to port.

2·5M

KØBENHAVN ØSTHAVN – MARGRETHEHOLM

This is yet another yacht haven with well over 700 moorings (2·5m, PD*, lit entrance), entered directly from the main channel

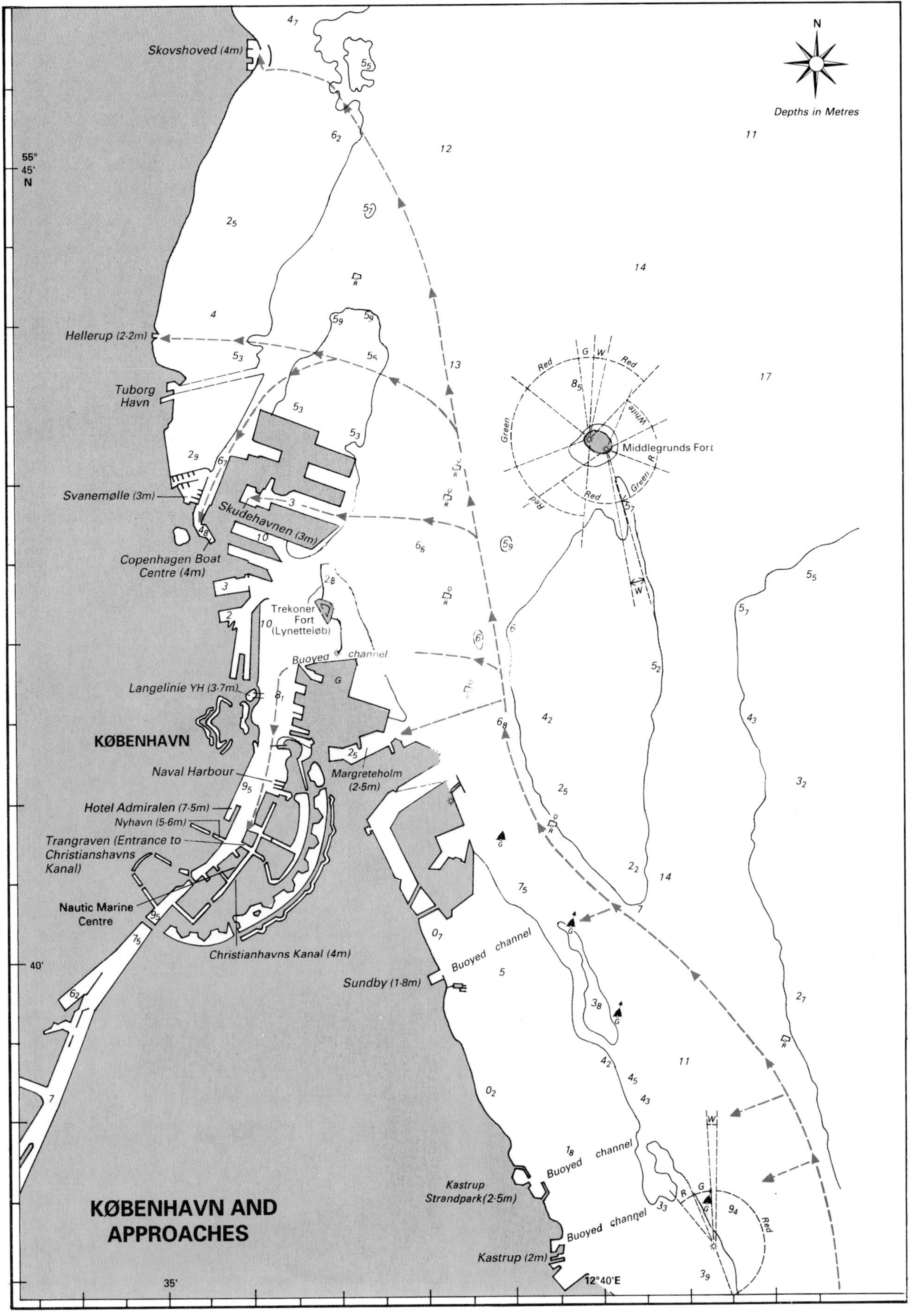
KØBENHAVN AND APPROACHES
Depths in Metres
N
Skovshoved (4m)
Hellerup (2·2m)
Tuborg Havn
Svanemølle (3m)
Copenhagen Boat Centre (4m)
Skudehavnen (3m)
Trekoner Fort (Lynetteløb)
Buoyed channel
Langelinie YH (3·7m)
KØBENHAVN
Naval Harbour
Margreteholm (2·5m)
Hotel Admiralen (7·5m)
Nyhavn (5·6m)
Trangraven (Entrance to Christianshavns Kanal)
Nautic Marine Centre
Christianhavns Kanal (4m)
Sundby (1·8m)
Kastrup Strandpark (2·5m)
Kastrup (2m)
Middlegrunds Fort
Red
Green
White
55° 45' N
40'
35'
12°40'E

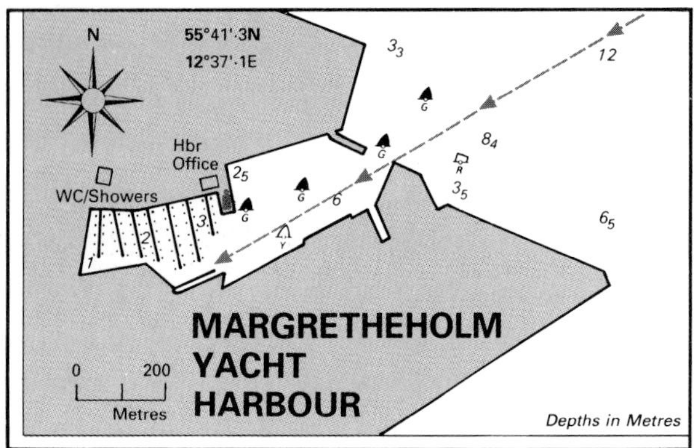

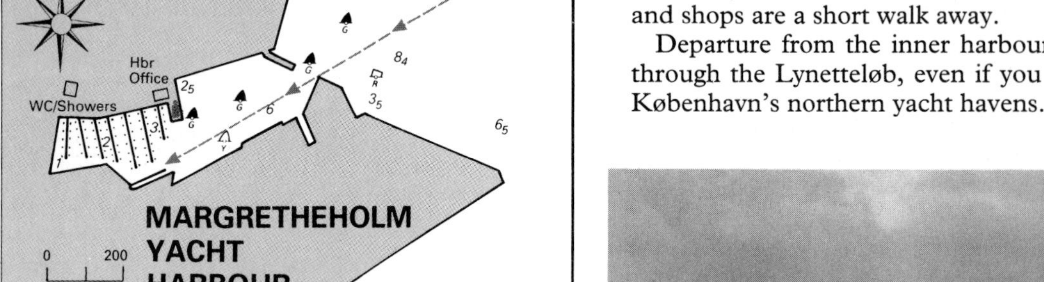

APPROACHES TO KØBENHAVN – LYNETTELØB CHANNEL

→ Some 0·6M from the Margretheholm outer channel buoys, and 0·35M before the prominent Trekroner fort with its sector light (white round tower, range 16–20M), the Lynetteløb buoyed channel (5m deep) opens to port. There is a sector light (2–4M range) at the gap in the Lynette breakwater, halfway along this channel, to make the passage easier. The channel leads directly into København harbour complex – further N, the Kronløb channel (10·1m) into the harbour is for big ships only.

3M (Nautic Marine Centre)

KØBENHAVN – INDERHAVNEN

Southwards from the Lynetteløb there are four main mooring possibilities. All have limited facilities, and the first three suffer from swell from ships and hydrofoils, but all are close to the city centre. **Langelinie** (3–3·7m, lit entrance) is on the W side. **Hotel Admiralen** (6–7m) is also on the W side; it is mainly for large yachts and suffers very considerable swell. Other possibilities are the N side of **Nyhavn** (over 5m), before the opening bridge and opposite the hydrofoil terminus, and the **Christianshavns Kanal** (3–4m) at the Nautic Marine Centre, the quietest moorings, in the dogleg entered almost directly opposite the Nyhavn. This area, with its canal bridges and gabled facades, is extremely reminiscent of Amsterdam's inner canals, and shops are a short walk away.

Departure from the inner harbour must again be through the Lynetteløb, even if you are heading for København's northern yacht havens.

København. Entrance to Langelinie yacht harbour.

København. Hotel Admiralen, an uncomfortable berth for small yachts.

København. Approaching Lynette Løb channel.

København. *Kylora* tucked away in Christianshavns Kanal near the Nautic Marine Centre.

Sightseeing in København

København has a population of around one and a half million. It has good bus and suburban train services, but many of the city's points of interest are easy to visit on foot, the main ones being the gardens, churches (Vor Frue Kirke, the cathedral, is near the Latin Quarter), palaces (Christianborg, Charlottenborg, Rosenborg, Amalienborg) and museums (Thorvaldsen, national, theatre, art, botanic, Freedom, Orlog, medieval history, toy, Tussaud's, the arsenal). These places, as well as the town hall and the government ministries, are all clustered between the canal and the W bank of Inderhavnen, stretching from Langelinie yacht haven to just S of the second bridge (Langebro) SW of Nyhavn. The Little Mermaid statue on Langelinie promenade is just S of Langelinie yacht haven at one end and the Tivoli Gardens amusement park is close NW of Langebro (and near the Central Station) at the other.

Trekroner fort from Lynette Løb channel.

Big ship and 'Little Mermaid'

By night the clustered fairy lights, winding walks and fireworks displays add a magical dimension to the Tivoli Gardens, while the Botanic Garden, 1·5 km further N, with its flower beds, woods, rock gardens and Palm House, is well worth visiting on a sunny day. Behind the Langelinie promenade is the Kastellet (citadel), dating from the 17th century. The main Strøget shopping area covers the southern half of the W bank area N of the Tivoli Gardens. On the E side of Inderhavnen, Christianshavn is a maze of streets, canals, old houses and water fortifications. There are ferry services from the harbour to Bornholm island, to Poland, to Landskrona (Sweden, 1 hour 30 minutes) and to Oslo.

KØBENHAVN NORDHAVNEN – SKUDEHAVNEN

⛵ This small yacht haven belonging to the Segelklub Sundet (3m, D) is approached from the Konge Dyb, crossing the busy traffic of the main Kronløb entrance to the inner harbour and then continuing

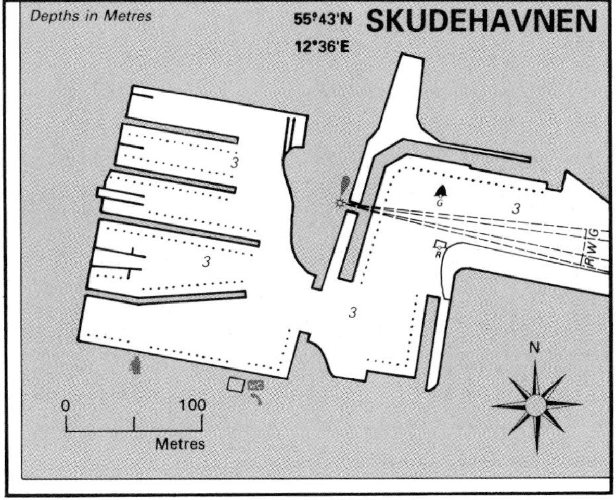

along a 0·5M-long basin, following a 3m-dredged buoyed channel. There is a sector light (range 5–7M) on the N wall of the inner entrance; the moorings are just before and after this entrance. There are container terminals nearby. The city centre is 3km away by rail.

5M (Copenhagen Boat Centre)

KØBENHAVN NORDHAVNEN – SVANEMØLLE/COPENHAGEN BOAT CENTRE (CBC)

Yet another vast yachting complex with all facilities; around 1,000 berths in Svanemølle (3m, PD*, lit entrance) and 300 in CBC (over 4m, D*, lights in line). In moderate weather the approach from Konge Dyb can cut across the 4·7–5·6m shoal patch N of the northern harbour complex. Round into Kalkbranderiløbet (over 6m) and continue south-westwards along this buoyed channel to CBC, with Svanemølle entrance to starboard (facing southwards) after passing the ferry harbour and with CBC a sharp turn to port at the head of the channel. The city centre is 3km away by rail.

About 1M N of Svanemølle is the small yacht haven of Hellerup (2·5m, lit entrance, short buoyed (unlit) channel 2·2m deep). Approach directly from offshore just N of the lit buoy at the northern end of the Kalkbranderiløbet channel – definitely not to be confused with the buoyed (lit) channel leading from this point to the industrial Tuborg Havn, just S of Hellerup, which is out of bounds to yachts.

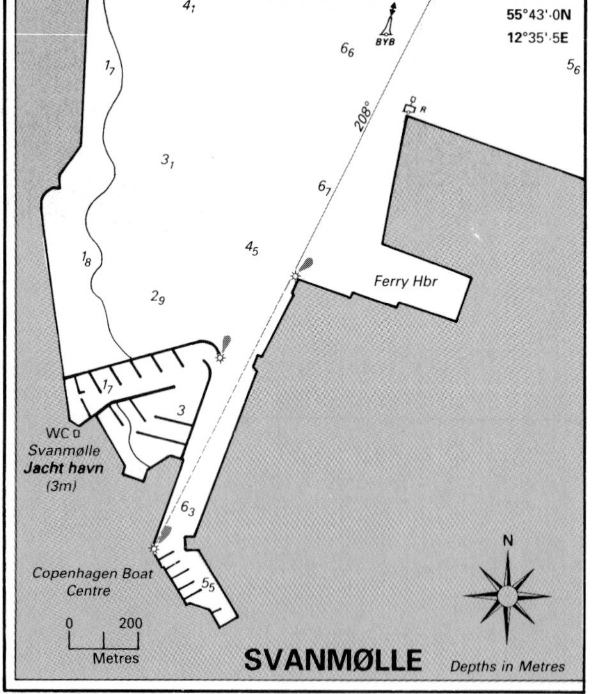

THE NORTHERN SOUND – WEST COAST

The bay from Skovshoved to Kronborg is exposed to winds from NNE through E to SSE, and passages in strong winds from these directions can be rough, particularly in the shallower depths over Tårbæk Rev and Nivå Flak and approaching any of the harbours. The northern entrance to the Sound funnels winds from the NW quadrant, and the shoals and harbour approaches on the Danish side are to be treated cautiously in these conditions, while the Helsingør narrows funnel strong winds from the S as well as from the NW.

This is not a good area for anchoring: shelter is available from only a limited number of wind directions, there is often considerable swell, and there is a busy coast road all the way from København to Gilleleje. All the anchorages suggested below should therefore be regarded as short-stay. Nevertheless, this is an easy area to cruise, with no fewer than 13 yacht havens on this side of the Sound over a distance of 33M (as far as Gilleleje at the northern entrance), and with distances between harbours ranging from 1M to 6M. Additionally, there are three yacht havens 5–7M offshore round Sweden's Ven island, which also has anchoring possibilities. There is also a large yacht haven at Råå, in Sweden, only 5M SE of Kronborg on the Danish coast.

→ The W side of the Sound to Helsingør exhibits typically Danish scenery, partly wooded, with many shoreside houses and occasional conspicuous churches. To remain in at least 5m of water, the passage route should be mainly (not entirely) about 1M offshore. It will need to be somewhat more (about 1·5M) in the middle of the bay off Nivå Flak, and it should be closer inshore rounding Kronborg point in order to keep out of the way of shipping in the Traffic Separation Scheme. There are two tricky pilotage areas in the N: a buoyed inshore passage close NW of Helsingør yacht haven between Lappegrund and Landgrund, and the shoal close N of Gilleleje yacht haven. There is a Traffic Separation Scheme in the narrows leading NW and southwards off Hälsingborg, with a central separation line marked by lit RW buoys, but with no charted outer-edge boundaries, although each side has a line of lit lateral buoys. Pleasure craft should keep inshore of these buoys when passing along the coasts here and cross only at right angles to the lanes. There is a ferry across the narrows between Helsingør and Hälsingborg.

There are 5 separate areas for regatta use charted offshore along this coast, each about 1M in diameter. It is useful to know these so that you can avoid them when you sight the crowds of sails on the horizon.

3·5M (from CBC)
SKOVSHOVED

The lit entrance, with a short offshore protective mole, is approached in 5m from the SE or the NE (where there are two yellow buoys offshore). Depth in the harbour is 3–4m (P★).

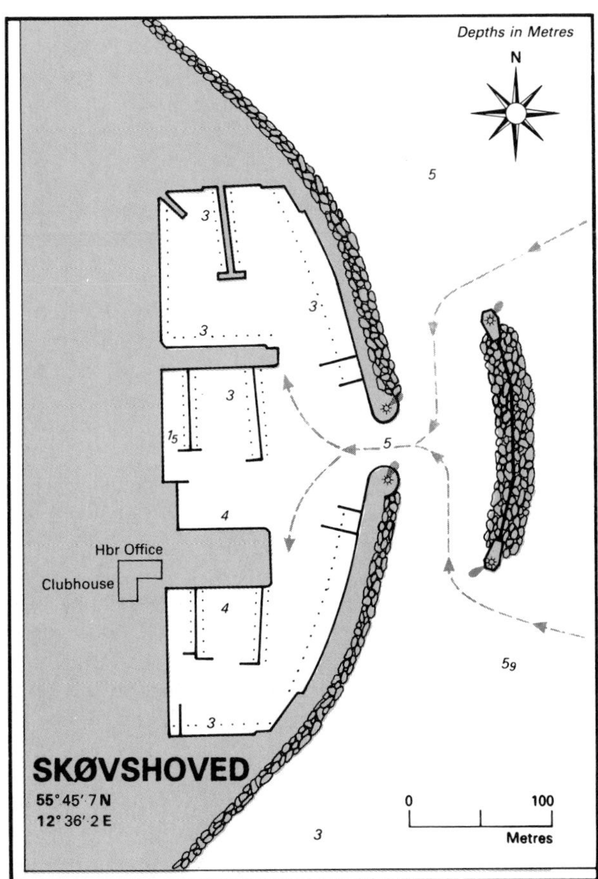

Tårbæk yacht haven (1·8m, lit entrance) is approached from directly offshore, with a 1·8m final approach. There is a lit cardinal buoy 2M offshore to the E.

⚓ In 3–4m over sand near the yellow buoy off the creek at Strandmøllen.

6·5M
VEDBÆK

This large yacht haven (over 400 berths, 2·5m, PD★) has a lit entrance, with a sector light on the northern end of the E mole and a red buoy just N of this. Approach from the NE, doglegging round this buoy into the NW-facing entrance.

4M
RUNGSTED

Yet another modern marina, with over 700 moorings (2–2·5m, PD★). The approach to its NW-facing entrance is very similar to that at Vedbæk. After the entrance buoys there is a sector light on the N end of the E mole; after the dogleg round this the harbourmaster's office is on the E mole.

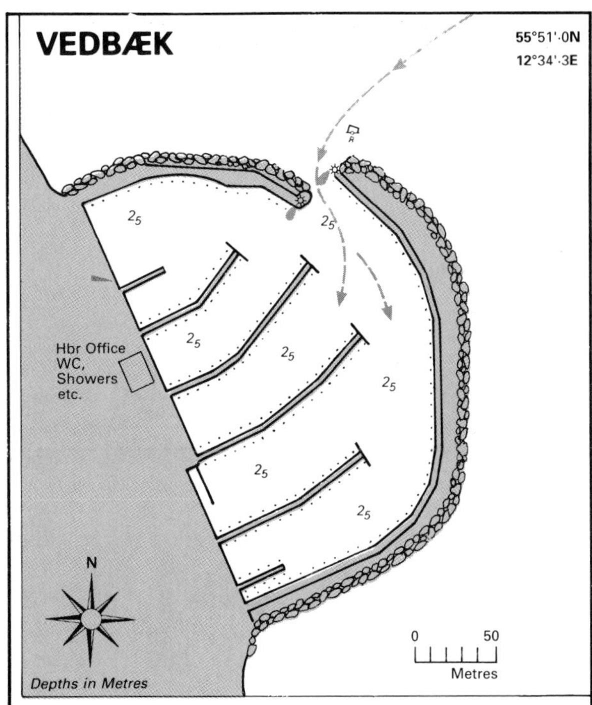

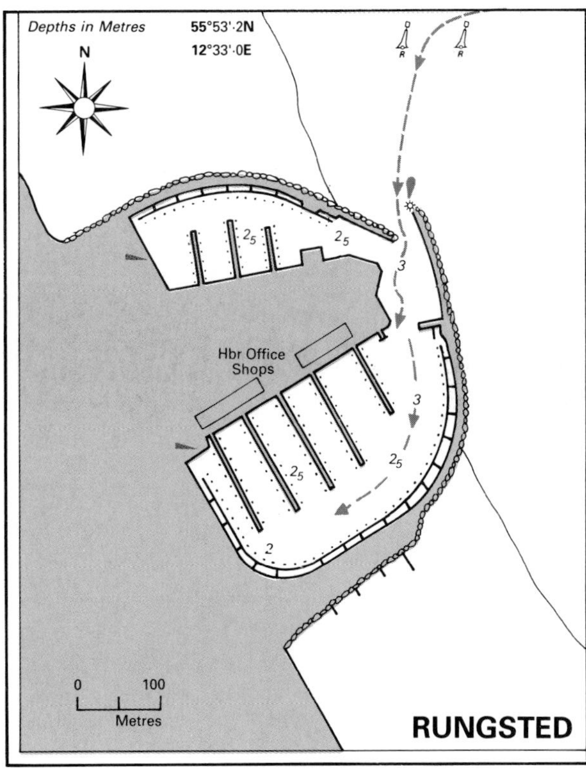

DIVERSION TO VEN ISLAND (SWEDEN)
(not included in total mileage)

→ The W coast of Ven is only 4·5M from Rungsted, mainly in deep water. The shoals round the island are steep-to, and a circumnavigation is no problem, the only tricky shoal patch (on the NW side) being well buoyed. This holiday island is a low, partially wooded 'table' of farmland with cliffs around it. There are three sector lights, on the N, E and S coasts, with ranges from 12–16M.

⛵ The three small fishing harbours have limited space and can be crowded. **Kyrkbacken** (3m, PD, sector light with 8–13M range on S mole of its directly approached entrance), on the W coast, is the largest. **Norreborg** (1·5m, unlit entrance, direct approach), on the N coast, is the smallest. **Bäckviken** (3m, lit entrance, directly approached) is on the E coast. In all of these you must moor head to the jetty with a kedge at the stern. The views are good and a tour of the island on a hired bicycle is well worth while.

Bäckviken harbour on Sweden's Ven island. Entrance.

⚓ If the weather and wind direction is right, the best anchorages are close inshore over sand on the S and E coasts.

3·5M
NIVÅ

⛵ This new medium-sized marina (over 300 places, 2–2·5m*) has a lit entrance with a lit offing buoy close by.

⛵ **Sletten** (1·1–3·1m) is a small fishing and yacht haven with a lit north-facing entrance approached from the NE.

⚓ In 3–4m over sand close N of Sletten yacht haven, or close S of Humlebæk yacht haven near the Louisiana museum of modern art and sculpture (well worth a visit). 1·5m sounding and a dangerous rock are charted about halfway between these anchorages.

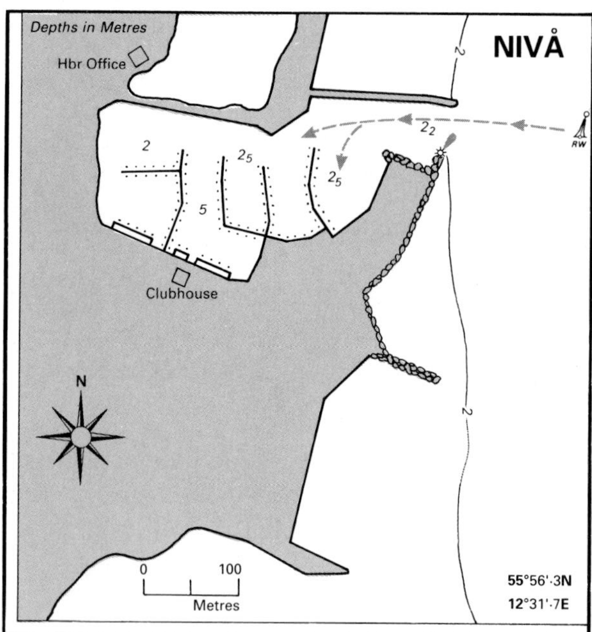

⛵ There follow three small fishing/pleasure-craft harbours with limited space for visitors: **Humlebæk** (0·9–2·5m, D, lit entrance approached in 2·5m from between two channel buoys (unlit) to the NE), **Espergærde** (2·5m, also with lit entrance approached in 2·5m from the NE), and **Snekkersten** (2·8m, lit entrance approached directly from the Sound; keep to N wall when rounding into harbour to avoid the shoals E of the E wall).

DIVERSION TO RÅÅ (SWEDEN)
(not included in total mileage)

⛵ The commercial and ferry harbours at Hälsingborg (Sweden) are out of bounds for visiting yachts, which must use the large **Råå yacht haven** (probably over 500 moorings, 2·5m, sector light on W mole of entrance, PD*), 3·5M S of the city centre along the coast. Hälsingborg city itself has an ancient centre, with a flight of steps up to Kärnan, a tower on the hill above. There is a ferry (25 minutes) to Helsingør. Råå harbour is easily approached from near Humlbæk yacht haven (7M across the Sound in Denmark), approximately following a line of three lit buoys across the southern end of the Traffic Separation Scheme. There is 3–4m depth near to the harbour entrance. This route is somewhat less hazardous than crossing the narrowest part of the separation scheme itself. There is a shopping centre near the yacht haven. Råå's fishing harbour, with its museum and nearby beautifully restored cottages, is also close to the yacht haven.

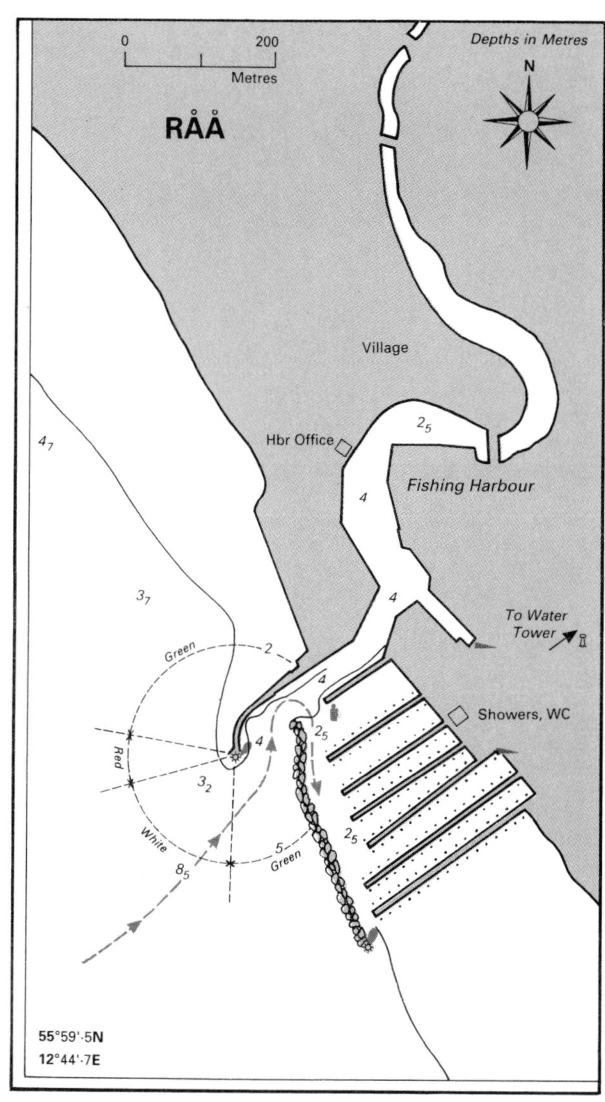

Approach to Råå yacht harbour, Sweden. The nearby huge ferry harbour of Hälsingborg is banned to yachts.

7·5M
HELSINGØR

Helsingør Statshavn is the commercial and ferry harbour on the S side of Kronborg point, and should not be mistaken for the yacht haven, since it is out of bounds. **Helsingør yacht haven** (1·1–3·8m, PD*, VHF Ch 16) is approached from about 0·5M offshore round Kronborg point, with its sector light (range 11–15M) on the NE corner of the prominent Kronborg castle. The haven has around 1,000 berths. The SE-facing lit entrance is best approached from the NE to keep in a minimum of 4m. There can be a strong crosscurrent.

Helsingør, Shakespeare's 'Elsinore', has a magnificent Gothic convent church, with spectacular paintings and hanging ship, as well as a British cannonball from the Nelson period protruding in an unlikely fashion from the inside roof of one of the chapels. There is a Carmelite convent housing a museum of the town's history; there are also many 16th-century buildings in narrow cobbled streets. Kronborg castle is a 16th/17th-century enlargement of the 15th-century Krogen castle; now housing a very extensive maritime museum, it was built originally to defend the Sound and levy tolls on passing shipping. A visit to the castle can include any or all of three features: the maritime museum, the royal

Råå, Sweden. The old fishing harbour.

Helsingør's 1000-boat marina, overlooked by Kronberg castle.

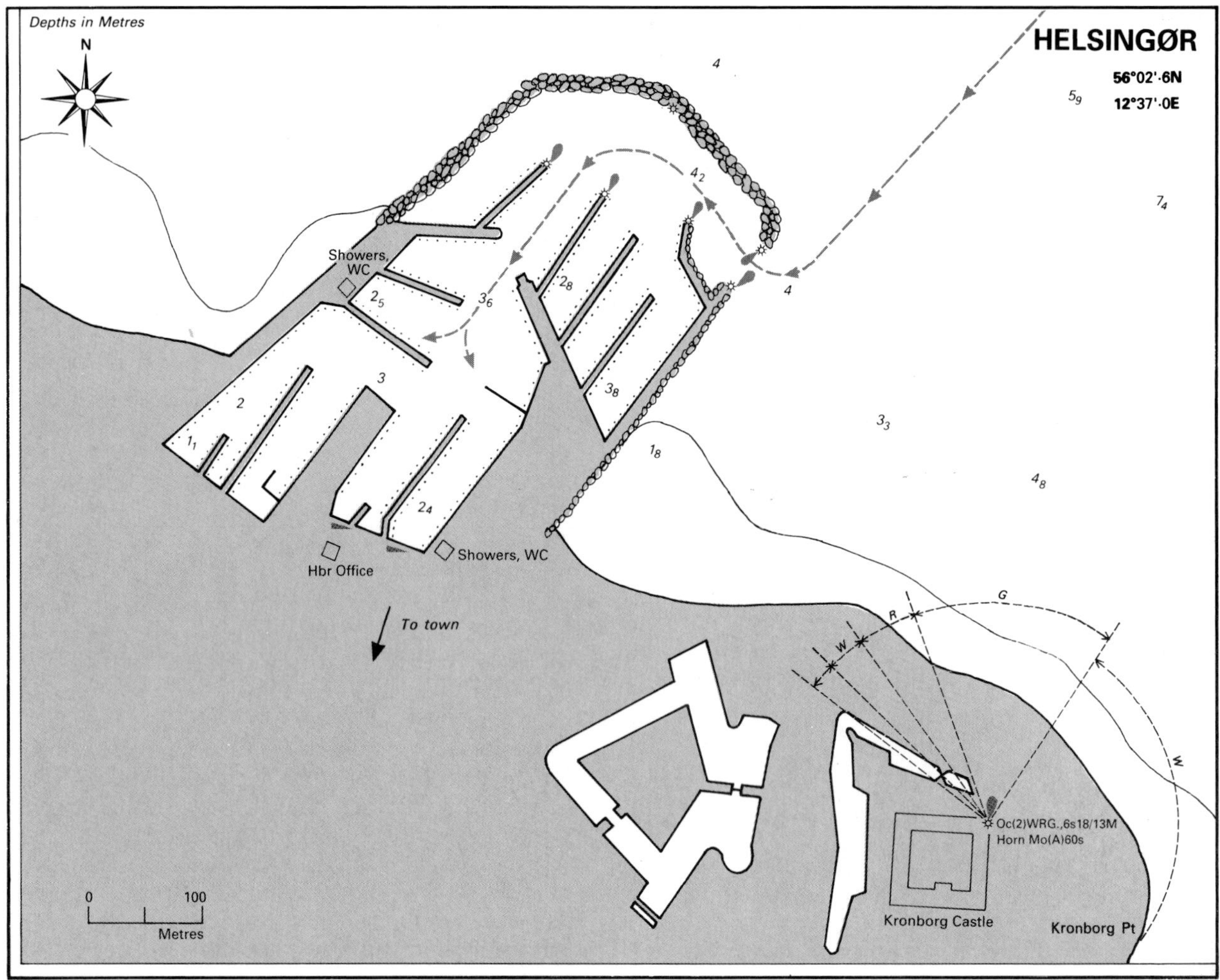

apartments, and the cellars, where the brooding seated statue of Holga Danske is housed, waiting to save Denmark from the enemy. The town also has a technology (including transport) museum; to the N of the town are the classical 16th-century Marienlyst palace and gardens, now part of the town's museum. There is a ferry (25 minutes) to Hälsingborg, Sweden.

→ Continuing westwards along the coast, after rounding the N mole of the yacht haven the course leads northwestwards, keeping in about 6–7m and passing between the two unlit buoys marking the Landgrund and Lappegrund shoals to the S and N of the course. To the W of this channel, Julebæk sector light (12–15M range, orange lantern) has a leading sector directly between these two buoys. Alternatively, in rough weather the shortest route out to the 10m contour can be taken from Helsingør entrance, continuing northwestwards in deep water and giving a reasonable clearance to the Traffic Separation Scheme, whose opposing traffic is on this side.

Hornbæk yacht haven (2·5–3m) is another small fishing and yacht harbour. Its lit, north-facing entrance is directly approached from between two channel buoys in about 3m, and has a swell which can be uncomfortable during or after strong winds. There are many old fishermen's cottages in the village.

A In 2–3m over sand close E of Hornbæk yacht haven.

→ If you are not visiting Gilleleje but heading round for the Isefjord or Roskilde, Nakkehoved, with its major long-range light (range 25M, prominent white square tower) and its offlying shoals, should be given a wide berth, passing outside the two unlit cardinal buoys on the northern edge (keeping in over 6m) before turning southwestwards round the steep cliff of Gilbjerg Hoved.

12·5M

GILLELEJE (SJÆLLAND)

About twice as large as Hornbæk, this fishing and yacht harbour (2·5–3m, D*) has a lit north-facing entrance, with a tricky approach. 1–2M N of the entrance there are shoals with exposed rocks, so approach from the NW, keeping W of a S cardinal buoy marking the S end of the westernmost of these shoals, and then running into the entrance from between two unlit channel buoys. It should be possible to keep in at least 3m by taking this route, but the crosscurrent and the swells over these shoals can

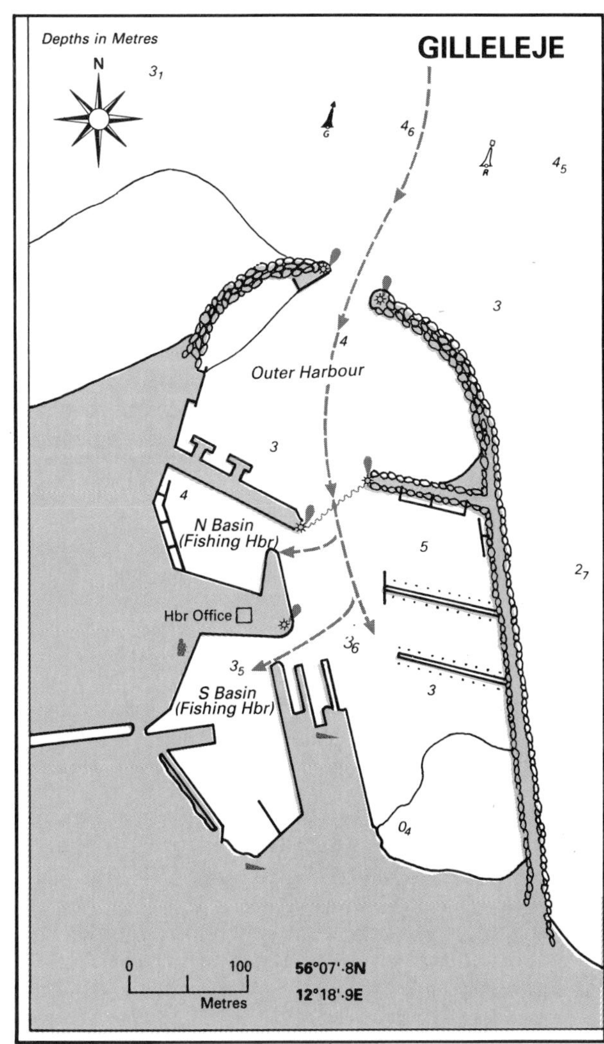

be uncomfortable in rough weather. Although the present harbour dates back only to the 1960s, there is a fishing museum in the nearby picturesque fishing village.

ISEFJORD AND ROSKILDE FJORD AND APPROACHES

Currents off the N coast of Sjælland are light, and are most noticeable in strong N to easterly winds (W-going) and strong S through to westerly winds (E-going). In settled weather there are regular tidal streams in the entrance to the Isefjord and in Kulhus Rende; in both cases the outward stream can be significant. Tidal streams are negligible inside the Isefjord and at the southern end of Roskilde Fjord. Inside these fjords, winds from N to W can raise sea level in some harbours by up to 1·3m and winds from between E and S can reduce them by up to 0·6–0·9m.

W Winds from the two northerly quadrants have a long fetch across the Kattegat. There is also a limited funnelling effect towards the sandbanks in the Isefjord entrance. In strong winds from these directions the shallow approaches from the offing buoy are to be avoided; more settled weather should be awaited. Both of these fjords are good, well protected cruising areas.

The passage southwestwards should be made about 3M offshore to keep S of the offshore explosives-dumping ground and clear the shoreside firing range, both marked by yellow buoys, before heading down to the lit offing buoy at the Isefjord entrance. There are steep cliffs near Tisvilde, with lower land on each side. According to the Admiralty *Pilot*, Tibirke church, 1M SSE of Tisvilde, is the last building remaining of a village buried by a sand drift in the 18th century.

Spodsbjerg sector light (range 11–18M, white square tower – not particularly conspicuous amongst the trees) is on the prominent point on the E side of the entrance. About 1M S of the offing buoy are the first of the closely spaced channel buoys (unlit) of the Osterløb, with a single lit buoy at the end of the channel (dredged to 6·4m). Yachts should have little difficulty in keeping just outside this channel, particularly necessary when the ferries are approaching. **Hundested** (3–5m, lit entrance, PD*) is a large fishing harbour directly entered from the N end of the channel in 5·5m. The entrance to the ferry (from Grenå, as well as local services) harbour is further S and should be avoided by yachts. The southern basin of the fishing harbour, and if this is full the southern side of the inner basin, are allocated to visitors. At the nearby lighthouse is a museum with souvenirs of the Polar explorer Knud Rasmussen, who lived here.

Hundested. E side of Isefjord entrance. In southwesterlies the entrance can be rough.

26M
LYNÆS

Approach this fishing and pleasure-craft harbour northeastwards from between the final lit Osterløb channel buoy and the cardinal buoy to its S, sounding round the Lynås Sand and approaching the entrance in over 5m. The large yacht haven (around 500 moorings, 1·8–2·5m, PD*), with a lit SE-facing entrance (the NE entrance is shallow and should be avoided by visitors), is NE of the much smaller fishing harbour with its outer mole (with a sector light at the head, 4–7M range) and its lit

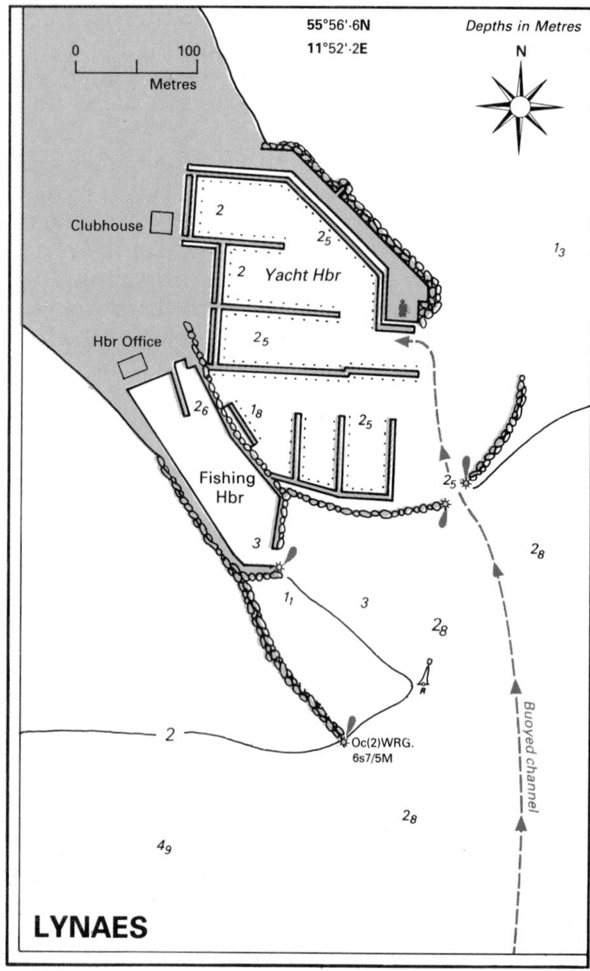

inner entrance. The course leads round the sector light and outside the red buoy northeastwards, following a short, spar-buoyed channel to the yacht-haven entrance in 2·5m. There are some picturesque fishermen's cottages and shops nearby. Hundested is a long walk unless you can borrow a bicycle from the harbourmaster.

DIVERSION TO ISEFJORD AND HOLBÆK

(not included in total mileage)

➞ There is space only to cover this diversion in summary. The distance from Hundested, at the entrance to Holbæk Marina in the S, is 15M.

The Isefjord consists of two *brednings*, with wide areas of 6–10m depths, connected by a buoyed channel (over 10m in places, with a sector light), Orø Vestre Løb, W of Orø island – Orø Ostre Løb, on the E side of the island, is less well buoyed and tricky for newcomers. Opening off the two *brednings* are three shallower inlets: Nykøbing Bugt, Lamme Fjord and Holbæk Fjord, the last with a buoyed channel (5·8m deep). The E side of the Yder Bredning is a charted Danish naval-exercise area which is to be avoided, particularly when the signal flags are flying ashore at the N and S boundaries. There is also a small, prohibited naval torpedo/mine area NE of Kongsøre point on the W side of the fjord.

⛵ In addition to the two at the entrance dealt with above, there are six yacht havens: **Rørvig** (1·2–2·5m*, lit entrance, tricky approach along buoyed Vester Løb entrance to Isefjord), which has a ferry service to Hundested; **Nykøbing** (two basins, 1·5–3·1m, lit entrance, buoyed approach, PD*); Orø (small, 2–3m, sector light on W molehead for approach in 3m); **Holbæk Marina** (the largest yacht haven in the area, of a similar size to Lynæs (above), 2–2·5m, sector light on molehead for approach, PD* – Holbæk's commercial harbour to the W is out of bounds to yachts and the old harbour further W is extremely small); **Hørby** (small, 1·7–2·1m, sector light on molehead for approach in 3m); and **Ejby Havn** (small, 1·4–1·7m, lit entrance, direct approach in 2m).

Both Nykøbing and Holbæk have good local museums and picturesque settings, and 2km SW of the latter town, at Tveje Merløse, is the oldest twin-towered church in Denmark.

⚓ There are many anchorages in 2–4m, some of which are within reach of landings, with bottoms ranging through sand, clay, mud and weed. These include (the following are by no means all) Skanse Bugt, at the head of the little bay E of Rørvig; Sidinge Fjord, off Lamme Fjord (keep along the N side away from the unmarked Egenås Hage); Lamme Fjord, near the dam (after sounding past Kisserup Hage, head for the northern sluice gate to avoid Avdebo Hage); Holbæk Fjord, close W of Holbæk old harbour or close W of Horby Havn; Munkholm, near the causeway across Bramsnæs Bugt (follow the E coast on approach); Bramsnæs Vig, close E of the headland or about 3 cables N of the head of the *vig*.

ROSKILDE FJORD (*Note* It is worth using the Danish hydrographic charts Nos *117* and *118* for pilotage in this difficult area.)

➞ The whole of this narrow fjord is marked, mainly with spar buoys and perches. Some are lit, particularly at the N end. The buoyed channel varies from 12m depths in the N through 5m off Frederikssund to as little as 2·5m near Eskilso. It is essential to follow the buoys carefully as there are wide shoal 'shelves' of less than 2m depth, particularly in the wider *brednings*. These are often covered with a maze of fishing stakes, with exposed rocks and boulders closer inshore in many places.

The N side of Kulhus Rende near the entrance channel has steep sand cliffs. Frederiksværk, further E, is in a wooded area with Maglehoj hill to its E. The N–S reaches of the fjord are bounded by scenic hills and woodlands, particularly on the W side and on both sides S of Frederikssund.

⛵ **Kulhuse** (1·5–2m) is a small ferry (to Sølager), fishing and pleasure-craft harbour, with an unlit entrance and direct approach in 2·2m, on the S promontory of the Kulhus Rende entrance.

➔ Visiting yachts which are newcomers to this area and which bypass Frederiksværk to continue on towards Frederikssund have a complicated channel to follow, with a 'slalom' double bend of spar buoys S of the Store Tørve Grund. S of this there are several isolated 1·8m boulder patches over a 2–4m-deep area. The channel to Frederiksværk, visiting the yacht haven and returning into the main channel E of the Store Tørve Grund, avoids this problem area.

Frederiksværk is an industrial harbour serving Frederiksværk steelworks (out of bounds to yachts). It is located in the NE corner of the first large bight in the fjord, on a buoyed (some lit) channel forming a large loop to and from the main channel, which continues on southeastwards. This is Denmark's only steel town, with steel-rolling mills and foundries on its outskirts. The older ironworks have now gone. There is a gunpowder museum in a water mill, and a local museum.

⛵ **Frederiksværk Havn** (2·5–3·5m, PD) is a tiny yacht haven close NW of the industrial harbour, at the head of a buoyed (unlit) channel which follows the SE side of a long mole (Slaggemole). The approach is tricky: from the lit buoy NE of Kulhuse point the main buoyed channel leads eastwards with a back transit (unlit) of a beacon with a yellow triangle near Sølager village on the N bank and the gable of a yellow building close W of this. 2·4M E of the lit Kulhuse buoy a buoyed channel leads NE past two lit buoys to the industrial harbour along a transit of two beacons (red triangles). Close W of the entrance to the industrial harbour are two channel spar buoys (unlit). A course between these leads round the deeper (4·5m) eastern side of the entrance, avoiding the foul area to the SE of the end of the Slaggemole; continue along the buoyed channel (unlit) to the yacht haven.

➔ The route southwards from Frederiksværk leaves the lit E cardinal buoy SSE of the entrance to starboard, then leaves to port a lit red buoy 1M further S, joining the main buoyed channel again along a transit (unlit triangular beacons) southeastwards past an E cardinal buoy marking Ølsted Grund shoals. A 2M reach (depth 7–10m) follows, with lit buoys at each end. At the southern end of this a closely buoyed channel leads to the opening bridge at Frederikssund, along two sets of lights in line, the second of which has its front leading light on the bridge.

⚓ There are few anchorage possibilities over the wide shallow sides of the northern part of the fjord below Frederikssund. On the W bank S of Dyrnås Hage, or close E of Øksneholm island, there are daylight anchorages over sand – take care to avoid the fishing stakes.

⛵ To the SW of the first of the channel buoys, before the fjord narrows, lies **Kignæs** or Neder Dråby, a small yacht haven (2·2m, lit entrance) between two long, northward-aligned moles. It has an east-facing entrance, approached along a 1·7m 0·8M-long channel marked by perches (unlit) and one offshore lit beacon.

Kronprins Frederiks bridge is a double-bascule road and rail bridge with 3·5m clearance when closed and a lit opening span. From 1 April to 30 September the bridge is opened on request from 5 a.m. to half an hour after sundown. In summer waiting times can be up to an hour; there is a pontoon on the W side of the channel on the S side of the bridge and there are piles to the N of the bridge. The N flag at the crosstrees (or the national flag at half-mast), or a long blast and a short blast on the horn, or VHF Ch 16 (working channels 12 and 13) obtains passage. Bridge signals: one F.R light, passage closed; 2 Fl.R lights, open for S-bound vessels; 3 Fl.R lights, S-bound vessels may pass through; 3 F.R lights, N-bound vessels may pass through.

Frederikssund, Roskilde Fjord. Kronprins Frederiks double bascule opening road/rail bridge.

➔ 0·7M along the buoyed channel is a disused railway bridge, with a gap for passage on the eastern side next to the south quay of Frederikssund commercial harbour (only available to large deep-draught yachts). Beyond this an overhead cable with a clearance of 27m spans the fjord.

13M

FREDERIKSSUND YACHT HAVEN

⛵ This medium-sized yacht haven (over 300 berths in two basins: Frederikssund 2–3m and Marbæk 1·7m, D★) is entered from the main channel by turning northeastwards close S of a red buoy, and then rounding the lit end of its southern breakwater, leaving two green buoys to starboard.

The town is a long way to walk, so you will need to hire a bicycle. A former medieval ferry town and trading centre, the town is well known for its outdoor Viking plays and feasts. There is also a museum of the works of J. F. Willumsen, the expressionist painter and sculptor.

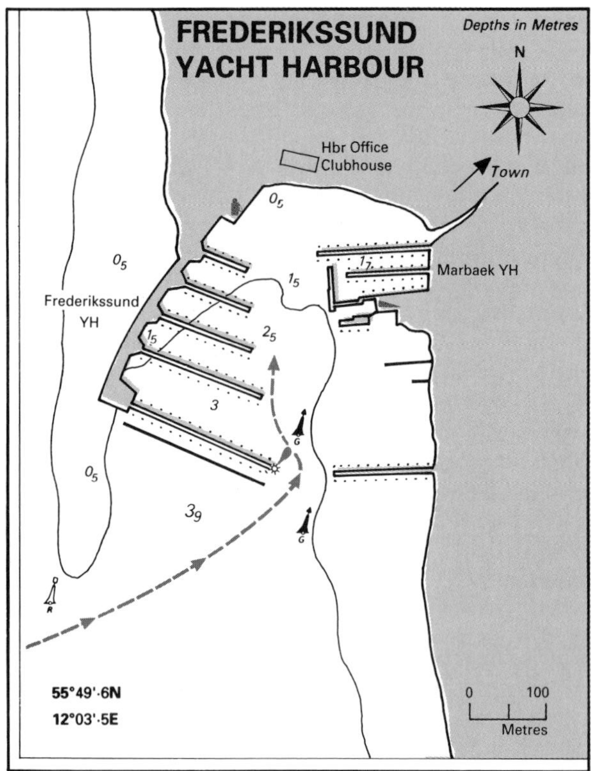

→ ⛵ ⚓ The next 6M of the channel to the southern end of Eskilso are narrow and winding, with scattered islands and rocks and charted depths of as little as 2·5m (we found less at times), so the spar buoys must be followed. **Skuldelev** (0·5–1·5m, unlit entrance) is a tiny, extremely shallow fishing harbour with few spaces on the W side of the channel. Near this point there is an overhead cable with 22m clearance across the fjord. Close S of the harbour entrance is a possible daytime anchorage over sand in about 3m.

5M (Jyllinge S)
ESKILSØ AND JYLLINGE N and S

→ At the lit buoy in the N approaches to Eskilsø island two alternative buoyed (unlit) channels branch off. One leads southeastwards in only 1·5m depth past the two Jyllinge yacht havens to a dead end with rocks and shoals. The main channel, with 2·5m depth, leads W of Eskilsø to a final red (occasional light) buoy at the northern edge of a wide area of fjord with 4·2–5·9m depths N of Roskilde.

⛵ ⚓ **Jyllinge north yacht haven** (1·7–2m, PD) is a small open harbour approached from the 1·5m channel (see above) directly from the green buoy to the SE of its unlit entrance. **Jyllinge south yacht haven** (1·5–2m, PD*) is a much larger harbour, with a W-facing (unlit) entrance to which the channel buoys lead directly after passing between Lilleø island and a tiny boat harbour on the mainland. There are anchorages S and N respectively of each of the harbour entrances, outside the marked channel over sand.

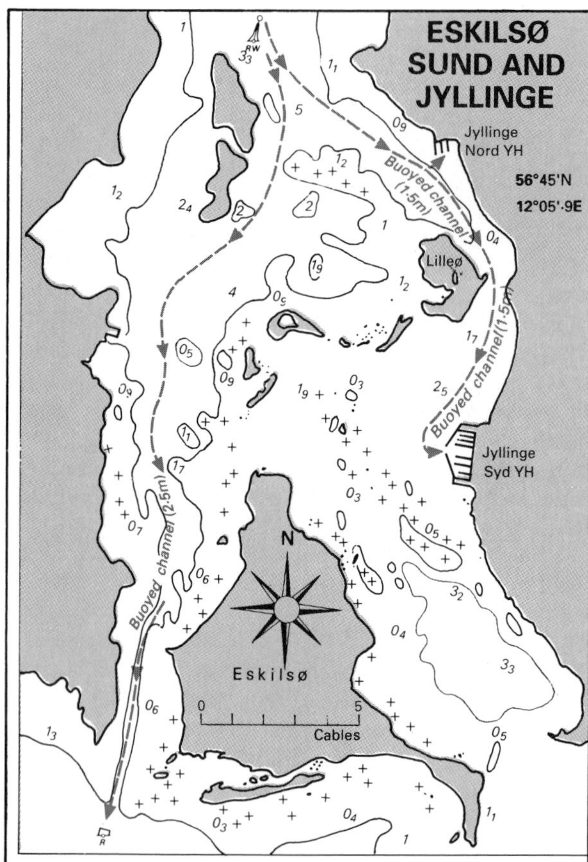

→ A course from the red (occasional light) buoy southwards across the fjord picks up the buoys (the first two with occasional lights) at the beginning of the channel (2·8m depth) to Roskilde in the SE corner of the fjord. Vestre Tue, a 1·6m isolated shoal, is marked by a red buoy eastwards of the first channel buoy. The channel buoys initially pass through rocky areas and must be followed carefully.

⛵ **Veddelev** (3m, lit entrance) is a small harbour on a promontory E of the channel; it is entered directly.

⚓ Kattinge Vig is a perfect natural harbour NW of Roskilde, entered from the main channel off Veddelev yacht haven via a narrow, buoyed channel (2·6m depth). There are several scenic anchorages over sand or mud in the various coastal indentations, and often a dinghy trip can be made ashore to scramble up the sand cliffs into the woods above or to barbecue on the beach. Anchor in Krage Vig, NE of Ringoen island, in one of the two bays S and E of the island, or in Smørvig, on the northern shore, E of the shallow Gade Kæret bay in the NW corner of the *vig*.

→ The main channel buoys are more widely spaced on the final approach to Roskilde across the wide basin N of the city, and there are lights in line to the entrance to the harbour. The city's two-spired

Kattinge Vig. A perfect anchorage near the head of Roskilde Fjord.

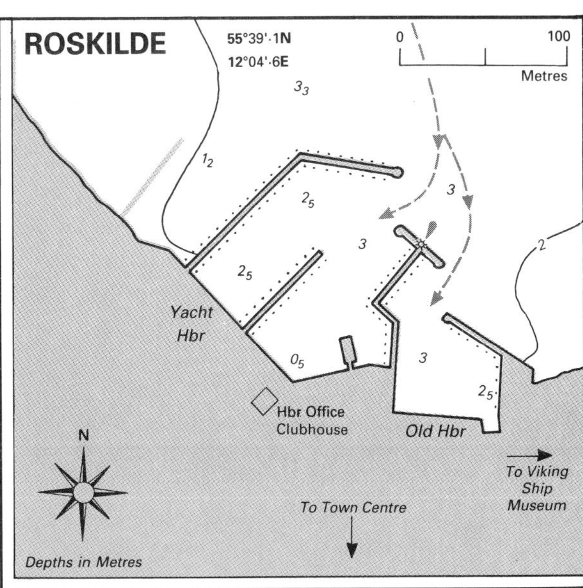

cathedral can be seen for a considerable distance on passage.

8·5M
ROSKILDE

The yacht haven and old harbour (0·5–3m) are entered on opposite sides of a central T-shaped mole, which is lit. Space inside is limited. If the harbour is full it is always possible to pick up a nearby mooring, or to anchor off the shore eastwards or westwards of the entrance in 2–4m; there are many landing jetties.

Sightseeing in Roskilde

Roskilde is one of Denmark's oldest towns. Founded in the 9th century, it was a royal residence and bishop's seat in the Middle Ages. Its prominent cathedral (St Luke's) is one of Denmark's major national monuments, containing the tombs of the kings and queens of Denmark. The second major point of interest is the Viking Ship Museum near the waterfront. An underwater ridge in the Roskilde Fjord, discovered much earlier by fishermen, was excavated in the late 1950s by the Danish National Museum, revealing several ships which had been sunk and covered with stones in the 11th century, probably to protect the approaches to the port from Norwegian marauders. Piecing together the remnants of the ships for the museum was a mammoth task. Five vessels are represented: a deep-sea trader (16·5m long) for trade with Greenland, Britain and Iceland, a Baltic merchant ship (13·3m), a small warship (18m), one of the dreaded longships (28m), and a 12m fishing or ferry boat. There is an accompanying film (in English as well as Danish) and an exhibition. Other attractions in Roskilde include Magle Kilde (a natural spring upon which much of Roskilde's industry was founded in the early 19th century), the 18th-century palace with its 'collections', several historic churches, the 19th-century town hall with its 500-year-old church tower, the Roskilde Museum, the delightful town park (overlooking the fjord), and the Games Museum (collection of games and playing cards).

→ The western section of the headwaters of Roskilde Fjord has two small yacht havens, but demands tricky shoal-water pilotage. The area of fjord in which the havens are located is approached from the gap on the W side of the deep-water basin

Roskilde Fjord. Entrance to Veddelev harbour near head of fjord.

Roskilde Fjord. Fishing stakes alongside the narrow channel.

Roskilde. Approaching the city with its twin-spired cathedral, burial place of Denmark's past rulers.

to the N of the Bognås peninsula. There is a long shoal patch across this gap from Skrivernåbbet point in the N to Fårgebrorev in the S, and there are two marked channels through this. One, midway along and marked by two occasional channel buoys, has only 1·4m depth; the other, in the S between Nørre Rev and Fårgebrorev, has 4m and is between the beacon (occasional light) on the southern end of Nørre Rev and a red (unlit) buoy close S. NE of the latter gap is **Gershøj** (1–1·5m only, D), a tiny fishing harbour with an unlit entrance entered directly round the harbour's NE corner. Southwards from the Nørre Rev channel a series of red buoys (one towards the end of the channel has an occasional light) leads round Agernæs peninsula to a somewhat larger harbour, **Herslev** (2m), with an unlit entrance directly entered from the N.

⚓ There are several picturesque anchorages in the long N–S bight W of Nørre Rev, mainly over sand in 2–3m. These include Møllekrog Vig, N of Gershøj Havn at the head of the bay (keep to the E side) with a landing jetty nearby (there is a 12th-century church at Skibby, 3km W of the head of the bay), the southern end in Lejre Vig, along the W coast off Lyndby, and Kransekrog and Uglekrog, to the N and S of Agernæs headland off the buoyed route to Herslev. Another superb anchorage E of the Nørre Rev is in Ølvig, in the W side of the bay 0·3M S of Nørrehoved point.

10. The German Baltic coast and Bornholm

Passage notes

The N German coastline from the Kieler fjord to the Polish border, and Denmark's outlying island of Bornholm to the N, is a huge and complex cruising area. The distance as the crow flies from the Kieler fjord entrance to Bornholm's E coast is 170M, which nearly doubles to around 300M of cruising coastline if all the indentations and island coasts are included. There are at least 50 feasible moorings at which to tie up and step ashore dryshod on the German coast, around 20 round Bornholm island, and at least another 40 on the Untertrave waterway and the N German lakes. An adequate guide to the area requires a book in itself, and this chapter gives cruise-planning notes rather than detailed pilotage information.

The greatest concentration of good yacht harbours is in the Fehmarnsund and Neustadter Bucht areas, in the former West Germany. Heiligenhafen, for example, has probably 1,000 berths, and a huge 1,600-berth marina is under construction at Neustadt. East of this area only Stralsund has extensive facilities, and although Bornholm has about 20 harbours, all are small.

Currents

In light weather the predominant currents in this area are SW to W-going with the outgoing Baltic stream, and there is a small anticlockwise back-eddy in Mecklenburg Bucht. However, wind-driven surface currents override this outflow, and these are predominantly parallel with the coast and into or out of the intervening bays and inlets. Winds from the E and N quadrants drive the currents westwards and southwards across the open sea areas (and also northwards into the Sound from Bornholm), down the Rügen coast and into Mecklenburg Bucht and its inlets. Winds from the W and S quadrants drive the currents eastwards and northwards, and out of the inlets. Seldom do these currents reach 2kn, but in exceptional gale conditions in the Fehmarn Bælt and Fehmarn Sund they can reach up to 4kn. There is also weak tidal flow in Fehmarn Sund in light conditions which can reach 1–2kn, but again wind is the main factor here, as in Strelasund, the channel S of Rügen.

Water levels

The N–E winds associated with a W-going current tend to increase water levels in this part of the Baltic, since the constricted necks of the Sound and the Belts to the W act as a 'dam' to the outgoing water. The S–W winds associated with an E-going current tend to do the opposite, reducing water levels, while again constricted channels and bays increase the effect more than in open-sea areas. Reduced water levels of 0·6–2m (the latter in the Trave) can occur, while increased levels tend to be greater and can range from 0·6m to as much as 3·3m (the latter in the Trave).

Weather

The length and warmth of the summer season do not change significantly moving eastwards along this coast from Kiel. Wind direction tends to be predominantly E–W aligned, but in the season winds tend to favour an eastward passage. In spring there is a window, when the proportions of easterly and westerly winds tend to equate. In summer, winds from the two western quadrants, but with more of a northwesterly tendency, predominate. In autumn the same applies, but with a southwesterly tendency.

Charts

German hydrographic *30, 39, 36, 40, 54, 55, 141, 142, 143, 159.*
NV *Sportschiffahrtskarten Series 1, 2* and ***4.*** These charts are often a little small in scale, and it is essential to have the pilot books, *Der Grosse NV Hafen Lotse, Bands 1, 2* and *4,* which accompany the chart sets for pilotage in the harbour entrances.
Danish hydrographic *189.*

THE GERMAN COAST FROM KIELER BUCHT TO THE POLISH BORDER

The western end of this coastline, i.e. the part in the former West Germany, is mainly low-lying, dyked farmland with only a few trees (particularly the island of Fehmarn). The Neustadter Bucht holiday-resort area, further E, is hilly and wooded. Yet further E, beyond the Trave estuary and across the former E German frontier, Mecklenburger Bucht has a more varied coastline with hills and woods in places, but even here one of the highest hills on its

Jutland
Kattegat
DENMARK
Lille Baelt
Odense
Fyn
Nyborg
Svendborg
Store Baelt
Sjaelland
Helsingør
Helsingborg
SWEDEN
The Sound
Landskrona
KOBENHAVN
Saltholm
Malmö
Falsterbo Canal
Drogden
Oc(3)WRG.15s
18-13M
Horn(3)60s
Oc.5s10M
Iso.WRG.8s16-12M
Falsterbørev
Iso.WRG.8s22-18M
Horn(2)30s
RC
Trelleborg
Gislövs Läge
Kullagrund
Iso.WRG.4s16-12M
Ystad
Ldg 2Iso.15M
Simrishamn
Aero VQ.40m
21M (occas)
Kaseberg
Sandhammaren
Fl.5s22M
Kivik
Sonderborg
Hanö
Tjarö
Karlskrona
N
Bornholmsgat
Hammerodde
Fl(2)18M
RC
Christiansø
Fl.19M
Bornholm
(Denmark)
Rønne
Svaneke
Fl(2)21M
Dueodde
Fl(3)20M
Horns
Baltic Sea
Rødvig
Praesto
Kalvehavn
Vordingborg
Møn
Møn
Fl(4)22M
Horn(4)60s
Stubbekøbing
Hestehoved
Oc(2)WRG.13/9M
Falster
Nakskov
Lolland
Rodby
Als
Sonderborg
Aro
Spodsbjerg
Langeland
Bagenkop
Keldsnor
Fl(2)20s25M
Flensburger Bucht
Flensburg
Falshöft
Oc(2)WRG.16s18/13M
Schleimunde
LFl(3)WR.20s14-6M
Schlei
Kieler Bucht
Kiel
Iso.WRG.6s
18-14M
Schleswig
Eckernförde
Bülk
Fl.WRG
Rendsburg
Kiel Canal
KIEL
Neuland
Fl(4)WR.30s
21 18M
Fehmarn Bucht
Oc.4s16M
Fehmarn
LFl.WR.10s
Fehmarn
Puttgarten
Marienleuchte
Fl(4)WR.15s22/18M
Heiligenhafen
Mecklenburger
Bucht
Dahmeshöved
Fl(3)12s23M
Neustadt
Lübecker
Bucht
Travemünde
LUBECK
Poel
Wismar
Buk
LFl(4)WR.45s
24/20M
Gedser
Gedser Odde
Fl(3)20s24M
RC
Wustrow
Oc(3)12s16M
Horn Mo(D)30s
Warnemünde
Fl(3+1)24s20M
Rostock
Darsser Ort
Fl(2+4)22s20M
Zingst
Saaler
Bodden
Ribnitz
Dornbusch
LFl.WR.10s21/15M
Stralsund
Arkona
Fl(3)17s22M
Ranzow
Fl.5s14M
Sassnitz
Oc.WG.6s10/6M
Rügen
Greifswalder
Bodden
Greifswalder Oie
Fl.3.8s26M
Greifswald
Freest
Peenestrom
Zatoka Pomorska
Wolgast
Usedom
Oc.WR.25M
RC
Swinoujście
Stettiner
Haff
Zalew
Szczeciński
Ueckermunde
Niechorz
Fl.10s20M
Kolobrzeg
Fl.3s.16M
RC
POLAND
Schleswig-
Holstein
Mecklenburg-Vorpommern
GERMANY
56°
55°
54°
N
10°
11°
12°E
13°
14°
15°

eastern coast, Diedrichshagener Berg, is only 128m. Further E still are pine woodlands and dunes, with the wooded island of Rügen and its barren cape, Arkona, protruding northwards. Church spires, lighthouses, occasional high bridges and the clustered buildings of the larger towns are the main landmarks throughout the area.

On a through passage, close-quarters shoal-water pilotage is required in Fehmarn Sund and round Fehmarn island generally, in Wismar Bucht, rounding the Darsser Ort headland, and in the Gellenstrom and Strelasund passages of Rügen (rounding Arkona Cape is straightforward).

The Baltic coast of Germany is of much more architectural and historic interest than the North Sea coast, with no less than four important historic Hanseatic League trading cities: Lübeck, Wismar, Rostock and Stralsund. In the Middle Ages the 'statutes of Lübeck', giving the city self-governing and free-trading rights, were adopted by at least a hundred other towns in the Baltic. Lübeck also built a canal link with the Elbe, bringing Hamburg, Bremen and Bruges into this league of mutual protection, which had its own fleet as well as a network of trading 'offices' abroad. Europe's fishing industry and trading fulcrum, however, gradually moved westwards, and the league declined, its last meeting being in Lübeck in 1630.

No visit to Travemünde, therefore, can afford to exclude a visit to Lübeck, with its beautifully restored buildings and historic ship harbour. Travemünde has excellent yachting facilities, but you can still visit Lübeck by train. Wismar, in the former East Germany, is a smaller but also interesting restored gabled trading town with limited yachting facilities. A visit to Warnemünde must take in a trip upriver to Rostock, of a similar size to Lübeck, but with few yachting facilities; if you do stay in Warnemünde's yacht harbour you can take the S-bahn to visit Rostock's maritime museum and Gothic buildings. Stralsund, the furthest E, is the most convenient of all the Hanseatic cities to visit, since it is directly on the through route and has extensive yachting facilities. Despite wartime damage it still has many ancient buildings, including its town hall and several churches.

There are many other historic towns and fishing ports along these coasts worth visiting.

There follows a list of all the main mooring possibilities, moving eastwards, together with pilotage notes where appropriate. In brackets after each is listed the type of harbour, my own rough estimate of the number of mooring places where possible (those without estimates are usually very small), the depths, and whether the entrance or the approach is lit.

Hohwachter Bucht

Lippe (yacht haven, 180, 0·6–2m, unlit, difficult entrance)

Fehmarn and Fehmarnsund

Heiligenhafen (yacht haven, 1,000 plus, 2·1–3·3m, lit)
Ortmühle (yacht haven, 100, 2·5m, lit approach)
Orth (commercial and yacht haven, 120, 2–3m, lit approach)
Lemkenhafen (yacht haven, 150, 2·5m, unlit)
Beelitz Werft (yacht haven, 110, 1·8–3m, unlit)
Grossenbrode-Fähre (yacht haven, 150, 2·5m, unlit)
Grossenbrode (2 yacht havens, 360, 1·9–2·2m, lit approach)
Burgstaaken-Burgetiefe (yacht haven, 650, 2–3m, lit approach)

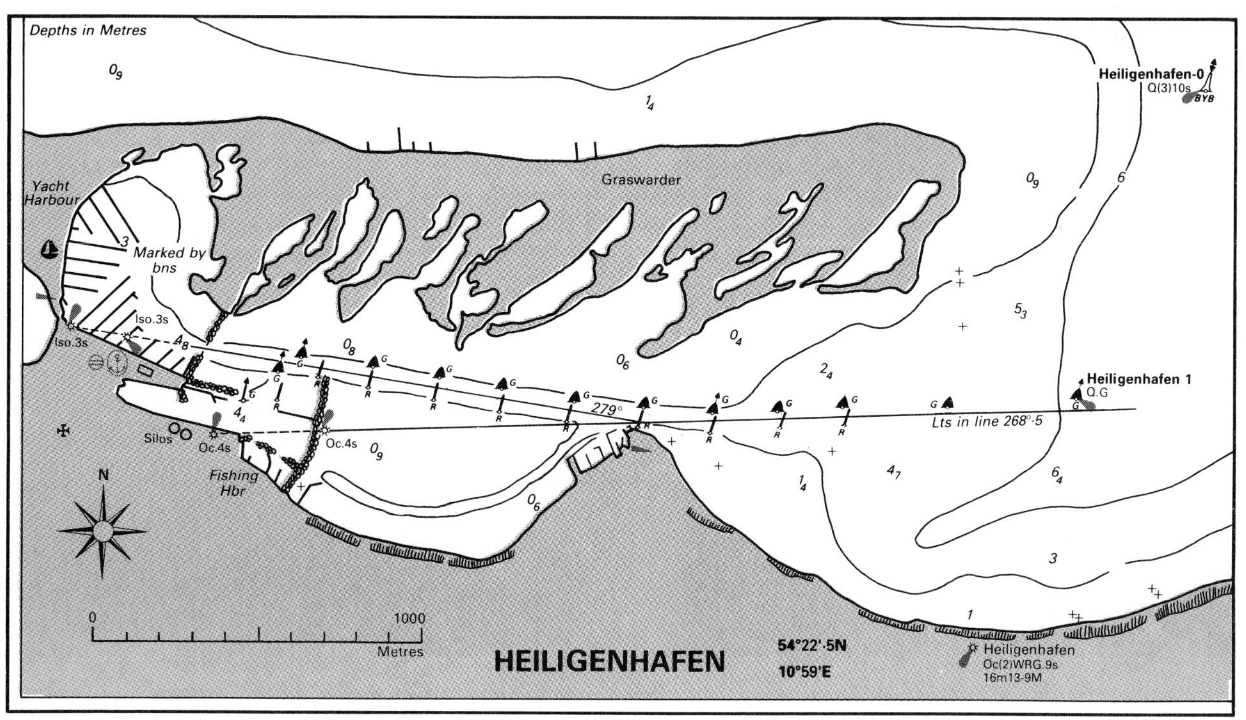

Heiligenhafen's entrance channel from the east is extremely well buoyed and lit, with a sector light for the initial approach and in daylight the unmistakeable, 134m high Warn F tower just over a mile south-southwest of the entrance. Although the town has a huge marina, it is also an interesting, long-developed holiday resort and active fishing port, with a town square and street cafés, small shops, good restaurants and a boating atmosphere.

Leaving Heiligenhafen the wide shoal areas in Fehmarnsund should be given a wide berth and the channel buoys followed whenever possible, particularly when approaching and leaving the Fehmarnsund bridge (23m clearance). From 'Fehmarnsund' red and white, lit offing buoy southeast of the bridge the passage to Neustadt is straightforward in 10m-plus water with no hazards other than clearing the cardinal buoys off the headlands at Dahmeshöved and Pelzerhaken.

The **Grossenbroder Binnensee** 3M S of Fehmarnsund has a good yacht harbour but also offers an excellent (given the usual water-skiers and bikes) virtually landlocked anchorage at its southern end in 2·2–2·6m. Its narrow entrance channel, though subject to frequent changes, was easily approached, lit (but daytime pilotage is advised) and well buoyed on our visit.

Neustädter Bucht

Grömitz (yacht haven, 800, 2–2·7m, lit)
Neustadt (2·5m, lit approach, new yacht haven with 1,400 berths, 2·5–3·5m)

Heiligenhafen. Heading down the approach channel.

Heiligenhafen entrance.

Fehmarnsund bridge (23m clearance) from the E.

Niendorf (yacht haven, 50, 2·4–3m, unlit)
Travemünde (three yacht havens plus varying moorings, 2,000 plus, 3–4m, lit approach)

The western side of Neustädter Bucht is an even more popular cruising area than Fehmarnsund in terms of numbers of marina berths, although this coast is rather exposed as a place to anchor.

Grömitz is an immaculate modern holiday resort with all facilities and a beach lined with *strandkorben* (seat baskets) like the Frisian resorts. Its modern yacht harbour (directly approached) is backed by low sand cliffs with footpath walks, and rolling farmland and woodland.

Neustadt. Entrance to the 1400-berth Ancora marina on the W side of the harbour approach.

Neustadt. Approach to the town harbour. The yacht harbour of NSV (Neustadter Segelvereines) is to the right.

Neustadt. Head of the fishing harbour. E side.

Neustadter SV yacht harbour.

Neustadt is approached from a red and white, lit offing buoy along a dead straight buoyed channel with lights in line, then turning either to port to the huge new **Ancora Marina** with its 1400 berths in two basins or to starboard and heading northwards into the old harbour. This marina, although useful for leaving a boat for long periods (which we did), is a long way from the interesting old town of Neustadt.

Much nearer to Neustadt, is the immaculate and friendly yacht club on the east side of the entrance to the old harbour, **Neustadter Segelvereines**, with around 250 berths (2–3m depth). Here the harbourmaster allocated us a berth (head-to) number through his voice trumpet as we doubled back from the entrance to sail past his office. The clubhouse toilet and restaurant facilities here are excellent.

Another option is to pick up one of the many municipal boxes along the east side of the old harbour or go right to the top of the harbour and lie alongside on either wall. Here you can step ashore for a *brötchen* with Bismark herring or a beer at one of the local *kneipen* (pubs) or restaurants. The shopping centre and square is up the hill east of the harbour.

Travemünde Another dead straight, buoyed channel with lights in line leads to Travemünde's northern breakwater with its sector light on the end. In daytime an enormous tower block can be seen well offshore east of the breakwater and, when closer in, the masts of the well preserved windjammer *Passat* in Passathafen to the east of the entrance.

There is a small fishing and yacht harbour, **Niendorf**, with a lit offing buoy about four miles west of Travemünde on Neustädter Bucht.

Travemünde's waterfront in the sunshine is a sight to warm the heart of any Mediterranean cruising person. Its shops, pavement cafés and restaurants are the core of the Holstein coast's fleshpots. There are probably at least 2000 box moorings in four places: all the way along the one mile long **waterfront** (if you can find one free); for large yachts in the **fishing harbour** (4–7m depth) at the west end of the waterfront; **Böbs-Werft** and **Baltica** marinas close west of the fishing harbour; and **Passathafen** (4m depth) on the south side of the entrance where you will need to take the ferry to visit Travemünde.

Die Untertrave

The first fixed bridge in Lübeck is eleven miles from Travemünde entrance along the main channel of the Untertrave and there are at least a dozen mooring possibilities along these reaches, including two large marinas at **Herreninsel** and **Schlutup**.

The most scenic part of this river is in the first half as far as Schlutup: here the DDR boundary,

Travemünde approach. The unmistakable tower block and, nearer the buoy, the masts of *Passat*.

Travemünde sea front. The Cannes of the Baltic.

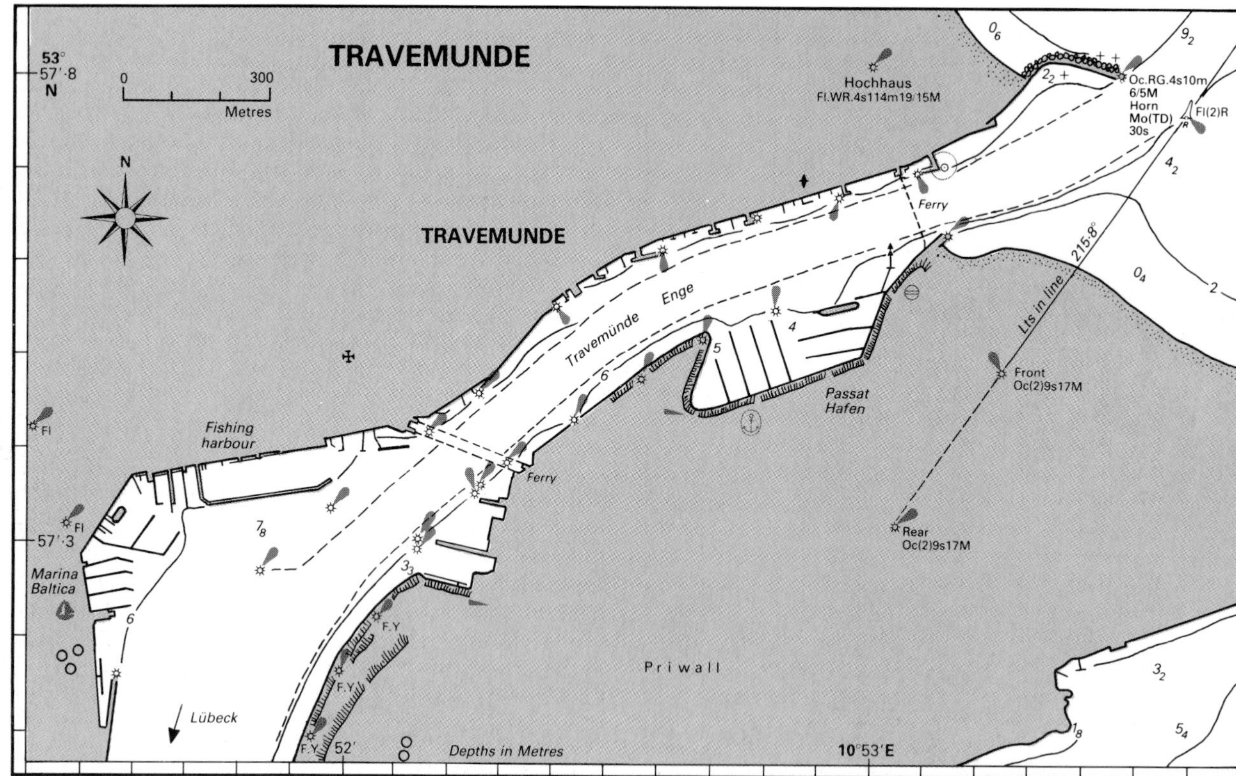

which used to follow the river from just north of Pötenitzer Wiek at the entrance (see plan) peeled off from the south bank southwestwards. There are numerous anchoring possibilities on the former East German side, including a bay, Pötenitzer Wiek and a lake, the Dassower See, in the initial reaches, and a series of bays along the south bank after the river curves westwards, as well as one at Silk on the north side. All of these are protected in various directions by wooded hills and occasional sand cliffs.

The most secluded of all is the Dassower See where, on our visit, we anchored south of Buchorst Island near an old, abandoned watch tower on the mainland. The neck of the entrance to this lake is marked by green, topmarked buoys, but you need to sound your way in carefully since it is only 2–3m in the middle and there are shallower patches. Here there is no fear of wash from passing traffic, although, in the main reaches of the river, shipping traffic in May proved sparse.

If you wish to lower your mast to pass through the **Elbe-Lübeck-Kanal**, the next, more industrial reaches are the place to do so, at the yards either at Schlutup where you can stay at the yacht harbour or on the west side of Teerhof Island, round which there are also many mooring boxes.

Lübeck The spires and buildings of Lübeck don't appear along the skyline until you pass Teerhof Island. Lübeck begins at the confluence of three waterways: the starboard-hand waterway (Wallhafen leading to the Stadtgraben) is the recommended route to the Canal (maximum clearance 4·4m); the middle waterway, Hansa Hafen, is where you can lie in up to 6m for a night or two alongside the south wall nearer its southwest end, but keeping clear of the riverboat terminal near the swing bridge; finally, the port-hand waterway at the confluence is spanned by a 5·5m clearance fixed bridge. There can be fluctuations of several feet in water level overnight so make sure there is some slack in your lines, while a short ladder may also be useful. There are no sanitary facilities in Hansa Hafen apart from a doubtful public toilet near the bridge, but you can go to the Seaman's Mission about halfway along the southern waterfront to borrow the shower or use the bar.

Lübeck. Hansa Hafen. Mooring is alongside the wall on the left in the distance.

A visit to Lübeck's completely water-surrounded city island is worth such hardships. From Hansa Hafen you can plunge straight into the medieval city to visit the churches, pubs, restaurants, market square and the large shopping centre. You can even take a local riverboat trip round the city.

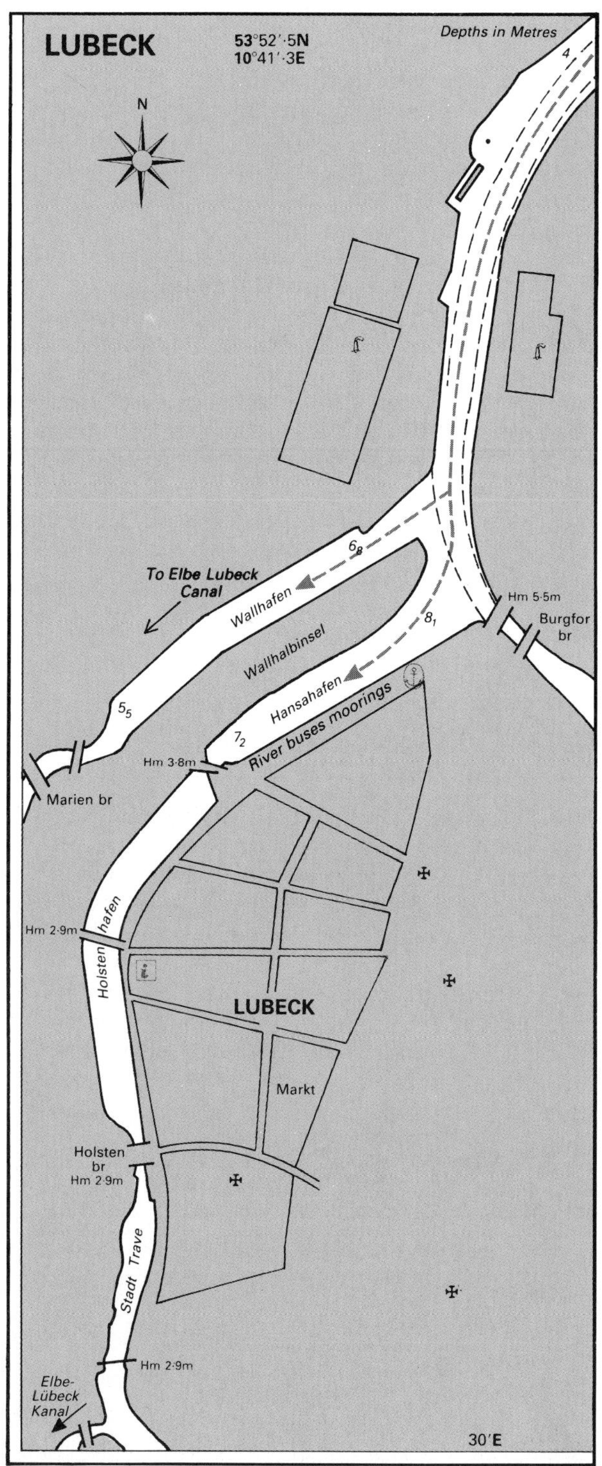

Lübeck. Vintage vessels in Holsten Hafen.

Wohlenberger Wiek and Wismar Bucht
Wohlenberg (jetty, 4·6–6·5m, lit)
Hohen Wieschendorf (jetty, 5·7–6·4m, lit approach)
Wismar (fishing harbour, 2·3m plus, lit)
Timmendorf (Poel island, fishing harbour, 1·6–3·3m, lit approach)
Kirchdorf/Niendorf (Poel island, fishing harbour, club jetty and quay, 3–3·5m, unlit)

The route from the western German side of Neustadter Bucht to Poel Island and Wismar in the former eastern sector is a straightforward one in deep water to begin with but ends up by cautiously following a buoyed channel into Wismar harbour since a shoal patch curtains the whole of the approaches to Wohlenburger Wiek and Wismar Bucht. Needless to say, these shoals can be extremely dangerous in strong onshore winds from east through north to west, so pick your weather. It is absolutely essential to pick up the 'Offentief' red and white, lit offing buoy and green and red unlit buoys which lead across the 5m 'neck' in the middle of the reef to the southeast of this buoy. Further southeast from these buoys the closely spaced, lit channel buoys into Wismar begin.

Above all, as a visitor, don't try to take the apparent short cut across the reef further southwest from Boltenhagen Bucht into Wohlenburger Wiek near the drying wreck. In calm weather we tried this and touched the ground, so I did the usual hard reverse and retraced our track out to sea to take the conventional route! Both of these beautifully rounded bays are well sheltered anchorages in winds from west through south round to east, particularly in Wohlenburger Wiek which is closed by shoals to the north. There is also a 4–6m depth jetty with a sector light and yellow buoys around it at **Wohlenburg** in the southwest corner of the bay, alongside which you can lie or simply use for landing – but don't forget, approach the bay from the Wismar fairway buoys to the northeast and not via the northwest shoals.

Along the main fairway to Wismar there are two mooring possibilities. The first is on the north or south walls (possibly with a stern kedge) of the small, somewhat westerly-exposed fishing harbour of **Timmendorf** (1·6–3·3m depth) on the west coast of Poel Island east of the first reach of the Wismar buoyed channel: this has a lit, red and white offing buoy, a lights in line approach and, for good measure, a sector light at the back of the harbour. The second possibility is alongside another jetty (5–6m depth) at **Hohen Wieschendorf** on the east coast of the peninsula of that name to the southwest of the second reach of the Wismar channel: there are shoals close around this and the approach must be directly in line with the jetty, which has leading marks/lights in line on it and red and green unlit buoys around marking the shoal edges.

For one night we anchored to the N of this reach of the Wismar channel in 3m just under the southern end of Poel Island and in the early hours were 'buzzed' by the *politzei.* A patrol launch shone its search light on our stern to read the name, but – the Cold War being over – trained no machine guns on us, did not hail us and simply motored off! I suppose we should have had our anchor light on even though this was well away from the main fairway in the shallows!

Kirchdorf is a fishing and ferry harbour on Poel Island at the northern end of the Kirch See which bites deeply northwards to almost split the island in two. The channel along this inlet is narrow, closely buoyed and although charted at 3m depth we found less than 2m at its edges, so keep to the middle between the buoys and allow for these being drifted by the wind in one direction or other. The harbour sports a brand new, 130m long, wooden jetty for pleasure craft, where we tied against the posts, but when the traffic here is busier you may have to use a kedge anchor head-to, or possibly stern-posts may be installed. The north quay was in use by fishing boats (you may also be able to lie alongside one of these) and by the ferry to Wismar. Poel is a delightful wooded tourist island with rolling hills and sandy beaches, best explored by hiring bicycles at Kirchdorf. On our explorations we had lunch at a restaurant in the tiny seaside village of Schwarzen Busch, and found a deserted barracks on the northern coast near Timmendorf and a smoked fish merchant on the east side of the harbour near Niendorf.

From the end of the Kirchdorf channel buoys it is best to return to follow the main Wismar channel to the west of the Walfisch sector light. There is a shallow (2·7m according to the chart) channel to Wismar charted to the east of Walfisch island, but this is only for those with local knowledge.

Wismar The industrial skyline and harbour cranes of Wismar are not inspiring but belie the more picturesque reality of the city and its Alter Hafen. The final reach of the channel is marked by lit dolphins and buoys, numerous boat moorings and a shallow (1·2m) yacht harbour to the west approached by a buoyed channel from the last green main channel buoy, No. 43. Southeast from this buoy four harbour basin entrances open up – the one for pleasure craft is the Alter Hafen, the second opening from the west. Mooring is alongside the east wall, south of the tripper boats with their *hafenrundfahrten.* There can be fluctuations in water level here of several feet, so make sure you have some slack on your lines and watch for chafe on the sharp wall edge – a short ladder may be useful. This mooring is convenient for the nearby restaurants and a visit to St Nikolai Kirche, a magnificent medieval brick church under restoration. The city is interesting for its contrasts while its facilities are being upgraded to match those of western German cities: the town centre square and occasional buildings in the side streets have been well restored, but the facades of many houses in the side streets were crumbling and the cobbled streets in a poor state of repair on our visit.

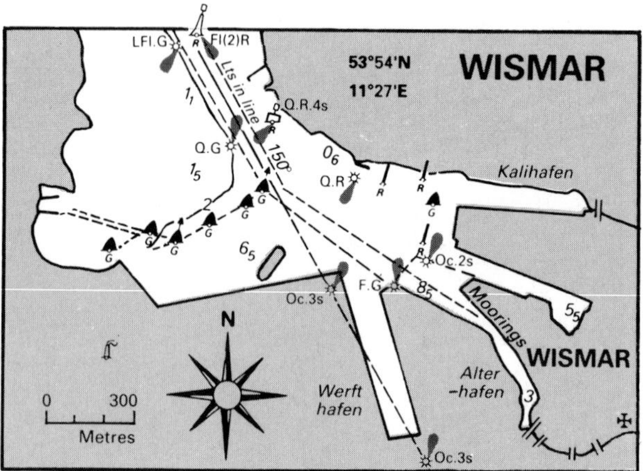

Wismar. Alter Hafen. *Kylora* moored alongside the E wall.

Mecklenburger Bucht E side

Warnemünde (club and quayside, 2·2–2·9m, lit approach)
Rostock (clubs, 1·5–2m, lit approach)
Darsser Ort (quayside, 5m, lit approach)

The whole of this side of Mecklenburger Bucht to the Darsser Ort is exposed to winds from approximately SW through NW to NE and the distances between harbours moderately long so passages need careful weather planning. There are four major navigational features.

i. Departure from Wismar bucht across its outlying shoals is via a northeastern buoyed (lit) channel.

ii. The Trollegrund spit, with 5·6m depths extending 1·5M N of the coast, needs a wide berth in rough weather and is largely unmarked apart from the 20/24M range Buk sector light well inland SW of Kühlungsborn. Anchoring and fishing is banned in a marked area N of the latter town.

Neustadter Bucht. Sailing off Grömitz.

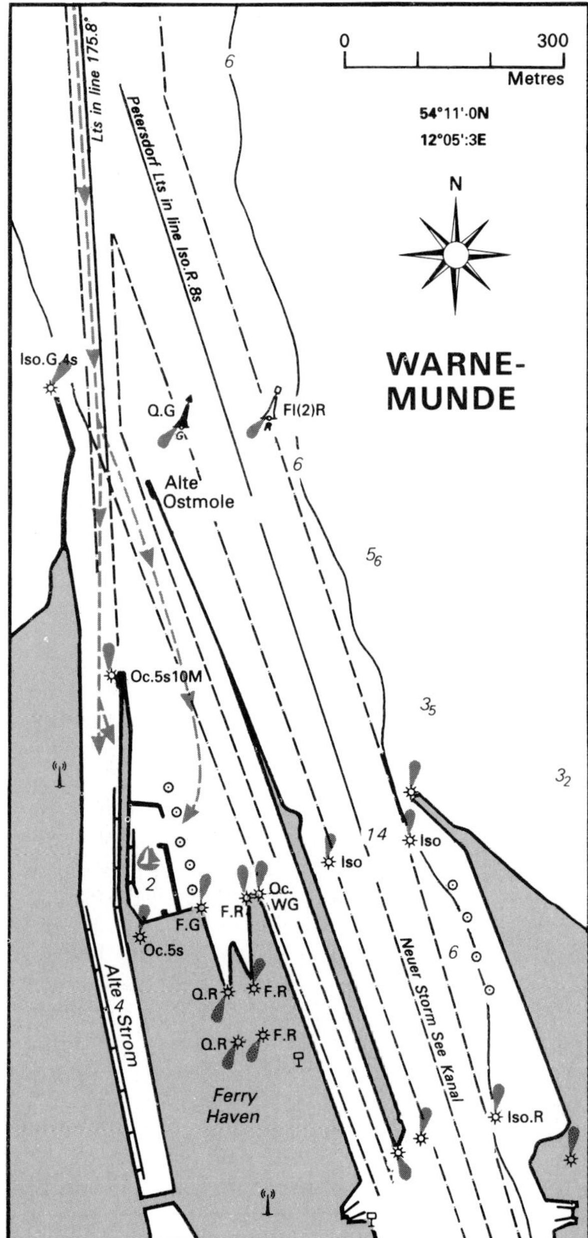

iii. A dead straight lit buoyed channel leads into Warnemünde for shipping, but small craft should avoid most of this danger by entering the channel near to the harbour entrance. Leaving or entering Warnemünde from the NE, however, there are extensive northeastern shoals which should be given a wide berth and at least a 2 mile offing is advisable all the way to the Darsser Ort.

iv. Darsser Ort haven, on the E side of this hooked peninsula has a tricky approach. The 17M-range light is the first major landmark, and the Darsser Ort E lit cardinal buoy to the NE should then be rounded before heading southwestwards to pick up the buoyed channel with lights in line.

Strelasund (through route)

Barhöft (pilots and patrol harbour, 1·2–5·1m, unlit)
Altefähr (landing stage, 1·7m at head, unlit)
Stralsund (yacht haven at lifting bridge, 1·1–2·7m, several hundred berths at 3 places, including yacht haven, lit approach)
Gustow (quayside, 4–5m, sector light)
Neuhof (quayside, 4·3m, lit approach)
Stahlbrode (fishing harbour, 1·5–5·5m, lit approach)
Puddemin (fishing harbour, 2·3–2·5m, unlit)
Glewitzer Fähre (quayside, 3·7m, lit approach)

It is a tricky 19M from Darsser Ort to the Gellenstrom entrance channel to Strelasund across 5–10m and, towards the end, 3–5m depth areas. In this area winds from the two northern quadrants are the most dangerous. The two major hazards are:

i. The Prerow Bank (4·2m) NE of Darsser Ort haven. A 1M offing from the coast for a distance of about 3M from leaving Darsser Ort keeps to the S of this.

ii. The approach should aim to pick up the first buoys at the northern end of the buoyed (lit) straight, but narrow, Gellenstrom channel. These are about 1·5M offshore in the white sector of the 10M range Gellen light (10m elevation white

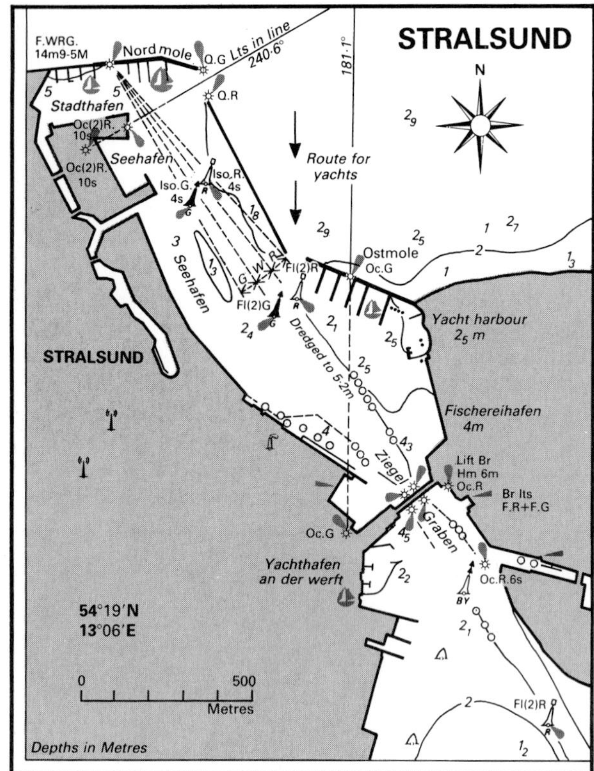

tower with red top) on the Gellen peninsula. From some 3M S of the outer buoys the passage is virtually a protected inland waterway with a lit buoyed channel past Stralsund and beyond to the Griefswalder Bodden, which itself is a huge, virtually inland lake.

Bodden and Grabow lakes

There are about a dozen places to moor in these lakes, which are entered at their eastern end through the Gellenstrom channel (dredged to 3·2m but liable to silting). This is also the entrance to the Strelasund through passage between Rügen and the mainland. All of these places are very small, mainly fishing and commercial harbours. There are no large marinas. Anchorages are plentiful. The lakes are 2–4m deep in their central areas and are connected by buoyed channels as little as an unreliable 2·5m deep.

The Rügen lakes

Also approached from the Gellenstrom, these are another complex of lakes E of Hiddensee island, with 2–7·5m depths in their central areas and interconnecting buoyed channels, some of which are an unreliable 2·5m deep. There are at least 15 limited mooring possibilities at jetties, fishing and small commercial harbours, including two very small yacht havens. Anchorages are plentiful.

N coast of Greifswalder Bodden and E Rügen (through route)

Lauterbach (commercial/fishing/yacht harbour, 2·6–5m, lit approach)
Vilm (island, two landing stages, 1·2–3·1m, unlit)
Sassnitz (fishing/ferry harbour, 4m, lit)
Seedorf (landing stages on sides of a harbour channel, 2·5m, unlit)
Baabe (quayside, 3m, lit approach)
Gager (fishing/ferry harbour, 2·9–3m, lit)
Zicker See (natural fishing harbour, several mooring jetties, dolphins and anchoring possibilities, 1·3–2·6m, lit approach)
Greifswalder Oie (island, tiny naval harbour, 3–4m, lit approach)

S coast of Greifswalder Bodden and Pommersche Bucht (through route)

Wiek (sides of harbour channel, 150, 1·2–3·4m, lit)
Greifswald Stadthafen (quayside, 2·2m, unlit)
Vierow (pier, 5·4–5·9m, lit)
Freest (50 plus, 1·6–1·9m, lit approach)
Ruden (island, fishing and pleasure-craft harbour, 2·9–4·7m, lit)
Swinoujscie/Swinemünde (town harbour quayside, 3m, lit approach)

Stettiner Haff and Vorpommern lakes

There are three entrances to these lakes: the 5m-dredged Peene channel at the western end in Germany, the Oder river/canal at Swinoujscie (Swinemünde in German), near the centre and on the Polish side of the border, and Dziwna, at the eastern end in Poland. The central lake areas are 2–7·2m deep and the two systems are connected by a buoyed 2·5m-dredged channel. There are at least a dozen possible mooring places on the German side alone, of which three are tiny yacht havens. One, along the Uecker river at Uekermünde on the SW side of Stettiner Haff, has two small yacht havens and riverside moorings with several hundred berths.

BORNHOLM AND CHRISTIANSØ ISLANDS

Bornholm is a granite island, partly wooded, with a high coastline and a number of coastal and inland hills ranging from 43m to 162m in height. It is most easily approached from København and along the Swedish coast, which is only about 10M away, possibly calling in at the Swedish harbours en route. From Arkona Cape in Germany the distance is around 25M. Ronne, the main town, is on the western promontory and is approached along lights in line. There are 18–21M-range all-round lights on each of the other three 'corners' of the island, and four other minor sector lights for various harbour approaches, as well as several other lights-in-line approaches.

The most dangerous part of the coast, with rocky shoals and offlying rocks, is from Hasle southwards past Rønne, all round the S coast and N along part of the E coast to Neksø. Throughout this area there are offlying cardinal and isolated-danger buoys. However, nearly all the harbours are on less hazardous parts of the E, NE and W coasts and can be approached directly.

Bronze Age rock carvings, Iron Age monoliths, rune stones, four fortified round churches – these give something of the flavour of this ancient island, which has a character different from that of the rest

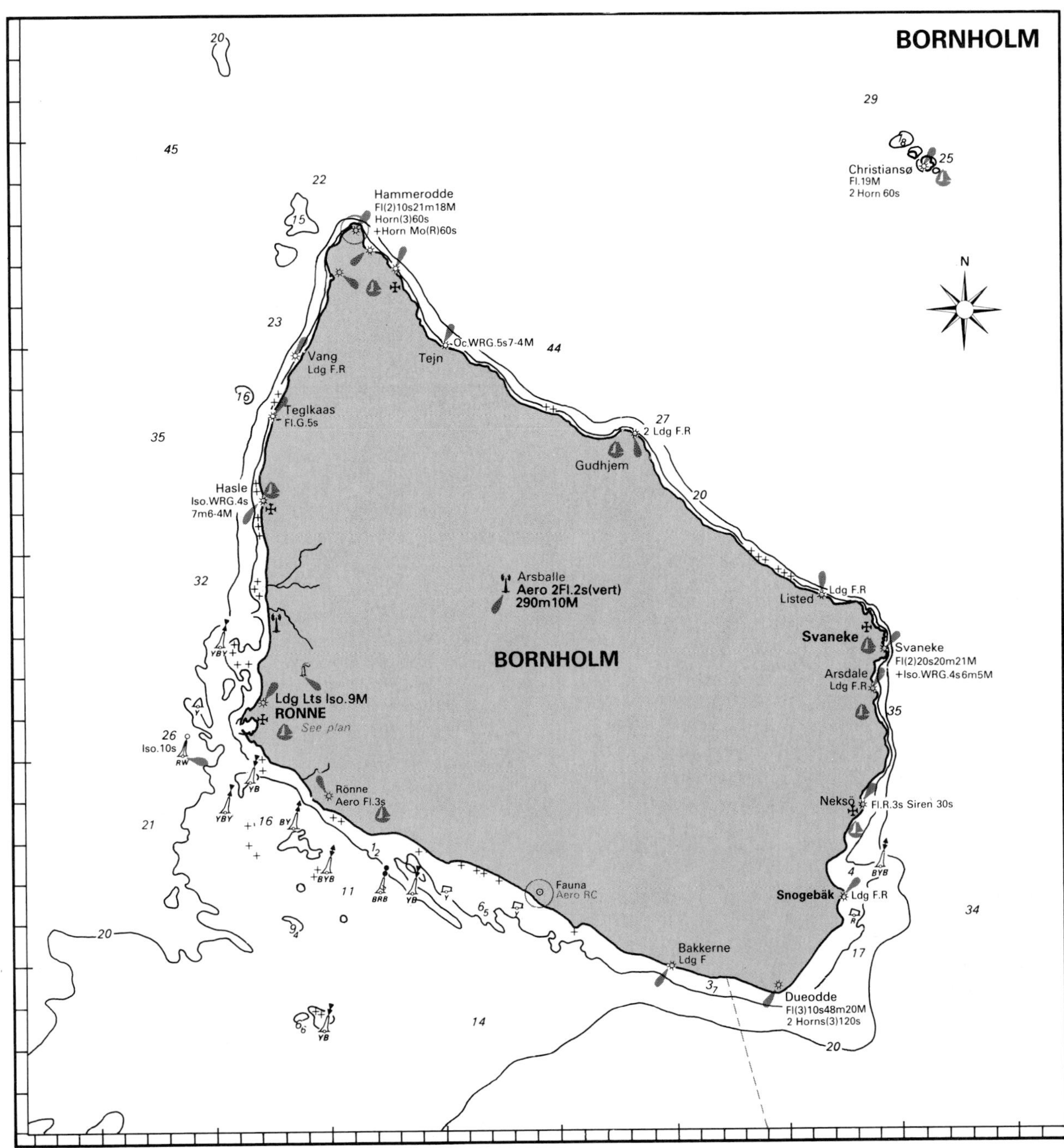

of Denmark, although it has probably been part of the country since the Viking period. Its nodal position in the Baltic allowed it to benefit from the Hanseatic trade, but it suffered badly in the 17th-century war with nearby Sweden. Germany occupied the island in the Second World War, and the Russians bombed the two main towns at the end of the war in the face of stiff German resistance and occupied the island for a year before handing it back to Denmark. Rønne, on the W coast, has a medieval quarter, but Neksø, on the E coast, has only a few ancient buildings left. There are many interesting inland villages and fishing hamlets on the island.

Ten miles off the NE coast, Christiansø and Fredericksø are twin islands, with a harbour in between, joined by a swing bridge. They were fortified by Denmark in the late 17th century after it lost its Swedish lands, and there is a defence tower on each island, one of which is now a museum. Grasholm island to the NW is a prohibited area.

With the exception of the small yacht havens of Nørre-Kås (near Rønne), Hasle and Tejn, each of the other mooring facilities on Bornholm can cater for relatively few visitors. There follows a list of all the main mooring possibilities, moving clockwise from Rønne. In brackets after each is listed the type of harbour, my own rough estimate of the number of mooring places where possible (those without estimates are usually very small), the depths, and whether the entrance or the approach is lit.

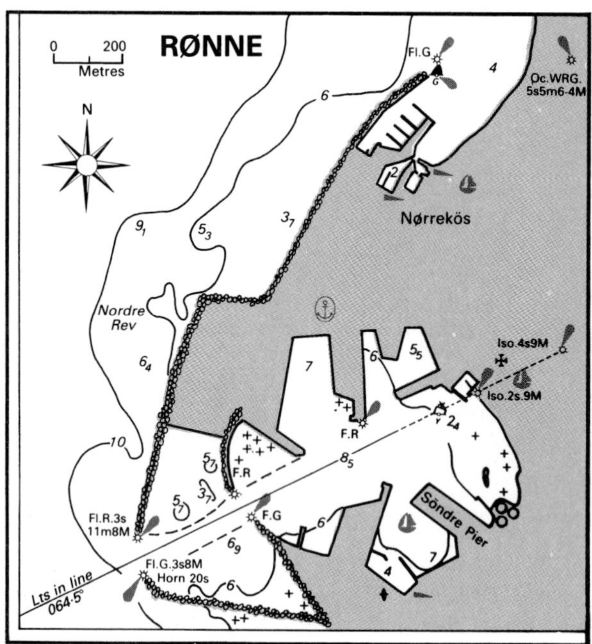

West coast

Rønne (commercial/ferry/fishing harbour, 80, 1·8–7m, lit)
Nørre-Kås (yacht haven close to Rønne, 150, 2m plus)
Hasle (yacht haven, 80, 1·5–3m, lit, VHF Ch 16, 12, 13)
Helligpeder (fishing harbour, 1–2·5m, lit occas.)
Teglkås (fishing harbour, 2·5m, lit)
Vang (commercial harbour, 30, 2·2–3·1m, lit)
Hammerhavn (commercial harbour, 60, 4m, lit)

Northeast coast

Sandvig (fishing harbour, 1·5–2·2m, lit approach)
Allinge (fishing/ferry harbour, 50, 4·4–4·7m, lit approach)
Tejn (fishing/yacht haven, 90, 1·5–3·5m, lit)
Gudhjem N (20, 3·6m, lit)
Gudhjem S (fishing harbour, 50, 4m, lit)
Melsted (fishing harbour, 40, 1·6m, lit)
Listed (fishing harbour, 2·8–3m, lit approach)
Svaneke (fishing harbour, 30, 3·5–4m, lit)

East coast

Årsdale (fishing harbour, 2·5–3m, lit approach)
Neksø (fishing harbour, 40, 3–5m, lit)
Snogebæk (small boat harbour, 40, 2m, lit approach)

South coast

Arnager (tiny fishing harbour, 1·5–2·2m, unlit)
Christiansø/Frederiksø (quayside, 3m, lit approach)

Appendix

I. Charts

British Admiralty Charts

Chart	*Title*	*Scale*
33	Approaches to Kieler Hafen	60,000
112	Terschellinger Gronden and approaches to Harlingen	50,000
126	Helgoland	15,000
185	Approaches to Swinoujscie and Szczecin	60,000
	Swinoujscie	24,400
	Szczecin	25,000
417	Grådyb	20,000
	Esbjerg harbour	10,000
598	Limfjord – Hals to Logstor	50,000
	Logstor	7,500
	Alborg	12,500
613	Mariager fjord, Randers fjord and Grenå	50,000
	Mariager: Hobro	5,000
	Randers: Grenå	10,000
	Approaches to Grenå	60,000
696	Kieler hafen	12,500
790	Approaches to Kobenhavn	40,000
892	Approaches to Göteborg	37,500
	Continuation to Kungen	37,500
1404	Esbjerg to Hanstholm including offshore oil and gasfields	375,000
1405	Terschelling to Esbjerg	375,000
1875	Die Jade to Norderpiep including German Bight light vessel	100,000
2114	The Kattegat	260,000
	Skagen	15,000
	Frederikshavn	35,000
2115	The Sound	150,000
2116	Little Belt and Kieler bucht	150,000
2118	Great Belt	150,000
2120	Samso Baelt, including Arhus bugt and Isefjord	150,000
	Holbaek	6,000
	Hundested	7,500
	Horsens	10,000
	Arhus	15,000
2150	Arkona to Ustka	200,000
	Kolobrzeg	10,000
2304	Karmö to Bergen	201,200
2322	Goeree to Texel	150,000
2360	Falsterbo to Oland	200,000
	Ronne	10,000
	Trelleborg. Ystad	20,000
2364	Fehmarn belt and Mecklenburger bucht	150,000
	Fehmarn sund	50,000
	Wismar and approaches	60,000
	Travemnnde	25,000
2365	Mecklenburger bucht to Greifswalder bodden	150,000
2469	Nord-Ostsee-kanal	50,000
	Brunsbüttel: Holtenau	12,500
	Rendsburg	20,000
2370	Warnemnnde and Rostock	20,000
2496	Limfjorden, Thyboron to Mors	60,000
	Thyboron Kanal	40,000
	Thyboron	8,000
	Lemvig	8,000
	Holstebro-Struer	8,000
	Oddesundbroens (Lifting span)	
2497	Limfjorden, Mors to Logstor	60,000
	Continuation of Lovns Bredning	60,000
	Thisted	8,000
	Thisted Annekshavn	8,000
	Nykobing Mors	8,000
	Glyngore	8,000
	Skive	8,000
2593	Texel to Borkum	150,000
2594	The Sound – northern part	60,000
	Helsingor	8,046
	Höganäs: Helsingborg: Sydhamnan and Kopparverkshamnan	15,000
	Landskrona	20,000
2596	Great Belt – northern portion	70,000
	Korsor	12,000
	Nyborg	15,000
	Kalundborg	25,000
2597	Great Belt – southern portion	70,000
	Agerso sund	50,000
2671	Skagerrak	350,000
	Hirtshals	12,500
	Hanstholm	15,000
2672	Listafjorden to Selbjornsfjorden including offshore oil and gas fields	350,00
2984	Approaches to Kristiansand	50,000
	Kristiansand havn	12,500
3194	Kobenhavns havn, Malmö and Limhamn	
	Kobenhavns havn	12,500
	Malmö	20,000
	Limhamn	20,000
3261	Die Elbe – Scharhörn riff to	50,000
	Medemgrund Cuxhaven	12,500
3262	Die Elbe – Medemgrund to Brokdorf	30,000
	Die Oste – Geversdorf to Osten	50,000
3266	Die Elbe– Brokdorf to Wedel	30,000
3268	Die Elbe – Port of Hamburg	15,000
	Die Elbe – Wedel to Seemannsh–ft	30,000
3368	Approaches to Die Jade and Die Weser	50,000
3369	Die Jade	50,000
	Wilhelmshaven	20,000
3405	Die Weser, Robbennordsteert to Nordenham	25,000
3406	Die Weser – Bremerhaven and Nordenham to Elsfleth	
	Brake	10,000
	Bremerhaven	12,500
	Nordenham to Elsfleth	25,000
3407	Die Weser, Elsfleth to Bremen	25,000
	Bremen harbour	12,500

3435	Plans on the southeast coast of Sweden	
	Oskarshamn:	15,000
	Karlskrona:	20,000
	Kalmar and the Narrows: Vastervik	25,000
	Kalmar sund – inner part:	
	Approaches to Oskarshamn:	
	Approaches to Vastervik	50,000
	Ronneby and approaches: Approaches to Karlskrona	50,000
3465	Little Belt – northern part	70,000
	Assens	6,000
	Vejle	8,000
	Haderslev: Fredericia	10,000
	Kolding	12,000
	Snaevringen	30,000
3509	Approaches to Die Ems	50,000
3510	Die Ems – Dukegat to Papenburg	25,000
	Emden	15,000
	Groningen	40,000
	Pogum to Papenburg	50,000
3562	Little Belt – southern part	70,000
	Abenra: Enstedvaerket: Sonderborg	15,000
	Flensburg	20,000
	The Narrows off Holnis	50,000
3663	Göteborg	12,500
3761	Borkumriff to Helgoland	150,000
3767	Süderpiep to Lister Tief, including Helgoland	130,000
	Approach to List	50,000
3768	Approaches to Esbjerg, including Lister tief and Horns rev	130,000

German Charts – *North Sea and Baltic Sea*

Chart	*Title*	*Scale*
2	Mündungen der Jade und Weser	50,000
	Dove Harle	25,000
3	Ansteuerung von Helgoland	50,000
4	Die Weser von Robbennordsteert bis Bremerhaven und Nordenham	25,000
	Häfen von Bremerhaven	12,500
5	Die Weser von Nordenham bis Farge	25,000
	Hafen von Brake	10,000
	Hafen von Elsfleth	10,000
	Die Hunte von Huntebrück bis Oldenburg	50,000
	Hafen von Oldenburg	20,000
	Huntemündung	10,000
6	Die Weser von Farge bis Bremen	nur Pläne
	Farge bis Osterort	25,000
	Vegesacker Kurve	12,500
	Häfen von Bremen	12,500
	Stephani-Brücke bis Hemelingen	25,000
7	Die Jade, innerer Teil	35,000
	Wilhemshaven	15,000
36	Gedser Odde bis Bornholm	200,000
	Ansteuerung von Trelleborg	25,000
	Ansteuerung von Ystad	20,000
	Hafen von Ystad	10,000
	Simrishamn	10,000
	Hafen von Klintholm	6,000
42	Nord-Ostsee-Kanal	50,000
	Hafenanlagen von Rendsburg	15,000
	Hafen-und Schleusen-anlagen von Holtenau	12,500
	Hafen-und Schleusen-anlagen von Brunsbüttel	12,500
44	Elbmündung	50,000
	Cuxhaven	12,500
46	Die Elbe von der Oste bis Brunsbüttel und Krautsand	30,000
	Die Oste von Geversdorf bis Osten	50,000
	Hafen-und Schleusenanlagen von Brunsbîttel	15,000
	Hafen von Glückstadt	10,000
	Dornbusch	30,000
	Die Stör von Wewelsfleth bis Itzehoe	30,000
47	Die Elbe von Krautsand bis Schulau	30,000
	Stadersand	15,000
48	Die Elbe von Schnulau bis Hamburg	nur Pläne
	Die Elbe von Schulau bis Teufelsbrück	30,000
	Häfen von Hamburg	15,000
84	Texel bis Borkum	150,000
85	Zeegat van Terschelling bis Harlingen	50,000
86	Zeegat van Ameland und Friesche Zeegat	50,000
	Nes	25,000
	Lauwersoog	25,000
87	Borkum bis Neuwerk und Helgoland	150,000
89	Juist bis Wangerooge	50,000
	Leybuch	50,000
	Hafen von Norddeich	20,000
	Hafen von Norderney	12,500
	Hafen von Langeoog	12,500
	Hafen von Bensersiel	12,500
	Dove Harle	25,000
90	Emsmündung	50,000
	Fischerbalje und Hafen von Borkum	15,000
	Eemshaven	20,000
91	Die Ems vom Dukegat bis Pogum	25,000
	Hafenanlagen von Emden	12,5000
	Dollard (Dollart)	50,000
92	Die Ems von Pogum bis Papenburg	25,000
95	Friesland Junction bis F-Schiff GW/Ems	150,000
103	Helgoland bis Rømø	150,000
104	Die Eider vom Eiderdamm bis Lexfähre	nur Pläne
	Eiderdamm bis Nordfeld	25,000
	Eidersperrwerk	10,000
	Hafen von Tönning	10,000
	Hafen von Friedrichstadt	10,000
	Nordfeld bis Lexfähre	50,000
105	Die Eider, Norder-und Süderpiep	50,000
	Hafen von Büsum	12,500
	Fahrwasser nach Friedrichskoog	50,000
106	Hever und Schmaltief	50,000
	Einfahrt nach Husum	25,000
	Hafen von Husum	12,500
	Hafen von Pellworm	12,500
	Strucklahnungshörn	12,500
107	Vortrapptief, Norder-und Süderaue	50,000
	Hafen von Hörnum	7,500
	Hafen von Amrum	25,000
	Hafen von Dagebüll	25,000
	Hafen von Wyj	7,500
	Schlüttsiel	12,500
108	Lister Tief	50,000
	Römö Havn	10,000
	Hafen von List	5,000
	Grådyb	20,000
	Esbjerg Nord	12,500
	Esbjerg Süd	12,500
109	Grådyb	20,000
138	Bornholm bis Oland und Stolpebank (Ławica Słupska)	200,000

139	Ahus bis Tärnö	50,000
	Hafen von Ahus	15,000
	Hafen von Sölvesborg	20,000
	Torsö	5,000
	Hällevik	10,000
	Nogersund	10,000
	Hanö	4,000
	Hörvik	5,000
	Pukavik	25,000
	Stillerydshamnen	15,000
	Karlshamn	15,000
140	Tärnö bis Utlängan	50,000
	Ronnebyhamn	10,000
	Hafen von Karlskrona	20,000
	Sandhamn	10,000
151	Arkona bis Kolberg (Kołobrzeg	150,000
	Hafen von Kolberg (Kołobrzeg)	10,000
159	Gewässer um Bornholm	100,000
	Christiansö	10,000
	Hafen von Rönne	212,500
	Hafen von Hasle	6,000
	Hammerhavnen	7,000
	Hafen von Allinge	3,000
	Hafen von Tejn	4,000
	Südhafen von Gudhjem	3,500
	Hafen von Svaneke	4,000
	Hafen von Neksö	6,000
	Hafen von Listed	3,000
	Arsdale	5,000
162	Gewässer zwischen Rügen und Møn	100,000
163	Mecklenburger Bucht, östlicher Teil	100,000
	Ansteuerung von Gedser	40,000
	Hafen von Gedser	7,500
289	Reede und Häfen von Kopenhagen	12,500
290	Heslingborg bis Råå	10,000
328	Sund, nördlicher Teil	70,000
	Hafen von Gilleleje	9,000
	Hornbäk	6,000
	Hafen von Helsingör	8,000
	Lappegrund	20,000
	Snekkersten	3,600
	Espergärde	2,800
	Humlebäk	4,0000
	Sletten	4,000
	Rungsted	9,000
	Vedbäk	5,000
	Hafen von Tårbäk	2,400
	Hafen von Skovshoved	7,400
	Mölle	15,000
	Höganäs	15,000
	Landskrona	20,000
	Barsebäckshamn	10,000
329	Sund, südlicher Teil	70,000
	Skanör	15,000
	Klagshamn	15,000
	Drogden	40,000
	Hafen von Dragör	8,000
	Jachthafen von Hvidovre	4,000
	Hafen von Mosede	2,500
	Hafen von Köge	10,000
	Jachthafen von Köge	6,000
330	Häfen von Malmö und Limhamn	12,000
477	Guldborg Sund und Karrebäk Fjord	
	Guldborg Sund	30,000
	Guldborg	3,500
	Hafen von Nyköbing	7,500
	Hafen von Nysted	3,500
	Karrebäk Fjord	30,000
	Hafen von Karrebäksminde	8,000
	Hafen von Nästved	8,000
478	Fakse Bugt und Bögeström	50,000
	Fakse Ladeplads	8,000
	Hafen von Rödvig	3,300
	Hafen von Nyord	2,700
	Hafen von Prästö	3,700
479	Grönsund und Storström	30,000
	Vordingborg Nordhavn	4,000
	Stubbeköbing	4,000
	Orehoved	6,200
	Hårbölle Havn	3,030
	Kalvehave	5,000
	Masnedsund	12,000
	Stege	4,000
	Storströmbrücke	
480	Smålandsfarvandet	70,000
	Kragenäs	5,000
	Bandholm	8,000
	Fejö Havn	2,800
	Vesterby	3,400
	Hafen von Femö	2,7800
	Hafen von Askö	2,500
	Oreby Bro	2,700
	Saksköbing	4,000
1511	Greifswalder Bodden, Ostansteuerung von Stralsund	50,000
	Anleger von Vierow	5,000
	Hafen von Wieck	5,000
1512	Peenestrom, nördlicher Teil	25,000
	Hafen von Peenemünde	7,500
	Hafen von Wolgast	10,000
1513	Peenestrom, südlicher Teil, und Kleines Haff	50,000
	Peenestrom südlich Wolgast	25,000
	Klotzow bis Mönchow	25,000
	Die Peene östlich #Anklam	50,000
	Die Ucker, nördlicher Teil	6,500
	Die Ucker, südlicher Teil	6,500
	Altwarp und Neuwarp (Nowe Warpno)	25,000
1514	Ansteuerung von Swinemünde (Swinoujście) und Großes Haff (Wielki Zalew)	50,000
	Hafen von Swinemünde (Swinoujście)	25,000
	Hafen von Ziegenort (Trzebiez)	10,000
1515	Die Oder von Ziegenort (Trzebiez) bis Stettin (Szczcin)	25,000
	Hafen von Stettin (Szczecin)	10,000
1516	Prorer Wiek	25,000
	Hafen von Saßnitz	10,000
	Fährhafen von Mukran	10,000
1578	Greifswalder Bodden, north sidel	25,000
	Hafen von Lauterbach	5,000
	Hafen von Gager	5,000
1579	Der Strelasund von Palmer Ort bis Stralsund	25,000
	Anleger von Glewitzer Fähre	5,000
	Hafen von Stahlbrode	5,000
	Hafen von Puddemin	5,000
	Anleger von Gustow	7,500
	Anleger von Neuhof	5,000
	Hafen von Stralsund	10,000
1621	Nödliche Rügensche Bodden	30,000
	Hafen vcon Kloster	4,000
	Hafen von Vitte	4,000
	Hafen von Schjaprode	4,000
	Hafen von Wiek	3,000
	Anleger von Vieregge	4,000
	Anleger von Vieregge	4,000
	Anleger von Ralswiek	5,000

	Martinshafen	4,000
	Hafen von Neuendorf	4,000
1622	Nordansteuerung Stralsund	25,000
	Hafen Stralsund'	10,000
1622	Nordansteuerung von Stralsund	25,000
	Hafen von Barhöft	4,000
	Hafen von Parow	5,000
	Hafen von Stralsund	10,000
	Hafen von Schaprode	4,000
1623	Boddengewässer Barhöft bis Ribnitz-Damgarten	50,000
	Hafen von Barth	5,000
1671D	Ansteuerung von Rostock	50,000
	Hafen von Barth	5,000
1672	Hafen von Rostock	12,500
	Warnemünde	5,000
	Marienehe bis Stadhafen	15,000

German Small Craft Charts

3002	Baltic planning	375,000
3003	Karten der Ostsee von Flensburg bis Kiel	
3004	Karten der Ostsee von Kiel bis Lübeck	
3005	Karten der Ostsee von Travemünde bis Stralsund	
3006	Karten der Ostsee von Stralsund bis Stettiner Haff (Zalew Szczeciński)	
3006	Karten der Ostsee. Gewässer um Rügen	
3007	Karten der Ostsee von Greiswalder Oie bis Stettiner Haff (Zalew Szczeciński)	
3009	Nord-Ostsee-Kanal und die Eider	
3010	Karten der Elbe von Cuxhaven bis Hamburg	
3011	Karten der Weser von der Mündung bis Bremen	
3012	Karten der Ems von Borkum bis Dörpen	
3013	Nordfriesische Inseln	
3014	Helgoländer Bucht	
3015	Ostfriesische Inseln mit Jadebusen	

Nautische Veröffentlichung

Four sets of yachtsmen's charts in plastic wallets.

Serie 1 Rund um Fünen – Kieler Bucht

Chart	*Title*	*Scale*
S1	Kieler Bucht	140,000
S2	Kieler Förde	40,000
S3	Kieler Bucht Süd-West	80,000
S4	Flensburger Förde	80,000
S5	Kleiner Belt Süd	80,000
S6	Kleiner Belt Mitte	80,000
S6a	Alssund u. Augustenborg	25,000
S7	Kleiner Belt Nord	80,000
S7a	Stromkarte Kleiner Belt	
S8	Nord Fünen	80,000
S9	Großer Belt Nord	80,000
S10	Großer Belt Mitte	80,000
S10a	Stromkarte Großer Belt	
S11	Großer Belt Süd	80,000
S11a	Nakskov Fjord	33,000
S12	Süd Fünen	80,000
S12a	Svendborgsund	15,000

Serie 2 Lübecker Bucht bis Bornholm und Kopenhagen

S13	Fehmarn	80,000
S14	Lübecker Bucht	80,000
S14a	Die Travemündung	17,000
S15	Mecklenburger Bucht	150,000
S16	Mön Südost	160,000
S16a	Wismar Bucht	33,000
S17a	Häfen von Rostock	25,000
S17	Smaalandsfahrwasser West	80,000
S18	Smaalandsfahrwasser Ost	80,000
S19	Grönsund	60,000
S19A	Guldborg Sund	60,000
S20	Fakse Bucht	60,000
S20a	Salzhaff	33,000
S21	Sund Mitte	80,000
S21a	Die Untertrave	15,000
S22	Hanö Bucht	260,000
S22a	Kopenhagen/Nakskov Fjord	40,000
S23	Sund Süd	140,000
S24	Klintholm bis Bornholm	220,000
S25	Bornholm	140,000

Serie 3 Gewässer um Samsö, Sund und Kattegat

Chart	*Title*	*Scale*
S26	Sund Nord	80,000
S26a	Oberflächenströmung im Sund	
S27	Isefjord	80,000
S28	Samsö Belt	100,000
S29	Aarhus Bucht	100,000
S30	Kattegat Süd	180,000
S31	Kattegat Mitte	180,000
S32	Kattegat Nord	180,000
S33	Mariager-Randers-Fjord	40,000
S34	Ansteuerungen und Hafenpläne	
S35	Ansteuerungen und Hafenpläne	

Serie 4 Rund um Rügen Boddengewässer-Stettin

Chart	*Title*	*Scale*
S36	Die Bodden südl. Zingst	60,000
S37	Strelasund Nord	60,000
S38	Hiddensee bis Jasmund	60,000
S39	Strelasund Süd	60,000
S40	Greifswalder Bodden West	60,000
S41	Greifswalder Bodden Ost	60,000
S42	Peenestrom Süd	60,000
S43	Stettiner Haff	80,000
S44	Die Oder bis Stettin	30,000
S45	Hiddensee bis Swinemünde	240,000

Der Nord – Ostsee Kanal – 2 charts at 1:55,000

Conversion tables

1 inch = 2.54 centimetres (roughly 4in = 10cm)
1 centimetre = 0.394 inches
1 foot = 0.305 metres (roughly 3ft = 10m)
1 metre = 3.281 feet
1 pound = 0.454 kilograms (roughly 10lbs = 4.5kg)
1 kilogram = 2.205 pounds
1 mile = 1.609 kilometres (roughly 10 miles = 16km)
1 kilometre = 0.621 miles
1 nautical mile = 1.1515 miles
1 mile = 0.8684 nautical miles
1 acre = 0.405 hectares (roughly 10 acres = 4 hectares)
1 hectare = 2.471 acres
1 gallon = 4.546 litres (roughly 1 gallon = 4.5 litres)
1 litre = 0.220 gallons

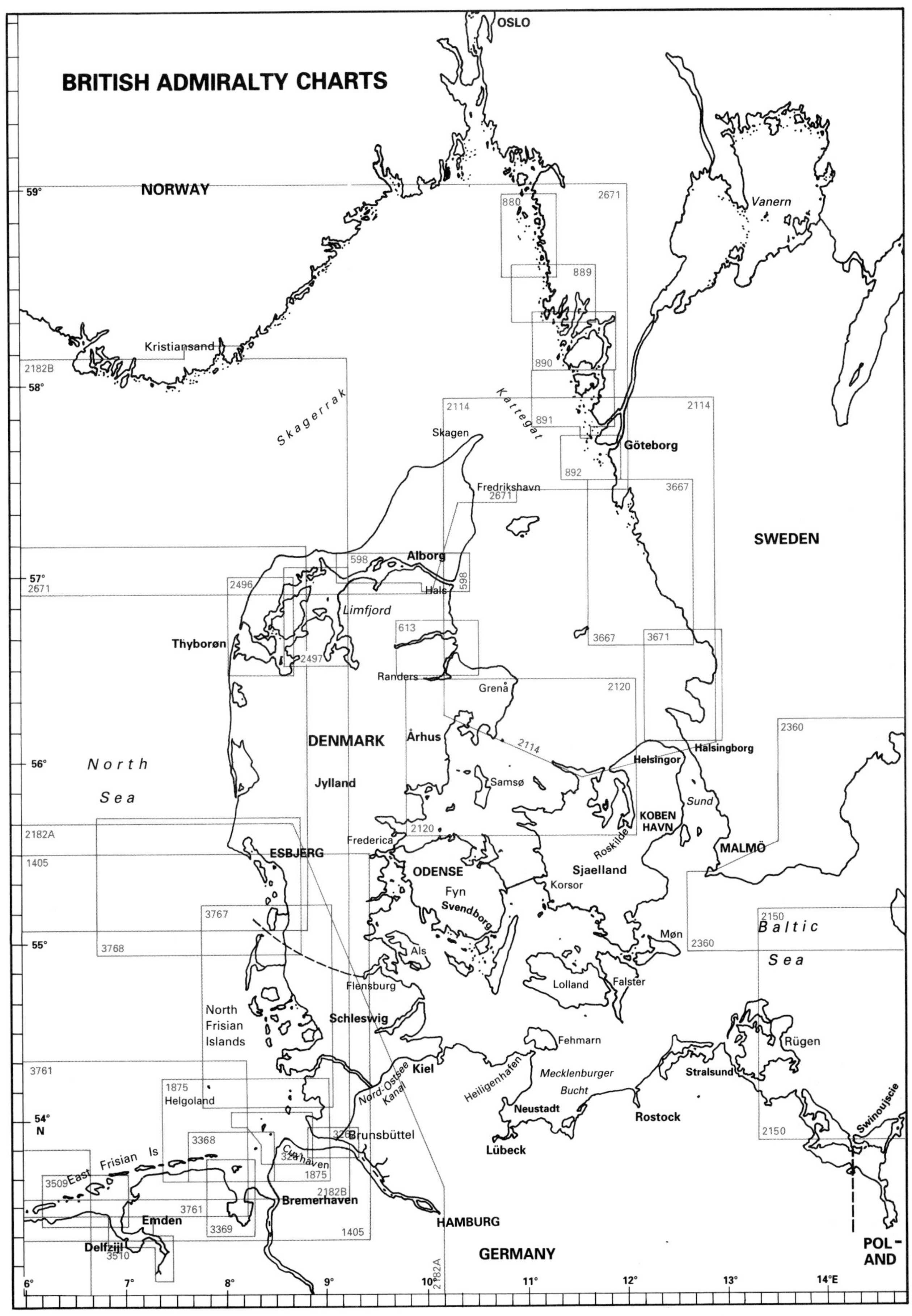
BRITISH ADMIRALTY CHARTS
OSLO
NORWAY
Kristiansand
Skagerrak
Kattegat
Skagen
Fredrikshavn
Göteborg
SWEDEN
Vanern
Alborg
Hals
Limfjord
Thyborøn
Randers
Grenå
Århus
DENMARK
Jylland
North Sea
Samsø
Hälsingborg
Helsingor
Sund
KOBEN HAVN
Roskilde
MALMÖ
Frederica
ESBJERG
ODENSE
Fyn
Svendborg
Sjaelland
Korsor
Møn
Baltic Sea
Als
Flensburg
Lolland
Falster
North Frisian Islands
Schleswig
Fehmarn
Rügen
Kiel
Nord-Ostsee Kanal
Heiligenhafen
Mecklenburger Bucht
Stralsund
Swinoujscie
Helgoland
Neustadt
Rostock
Brunsbüttel
Lübeck
East Frisian Is
Cuxhaven
Bremerhaven
Emden
HAMBURG
Delfzijl
GERMANY
POL-AND
59°
58°
57°
56°
55°
54° N
6°
7°
8°
9°
10°
11°
12°
13°
14°E
880
889
890
891
892
2671
2114
3667
3671
2120
2360
2150
2182B
2182A
598
613
2496
2497
1405
3767
3768
3761
1875
3368
3369
3509
3510

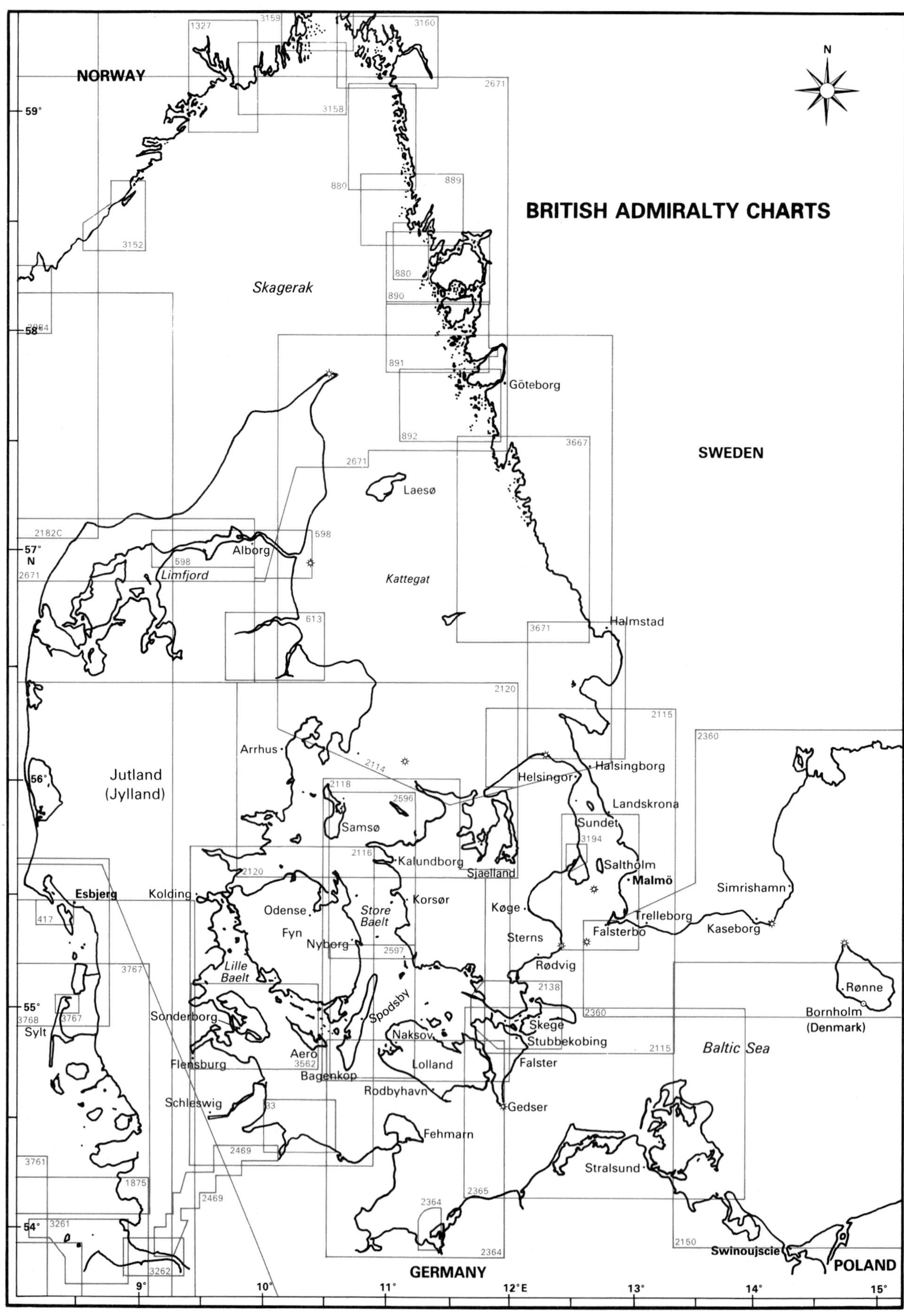
BRITISH ADMIRALTY CHARTS
N
NORWAY
SWEDEN
GERMANY
POLAND
Skagerak
Kattegat
Baltic Sea
Jutland
(Jylland)
Göteborg
Laesø
Alborg
Limfjord
Halmstad
Arrhus
Helsingor
Halsingborg
Landskrona
Sundet
Saltholm
Malmö
Samsø
Kalundborg
Sjaelland
Korsør
Odense
Fyn
Store
Baelt
Nyborg
Lille
Baelt
Kolding
Esbjerg
Sonderborg
Flensburg
Schleswig
Aero
Bagenkop
Spodsby
Naksov
Lolland
Rodbyhavn
Fehmarn
Køge
Sterns
Rødvig
Skege
Stubbekobing
Falster
Gedser
Trelleborg
Falsterbo
Kaseborg
Simrishamn
Rønne
Bornholm
(Denmark)
Stralsund
Swinoujscie
Sylt
59°
58°
57°
N
56°
55°
54°
9°
10°
11°
12°E
13°
14°
15°
1327
3159
3160
2671
3158
880
889
3152
880
890
2984
891
892
3667
2671
2182C
598
598
2671
613
3671
2120
2115
2360
2114
2118
2596
2116
2120
417
2597
3767
3768
3767
2138
2360
2115
3562
33
2469
2469
3761
1875
3261
3262
2364
2365
2364
2150
3194

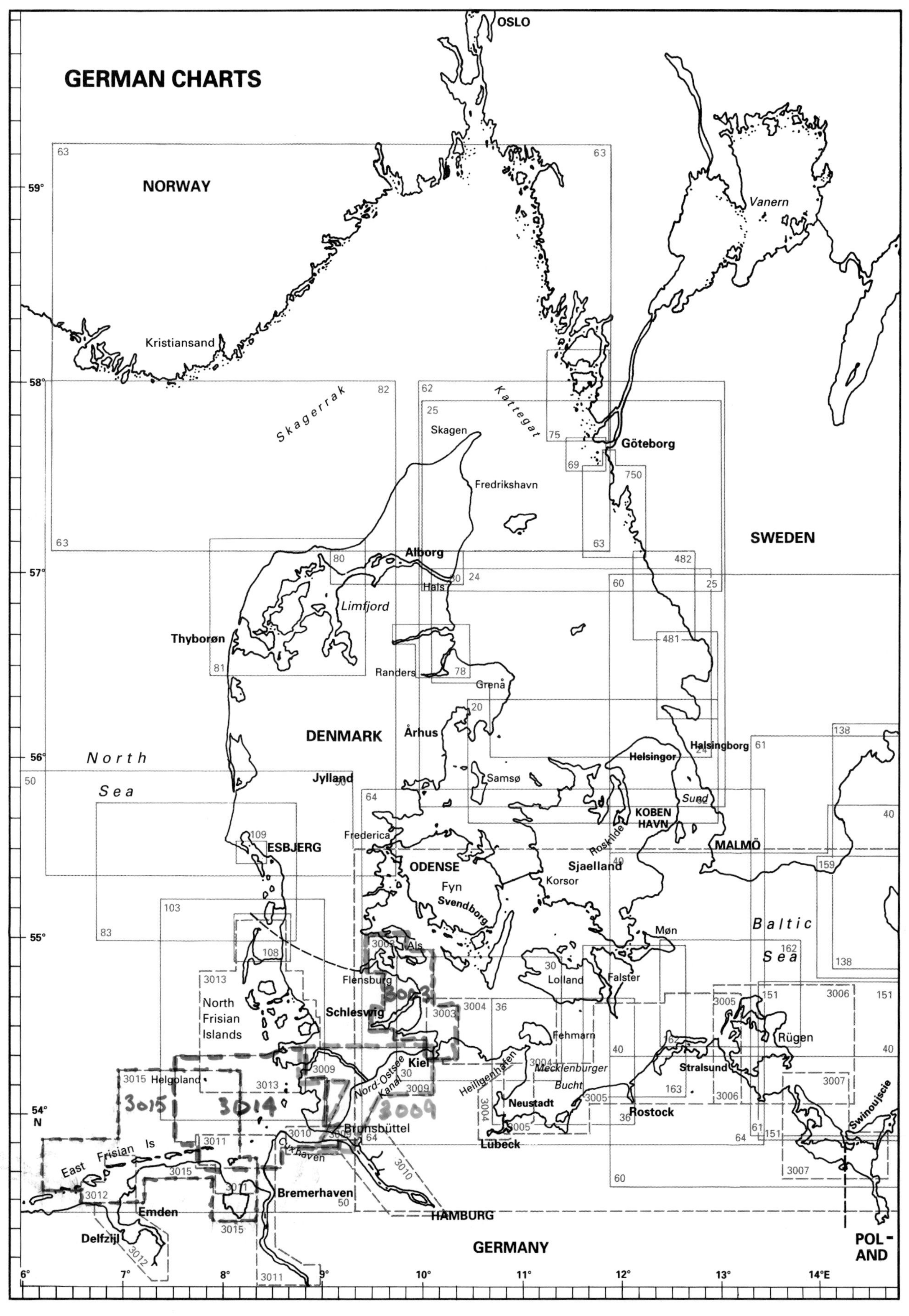
GERMAN CHARTS
NORWAY
DENMARK
SWEDEN
GERMANY
POL-AND
OSLO
Kristiansand
Skagerrak
Kattegat
Skagen
Fredrikshavn
Göteborg
Vanern
Alborg
Hals
Limfjord
Thyborøn
Randers
Grenå
Århus
Jylland
Samsø
Helsingor
Halsingborg
Sund
KOBEN HAVN
Roskilde
MALMÖ
North Sea
ESBJERG
Frederica
ODENSE
Fyn
Svendborg
Sjaelland
Korsor
Møn
Baltic Sea
Als
Flensburg
Schleswig
North Frisian Islands
Lolland
Falster
Fehmarn
Kiel
Nord-Ostsee Kanal
Heiligenhafen
Mecklenburger Bucht
Neustadt
Lübeck
Rostock
Stralsund
Rügen
Swinoujscie
Helgoland
East Frisian Is
Brunsbüttel
Cuxhaven
Bremerhaven
Emden
Delfzijl
HAMBURG
59°
58°
57°
56°
55°
54° N
6°
7°
8°
9°
10°
11°
12°
13°
14°E

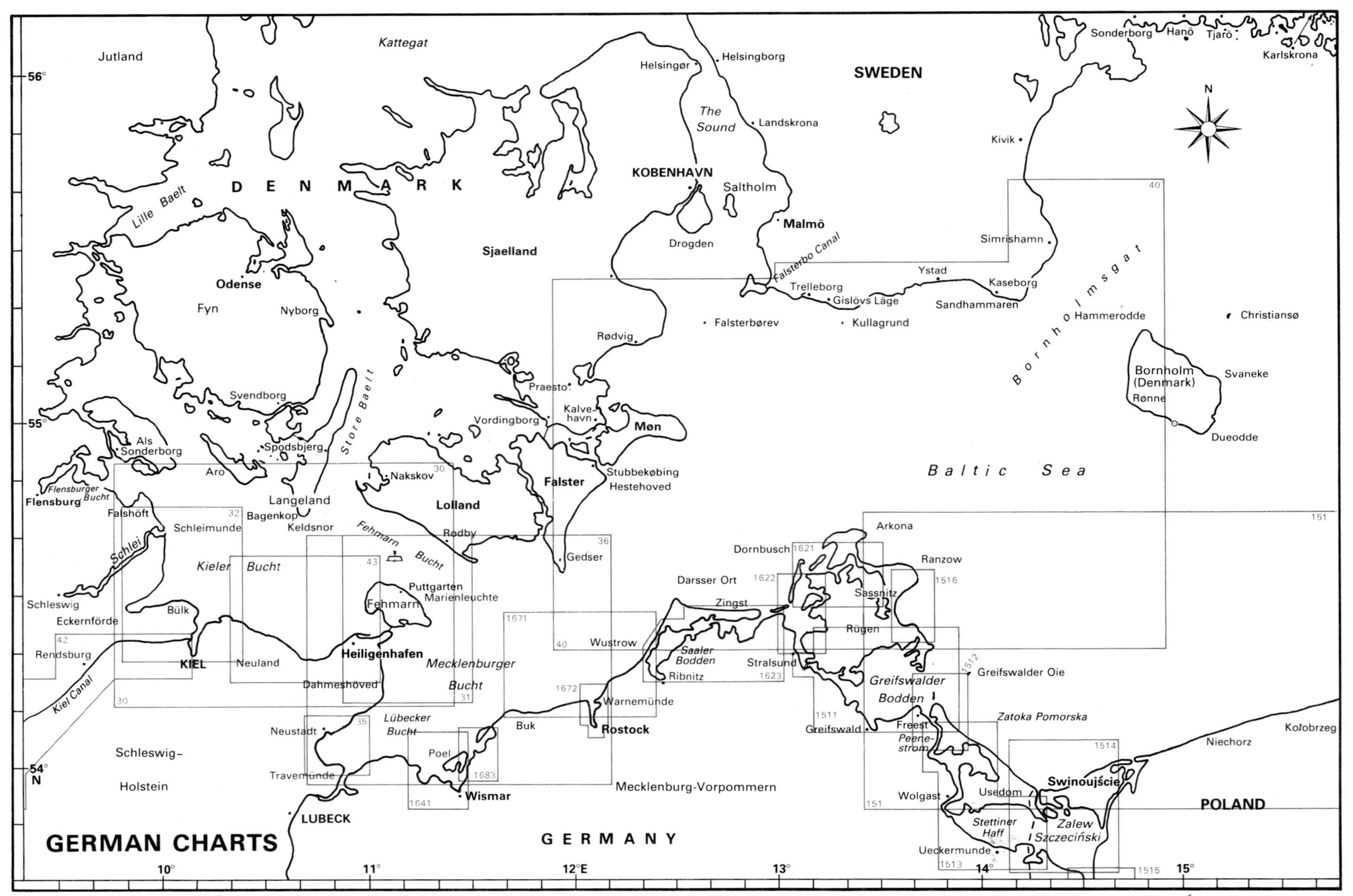
GERMAN CHARTS
SWEDEN
DENMARK
GERMANY
POLAND
Baltic Sea
Kattegat
The Sound
Bornholmsgat
Store Baelt
Lille Baelt
Jutland
Sjaelland
Fyn
Lolland
Falster
Møn
Langeland
Als
Bornholm (Denmark)
Rønne
Svaneke
Dueodde
Christiansø
Hammerodde
Karlskrona
Tjärö
Hanö
Sonderborg
Kivik
Simrishamn
Kaseborg
Sandhammaren
Ystad
Gislövs Läge
Kullagrund
Trelleborg
Falsterbo Canal
Falsterbørev
Malmö
Landskrona
Helsingborg
Helsingør
Saltholm
KOBENHAVN
Drogden
Rødvig
Stubbekøbing
Hestehoved
Kalvehavn
Praesto
Vordingborg
Gedser
Rødby
Nakskov
Odense
Nyborg
Svendborg
Spodsbjerg
Bagenkop
Keldsnor
Aro
Sonderborg
Falshöft
Flensburg
Flensburger Bucht
Schlei
Schleswig
Eckernförde
Rendsburg
Kiel Canal
Bülk
KIEL
Schleimunde
Kieler Bucht
Neuland
Dahmeshöved
Heiligenhafen
Fehmarn
Fehmarn Bucht
Puttgarden
Marienleuchte
Mecklenburger Bucht
Lübecker Bucht
Neustadt
Travemünde
LUBECK
Poel
Wismar
Buk
Warnemünde
Rostock
Wustrow
Ribnitz
Saaler Bodden
Zingst
Darsser Ort
Dornbusch
Stralsund
Rügen
Sassnitz
Arkona
Ranzow
Greifswald
Greifswalder Bodden
Greifswalder Oie
Freest
Peenestrom
Wolgast
Usedom
Stettiner Haff
Ueckermunde
Zalew Szczeciński
Swinoujście
Zatoka Pomorska
Niechorz
Kołobrzeg
Schleswig-Holstein
Mecklenburg-Vorpommern
56°
55°
54° N
10°
11°
12°E
13°
14°
15°
151
40
1515
1514
1512
1513
1516
1621
1622
1623
1511
36
1672
1671
1683
1641
31
30
35
43
32
42

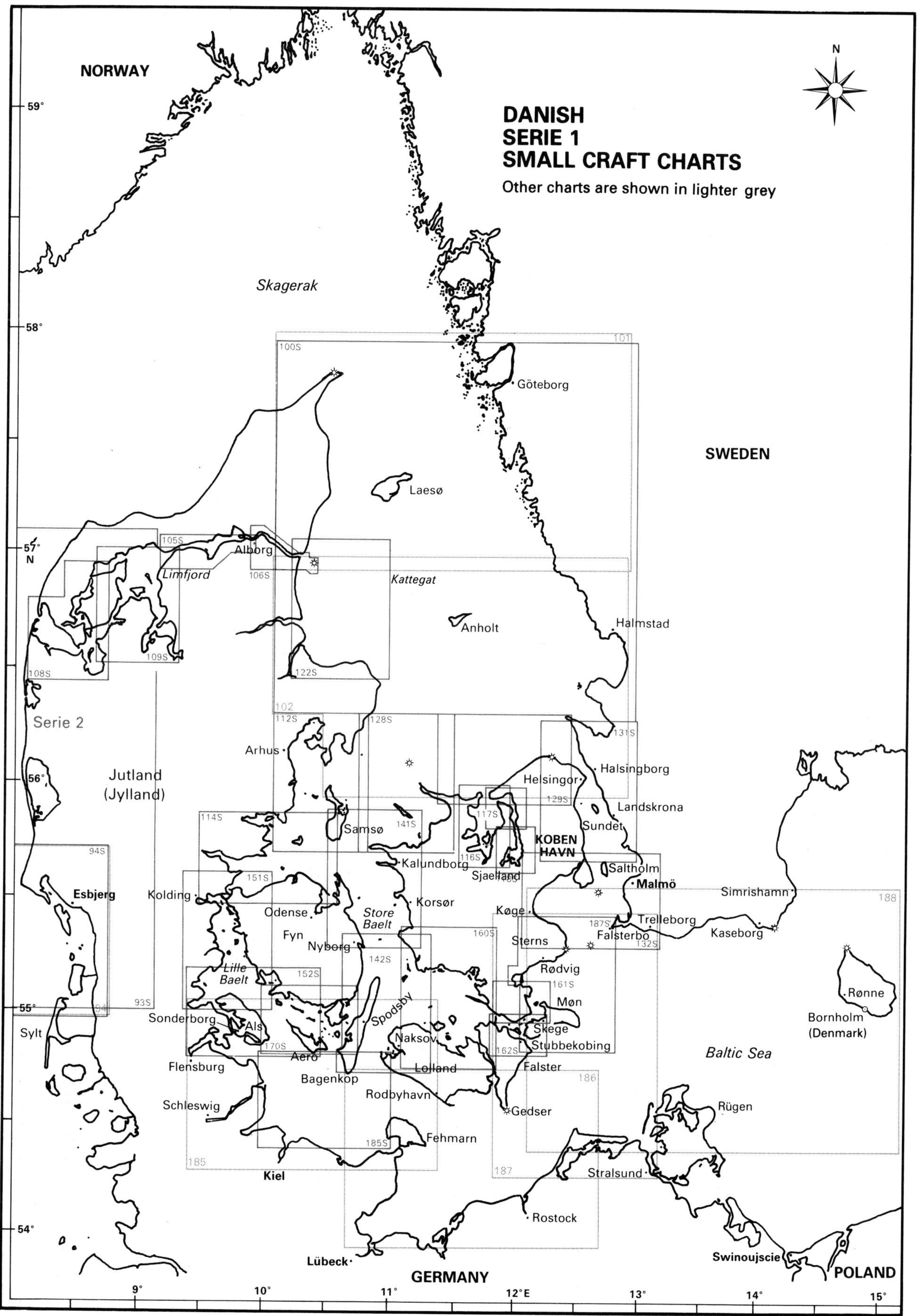
DANISH
SERIE 1
SMALL CRAFT CHARTS
Other charts are shown in lighter grey
N
NORWAY
Skagerak
SWEDEN
Göteborg
Laesø
Kattegat
Anholt
Halmstad
Limfjord
Alborg
Serie 2
Jutland
(Jyllland)
Arhus
Helsingor
Halsingborg
Landskrona
Sundet
KOBEN HAVN
Saltholm
Malmö
Samsø
Kalundborg
Sjaelland
Esbjerg
Kolding
Odense
Fyn
Store Baelt
Korsør
Nyborg
Køge
Simrishamn
Trelleborg
Falsterbo
Kaseborg
Sterns
Rødvig
Lille Baelt
Møn
Rønne
Bornholm
(Denmark)
Sonderborg
Als
Sylt
Spodsby
Naksov
Skege
Stubbekobing
Baltic Sea
Flensburg
Aero
Bagenkop
Lolland
Falster
Rodbyhavn
Schleswig
Gedser
Rügen
Fehmarn
Kiel
Stralsund
Rostock
Lübeck
GERMANY
Swinoujscie
POLAND
59°
58°
57° N
56°
55°
54°
9°
10°
11°
12°E
13°
14°
15°
100S
101
102
105S
106S
108S
109S
112S
114S
116S
117S
122S
128S
129S
131S
132S
141S
142S
151S
152S
160S
161S
162S
170S
185S
185
186
187
187S
188
93S
94S

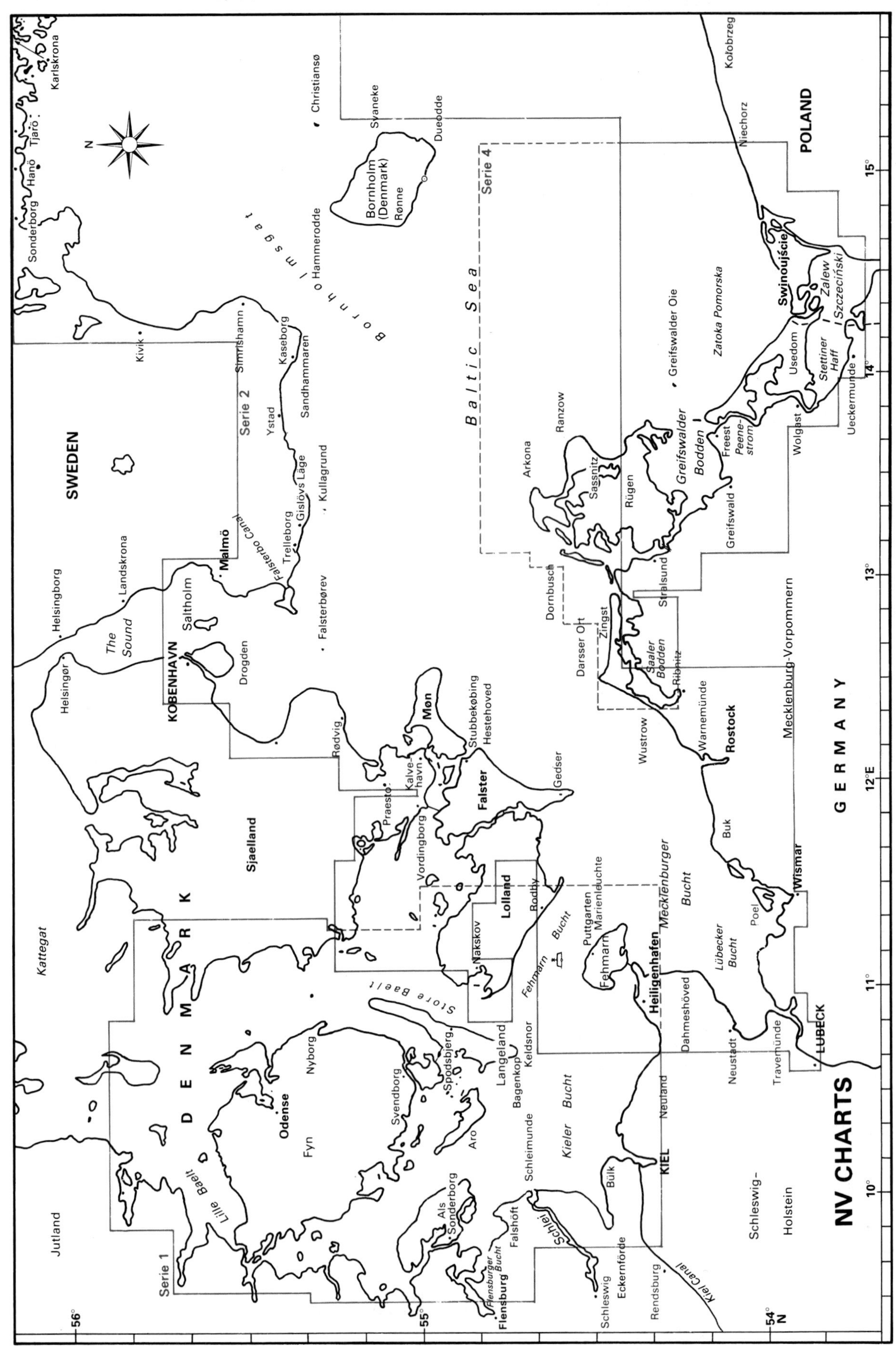

NV CHARTS
SWEDEN
DENMARK
GERMANY
POLAND
Baltic Sea
Kattegat
The Sound
Bornholmsgat
Store Baelt
Lille Baelt
Kieler Bucht
Fehmarn Bucht
Mecklenburger Bucht
Lübecker Bucht
Greifswalder Bodden
Zatoka Pomorska
Stettiner Haff
Zalew Szczeciński
Saaler Bodden
Peene-strom
Kiel Canal
Falsterbo Canal
Serie 1
Serie 2
Serie 4
Jutland
Fyn
Sjaelland
Lolland
Falster
Møn
Als
Langeland
Fehmarn
Rügen
Usedom
Poel
Zingst
Bornholm (Denmark)
Rønne
Svaneke
Dueodde
Hammerodde
Christiansø
Karlskrona
Tjärö
Hanö
Sonderborg
Kivik
Simrishamn
Kaseborg
Sandhammaren
Ystad
Gislövs Läge
Kullagrund
Trelleborg
Falsterbørev
Malmö
Landskrona
Helsingborg
Helsingør
Saltholm
KØBENHAVN
Drogden
Rødvig
Stubbekøbing
Hestehoved
Kalvehavn
Praestø
Vordingborg
Gedser
Rødby
Nakskov
Spodsbjerg
Bagenkop
Keldsnor
Nyborg
Svendborg
Odense
Aro
Sønderborg
Schleimunde
Falshöft
Flensburger Bucht
Flensburg
Schlei
Schleswig
Eckernförde
Rendsburg
Bülk
KIEL
Neuland
Dahmeshöved
Heiligenhafen
Puttgarten
Marienleuchte
Neustadt
Travemünde
LÜBECK
Wismar
Buk
Warnemünde
Rostock
Wustrow
Ribnitz
Darsser Ort
Dornbusch
Stralsund
Arkona
Sassnitz
Ranzow
Greifswald
Freest
Greifswalder Oie
Wolgast
Ueckermünde
Swinoujście
Niechorz
Kołobrzeg
Schleswig-Holstein
Mecklenburg-Vorpommern
56°
55°
54° N
10°
11°
12° E
13°
14°
15°

II. Water levels in the southwest Baltic harbours. Routes 4, 5, 6, 7

Location	*Tidal range MHW–MLW metres*	*Rise with strong wind: direction/ metres*	*Fall with strong wind: direction/ metres*
Route 4. Kiel to the Limfjord entrance via the Lille Bælt			
(S–N by direction of passage)			
Kieler Förde			
Kieler Förde	n/a	NE 2	SW 2
Eckenförde			
Eckenförde Hafen	n/a	NE 0·9	SW 1·2
Schlei Förde			
Schleimunde	n/a	NE–ENE 3·5	W 2
Arnis	n/a	n/a	W 1
Marina Brodersby	n/a	n/a	W down
Kleine Breite	n/a	E 0·1	W 1·2
Flensburger Förde			
Marina Minde	0·5	NE 1	SW 1
Egernsund	1·4	N–NE 1·5	W–SW 1·5
Gråsten	0·3	E 1	W 1
Flensburg	n/a	E 3	W 2
Als Sund			
Hørup Hav	0·1	NE 1·2	NW 1·2
Sonderburg harbour	0·1	E 1·2	W 1·2
Sottrupskov	0·1	E 1·2	W 1·2
Augustenborg	0·2	NE 1	NW 1
Dyvig	0·8	E 1	W 1
Åbenra Fjord			
Varnæs Vig	0·3	NE–E 1	SW–W 1
Åbenrå (Apenrade)	1·0	NE–SE 1·5	SW 1
Genner Fjord			
Kalvø	0·5	W 1	SE 1
Årosund			
Årø	0·3	NE 1·5	NW 1·5
Årøsund	0·3	NE 1–1·6	SW 0·6–1·6
Haderslev Fjord			
Haderslev	0·2	E 1·3	W 1·3
Lille Bælt			
Assens (marina)	0·3	NW–NE 1·4	S–W 1
Bågø	0·5–1	NE 1·2	NW 1·6
Hejlsminde	1·0	E–NE 1·5	W–SW 1
Kolding Fjord			
Kolding	0·2	E 1·5	W 1·5
Skærbæk	0·2	E 1	W 0·8
Snaevringen			
Middelfart Sportbhfn	0·5	E–SE 1	n/a
Strib	0·4	NE 1	S–SW 0·8
Fredericia Sportbhfn	0·4	NE 1·4	S–SW 1·6
Fyn			
Bogense	0·5	N–NE 1·6	S–SW 1·6
Vejle Fjord			
Vejle	0·6	NW–NE 1·6	S–SW 1·4
Rosenvold	0·4	NW–NE 1·5	SE–SW 1·5
Juelsminde	0·4	NW–NE 1·5	SE–SW 1
Horsens Fjord			
Snaptun	0·5	NW–N 1·2	S 1·2
Hjarnø	0·5	NW–N 1·2	S 1·2
Horsens	0·4	NW–N 0·5–1·5	SW–S 0·5–1·0
Samsø			
Kolby Kås	0·6	NW–N 1	SE–S 1
Ballen	0·3	NW–N 1	E–SE 1
Langør	0·6	NW–NE 1	SW–SE 1
Mårup	0·6	NW–NE 0·9	SW–SE 0·9
Århus Bucht			
Hov	1·0	N 0·4	SW 0·3
Tunø	0·8	NW–NE 0·5	SW 0·5
Norsminde	n/a	N 1	S 1
Marselisborg	0·3	W–NW 1	SE 0·8
Århus	0·3	W–NW 1	SE 0·8
Egå Marina	0·3	NW 1	SE 0·6
Kaløvig	0·5	W 1	SE 1
Nappedam	0·3	NW–NE 1·5	SE–E 0·6
Knebel Vig	0·2	NW–N 1·2	SE–S 0·5
Skødshoved	0·6	NW 0·8	SE 0·8
Ebeltoft	0·3	WNW 1·3	ESE 0·9
Ålborg Bugt			
Grenå (commercial harbour)	0·3	NW–W 1·1	SE–E 1·2
Bønnerup	0·5	W 1	SE 0·5
Anhol	0·4	W 1	E 0·8
Randers Fjord			
Udbyhøj	0·8	NW–NE 0·7	SE–SW 0·7
Mellerup	0·5	NW–NE 1·6	S–SE 1
Uggelhus	0·5	N 0·6	S 0·6
Dronningborg	0·5	NW–NE 1·8	S–SE 1
Randers	0·5	NW–NE 1·8	S–SE 1
Mariager Fjord			
Hadsund	0·2	NW–W 0·6	SE–SW 0·6
Mariager	0·3	NW–NE 1·4	SE–SW 0·4
Hobro	0·3	NW–NE 1	SE–SW 0·5
Limfjord entrance			
Egense	0·3	W 1·2	E 0·5
Hals	0·3	W 1	E 0·5
Kattegat			
Vesterø	0·5	W 1	E 0·9
Sæby	0·4	W–NW 1	E–SE 1
Frederikshavn			
Seesp'hn	0·3	W 1·2	E 0·8
Route 5. The Limfjord			
(E–W, then return to Thisted by direction of passage)			
Limfjord E entrance			
Hals	0·3	W 1·0	E 1·5
Egense	0·3	W 1·2	E 0·5
Alborg to Løgstør			
Nørre Sundby (Ålborg)	0·3	W 1·0	E 0·5
Gjøl	0·3	NW 0·5	E 0·5
Nibe	0·1	W–NW 1·0	E–SE 0·3
Attrup	0·1	W–SW 0·9	E 1·0
Løgstør	0·2	W 1·6	E 0·9
Løgstør Bredning			
Rønbjerg Havn	0·1–0·2	W 1·0	E 0·9
Livø	0·1–0·15	SW 1·2	NE 1·5
Risgårde Bredning			
Hvalpsund Marina	1·0	W–NW 1·0	NE–E 1·0
Virksund and Hjarbæk Fjord			
Virksund harbour	0·25	W–NW 1·8	E–SE 0·7
Hjarbæk harbour	0·1	E 0·3	W 0·3
Skive Fjord			
Skive Søsportshavn	1·1	W–NW 1·7	E 0·8
Fur Sund and Salling Sund			
Fur	0·6	W 1·3	E 1·0
Nykøbing harbour	0·5	W 1·5	E 0·9
Glyngøre	0·5	W 0·8	E 0·8
Kås Bredning			
Sillerslev	0·5	W 1·0	N–E 1·0
Jegindø	1·0	SW–W 1·0	E 1·0
Venø Bugt and Venø Sund			
Gyldendal	0·1	W 0·8	E 0·3
Struer	0·2	SW–NW 1·5	NE–SE 1·5

Venø	0·9	N–NW 1·5	E–SE 1·0
Oddesund	0·6	SW 0·8	E 0·5
Nissum Bredning			
Lemvig Marina	0·2	SW–NW 1·7	SE–NE 0·8
Thyborøn	0·5	SW–W 1·0	NE–SE 1·0
Agger	0·3	SE–SW 1·0	NW–NE 0·5
Bølore Hage to Løgstør Bredning			
Doverodde	1·0	W 1·0	E 1·0
Vilsund Havn	0·4	W 0·8	E 0·8
Thisted harbour	0·3	SW 1·5	ENE 1·0
Amtoft	0·1–0·2	SW 0·8–1·2	E 0·3–0·5

Route 6. Kiel to Odense via South Fyn and the Store Bælt

(S–N by direction of passage)

Ærø and nearby islands			
Marstal	0·5	NE–E 1·2	SE–SW 1·2
Strynø	0·0	NE 1·2	SW 0·9
Ristinge	0·2	N–NE 1·6	SE–SW 1·6
Birkholm	n/a	NE 1·0	SW 1·0
Ærøskøbing	0·1	E–SE 2·0	W–SW 1·5
Hjortø	n/a	E–NE 1·1	W 1·1
Drejø pier	1·0	E–NE 1·0	W–SW 1·0
Drejø Havn	0·3	N–NE 1·0	SW reduced
Søby	0·1	NE 1·5	SW 1·5
South Fyn and nearby islands			
Bøjden pier	n/a	E–NE 1·0	W–SW 1·0
Faldsled	1·0	N–E 0·6	S–W 0·5
Lyø	0·5	E 1·0	W 1·0
Dyreborg	0·9	NE 1·5	NW 1·0
Fåborg	0·0	NE 1·0	SW 1·0
Bjørnø	0·2	NE 1·0	SW 1·0
Korshavn pier	0·3	n/a	n/a
Fjællebroen	0·3	N–E 1·0	W 1·0
Ballen	0·4	E 1·0	W 1·0
Rantzausminde	0·4	E 1·2	NW 1·2
Svendborg Sund			
Svendborg yacht haven	0·5	N–NE 1·5	S–SW 1·5
Vindeby yacht haven	0·3	NE 1·0	SW 1·0
Svendborg commercial harbour	0·5	N–NE 1·5	S–SW 1·5
Svendborg Sund Marina	0·7	N 1·0	S 1·0
Gambøt	0·5	NW–NE 1·4	E–SW 1·4
Troense	0·3	S–SW 0·9	N–NE 1·2
Channel between Fyn and Langeland			
Rudkøbing	0·1	NW–NE 0·6	S–W 1·2
Daggeløkke	0·1	N 0·8–1·2	S–SE 0·9
Lundeborg	0·6	N–NW 0·6	S–E 0·6
Lohals Havn	0·1	SW 1·2	NE 1·3
Store Bælt			
Nyborg	0·3	WNW–NE 1·0	SSW–SE 0·7
Vasebro	0·5	N 1·2	S 0·6
Skælskør yacht haven	0·5	NW–NE 1·0	SE–SW 0·6
Korsør	0·3	NW–NE 1·2	S 0·8
Kerteminde	0·5	NW–NE 1·0	S 0·8
Mullerup	0·4	N–NW 1·3	S–SE 0·8
Reersø	0·6	N 1·5	SE 0·9
Kalundborg	0·4	NW 1·3	SE 0·9
Odense Fjord			
Korshavn	0·3	n/a	n/a
Otterup	0·6	W–N 0·6	E–S 0·6
Bregnør	0·6	NE–N 1·0	S 1·0
Stige	0·4	W–NE 1·8	E–SW 1·5
Odense	0·4	W–NE 1·8	E–SW 1·5

Route 7. Kiel to Roskilde via Smålands Farvandet and the Sund

(S–N by direction of passage)

Langeland			
Marstal Bugt	n/a	NE 1·2	SW 1·2
Bagenkop (Langeland)	0·0	NE 1	SW 1
Lolland			
Langelands Bælt	n/a	NE 1·5	SW 1·5
Nakskov Fjord	n/a	ENE–ESE 1·2	SW 1·2
Nakskov (Lolland)	0·2	NE–E 1·5	SW–W 1
Smålands Farvandet			
Vejrø	0·4	W 0·6	S 0·6
Vordingborg (Sjælland)	0·4	W–NW 1·4	E–SW 1
Kalvehave (Sjælland)	0·6	W followed by E storm 1·2	W 0·8
Gåbense	0·4	NW–NE 1·0	SE–SW 1·3
Stubbekøbing	0·3	NE–N 1·1	S–SW 1·1
Hårølle	0·7	NE 1·0	SW 1·0
Stege Bugt			
Stege (Sjælland)	0·4	NE 1	S–SW 1
Nyord	0·2	NE 0·6	W 0·3
Sandvig (Sjælland)	0·5	E 1·7	W 1
Fakse Bugt			
Præsto (Sjælland)	0·7	E 1·5	W 1
Fakse Ladeplads	0·5	E 1·5	W 1·5
Rødvig	0·6	E–NE 1·3	W–NW 1·3
Køge Bugt			
Bøgeskov	1·0	NE–E 0·8	SW–W 0·6
Køge (Sjælland)	0·4	NE–SE 1·6	W 0·9
Hundige (Sjælland)	0·5	SE storm + or – 0·5	
Ishøj (Sjælland)	0·5	E 0·2	W 0·2
Brøndby (Sjælland)	0·5	E–NE 1	W 1
København Sydhavn	0·2	W–NW 1·4	E–S 1·1
Drogden			
Dragør (Sjælland)	0·6	NE 1·4	SE 1
Flakfortet	0·2	WNW–NNE 1·2	NE–SSE 1·2
Kastrup Strandpark	0·5	NW–NNE 1	SE 1
Sundby Sejl Forening	0·6	NW 0·6	SE 0·6
København			
Østhavnen	0·5	NW–NE 0·9	E–S 0·9
Nordhavnen and Innenhavnen	0·2	W–NW 1·4	E–S 1·1
Malmø			
Malmø Hamn	n/a	NW–N 1·2	S–SE 1·3
The Sound			
Skovshoved (Sjælland)	0·2	N–NW 1·3	S–SE 0·9
Vedbæk (Sjælland)	0·5	NW 1	SE 0·7
Rungsted (Sjælland)	0·3	NW 1·3	S–SW 0·8
Nivå (Sjælland)	0·3	NW 0·6	S–SE 0·5
Helsingør (Sjælland)	1·0	NW 1	SE 0·6
Råå (Sweden)	n/a	NW 1·5	SE 1
Gilleleje (Sjælland)	0·5	NW 2	SE 1·5
Roskilde Fjord			
Lynæs	0·5	N–NW 1	SE 1
Fredrikssund Yachthafen	0·5	NW 1·1	E–SE 1
Jyllinge N	0·3	N 0·3	S 0·3
Jyllinge S	1·0	NW 1	SE–S 0·5
Roskilde	0·1	W–N 0·5–1·6	E–S 0·3–0·9

III. Telephone numbers of harbours

(Routes 1 to 7 only. It is suggested that you ring in normal office hours, say from 1000–1600.)

DENMARK

Note These are harbour offices on the routes examined, unless otherwise described. (Some Swedish harbours are included from Route 7.)

Åbenrå ☎ 74 62 89 85
Agersø ☎ 53 59 81 24
Agger (Limfjord) ☎ 97 94 24 01
Aggersund (Limfjord) ☎ 98 67 13 00
Ålborg (Limfjord) Marina Strandpark ☎ 98 10 25 75
Ålborg (Limfjord) Norre Sundby Bådehavn ☎ 98 17 60 17
Ålborg (Limfjord) Skudehavnen ☎ 98 13 85 48
Ålborg (Limfjord) Vestre Bådehavn ☎ 98 12 81 72
Amtoft (Limfjord) ☎ 97 99 34 46
Anholt (island) ☎ 86 31 90 08
Århus ☎ 86 19 15 90
Åro (island) ☎ 74 58 49 70
Æroskøbing (Æro) ☎ 62 52 12 53
Årosund ☎ 74 58 45 95
Assens (Fyn) ☎ 64 71 31 65, marina ☎ 64 71 35 80
Attrup (Limfjord) ☎ 98 23 30 99
Augustenborg (Als) ☎ 74 47 15 62
Bäckviken (Ven, Sweden) ☎ (0418) 721 92
Bågo (island) ☎ 64 71 8 86
Bagenkop ☎ 62 56 18 61/40 16 05 63
Ballen (Samsø) ☎ 86 59 12 03
Bjørnø (island) ☎ 62 61 14 22
Bøgeskov (Sjælland) ☎ 53 70 00 95
Bønnerup ☎ 86 38 60 83/61 33
Bogense (Fyn) ☎ 64 81 21 15
Bregnør (Fyn) ☎ 65 32 20 57
Brejning ☎ 75 86 23 52
Brøndby (Sjælland) ☎ 42 73 61 00
Christiansø (island) ☎ 53 96 20 01
Dageløkke (Langeland) Marina ☎ 62 59 13 10
Doverodde (Limfjord) ☎ 97 95 90 23
Dragør (Amager) ☎ 31 53 05 32
Dronningborg ☎ 86 43 72 55
Dyreborg (Fyn) ☎ 62 61 89 27
Dyvig (Als) Kro ☎ 74 45 14 90, Bådelaug ☎ 74 45 02 00
Ebeltoft ☎ 86 34 30 08/25 11/22 35
Egå Marina ☎ 86 22 55 51
Egense (Limfjord ent) ☎ 98 31 00 57
Egernsund Gråsten Turistbureau ☎ 74 65 09 55
Endelave (Samsø) ☎ 75 68 91 50
Esbjerg ☎ 75 12 92 00
Espergærde (Sjælland) ☎ 42 23 26 73
Fåborg (Fyn) ☎ 62 61 16 87
Fakse Ladeplads (Sjælland) ☎ 53 71 62 32/63 57
Faldsled (Fyn) ☎ 62 68 11 51
Fanø (island) Sejlklub ☎ 75 16 25 65
Femø (island) ☎ 53 91 50 74
Fjællebroen (Fyn) ☎ 62 61 64 44
Flakfortet (island) Restaurant Sct Thomas ☎ 30 22 40 58
Fredericia ☎ 75 92 02 55, Lystbådehavn ☎ 75 93 46 99
Frederikshavn Søsportshavn ☎ 98 43 28 56
Frederikssund (Sjælland) ☎ 42 31 55 04, Marbæk ☎ 42 31 20 66
Frederiksværk (Sjælland) ☎ 42 12 10 06
Fur (Limfjord) ☎ 97 59 32 01
Gåbense (Falster) ☎ 53 84 63 47
Gershøj (Sjælland) ☎ 42 32 87 61
Gilleleje (Sjælland) ☎ 48 30 16 63
Gjøl (Limfjord) ☎ 98 27 72 82
Glyngøre (Limfjord) ☎ 97 73 18 80
Gråsten ☎ 74 65 11 60
Grenå Lystbådehavn ☎ 86 32 72 55
Haderslev ☎ 74 52 00 47
Hadsund fishing harbour ☎ 98 57 23 43, yacht haven ☎ 98 57 24 39/18 98
Hals (Limfjord ent) ☎ 98 25 28 09
Hårbølle (Møn) ☎ 55 81 74 41
Hellerup (Sjælland) ☎ 31 62 07 61/88 03
Helsingør (Sjælland) Nordhavnen ☎ 42 10 10 55
Herslev (Sjælland) ☎ 42 40 24 39
Hestehoved (Lolland) ☎ 53 92 48 74
Hjarbæk (Limfjord) ☎ 86 64 24 04
Hjarnø (island) ☎ 75 68 33 45
Hjortø (island) ☎ 62 54 15 18
Hørby (Sjælland) ☎ 53 46 01 23
Hørup Hav (Als) ☎ 74 41 61 20
Hobro ☎ 98 52 12 00, Sejlklubs Havn ☎ 98 52 53 27
Holbæk (Sjælland) ☎ 53 43 01 61, Marina ☎ 53 43 88 77
Horsens ☎ 75 62 14 33
Hov ☎ 86 55 61 19
Humlebæk (Sjælland) ☎ 42 19 06 53
Hundested (Sjælland) ☎ 42 33 72 34
Hundige (Sjælland) Hejren ☎ 42 90 86 18, Mågen ☎ 42 90 67 59
Hvalpsund (Limfjord) Marina ☎ 98 63 80 01
Hvide Svaner (Sjælland) ☎ 55 44 24 15/23 53
Hvide Sande ☎ 97 31 16 32
Ishøj (Sjælland) ☎ 42 73 00 04, Vallensbæk ☎ 42 54 35 75
Jegindø (Limfjord) ☎ 97 87 90 32/90 33
Juelsminde ☎ 75 69 35 81
Jyllinge (Sjælland) Nordhavn ☎ 46 78 80 06
Jyllinge (Sjælland) Lystbådehavn ☎ 46 78 93 48
Kaløvig ☎ 86 99 19 67
Kalundborg (Sjælland) ☎ 53 51 01 88
Kalvehave (Sjælland) ☎ 53 78 84 60
Kalvø ☎ 74 69 87 58
Karrebæksminde (Sjælland) ☎ 55 44 20 45
Kastrup Strandpark (Sjælland) ☎ 31 50 21 27
Kerteminde (Fyn) ☎ 65 32 37 33
Kignæs (Sjælland) ☎ 42 33 18 11
København Copenhagen Boat Centre ☎ 31 18 31 22
København Inderhavn ☎ 33 12 20 63
København Langelinie Lystbådehavn ☎ 31 26 23 38
København Nord Svanemollen ☎ 31 20 22 21
København Øst Københavns Motorbådsklubs Havn ☎ 31 95 86 08
København Øst Margretheholm ☎ 31 57 57 78
København Syd Fiskerihavnen ☎ 36 30 06 37
Køge (Sjælland) ☎ 53 66 16 89
Kolby Kås (Samsø) ☎ 86 59 10 11
Kolding ☎ 75 53 27 22
Kongebro (Fyn) ☎ 64 41 29 65
Korshavn (Fyn) ☎ 65 34 19 33
Korshavn (Avernakø) ☎ 62 61 17 43
Korsør (Sjælland) ☎ 53 57 59 30
Kulhuse (Sjælland) ☎ 42 33 05 40/42 50 35 30
Kyrkbacken (Ven, Sweden) ☎ (0418) 722 22/87
Lagunen (Sweden) ☎ (040) 16 04 30
Langø (Lolland) ☎ 53 94 81 18
Langør (Samsø) ☎ 86 59 63 15
Lemvig ☎ 97 82 01 06, Marina ☎ 97 82 04 88
Limhamn (Sweden) ☎ (040) 15 20 24
Livø (Limfjord) ☎ 98 67 69 19
Løgstør (Limfjord) ☎ 98 67 11 08
Lohals (Langeland) ☎ 62 55 13 85
Lundeborg (Fyn) ☎ 62 25 18 47
Lübeck WerFr Grell (boatyard) ☎ (0451) 6 99 23
Lynæs (Sjælland) ☎ 42 33 91 19
Lyø (island) ☎ 62 61 92 86
Mariager ☎ 98 54 13 22
Marina Minde ☎ 74 42 31 43
Marselisborg ☎ 86 19 86 44
Marstal (Æro) ☎ 62 53 10 93
Mårup (Samsø) ☎ 86 15 66 49
Mellerup ☎ 86 44 15 17
Middelfart (Fyn) ☎ 64 41 02 53, Lystbådehavn ☎ 64 41 29 65
Mosede (Sjællan) ☎ 42 90 06 01
Mou (Limfjord) ☎ 98 31 10 49
Mullerup (Sjælland) ☎ 53 55 86 75
Nakskov (Lolland) ☎ 53 92 03 13
Nappedam ☎ 86 37 20 89
Næstved (Sjælland) ☎ 53 72 00 56/25 43
Nibe (Limfjord) ☎ 98 35 30 25
Nivå (Sjælland) ☎ 42 24 48 76
Nørre Uttrup (Limfjord) ☎ 98 19 04 43
Norreborg (Ven, Sweden) ☎ (0418) 723 33
Norsminde ☎ 86 93 16 54
Nyborg (Fyn) ☎ 65 31 05 87
Nykøbing (Sjælland) ☎ 53 41 00 77
Nykøbing (Mors Limfjord) ☎ 97 72 00 49
Nyord (island) ☎ 55 81 85 80

Øer ☎ 86 34 02 22
Oddesund (Limfjord) ☎ 97 87 50 20
Odense (Fyn) ☎ 66 12 00 25
Omø (island) ☎ 53 59 90 90
Onsevig (Lolland) ☎ 53 93 21 28/22 61
Orø (Sjælland) ☎ 53 47 04 19
Otterup (Fyn) ☎ 64 82 12 60
Præstø (Sjælland) ☎ 53 79 10 72
Råå (Sweden) ☎ (042) 10 76
Randers ☎ 86 42 10 57
Rantzausminde (Fyn) ☎ 62 21 14 92
Reersø (Sjælland) ☎ 53 55 94 45
Ringkøbing ☎ 97 32 13 02
Ristinge (Lolland) ☎ 62 57 16 50
Rødvig (Sjælland) ☎ 53 70 60 07
Rømø ☎ 74 75 52 45
Rønbjerg (Limfjord) ☎ 98 67 65 36
Rørvig (Sjælland) ☎ 59 91 93 36
Rosenvold ☎ 75 69 13 07
Roskilde (Sjælland) ☎ 42 35 10 00
Rudkøbing (Langeland) ☎ 62 51 13 39/40 53
Rungsted ☎ 42 86 83 11
Sakskøbing (Lolland) ☎ 53 89 41 34
Sandvig (Sjælland) ☎ 53 79 77 02
Sillerslev (Limfjord) ☎ 97 76 43 26
Skælskør (Sjælland) ☎ 53 59 42 04
Skærbæk ☎ 75 56 34 27
Skarø (island) ☎ 62 21 58 09
Skive (Limfjord) Søsportshavn ☎ 97 52 73 33
Skødshoved ☎ 86 35 15 82
Skovshoved (Sjælland) ☎ 31 64 13 88
Skuldelev (Sjælland) ☎ 42 32 06 59
Sletten ☎ 42 19 43 86
Snaptun ☎ 75 68 32 64
Snekkersten (Sjælland) ☎ 42 22 46 34
Søby (Æro) ☎ 62 58 14 30
Sønderborg ☎ 74 42 27 65, Lystbådehavn ☎ 74 42 93 92
Stege (Møn) ☎ 55 81 55 25
Stige (Fyn) ☎ 66 17 86 23
Strib (Fyn) ☎ 64 40 64 56
Struer (Limfjord) ☎ 97 85 02 28
Strynø (island) ☎ 62 51 53 12
Stubbekøbing (Falster) ☎ 53 84 10 92
Sundby Sejl Forening (Amager) ☎ 31 59 35 80
Svendborg Sund Marina (Fyn) ☎ 62 21 67 22
Svendborg (Fyn) ☎ 62 21 06 57, Lystbådehavn ☎ 62 21 14 92
Tårbæk (Sjælland) ☎ 31 63 03 09
Thisted (Limfjord) ☎ 97 91 14 00
Thyborøn (Limfjord ent) ☎ 97 83 10 50
Torsminde ☎ 97 49 70 44
Troense (Tåsinge) ☎ 62 22 59 39
Tunø (island) ☎ 86 55 30 92/16
Udbyhøj Nord ☎ 86 47 21 05, Syd ☎ 86 48 52 41
Uggelhuse ☎ 86 49 55 81
Vedbæk (Sjælland) ☎ 42 89 12 23
Veddelev (Sjælland) ☎ 42 36 45 69
Vejle ☎ 75 82 59 42
Vejrø (island) ☎ 53 91 32 50
Venø (Limfjord) ☎ 97 86 80 26
Vesterby (Fejø) ☎ 53 93 52 21
Vesterø (Læsø) ☎ 98 49 93 37
Vilsund (Limfjord) ☎ 97 93 16 63
Vindeby (Tåsinge) ☎ 62 22 59 14
Virksund (Limfjord) ☎ 97 53 94 24
Vordingborg (Sjælland) ☎ 53 77 17 11

GERMANY

Accumersiel (Dornum) YC-Stpt-Leiter ☎ (04943) 7 20, Hafenwart ☎ (04933) 24 40
Altenbruch ASV ☎ (04722) 23 54
Amrum town administration ☎ (04682) 8 61
Arnis Yacht-und-Bootswerft Matthiessen & Paulsen GmbH ☎ (04642) 23 166
Baltrum Stpt-Leiter ☎ (04939) 2 02, Hafenamt ☎ (04939) 4 48
Bensersiel Seglerverein ☎ (04941) 1 00 76, HM ☎ (04971) 17 44/32 53
Borkum Yachthafen ☎ (04922)·38 80, HM ☎ (04922) 34 40
Brunsbüttel Kanaljachthafen Hfn-Kpt ☎ (04852) 88 53 60, Hafenwart ☎ (04852) 32 56
Brunsbüttel Alte Hafen Seglerverein ☎ (04852) 31 07
Büsum Segelverein ☎ (04834) 29 97, HM ☎ (04834) 36 07
Cuxhaven HM ☎ (04721) 3 41 11, Yachthafen ☎ (04721) 4 89 60
Damp 2000 Ostseebad ☎ 0 43 52 80 01
Düsternbrook Kieler Yacht-Club e.V. ☎ (0431) 8 50 21
Eckenförde Segelclub Eckernförde e.V. ☎ (04351) 8 11 12/8 11 43
Eidersperrwerk locks office ☎ (04833) 22 11
Farensort Flensborg yacht club e.V. (Clubhouse Fahrensodde) ☎ (0461) 3 51 17
Flensburg Flensburger Yachtservice GmbH ☎ (0461) 1 77 27
Friedrichskoog HM ☎ (04854) 3 90, Liegeplätze ☎ (04854) 3 01
Gelting Faaborg-Gelting Autofähre nach Dänemark ☎ (04643) 7 93
Glücksburg Flensburger Segel Club ☎ (04631) 80 50
Hamburg City-Sport Hafen ☎ (040) 36 42 97
Hamburger Jachthafen, Wedel HM ☎ (04103) 44 38
Harlesiel HM ☎ (04462) 55 25
Heiligenhafen Hfn Mstr Jachthafen 4. ☎ (04362) 500 72/500 74
Helgoland Wss-Sportclub ☎ (04725) 5 85, HM ☎ (04725) 78 92
Hooksiel WSC e.V. ☎ (04421) 20 19 04, Hfn Mstrs ☎ (04425) 2 85/6 87/4 30
Juist Segel-Klub e.V. ☎ (04935) 3 77, HM ☎ (04935) 7 24
Kappeln-Grauhöft ☎ (04642) 48 58
Laboe Yachtclub Laboe e.V. ☎ (04343) 16 65
Langeoog SVH Langeoog ☎ (04972) 5 26, HM ☎ (04972) 3 01
List (Sylt) Hafenamt ☎ (04652) 3 74
Maasholm Monika Pauls Bootservice (AmJachthafen) ☎ (04642) 60 94
Meldorf MSV ☎ (04832) 76 58/14 68, Schleuse ☎ (04832) 71 81/21 05
Neuharlingersiel HM ☎ (04974) 2 89
Neustadt Hfn Mstr Neustadt SV ☎ (04561) 3271/3255
Nordeich Yacht-Club ☎ (04931) 30 05, HM ☎ (04931) 80 60
Norderney Hafenwart ☎ (04932) 37 98, Bootshaus ☎ (04932) 28 50
Nordfeld Schleuse ☎ (04881) 3 95
Oste Brückenwarter ☎ (04753) 4 22
Otterndorf Schleusenmeister ☎ (04751) 21 90, Hafenwart SV des TSV ☎ (04751) 1 31 31
Rendsburg Regatta-Verein Rendsburg ☎ (04331) 2 39 61
Schleswig Wiking Yachthafen ☎ (04621) 3 56 66
Spiekeroog Hfn Mstrs ☎ (04976) 2 72/2 17/4 38
Stickenhörn British Kiel Yacht Club ☎ (0431) 39 88 33
Strande Hafen Mstr ☎ (04349) 89 88
Tönning HM ☎ (04861) 14 00, TYC e.V. ☎ (04861) 7 54
Travemünde Marina Baltica ☎ (04502) 86 01 20
Wangerooge WYC ☎ (04469) 4 71, Hafenwart ☎ (04469) 4 16
Wendtorf Marina Wendtorf ☎ (04343) 90 99
Wilhelmshaven, S'Gazellenbrücke Yachtclub ☎ (04421) 4 41 21, Marina ☎ (04421) 4 34 15
Wyk (Föhr) town administration ☎ (04681) 50 40

IV. Bibliography

UK Hydrographic Office

Admiralty List of Lights and Fog Signals
Vol B Southern and Eastern Sides of the North Sea (NP 75)
Vol C Baltic Sea (NP 76)
Admiralty List of Radio Signals
Vol 1 Part 1. Coast Radio Stations (NP 281(1))
Vol 2 Radio Navigational Aids (NP 282)
Vol 3 Radio Weather Services (NP 283)
Vol 6 Part 1. Port Operations, Pilot Services and Traffic Management (NP 286(1))
Admiralty Sailing Directions
North Sea (East) Pilot (NP 55)
Baltic Pilot Volume 1 (NP 18)
Admiralty Tidal Stream Atlas. North Sea. Eastern Part (NP)
Admiralty Tide Tables Vol, European Waters (NP 201)
Admiralty Notices to Mariners: weekly edition

Other pilot books from Imray

North Sea Passage Pilot. Harbours and pilotage on the east coast of England, France, Belgium & the Netherlands. Navin. Imray, Laurie, Norie & Wilson Ltd.
Cruising Guide to the Netherlands. Navin. Imray, Laurie, Norie & Wilson Ltd.
The Baltic Sea. Germany, Poland, the Baltic States, Russia, Finland, Sweden and Denmark. RCC Pilotage Foundation. Imray, Laurie, Norie & Wilson Ltd.

Other pilots and guides

Nordseeküste (Vols 1 and 2). Werner. Delius Klasing Verlag.
Deutsche Nordseeküste. Bahnsen and Schaper. DK Edition Maritim.
[1]*Deutsche Ostseeküste.* Bahnsen and Schaper. DK Edition Maritim.
[1]*Der Grosse NV Hafenlotse (Bands 1, 2, 3, 4).* Nautische Veröffentlichung.
Der NV Landganglotse (Bands 1, 2, 3, 4). Nautische Veröffentlichung.
Komma's Havnelods. Aschehougfakta. There is a German version of this: *Hafenführer Dänemark,* DK Edition Maritim.
Ankerplätze in Dänemark. Werner. DK Edition Maritim.
Ankern in Dänemark. Claussen. Die Barque GmbH.

Tourism

Insight Guides: Denmark. APA Publications (HK) Ltd.
The Visitor's Guide to Denmark. Constance. Moorland Publishing Co Ltd.
Baedeker's Denmark. Prentice Hall Press.
West Germany: the Rough Guide. McLachlan, Norton.
Michelin Deutschland. Michelin Reifenwerke KG.

The Danish Tourist Board/*Danmarks Turistråd* in København (it also has a London office) has a wide range of tourist offices in most towns in Denmark, many of which provide leaflets about their local area. In writing to one of these offices, it is sufficient to address the letter to *Turistbureauet* followed by the postal code and name of the town.

[1]These guides correspond to the four NV *Sportschiffahrts-karten.*

V. Glossary

Chart and navigational terms

Danish. English. *German*

Å. River. *Fluss*
Bæk. Rivulet. *Au*
Båke. Beacon. *Bake*
Bjerg. Mountain. *Berg*
Bredning. Broad. ...
Bro. Pier, bridge. *Brücke*
Brygge. Quay, wharf. *Kai*
Bugt. Bay. *Bucht/wiek*
By. Town, city. *Stadt*
Dæmning. Dam. *Damm*
Dige. Dyke. *Deich*
Duc d'albe. Dolphin. *Dalbe*
Dyb. Deep. *Tief*
Færge. Ferry. *Fähre*
Farvandet. Fairway. *Fahrwasser*
Fjord. Inlet/loch. *Förde*
Flak/grund. Shoal. *Grund*
Gab. Mouth. *Münding*
Gamle Old. *Alt*
Hage. Spit. *Spitze*
Havn. Harbour. *Hafen*
Høj. Hill. *Hügel*
Høj. Height. *Höhe*
Hoved. Head. *Höved/höft*
Huk. Point. *Huk*
Inder/indre. Inner. *Binnen*
Indløb. Entrance. *Einfahrt*
Kap. Cape. *Kap*
Klint. Cliff. *Kliff/Klippe*
Klit. Dune. *Düne*
Lille. Little. *Klein*
Løb. Channel. *Fahrwasser*
Lods. Pilot. *Lotse*
Mølle. Mill. *Mühle*
Munding/minde. Mouth. *Münding/münde*
Næs. Point, headland. *Nis*
Nørre/nord/nordre. North. *Nord*
Nor. Shallow inlet, lake. *Noor*
Ny. New. *Neu*
Ø. Island. *Insel*
Odde. Point. *Huk*
Ost/oster/østra. East. *Ost*
Östersjön. Baltic. *Ostsee*
Plade. Shoal. *Untiefe*
Pulle. Shoal. *Untiefe*
Pynt. Point. *Spitze*
Rådhus. Town hall. *Rathaus*
Red. Road, roadstead. *Reede*
Rende. Channel. *Rinne*
Rev/revle. Shoal, reef. *Riff*
Rød. Red. *Rot*
Røn. Rock. *Stein*
Skov. Wood. *Holz/wald*
Slot. Castle. *Schloss*
Slot. Castle. *Borg*
Snævringen. Narrows.
Sø. Sea. *See*
Sønder/sødre/syd. South. *Sud*
Sort. Black. *Schwartz*
Stor. Great. *Gross*
Strøm. Stream, current. *Ström*
Tør. Dry. *Trocken*
Vest/vester/vestre. West. *West*
Vrag. Wreck. *Wrack*
Yder. Outside. *Aussen*

German. ***Danish***. English

Alt. ***Gamle***. Old
Au. ***Bæk***. Rivulet
Aussen. ***Yder***. Outside
Bake. ***Båke***. Beacon
Berg. ***Bjerg***. Mountain
Binnen. ***Inder/indre***. Inner
Borg. ***Slot***. Castle
Brücke. ***Bro***. Pier, bridge
Bucht/wiek. ***Bugt***. Bay
Dalbe. ***Duc d'albe***. Dolphin
Damm. ***Dæmning***. Dam
Deich. ***Dige***. Dyke
Düne. ***Klit***. Dune
Einfahrt. ***Indløb***. Entrance
Fähre. ***Færge***. Ferry
Fahrwasser. ***Farvandet***. Fairway
Fahrwasser. ***Løb***. Channel
Fluss. ***Å***. River
Förde. ***Fjord***. Inlet/loch
Gross. ***Stor***. Great
Grund. ***Flak/grund***. Shoal
Hafen. ***Havn***. Harbour
Höhe. ***Høj***. Height
Holz/wald. ***Skov***. Wood
Höved/höft. ***Hoved***. Head
Hügel. ***Høj***. Hill
Huk. ***Huk***. Point
Huk. ***Odde***. Point
Insel. ***Ø***. Island
Kai. ***Brygge***. Quay, wharf
Kap. ***Kap***. Cape
Klein. ***Lille***. Little
Kliff/klippe. ***Klint***. Cliff
Lotse. ***Lods***. Pilot
Mühle. ***Mølle***. Mill
Münding. ***Gab***. Mouth
Münding/münde. ***Munding/minde***. Mouth
Neu. ***Ny***. New
Nis. ***Næs***. Point, headland
Noor. ***Nor***. Shallow inlet, lake
Nord. ***Nørre/nord/nordre***. North
Ost. ***Ost/oster/østra***. East
Ostsee. ***Östersjön***. Baltic
Rathaus. ***Rådhus***. Town hall
Reede. ***Red***. Road, roadstead
Riff. ***Rev/revle***. Shoal, reef
Rinne. ***Rende***. Channel
Rot. ***Rød***. Red
Schloss. ***Slot***. Castle
Schwartz. ***Sort***. Black
See. ***Sø***. Sea
Spitze. ***Hage***. Spit
Spitze. ***Pynt***. Point
Stadt. ***By***. Town, city
Stein. ***Røn***. Rock
Ström. ***Strøm***. Stream, current
Sud. ***Sønder/sødre/syd***. South
Tief. ***Dyb***. Deep
Trocken. ***Tør***. Dry
Untiefe. ***Plade***. Shoal
Untiefe. ***Pulle***. Shoal
West. ***Vest/vester/vestre***. West
Wrack. ***Vrag***. Wreck

English. ***Danish***. *German*

Baltic. ***Östersjön***. *Ostsee*
Bay. ***Bugt***. *Bucht/wiek*
Beacon. ***Båke***. *Bake*
Black. ***Sort***. *Schwartz*
Broad ***Bredning***. ...
Cape. ***Kap***. *Kap*
Castle. ***Slot***. *Schloss*
Castle. ***Slot***. *Borg*
Channel. ***Rende***. *Rinne*
Channel. ***Løb***. *Fahrwasser*
Cliff. ***Klint***. *Kliff/klippe*
Dam. ***Dæmning***. *Damm*
Deep. ***Dyb***. *Tief*
Dolphin. ***Duc d'albe***. *Dalbe*
Dry. ***Tør***. *Trocken*
Dune. ***Klit***. *Düne*
Dyke. ***Dige***. *Deich*
East. ***Ost/oster/østra***. *Ost*
Entrance. ***Indløb***. *Einfahrt*
Fairway. ***Farvandet***. *Fahrwasser*
Ferry. ***Færge***. *Fähre*
Great. ***Stor***. *Gross*
Harbour. ***Havn***. *Hafen*
Head. ***Hoved***. *Höved/höft*
Height. ***Høj***. *Höhe*
Hill. ***Høj***. *Hügel*
Inlet/loch. ***Fjord***. *Förde*
Inner. ***Inder/indre***. *Binnen*
Island. ***Ø***. *Insel*
Little. ***Lille***. *Klein*
Mill. ***Mølle***. *Mühle*
Mountain. ***Bjerg***. *Berg*
Mouth. ***Munding/minde***. *Münding/münde*
Mouth. ***Gab***. *Münding*
Narrows. ***Snævringen***.
New. ***Ny***. *Neu*
North. ***Nørre/nord/nordre***. *Nord*
Old. ***Gamle***. *Alt*
Outside. ***Yder***. *Aussen*
Pier, bridge. ***Bro***. *Brücke*
Pilot. ***Lods***. *Lotse*
Point. ***Pynt***. *Spitze*
Point, headland. ***Næs***. *Nis*
Point. ***Huk***. *Huk*
Point. ***Odde***. *Huk*
Quay, wharf. ***Brygge***. *Kai*
Red. ***Rød***. *Rot*
River. ***Å***. *Fluss*
Rivulet. ***Bæk***. *Au*
Road, roadstead. ***Red***. *Reede*
Rock. ***Røn***. *Stein*
Sea. ***Sø***. *See*
Shallow inlet, lake. ***Nor***. *Noor*
Shoal, reef. ***Rev/revle***. *Riff*
Shoal. ***Plade***. *Untiefe*
Shoal. ***Flak/grund***. *Grund*
Shoal. ***Pulle***. *Untiefe*
South. ***Sønder/sødre/syd***. *Sud*
Spit. ***Hage***. *Spitze*
Stream, current. ***Strøm***. *Ström*
Town, city. ***By***. *Stadt*
Town hall. ***Rådhus***. *Rathaus*
West. ***Vest/vester/vestre***. *West*
Wood. ***Skov***. *Holz/wald*
Wreck. ***Vrag***. *Wrack*

Index

Abbenfleth, 44
Åbenrå (Apenrade), 93
  fjord, 81, 82, 93
Accumer Ee, 17
Accumersieler Balje, 28-9
Achtenwehrer Schiffartskanal, 64
Admiralty, books, 3; *see also charts*
Adsbøl, 90
Æro island, 132, 134-5
Æroskøbing, 134-5
Agersø Sund, 142-3
Agger, 129
Albæk, 115
Ålborg, 119-20
  Bugt, 110, 114
Albuen, 152
Allinge, 188
Als Fjord, 93
  island, 81, 82
  Odde, 112
  Sund, 91-3
Altefähr, 185
Altenbruch, 41
Amager island, 159, 160
Amrum, 50
Amtoft, 130
anchoring in the Baltic, 73-4
Ancora Marina, 181
Andersen, Hans Christian, 5, 148
Angeln, 81
Anholt island, 109-10
Apenrade *see* Åbenrå
Århus, 82, 105-6
  Bugt, 104
Arkona, 179
Arnager, 188
Arnis, 87
Arnisser Segelclubs, Kappeln, 87
Årø, 95
Årøsund, 94-5
Årsdale, 188
Aså, 115
Askø island, 149, 153
Assens, 96
Astrup vig, 123
Asvig, 100, 101
Attrup, 121
Augustenborg fjord, 91, 92
Avernakø island, 136-7

Baabe, 186
Bäckviken, 168
Bagenkop, 151-2
Bågø, 96
  Sund, 96
Ballen (Samsø), 81, 102-3
Ballen (Svendborg Sund), 138
Baltica Marina, 181
Baltrum, 27-8
  approaches, 16-17, 19
Baltrumer
  Balje, 28
  Wattfahrwasser, 28
Barakkebo, 160
Barhøft, 185
Barnkruger Loch, 43
Båring Vig, 98-9
Baurs Park, 45
Beelitz Werft, 179
Begtrup vig, 107
Bensersiel, 29, 30
bibliographies, 1, 3, 203
Bielenburg, 43
Binneneider, 59, 71
Birkholm island, 134
Bjørnø, 136-7
Bjornsholm Bugt, 122
Blankenese, 45
Blaue Balje, 15, 17, 32
Blåvandshuk, 18
Böbs-Werft marina, 181
Bodden lakes, 186
Bogense, 99
Bøgeskov, 157
Bøgestrøm, 149, 155-6
Bohnert Hülsen, 88
Bøjden, 142
Bøløre Hage narrows, 129
Bønnerup, 110
books and pilots, 1, 3, 203
Borgstedter See, 59, 63-4
Borgwedel, 88
Borkum, 24-5
  approaches, 16, 19
Bornholm island, 177, 186-8
Bramsnæs Vig, 172
Bredningen, 96
Bregnør, 148
Brejning, 100
Bremerhaven, 19-21, 36-7
Bremervørde, 41
Brodersby, Marina, 88
Brøndby, 158-9
Brunsbüttel, 41, 62
Brunshausen, 44
buoys, SW Baltic, 77-8
Burgstaaken-Burgetiefe, 179
Busetief, 16, 25, 27
Büsüm, 18, 47, 48, 49

Carolinensiel, 32
Carolinensieler Balje, 32
Central European Time, 1
chart agents, 2
charts, 2-3, 189-98; *see also start of each chapter*
Childers, Erskine (Riddle of the Sands), 19, 30, 81
Christianshavns kanal, 164
Christiansø island, 187, 188
City-Sport Hafen, Hamburg, 45
coast radio stations
  German Bight, 14
  SW Baltic, 79
coinage, 1
collision rules, 3
currency, 1
currents
  German Bight, 7-11
  SW Baltic, 75-6
  see also start of each chapter
customs formalities, 3
Cuxhaven, 19, 21, 39
  to Süderpiep, 49

Daggeløkke, 140-1
Damp, 86
Dänevirke, 4, 81
Darsser Ort, 185
Dassower See, 182
Decca coverage
  German Bight, 14
  SW Baltic, 79
Denmark, *history* 4-6, 81-2
Dietrichsdorf, 85
Dietrichshagener Berg, 179
Djursland peninsula coast, 108
Dornumer Accumerseil, 28-9
Dove Harle, 31
Dove Tief, 16
Doverodde, 129
Dragør, 159-60
Dragstrup Vig, 129
Drejø, 135
Drogden, 162
Dronningborg, 111
drove roads, 4
Düne, 37
Düsternbrook, 59, 85
Dwarsloch, 44
Dybbøl hill battle, 5, 81
Dybvig (Fejø Havn), 153
Dyreborg, 136
Dyvig, 82, 91, 93
Dziwna, 186

East Frisian islands
  approaches, 15-16
Ebeltoft, 107
  Vig, 107-8
Eckernförde, 86
Egå Marina, 105-6
Egens Vig, 106
Egense Dyb, 147
Egense yachthaven, 113, 114
Egernsund, 90
Eider, river, 49-50, 59, 61
Eiderkanal, 59
Eidersperrwerk, 49, 61, 67
Ejby Havn, 172
Elbe, 39-45
  approaches, 15, 17-18, 19, 21
  to Süderpiep, 48
Elbe-Lübeck-Kanal, 45, 182
Elsinore (Helsingør), 4, 149, 169-70
Emden, 21, 22, 23-4
Ems, river, 15, 16-17, 24
Endelave, 102
Enehøje island, 152
Esbjerg, 47, 54-5
  approaches, 15, 18
Eskilsø, 174
Espergærde, 168
Este, river, 44-5

Fåborg, 136
  fjord, 136-7
Fægerstrøm, 155
Fænø Sund, 96-7
Færker Vig, 124
Fævig, 129
Fahrdorf, 88
Fakse Bugt, 156, 157
Fakse Ladeplads, 157
Falsled, 136
Falster island, 149
Fanø, 53, 54
  offshore of, 53
Farensort, 90
Fedderwarder Fahrwasser, 36, 37
Fedderwardersiel, 36
Feggesund, 130
Fehmarn Bælt, 75
  island, 179
  Sund, 179, 180
Fehmarnsund bridge, 180
Fejø island, 149, 153
Femø island, 149, 153, 154
fishing stakes and buoys
  SW Baltic, 78
Fjællebroen, 137
Flakfortet, 162
Fleckeby, 88
Flemhuder See, 59, 64
Flensburg, 6, 91
Flensburger Förde (Flensborg fjord), 81, 82, 90-1
fog
  German Bight, 13
  SW Baltic, 76, 77
Föhr, 51
Föhrer Ley, 51
formalities, 3
Fredericia, 98-9
Fredericksø island, 187, 188
Frederikshavn, 115
Frederiksværk Havn, 173
Fredrikssund Yacht Haven, 173-4
Fredskov bridge, 155
Freest, 186
Freiburg, 41
Friedrichstadt, 6, 59, 61, 67, 69-70
Frisian islands, approaches, 15-16, 18
Fünen see Fyn
Fur, 124
  Sund, 124-5
Fyn (Fünen), 81, 82, 96, 131-48

Gåbense, 155
Gager, 186
Gamborg fjord, 96
Gambøt, 139
Gellenstrom channel, 185, 186
Gelting, 90
Genner fjord, 82, 93-4
Germany, north
  history, 4-6

Gershøj, 176
Gezeiteneider, 69
Gieselau, 59
  Kanal, 59, 61, 62, 71
Gilleleje, 5, 170-1
Gjøl, 120
  Bredning, 120
Glewitzer Fähre, 185
Glomstrup vig, 129
glossary, 204
Glücksburg, 90
Glückstadt, 43
Glyngøre, 126
Grabow lakes, 186
Grådyb, 53, 55
Grasholm island, 187
Gråsten, 90
Grauhöft, 87
Greetsiel, 25, 26
Grenå Havn, 108-9
Griefswald Stadthafen, 186
Griefswalder Bodden, 186
  Oie, 186
Grömitz, 180, 185
Grossenbrode, 179
  Fähre, 179
Grossenbroder Binnensee, 180
Grosser, 16
Gryndeløb, 136-7
Gudhjem, 188
Gustow, 185
Gyldendal, 126

Haddeby *see* Haitabu
Hadderber Noor, 81
Hadelner canal, 41
Haderslev, 95
  fjord, 81, 95
Hadsund, 112
Hafen von Wyk, 51
Hagedyb, 121
Haitabu (Haddeby, Hedeby), 81, 88
Hals, 114
Hälsingborg, 168
Hamburg, 5, 19, 21, 39, 44-5
Hamburger Jachthaven, 44
Hammerhavn, 188
Hansa Hafen, Lübeck, 182
Hanseatic League, 6, 37, 179
Hantsholm, 58
Hårbølle, 155
Harlesiel, 32
Harlesieler Wattfahrwasser, 17, 31
Harre Vig, 126
Harrisleer Segelclubs, 90
Haseldorf, 44
Hasle, 187, 188
Haupt-Kanal, Bremerhaven, 37
Heijlsminde, 96
Heiligenhafen, 179, 180
Helgoland, 15, 37-8
  to Büsüm, 48
Helligpeder, 188
Helnæs Bugt, 135-6
Helsingør (Elsinore), 4, 149, 169-70
Herreninsel, 181
Herslev, 176
Hestehoved yacht haven, 152
Hetlinger Schanze, 44
Hedeby see Haitabu
Heverstrom, 47
Hirsholm island, 115
Hirtshals, 58
Hjarbæk fjord, 123
Hjarno, 101
Hjelm island, 108
Ho Bugt, 54
Hobro, 112-14
Hochdonn, 62
Hohen Wieschendorf, 183, 184
Hohewegrinne, 17, 36
Hohwachter Bucht, 179
Holbæk, 172
Holckenhavn fjord, 141
Holingsted, 4
Holknobsloch, 52
Høllet, 112
Holsterbro, 126-7
Holtenau, 61, 64, 65, 85
Hook Meer, 33
Hooksiel, 33
Hørby, 172
Hornbæk, 170
Horns Rev, 55
Hörnum, 51-2
Horsens, 101
  fjord, 81, 101
Horumersiel, 32
Hørup Hav, 90
Hotel Admiralen, København, 164
Hou, 115
Hov, 104
Hovsør Havn, 130
Hubertgat, 16
Hulbalje, 30
Humlebæk, 168
Hundersted, 171
Hundige, 158
Husum, 47
Hvalpsund Marina, 122
Hvide Sande, 55-6
Hvide Svaner, 154
Hvidovre, 159

ice
  German Bight, 13
  SW Baltic, 76
inshore traffic zone, 15
Isefjord, 171-2
Ishøj, 158, 159

Jade estuary, 32-5
  approaches, 17, 19, 32
Jammer Bugt, 58
Jarsshumerhafen, 23
Jegindø, 126
Juelsminde, 100
Juist, 16, 26
Juister Riff, 16
Jyllinge, 174

Kaiser Wilhelm Kanal, 59
Kaiserbalje, 36
Kaløvig, 106
Kalundborg, 105, 146-7
  fjord, 147
Kalvebod Løb, 159
Kalveboderne, 159
Kalvehave, 155
Kalvø, 94
Kampen, 52
Kanhave canal, 103
Kappeln-Grauhöft, 7, 87
Karby Odde, 129
Karrebæksminde, 154
Karschau, 87
Kås Bredning, 126
Kastrup, 162
Kattegat, 75, 76, 78, 109
Kattinge Vig, 174
Kattinger Watt, 67
Kerteminde, 145
  Bugt, 145, 146
Kiel, 84-5
  canal *see* Nord-Ostsee-Kanal
  Wik, 85
Kieler Bucht, 133, 151-2
  Förde, 84-5
Kignæs, 173
Kirchdorf, 183, 184
Kisserup Hage, 172
Klintebjerg, 148
Knebel Vig, 82
Kniep, 51
Kobberdyb channel, 141
København, 4, 149, 162-6
Køge, 157-8
  Bugt, 157
Köhlfleet, 45
Kolby Kås, 102
Kolding, 75, 82, 98
  fjord, 97
Kollmar, 43
Konge Dyb, 162
Kongebro, 98
Kongsdale, 112
Kopperby, 87
Korshavn, 137
Korsør, 144
Krage Vig, 174
Kragenæs, 153-4
Kranskrog, 176
Krik Vig, 129
kroer, 4
Kronborg castle, 4, 5, 169, 170
Kronen Loch, 49
Kronprins Frederiks bridge, 173
Krückau, river, 43
Krückaumündung, 43
Kulhuse, 172
Kyrkbacken, 168

Laboe, 85
Læso island, 75, 114
Lagunen, 160
Lamme fjord, 172
Landbalje, 31
Langballigau, 90
Langeland, 140-1, 151-2
  Bælt, 152
Langelinie, 164, 165
Langeoog, 29-30
  approach, 17
Langeooger Wattfahrwasser, 30
Langerak, 119
Langø, 152
Langør, 102-3
Lauenburg, 45
Lauterbach, 186
Lejre Vig, 176
Lemkenhafen, 179
Lemvig, 127-8
Lexfähre, 59, 70, 71
Leybucht, 25
lifeboat stations
  German Bight, 14-15
  SW Baltic, 79
lights, major
  German Bight, 14
  SW Baltic, 77-8
Lille Bælt, 81, 98-102, 135-6
Limfjord, 117-30
  eastern entrance, 113-14
  western entrance, 58
Limnhamn, 160-1
Lindaunis, 87
List, 52, 53
  Land, 52, 53
Listed, 188
Lister Landtief, 52
  Ley, 53
  Tief, 52, 53
Livø, 121-2
Løgstør, 121, 130
  Bredning, 121
Løgten Bugt, 106
Lohals, 141
Lolland island, 149
Lovns Bredning, 122
Lübeck, 6, 179, 181, 182-3
  Kanal, 45, 182
Lühe, 44
Lundeborg, 141
Luneort-hafen, Bremerhaven, 37
Lynetteløb channel, 164
Lynæs, 171-2
Lyø, 136
  Krog, 136
Lysen Bredning, 126

Maasholm, 87
Magerodde, 129
Malmø, 159, 160-1
Margretheholm, 162, 164
Mariager, 112
  fjord, 111-12
Marina Brodersby, 88
Marina Minde, 90
Marselisborg, 104-5
Marstal, 133
Mårup, 103
  Vig, 103
Masned Sund, 154-5
Mecklenburger Bucht, 177-8, 185
Meldorf, 47
Meldorfer Bucht, 49
Mellerup, 111
Melsted, 188
Memmert, 25
Middelfart, 82, 97, 98
Minde, Marina, 90
Minsener Balje, 32
Minsener Oog, 17, 19
  Wattfahrwasser, 32
Missunder Yachtclub, 88
Mittelhever, 50
Mittelrinne, 17, 36
Möllegab channel, 134
Møllekrog Vig, 176
Möltenort, 85
Mon island, 149
Mönkeberg, 85
mooring in the Baltic, 73-4
Mörkedyb channel, 134
Mors (Nykøbing), 125-6
Mosede, 158
Mou, 119
Mühlenberg, 45
Mullerup, 147
Munkholm, 172
Musholm Havn, 147

Næstved, 154
Nakkebølle fjord, 137
Nakskov, 152-3
fjord, 152
Nappedam, 106-7
Nassau Hafen, 33
nature reserves, 15, 17
Navtex
German Bight, 14
SW Baltic, 79
Neder Dråby, 173
Nees Vig, 129
Neksø, 187, 188
Nesskanal, 45
Neuenschleuse, 44
Neuharlingersiel, 30
Neuhaus, 41
Neuhof, 185
Neustadt, 180-1
Neustädter Bucht, 177, 180, 185
Segelvereines, 181
Nibe, 120-1
Bredning, 120
Niendorf, 180, 181, 183
Niro Petersen, Flensburg, 91
Nissum Bredning, 127
Nivå, 168
Nord-Ostsee-Kanal, 15, 59-66
Nordby, 53, 54
Norddeich, 21, 27
Norderaue, 51
Norderelbe, 49
Norderney, 16, 21, 26
Norderneyer Wattfahrwasser, 27
Norderspiep, 49-50
Nordfeld, 59, 61, 67
Lock, 70
Nordsee-Marina, Bremerhaven, 37
Normands Dyb, 55
Nørre Rev, 176
Nørre Uttrup, 119
Nørre-Kås, 187, 188
Norreborg, 168
Norsminde, 75, 104
North Frisian islands, approaches, 18
Nybøl Nor, 90
Nyborg, 141, 142
Nykøbing (Isefjord), 172
Nykøbing (Mors), 125-6
Nyord, 156
Nysø, 156

Obereidersee, 59, 62-3
Odby Bugt, 127
Oddesund, 127
narrows, 127
Odense, 5, 142, 145, 148
fjord and kanal, 147
Oder, river/canal, 186
Øer yachthaven, 108
Okseør islands, 82, 90
Ølvig, 176
Olympiahafen Schilksee, 85
Omø island, 149
Onsevig, 153
Øresund *bridge and tunnel project*, 6
Orø island, 172
Orth, 179
Ortmühle, 179
Oste, river, 41
Øster Hurup, 114
Osterems, 15, 25
Østerrenden, 145
Otterndorf, 41
Otterup, 147
Otzumer Balje, 17

Pahlen, 59
Pahlhude, 70, 71
Passathafen, 181
Peene channel, 186
pilot guides, 1, 203
Pinnau, river, 43
Pinnaumündung, 43-4
Poel island, 183, 184
Poland, 186
Pommersche Bucht, 186
Potenitzer Wiek, 182
Pouls Vig, 154
Præsto, 156-7
fjord, 149, 156-7
precipitation, SW Baltic, 77
Puddemin, 185
Pulse Vig, 125

Råå, 168-9
radiobeacons
German Bight, 14
SW Baltic, 78
rain, SW Baltic, 77
Randers, 111
fjord, 77, 110-11
Randzelgat, 16, 25
Rantzausminde, 138
Ratsdelft, Emden, 23
Reersø, 147
regulations, 3
Rendsburg, 6, 59, 62-3
rescue services, 80; *see also lifeboat stations*
Revkrog, 137
Riddle of the Sands (Childers), 19, 30, 81
Riffgat, 25, 27
Ringkøbing, 56
fjord, 56
Ringoen island, 174
Risgårde Bredning, 122
Ristinge, 134
Rødvig, 157
Rømø Dyb, 53
island, 53
Rønbjerg Havn, 121
Rønne, 187, 188
Rønnershavnen, 115
Rørvig, 172
Rosenvold, 100
Roskilde, 4, 149, 175-6
fjord, 149, 171, 172-6
Rostock, 6, 179, 185
Rov Vig, 129
Ruden, 186
Rudkøbing, 140
Løb, 139, 140
Rügen, 179, 186
lakes, 186
Rungsted, 167
Rüschkanal, 45
Rüstersiel, 33
Rütergat, 50
Ruthenstrom, 43

Sæby, 115
Sakskøbing, 154
Salling Sund, 125
Samsø, 81, 102-3
Sandbjerg Vig, 82, 100
Sandvig (Bøgestrøm), 156
Sandvig (Bornholm), 188
Sassnitz, 186
Schnausende, 90
Schilbalje, 30-1
Schilksee, 85
Schlei fjord, 81, 87-8
Schleimünde, 86
Schleswig, 6, 81, 87-8
Schleswig-Holstein, 47-53
history, 5
Schleswiger Jachthaven, 88
Schleswiger Holm, 88
Schluchter, 16
Schlutup, 181
Schmaltief, 50
Schwarzen Busch, 184
Schwentine, 85
Schwinge, river, 44
Seedorf, 186
seegats, 15-16, 19
Siesby, 87
Silk, 182
Sjælland, 143-7, 149-76
Skælskør, 143
Skærbæk, 97-8
Skagen, 58, 75, 115
Skagerrak, 57, 75
Skalø, 153, 154
Skanse Bugt, 172
Skarø, 138
Skibby, 176
Skibsted Vig, 129
Skive fjord, 123-4
Skødshoved, 107
Skovshoved, 167
Skudehavnen, 165
Skuldelev, 174
Sletten, 168
Slugen, 55
Smålands Farvandet, 75, 149-51, 153
Smørvig, 174
Snævringen, 75, 76, 82, 97, 98
Snaptun yacht haven, 101
Snekkersten, 168
Snogebæk, 188
Søby, 135
Sønderborg (Sonderburg), 81, 91
Sønderho, 53
Søndre Arbejdshavn, 128
Søndre Løb, 159
Søren Bovbjergs Dyb, 55
Sottrupskov, 92
Sound (Sund), 5, 6, 149-51, 157-70
Sperrwerk Leysiel lock and bridge, 25
Spiekeroog, 17, 21, 30-1
St Margarethen, 41
Stahlbrode, 185
Stavreby, 156
Steendiekkanal, 45
Stege, 156
Bugt, 155-6
Stettiner Haf, 186
Stexwig, 88
Stickenhörn, 85
Stollergrundrinne, 85
Stör, river, 41
Störloch, 41
Store Bælt, 131, 142-6, 152
bridge and tunnelling project, 6, 145
Storstrøm bridge, 154
Stralsund, 6, 179, 185, 186
Strandby, 115
Strande, 85
Stranderød Bucht, 90
Strelasund, 185-6
Strib, 98
Struer, 126-7
Strynø, 134
Stubbekøbing, 155
Stüverslegde, 30
Suchsdorf, 64
Süderpiep, 49
Süderstapel, 71
Sundby Sejl Forening, 162
Svaneke, 188
Svanmølle, 166
Svendborg, 138-9
Sund, 137-9
Sweden, 160-1, 168
Swinoujscie (Swinemünde), 186
Sylt, 47, 51-3

Tambosund, 129
Tannis Bugt, 58
Tårbæk, 167
Tæsinge island, 139-40
Teerhof island, 182
Tegeler Rinne, 17
Teglkås, 188
Tejn, 187, 188
Telegraphenbalje *see* Wangerooger Wattfahrwasser
telephone numbers of harbours, 201-2
telephoning, 1
temperatures, 76, 77
Teufelsbrücke, 45
Thisted, 130
Bredning, 129-30
Thyborøn, 57-8, 128
tidal heights and ranges
German Bight, 7-11
SW Baltic, 75-6, 199-200
see also start of each chapter
tidal streams and currents
German Bight, 7-11
SW Baltic 75-6
see also start of each chapter
Time, Central European, 1
Timmendorf, 183, 184
Tönning, 50, 59, 61, 67-8
Torsminde, 57
tourist guides, 203
tourist information addresses, 1-2
traffic separation schemes, 15
Tragten, 98-9
Tranebjerg, 81, 102
Travemünde, 179, 180, 181-2
Troense, 139
Tunø island, 81, 103-4

Udbyhøj Nord, 111
Sud, 111
Uecker, river, 186
Ueckermünde, 186
Uggelhuse, 111
Uglekrog, 176
Untertrave, river, 181

Vang, 188
Vedbæk, 167
Veddelev, 174
Vierow, 186
Vejle, 100
fjord, 81, 99-100

Vejrø island, 149, 153
Vemmingbund, 90
Ven island, 168
Venø, 127
  Bugt, 126
  Narrows, 127
  Sound, 127
Vesterby, 153
Vesterø, 114
Vikings, 4
Vilm, 186
Vilsund, 129
Vindeby yachthaven, 138
Virksund, 123
Visby Bredning, 129
Voer, 111
Vordingborg, 154-5
Vorpommern lakes, 186
Vortrapptief, 51, 52

Wackerballig, 90
Wangerooge, 31-2
  approaches, 15, 16, 17
Wangerooger Wattfahrwasser, 17, 32
Wangersiel, 32
Warnemünde, 179, 185
Wattfahrwassen (watt channels), 19
weather
  German Bight, 13
  SW Baltic, 75, 76-7
  see also start of each chapter
weather forecasts
  German Bight, 2, 14
  SW Baltic, 2, 79
Wedel, 44, 45
Weiche Dückerswisch, 62
Wendtorf, 85
Wenningstedt, 52
Weser estuary, 17, 34, 35-7
Westerbalje, 17
Westerems, 15, 16
Westerland, 52-3
Wewelsfleth, 41
Wichter Ee, 15, 16-17, 19
Wiek, 186
Wiking Jachthafen, Schleswig, 88
Wilhelmshaven, 5, 21, 33-5
winds
  German Bight, 12-13
  Limfjord, 117
  SW Baltic, 75, 76, 77
Wischhafen, 41
Wismar, 179, 183, 184
  Bucht, 179, 183
withy markers, 19
Wittdün, 50
Wohlenberg, 183, 184
Wohlenberger Wiek, 183-4
Wyk island, 51

yachting associations, 1-2
Yachtzentrum Nord, 90

Zehnerloch, 48-9
Zicker See, 186
Zone 1 nature reserves, 15, 17